The Natural History *of* Love

The NATURAL HISTORY *of* LOVE

Revised and Updated Edition

MORTON HUNT

ANCHOR BOOKS
DOUBLEDAY
New York London Toronto Sydney Auckland

AN ANCHOR BOOK
PUBLISHED BY DOUBLEDAY
a division of Bantam Doubleday Dell Publishing Group, Inc.
1540 Broadway, New York, New York 10036

ANCHOR BOOKS, DOUBLEDAY, and the portrayal of an anchor are trademarks of
Doubleday, a division of Bantam Doubleday Dell
Publishing Group, Inc.

The Natural History of Love was originally published in hardcover by Alfred A. Knopf,
Inc., in 1959. This revised and updated edition was published by arrangement with the
author.

Library of Congress Cataloging-in-Publication Data

Hunt, Morton, 1920–
The natural history of love/Morton Hunt.—1st Anchor Books ed.
p.   cm.
Includes bibliographical references (p.   ) and index.
1. Sex customs—History.   2. Love—History.   3. Man-woman
relationships—History.   I. Title.
HQ12.H75   1994
306.7′09—dc20   93-33361
CIP

To Bernice,
because this book is about love

A PREFATORY NOTE
TO THIS EDITION

❀   ❀

❀

I COULD NOT HAVE FORESEEN, when writing this book in the late 1950s, the vast social upheavals just ahead that would transform the practices and meaning of love—the sexual revolution, the women's movement, the revolt of the young against the values of their society, the commune movement, open marriage, gay liberation, and AIDS.

I could not have imagined that history would move so swiftly that in my own time I would see vast changes in the patterns of love and marriage I had portrayed as the outcome and product of 2,500 years of social evolution.

I could not have guessed how much satisfaction it would give me to find that, nevertheless, many of the judgments I had reached and predictions I had hesitantly made were sound and had held up in the maelstrom of change.

I have extensively revised Chapter X—formerly the final chapter —recasting it as part of the portrait of past times, and written a new chapter, XI, showing how the tumultuous movements mentioned above threatened, for a time, to radically devalue love or even scrap it altogether—and in the end did no such thing but modified it in a number of ways that made it suit the times and continue to meet the deepest needs of men and women.

What love will become in the decades ahead I will never know; I have managed to live this long but someone else must be the chronicler from here on. To him or her, good luck; may you enjoy your labors as much as I have mine.

A PREFATORY NOTE
TO THE FIRST EDITION

❁   ❁

❁

WHEN I FIRST READ Boswell's *London Journal* some years ago, I was fascinated by the details of his love affair with a young actress named Louisa Lewis. The words, the manners, and the intimate details of his report on that peccadillo seemed to me infinitely more real and convincing than those of almost any novel or play. Though I might have been more deeply moved by a work of fiction, I *believed* what Boswell wrote; his reportorial account allowed me the unforgettable experience of living with him in his own time and almost in his own skin. I wondered if it were possible to learn about other men in other times from sources equally credible and equally intimate, and so got the idea of writing this book—an attempt to recreate, from historical materials, a series of realistic portraits of love in each of the major eras of Western history.

Love, to be sure, is a quicksilver word; though you see plainly where it is, you have only to put your finger on it to find that it is not there, but someplace else. What I do not mean by it in this book is, at least, clear enough: this is neither a *Perfumed Garden* nor a historian's Kinsey Report, but primarily the history of emotional relationships between the sexes. Sexual behavior plays a large part in it, to be sure, but what I have wanted most to show is how people have felt about each other. Making this invasion of their private lives has both gratified my curiosity about other people's business and helped me understand, to some degree, what has made modern love the thing it is. The reader need not share the latter motive; I would be delighted if he merely came here seeking enjoyment, and found it.

SOURCES

ANYONE who undertakes to write on love naturally faces the hazard of being challenged by scholars and experts; what is worse, he is apt also to be challenged by everyone else, for what man does not consider himself qualified to argue about love? I have, therefore, from time to time indicated in a footnote the source of some hard-to-believe quotation or the justification for some controversial interpretation. For the rest, the more useful and important works drawn upon in each chapter are named in the section at the back of the book entitled "Notes on Sources."

THANKS

TO THOSE learned and busy people who were good enough to read various chapters and give me their suggestions, I owe thanks for ferreting out at least some of my errors. I am grateful to Professor Richard Haywood of New York University for his comments on Chapters II, III, and IV; to Professor Helaine Newstead of Hunter College for hers on Chapter V; to Professors Garrett Mattingly and Peter Gay of Columbia University, the former for his comments on Chapters VI and VII, and the latter for his on IX; to Professor Raymond G. Carey of the University of Denver for his on Chapter VIII; and to Dr. Abraham Stone, Director of the Margaret Sanger Research Bureau, for advising me on Chapter X.

I am indebted more than I should reveal to my friend Robert L. Heilbroner for putting aside his own writing and providing me with a meticulous and invaluable critique of the style and content of every chapter. Of the several people who assisted me in research, Dr. Katharine M. Rogers deserves my special thanks for her persistence and professional skill in verifying worrisome points and relocating mislaid or missing references.

ACKNOWLEDGMENTS

GRATEFUL acknowledgment is hereby made to the following publishers and persons for permission to reprint the materials specified:

Elizabeth Barnett, literary executor of the estate of Norma Millay Ellis: "I Shall Forget You Presently, My Dear," by Edna St. Vincent Millay, from *Collected Poems* (HarperCollins), copyright © 1922, 1950 by Edna St. Vincent Millay;

Cambridge University Press: lines from R. C. Trevelyan's translation of *Idylls of Theocritus* (1925);

Curtis Brown, Ltd.: the lines from Catullus' *Carmine* Nos. 8, 11, 68, and 85, as translated by Gilbert Highet in his *Poets in a Landscape* (Alfred A. Knopf), copyright © 1957 by Gilbert Highet;

Little, Brown & Co.: selections from *Revolution from Within: A Book of Self-esteem* by Gloria Steinem;

Routledge: selections from B. P. Moore's translation of Ovid's *Ars Amatoria* (Blackie & Son, Ltd., 1935); lines from No. 72 of Catullus' *Carmine*, as translated by F. A. Wright in *Catullus: The Complete Poems* (Routledge & Kegan Paul, 1926);

Yale University Press: excerpts from the *Yale Edition of Horace Walpole's Correspondence* (1937–1955).

CONTENTS

❁   ❁

❁

Chapter I

INTRODUCTION

I

The Trouble with a Word

❋   ❋

❋

*V*oi, *che sapete, che cosa è amor?"* asked Cherubino in Mozart's
Marriage of Figaro. "Tell me, you who know, what is this
thing, love?" Cherubino was still a beardless adolescent and did not
know the answer, but he took it for granted there was one. So have
most other people, and many of them have tried to give it, but the
most noteworthy feature about all their answers is how thoroughly
they disagree. Sometimes, it seems, they cannot possibly be referring
to the same phenomenon, or even to related ones; after a while one
wonders whether there is something wrong with the question itself, or whether perhaps it employs a word of no fixed meaning and
can have no fixed answer.

Poets have written more about love than almost anyone else and
are somehow thought to be experts on it, but they continually con-
tradict each other in hopelessly irreconcilable terms. Some call it
"the sweetest thing on earth," while others assure us that it is "a
mighty pain" and "a sickness full of woes"; another calls it "a proud
and gentle thing" while yet another insists it is "an abject intercourse between slaves and tyrants." A poet will even disagree with
himself, with never a sign of discomfort. Shakespeare on one occasion answered Cherubino's question in the tones of an amiable and
slightly wicked satyr:

> *What is love? 'tis not hereafter;*
> *Present mirth hath present laughter;*
> *What's to come is still unsure;*
> *In delay there lies no plenty:*
> *Then come kiss me, sweet and twenty,*
> *Youth's a stuff will not endure.*

[3]

But another time he fervently and a trifle righteously took this higher view:

> *Love's not Time's fool, though rosy lips and cheeks*
> *Within his bending sickle's compass come;*
> *Love alters not with his brief hours and weeks,*
> *But bears it out even to the edge of doom.*

Poets, of course, are a notoriously flighty lot, but sober philosophers have come no closer to agreeing with each other on the ultimate truth of love. Plato, for instance, held it to be an appreciation of beauty, especially that of abstract ideas and mathematical concepts. Descartes, seeking to avoid this rather static view, injected some desire and action into it; love, he said, is an emotion in which the soul is incited to join itself willingly to objects which appear agreeable to it. In our own time Ortega y Gasset analyzed such philosophizing, and on the basis of modern psychology found it wanting; in his little volume, *On Love*, he produced his own definition of love as "a centrifugal act of the soul in constant flux that goes towards the object and envelops it in warm corroboration, uniting us with it, and positively reaffirming its being." Even without an exegesis—which we clearly need to make anything of all that—we can guess that he is talking about something else again. So it is with the great minds; no wonder, then, that the average man feels himself fully justified in having his own opinions on the subject.

But whatever the definition, is there not at least some agreement as to the extent of love's power and influence? Not a bit. Dante, in the closing line of his giant work, saw it as a macrocosmic force— "love that moves the sun and the other stars." Marlowe's Faustus, though not similarly cosmological in his outlook, nevertheless expected Helen to make him immortal with a single kiss, and Sir Walter Scott epitomized the viewpoint of all the romantics who have ever believed love to have an incomparable power over men's lives:

> *Love rules the court, the camp, the grove,*
> *And men below, and saints above;*
> *For love is heaven, and heaven is love.*

Quite a few other men, however, have considered such talk to be the purest nonsense. Francis Bacon tartly remarked that among the great people of history "there is not one that hath been transported to the mad degree of love." Samuel Johnson, a soul mate of his in a later century, believed that love "has no great influence upon the sum of life," and in modern times H. L. Mencken, as good a scoffer as any, called it merely "a state of perceptual anesthesia."

Semantic troubles with the word "love" are one of the main reasons for confusion and disagreement on the subject. Having remained undifferentiated, the single noun is freely used to refer to any one of several distinct entities. There is "making love" and "being in love," which are quite dissimilar ideas; there is love of God, of mankind, of art, and of pet cats; there is mother love, brotherly love, the love of money, and the love of one's comfortable old shoes. People who study animals have a particular weakness for applying the word to behavior which only externally resembles human love, and then drawing conclusions which they think should hold good for human beings. A Philadelphia psychoanalyst named Leon J. Saul wrote not long ago that birds, since they feed and care for their young with no thought of personal ambition or of being supported in old age, provide us with the perfect model of "true love." Unromantic biologists, however, know that much of this loving behavior consists of purely instinctive responses to "releasers," which are visual or other stimuli that cause the bird to respond automatically. Many songbirds will feed a painted, gaping, artificial mouth just as readily as a real one. Moreover, if a cuckoo, born in a songbird's nest, pushes the baby songbirds out, the loving parents will ignore the fallen ones and feed only the cuckoo; true love seems to be aroused only by the sight of baby-bird-within-nest.

Still, many naturalists have been unable to refrain from seeing human emotions throughout the animal world. In 1900 a German science-popularizer named Wilhelm Bölsche wrote rapturously of the "spiritual impetuosity" of the salmon who even goes hungry in order to find his beloved mate, while the Italian anthropologist, Paolo Mantegazza, a generation earlier offered in the name of natural history such lyrical rhapsodies as this in his book, *The Physiology of Love:*

> Fondly they caress each other with their wings. . . . The wing of one softly and slowly kisses the silk and velvet of his companion. . . . Two creatures, nude yet clothed, passionate and chaste, that love but once and one creature only, that kiss on earth and mate in the skies. . . . Why do we not also love in this way?

For good reason: we do not fly, and anyhow our clothes can come off, neither of which is true of the small brown butterflies he was discussing.

But butterflies were not the end; Professor Mantegazza claimed that flowers also had the power to caress each other, Bölsche held that even the bacillus has a love life, and a series of others reached the logical conclusion that the chemical bonds holding atoms together in molecules were the ultimate form of love. "Potassium and phosphorus entertain such a violent passion for oxygen," wrote a German physician and science writer named Büchner in 1885, "that even under water they burn, that is, unite themselves with the beloved object." Similar ideas are current today, though couched in less incandescent prose; even the learned anthropologist M. F. Ashley Montagu recently wrote that the tendency of matter to cohere is the most primitive form of love. The nuclear binding forces of the atom, he says, are a form of "cooperation," while the bonds holding atoms together in a molecule exemplify "interdependence"; these same characteristics are variously manifested by the amoeba, the plant, the animal, and man, and in the latter are called love.[1]

Perhaps we can simply ignore most of these excursions in meaning; neither Cherubino nor most of the other people who have been fascinated by love have had in mind anything but the love of human beings. Even so, the subject remains marvelously confounded by the variant uses of the word. One of the most famous books on love is the *Ars Amatoria* of Ovid, but he meant by it only a delicious game of seduction, with never a bit of nonsense about centrifugal acts of the soul. Almost at the same time, Platonists and Neoplatonists were using the same word to mean something spiritually ennobling and capable of leading the mind toward divinity. The early Christians fretted about the fact that in their time the name of love was applied with equal ease to pagan sexual orgies and to the Christian feeling for God; after several centuries they more or less succeeded in getting all sexual expression (even within marriage) referred to as "lust," while "love" referred only to religious and benevolent emotions. But the dichotomy would not hold; by the eleventh century men and women had re-appropriated the word for

---

[1] *The Meaning of Love*, pp. 12–16. But in his later and far more profound study of love, *The Direction of Human Development*, he omitted the atomic and molecular analogies.

feelings they had about each other, and since then it has been freely used to refer to everything from the lecheries of Restoration rakes to the domestic sentimentality of the Victorians. Afoot in this semantic jungle, we can have only sympathy for the anonymous compiler of *The Ladies Dictionary* of 1694, who hacked away briefly at the question and then hastily backed out:

> *Love,* what is it? Answ. 'Tis very much like light, a thing that everybody knows, and yet none can tell what to make of it. 'Tis not money, fortune, jointure, raving, stabbing, hanging, romancing, flouncing, swearing, ramping, desiring, fighting, dicing, though all those have been, are, and still will be mistaken and miscalled for it. . . . 'Tis extremely like a sigh, and could we find a painter who could draw one, you'd easily mistake it for the other.

And thus the question "What is this thing, love?" may be incapable of any good answer as long as it implies that there is a single entity. What, then, will this book be about? Not about the love of art, money, or pets; not about the love of God, mankind, or shoes; not about the loves of salmon, butterflies, or atoms. There is a simple criterion—not a definition, but merely a litmus-paper test—of love as it is meant in this book, and as it is thought of, I believe, by most people when they hear the word: it will be any and every form of relationship between human beings which makes sense when used in conjunction with the phrases "falling in love" or "being in love with."

So we must reword Cherubino's question for him a little, making it: "What are these things that have been called love?" In this somewhat inelegant form, the question might find an answer; and that, in fact, is precisely what this book will try to do.

2

Love in the Butterfly Net

❀   ❀

❀

I have called this a "natural history" of love. The term, to be sure, ordinarily refers to the scientific study of animals other than man; I have used it nevertheless because this is to be a data-gathering field expedition in which the author and his readers are the naturalists, the various eras of Western history are the jungles and plains we shall visit, mankind is the fauna that inhabit those regions, and his ways of loving are what we hope to observe and collect examples of.

Most of the learned people who write about love seem to equip themselves in advance with a special theory; with this as a kind of butterfly net, they then sally forth and attempt to capture cases to prove or exemplify their point. But with a single net one can bag only a very narrow range of creatures; if the mesh is the right size for butterflies, it will be too coarse to catch midges and singularly inappropriate for taking elephants. Moralists like Ortega y Gasset and psychoanalysts like Erich Fromm insist that love is not selfish, not a question of desire to possess, but involves a selfless, generous wish to give, to benefit, and to succor the beloved; with such a theory, however ethical it may sound, one cannot capture the love of Catullus for Lesbia, King Henry for Anne Boleyn, or indeed a great many others throughout history. Freudians explain love as arising from inhibited or delayed sexuality, but both pagan Romans and Catholic priests of the Dark Ages often fell deeply in love with their concubines after having uninhibitedly slept with them for months or years. The Marxist's critique of love, the marriage counselor's picture of love, the anthropologist's meaning of love,

[8]

are all useful and stimulating, but each manages by itself to encompass only some kinds of evidence and to miss the others.

We, on the other hand, will venture forth generously equipped with nets both large and small, plus a complete array of lenses, field glasses, stoppered bottles, traps, chains, and cages, so that we need miss nothing. Most important of all, we will take with us a wide-eyed readiness to observe the creatures just as they are, living and making love in their own surroundings.

Even so, there are limits to what we will undertake. We will pass up, for instance, the temptation to explore the curious jungles of primitive love, for here the creatures are so unlike ourselves that we may find it quite impossible to feel their emotions vicariously or assess the meaning of love in any but the most detached fashion. Even when the primitive man speaks as directly and as eloquently as he can, his words hardly help us; most primitive languages are so remote from modern Indo-European language in their structure that the thought processes and undercurrents of meaning can scarcely be translated, while the emotional significance of every object and action is too alien to convey a mood to any but the professional anthropologist. This, for example, is how an intelligent young Trobriand chieftain described a typical romantic rendezvous to the anthropologist Bronislaw Malinowski:

> We make love: our fire, our lime gourd, our tobacco; food no, shame. We go, we go one tree tree big; we sit, we louse and eat; we tell to woman: "We copulate." It is finished, we go to village; in village we go to bachelors' house, we lie, we chatter. Supposing we are alone, we undo pubic leaf ours she undoes skirt we sleep.

Malinowski, recognizing the unintelligibility to outsiders of this transcript, also made a free rendering, padded out with civilized words and explanations, which went as follows:

> When we go out on a love-making expedition, we light our fire; we take our lime gourd (and chew betel-nut), we take our tobacco (and smoke it). Food we do not take, we would be ashamed to do so. We walk, we arrive at a large tree, we sit down, we search each other's heads and consume the lice, we tell the woman that we want to copulate. After it is over we return to the village. In the village we go to the bachelors' house, lie down, and chatter. When we are alone he takes off the pubic leaf, she takes off her fiber skirt: we go to sleep.[2]

[2] B. Malinowski: *The Sexual Life of Savages in Northwestern Melanesia*, pp. 335-6.

It is certainly less formidable, grammatically speaking, but it is still emotionally impenetrable; the reader may be pardoned for saying, like the waspish Byron: "I wish he would explain his explanation."

And anthropologists do so, in the form of intensive, detailed descriptions of puberty rites, mate-selection, courtship, sexual practices, and married life among primitive peoples. But in the great mass of such writings there is almost nothing that seems to refer to love as Western man knows it. Primitive love has perhaps a hundred, perhaps more, different forms, but only a few resemble Western love at all; those few do so only superficially and usually only in certain aspects of sexual practice. For by and large, the clanship structure and social life of most primitive societies provide a wholesale intimacy and a broad distribution of affections; Western love, with its especially close and valued ties between two isolated individuals, is neither possible nor needed. Furthermore, most primitive peoples fail to see any great difference between individuals, and hence do not become involved in unique connections in the Western fashion; any number of trained observers have commented on the ease of their detachment from love objects, and their candid belief in the interchangeability of loves. Dr. Audrey Richards, an anthropologist who lived among the Bemba of Northern Rhodesia in the 1930's, once related to a group of them an English folk-tale about a young prince who climbed glass mountains, crossed chasms, and fought dragons, all to obtain the hand of a maiden he loved. The Bemba were plainly bewildered, but remained silent. Finally an old chief spoke up, voicing the feelings of all present in the simplest of questions: "Why not take another girl?" he asked.

Leaving such questions to be answered by the anthropologist, or anyone else who cares to try, we shall explore only the domain of civilized man, and in fact only Western civilized man, in the past 2,500 years. Even so, it will not be possible to do justice to all who lived in that period; of the love lives of the illiterate and the oppressed, for instance, very little record remains in most of history. We will therefore consider as love in each era that which the era itself meant by the word—the dominating ideas of the dominating classes.

About them, of course, there is plenty of information. But not all of it is reliable, and even the most acquisitive naturalist must have some rules as to what he will consider an acceptable specimen. It is generally supposed that great fiction and great drama bare the human soul and portray the secrets of the heart. But whose soul and whose heart? Those of the author or of his subject? Those of the era of the plot, or the era of the author's own life? The tale of Tristan and Iseult is often thought to convey transcendent truths concerning love, but if one tries to label them and identify them, they vanish or change form before his very eyes. Generations of high-school pupils have learned, through Tennyson, what the world of King Arthur was like in which Tristan and Iseult lived;[3] it greatly resembled a parcel of Victorian gentlemen in medieval costume. The college student, being more sophisticated, reads Sir Thomas Malory and learns that Arthur and his knights were actually rather like fifteenth-century English noblemen in medieval costume. The still more sophisticated graduate student reads Chrétien de Troyes and learns that in fact they were very much like the courtiers of twelfth-century France in medieval costume (and quite properly so). But the historical Arthur was only a minor chieftain rather than the king of a great civilization, and the events he is supposed to have played a part in took place in the sixth century, not the twelfth. He and his men, or their real counterparts, were uncouth Celtic warriors, while the real Tristan, or Drustan, was very likely an equally uncouth Pictish chieftain; neither Arthur, Tristan, nor Iseult could have been anything like the twelfth-century aristocrats in dress, morals, and culture, and their love patterns could not by any stretch of the imagination have been like those portrayed by Chrétien, much less Malory, and still less Tennyson.

Similarly, some of the most vivid characterizations of the seventeenth-century Puritans of New England are the figures created by Nathaniel Hawthorne, who lived two centuries after they did and saw them in retrospect as tormented, brooding, inhibited people. But the historian Henry Cabot Lodge (grandfather of the present Ambassador Lodge) remarked that he had looked on every page of New England history for Hawthorne's characters and never found them. When the diary of Judge Samuel Sewall, the Puritan equivalent of Samuel Pepys, was at last published in 1878, Lodge once again hoped he would discover the originals of Hawthorne's types, but could find not one in all its pages. The Puritan of fiction was, in large part, a fiction.

[3] Tristan (whom Tennyson calls Tristram) did not originally live in it at all, and his story had no connection with the Arthurian court. But by the Middle Ages he and Iseult had been enveloped by the growing Arthurian legend, and Tristan had been made into a knight of the Round Table.

So we will be chary of accepting the word of creative literature as primary evidence. It will surely be valuable, but more by way of corroboration and amplification than otherwise. Primarily we will look to biography, private correspondence, diaries, and the anecdotes and trivia recorded by chroniclers and amateur historians. The advice of fathers to their sons and daughters will be useful, and so will old books of domestic conduct, manuals of courtship technique and sexual methodology, the laws of adultery, divorce, and dowry, and the rules of etiquette. Even palace gossip may sometimes be illuminating; one senses a whole chapter of light-hearted cynicism in a little story about the father of Alexander the Great, repeated centuries later by Plutarch: "What said a woman to King Philip that pulled and hauled her to him by violence against her will? 'Let me go,' said she, 'for when the candles are out, all women are alike.' "

And now, having taken thought for the problems of gathering our specimens, and having outfitted ourselves with all the apparatus of an open mind, we are at last ready to embark on our expedition. The tide is full and it is time to cast off. With luck, we may bring back a museumful of treasures and a fat sheaf of field notes; then let who will visit our museum of love, see what we have collected, and make theories to suit himself.

Chapter II

DILEMMA IN GREECE

I

The Invention of Love

❀   ❀

❀

No wonder the Greeks had a word for nearly everything—
they invented nearly everything. Or, at any rate, a great
many of the things that have been important to Western civilization
ever since: the theory of atoms and the principles of punctuation,
democratic procedure and political dictatorship, metaphysics and
the forms of the drama, scientific terminology and a love of bathing,
and some of the oldest jokes in the world, as, for instance:

Talkative barber: How shall I cut your hair, sire?
King Archelaus of Macedon: In silence.

And that was not all; they also invented love, gave it two names—
eros (carnal love) and *agape* (spiritual love)—and elaborated upon
both its theory and its practice.

Love has never since divested itself of its Greek trappings. Cupid
(Eros) and his arrows are a Greek conceit; Sappho drew up a
formal symptomatology of lovesickness which has been faithfully
adhered to by lovers for twenty-five centuries; Platonic love, that
long-discussed and marvelously misapplied term, originated with
Plato's own attempts to build incorporeal metaphysics out of the
desires of the flesh; and a whole set of familiar love tales emerged
from Greek sources—Odysseus and Penelope, Daphnis and Chloe,
Cupid and Psyche, Dido and Aeneas, Hero and Leander, and many
others.[1] Greek literature of earlier times had been made up chiefly
of heroic histories, political diatribes, religious hymns, philosophic
inquiries, and the like, but beginning with the Golden Age (about

[1] And later many fictional love stories
with Greek backgrounds came to be
thought truly Greek; the legend of
Troilus and Cressida, for instance, originated in the Middle Ages in Western
Europe, but is often taken for a genuine
Trojan legend.

480 B.C. to 399 B.C.) it became progressively diluted with an ever greater admixture of love lyrics, amorous laments, and protracted romances ending either in bliss or misery. In some of these—even in the briefest epigrams—love sentiments occasionally achieved a quality quite unknown to the primitive peoples who preceded the flowering of Athenian culture:

> *My soul was on my lips, as I kissed Agathon;*
> *It came there (poor soul!) longing to cross over to him.*

Yet for all its familiar aspects, love in classic Greece was peculiarly, and even startlingly, different in character from later and contemporary Western conceptions of love. For it was considered not so much an ennobling and transforming goal of life, but an amusing pastime and distraction, or sometimes a god-sent affliction. And its heartfelt expressions were poured forth not by young men and women who desired each other as mates, but by married men serenading courtesans, and by homosexuals (or lesbians) wooing others of their kind. It is therefore a paradox of no mean order that modern love began with Greek love and owes so much to it, although the forms and ideals of Greek love are considered immoral and, to a large extent, illegal, in modern society.

2

Love Life of an Insolent Hero

❀   ❀

❀

The tastes and preferences of the Athenians of the time of Socrates were not as uniformly noble and elevated as they often seem in romantic perspective. They admired wisdom, it is true, but they admired physical beauty even more, even when it was accompanied by no wisdom whatever; they esteemed moderation and self-control, but they vastly admired *hybris* (insolent pride) and fiery passion; and though they praised virtue, they were entranced by cunning and trickery. In the realm of love it was much the same: they studied it, argued about it, exalted its pleasures, and lamented its pains—but in the main were able to feel it only for prostitutes and pederasts.

In an extreme form all this is well exemplified by the man who helped tarnish the luster of the Age of Pericles—his own foster son, Alcibiades, that man of extreme contrasts: pupil of Socrates and vulgar roisterer, superb warrior and idle wastrel, master politician and common lawbreaker, patriot and traitor, devotee of philosophy and oratory, and passionate lover of whores and boys.[2]

Born in 450 B.C. of a wealthy noble family, Alcibiades lost his father early, and was raised by his mother's kinsman Pericles, the great statesman and leader of Athens in her democratic zenith. In his teens, Alcibiades blossomed out as the tallest and handsomest youth in Athens, and soon was everywhere accompanied by a swarm of men who, in the fashion of the time, courted and flattered him as though he were a beautiful girl. He played the role of *demimondaine* expertly, taunting, flirting, and frustrating his lovers, and allowing homosexual favors when it pleased or profited him. Youths aped his manners, his lisp, and his special style of shoes, and his latest pranks and dissipations were always the talk of the town.

Yet Alcibiades had a brilliant mind and a strain of moral sensibility. He studied with Socrates, and when the philosopher spoke to him of the virtuous life, tears would run from the lad's eyes. "If I did not shut my ears against him, and fly as from the voice of the siren," Alcibiades later said, "my fate would be like that of the others—he would transfix me, and I should grow old sitting at his feet. For he makes me confess that I ought not to live as I do. . . . And therefore I run away and fly from him." Fleeing from Socrates again and again, he reveled in dissolute pleasures and played discreditably at politics; yet he was brave and manly, and fought well at Potidaea at the age of twenty (though Socrates had to save his life on the battlefield), and six years later did still better at Delium (where he returned the favor).

---

[2] The principal classical sources of information about Alcibiades are Plutarch's "Life of Alcibiades," Xenophon's *Memorabilia*, and two dialogues of Plato; many other writers mention him, but anecdotally and often unreliably.

In the full flush of his youthful popularity, Alcibiades was atrociously insolent, but he always went completely unpunished. When Pericles said that he too, like Alcibiades, had talked too cleverly and dogmatically of politics in his youth, his foster son sneered: "Would that I had conversed with you, Pericles, when you were still acute in such discussions!" Anytus, a wealthy lover of his, invited him to a banquet; Alcibiades came only as far as the door, and wickedly ordered his slaves to pick up and carry home half of the gold and silver vessels spread before the other guests. The banqueters were furious and protested to Anytus that Alcibiades had acted outrageously, but the lovesick man replied: "Not so, but moderately and kindly; he might have taken all there were; he has left us half."

To meet the dare of fellow roisterers, Alcibiades once publicly punched Hipponicus, one of the richest and most powerful citizens of Athens, in the face, but the next morning he came to Hipponicus' house, bared his body, and begged the older man to whip him. Hipponicus was overcome. He not only forgave the youth, but offered him his daughter, Hipparete, in marriage, with a dowry of ten talents ($60,000)—which the glib Alcibiades promptly persuaded him to double when she should become a mother. To Alcibiades' way of thinking, this was just about his wife's only attraction. After marrying her, he paid no attention to her except to give her household orders. With her dowry money, he filled his house with costly furniture, had artists paint pictures on the walls, held elegant banquets, and lived in luxury and splendor such as were rare in Athens at that time. His wife's role in all this remained merely that of his housekeeper—one who took orders, and was ignored except when inefficient in serving him.

Alcibiades' attitude toward her was not the result of homosexuality. Like most upper-class Athenian men of his time, he was equally attracted by both sexes. The women who intrigued him, however, were those who sold their favors; these he liked thoroughly, from elegant courtesans to common brothel inmates, and at all levels they were fond of him and much impressed by him. But this did not in the least interfere with his continuing affection for other men and for boys. In fact, so successful was he on all fronts that he chose not an ancestral device for his shield, but a design of Eros holding a thunderbolt, to indicate his own invincibility in love.

When Hipparete could stomach all this no longer, she returned to her father's house and prepared to divorce Alcibiades, but the day she appeared in court he and some of his friends burst in, snatched her up, and carried her off. No one protested or tried to free her, and she passively accepted the situation, remaining in his house quietly until her death a short time later. His reasons for carrying her off had nothing to do with hidden affection. Under Athenian law, when a wife divorced her husband, he had to return the dowry—and this Alcibiades had no intention of doing.

His political and military biography, entangled as it is with the complex Peloponnesian War, is too involved to bear telling here, but a few highlights of it will illuminate his personality. Through political and military exploits, he rose to be one of Athens' ten generals and successfully preached the need for a war against Syracuse in order to expand the Athenian economy. The Assembly endorsed his plan and in 415 B.C. built a great armada and dispatched an army in it, with Alcibiades as one of its two commanders. But a few days after its departure they sent a swift ship ordering him back to stand trial for the mischievous mutilation of the ears, noses, and phalli of the city's many statues of Hermes, as well as for certain religious impieties. The doughty general denied the charges, but jumped ship rather than stand trial. He then made his way to Sparta and appeared before its Assembly, arguing that Sparta should join Syracuse in the war against Athens. The Spartans listened and were impressed; unfortunately, before Alcibiades could fulfill the dream of conquering his own city at the head of an enemy army, he indulged in a love affair with the Spartan Queen, Timaea, and had to flee the wrath of King Agis. In this extremity he turned to the Persians, the traditional enemies of all Greeks, and found shelter among them.

The military fortunes of Athens declined seriously in the following years. After a series of overturns of the government, the democracy came back into power; the Athenian Assembly offered Alcibiades an amnesty after ten years' absence if he would return and take charge of their military forces. He heeded the call, promptly defeated two Spartan fleets, and entered Athens to the accompaniment of frenzied adulation, all his sins forgotten. But then came an unexpected naval defeat as a result of his temporarily leaving his post of command, whereupon the fickle Assembly turned upon him again. Once more he fled the city, and when the Athenian fleet, lacking his leadership, was completely destroyed by the Spartans, he had to flee still farther—as before, to the Persians. In Phrygia he put himself under the protection of General Pharnabazus, who lent

him a house in which he lived, plotting and consoling himself with
one, or some say two, courtesans. The Persian King, meanwhile, in
order to curry favor with the conquering Spartans, secretly ordered
Pharnabazus to kill his guest, and one day in 404 B.C. two assassins
set fire to Alcibiades' house and riddled him with arrows and jave-
lins as he ran forth naked, sword in hand—still brave, still beautiful,
still full of *hybris*.

More fascinated than horrified by him, the Greeks made him a
favorite subject of biographical and philosophic writing. At least
half a dozen dialogues, including one doubtfully ascribed to Plato,
bore his name in classic times, and he appeared briefly in scores of
other works. Forgetful of his crimes but mindful of his charm, they
set up a monument at his Phrygian grave; so great was his appeal
even five centuries later that the Roman Emperor Hadrian had a
marble statue of him put up at the monument and ordered an ox
sacrificed there every year. This was the man the Athenians admired
to distraction, and who wore into battle the likeness of Eros on his
shield.

3

"Marriage Brings a Man Only Two Happy Days"

Not every Greek was an Alcibiades, but even those who were
law-abiding, gentle, and kindly tended to look upon their
wives as a necessary burden and expected to find love only outside
the home. Their relationships with the women they married can be

hesitantly inferred from drama and comedy, but neither hesitancy nor inference is necessary, for among the Greek writings that survived the Roman conquest and the Dark Ages there is one detailed, authentic nonfictional portrayal of the life of the upper-class Athenian woman. It comes from the prolific historian Xenophon, who found time among his more ambitious projects to dash off a brief handbook on home and farm economics which he called *The Economist*.[3] It gives advice on the management of a household, the control of slaves and servants, and the proper techniques of farming; and when it deals with the handling and training of a wife, it provides us with the best existing description of the well-to-do woman's life in Athens at the end of the fifth century B.C. *The Economist* is written in the form of a dialogue, most of it taking place between Socrates (under whom Xenophon had studied) and an excellent young man named Ischomachus. As with all dialogues, it undoubtedly employs much literary artifice, but basically it is not a work of fiction; it is a practical manual, offering a blueprint of the well-run normal household.

In chapter seven Socrates first asks Ischomachus whether his wife came to him well prepared for her role. "My dear Socrates," Ischomachus replies, "how could she have had sufficient knowledge when I took her, since she came to my house when she was not fifteen years old, and had spent the preceding part of her life under the strictest restraint in order that she might see as little, hear as little, and ask as few questions as possible?" Since his bride was only an ignorant child, without glamour, sophistication, intellectuality, or experience in the ways of attracting men, it is little wonder that Ischomachus has almost nothing to say about loving her; love, in fact, had nothing whatever to do with their marriage, as he himself pointed out to the girl soon after their wedding.

"Tell me, my dear wife," he said one day, after the girl had become somewhat accustomed to him, "have you ever considered with what view I married you, and with what object your parents gave you to me? For I am sure it is as evident to you as to me that there was no lack of other persons with whom we might have shared our respective beds. But when I took thought for myself, and your parents did for you, whom we might select as the best partner for a

---

[3] The title, in English, has a misleading sound; the Greek, *Oeconomicus*, implied one who was expert not in theoretical economics, but in the management of his farm and estate.

house and children, I preferred you, and your parents, it appears, preferred me." With this unromantic preamble, he began to explain the purpose of marriage, telling her that it rested first of all on co-operation in managing their common fortune and property.

"But in what respect could I co-operate with you?" asked the girl with due humility. "What power have I? Everything lies with you. My duty, my mother told me, was to conduct myself discreetly."

This being a modest and proper answer, Ischomachus generously said that she could indeed help him. The gods had made man and woman different so as to be of the greatest use to each other. By their union, man and woman produce offspring and keep the race alive, but even more important, they profit by a division of labor. There are two general kinds of work—outdoor and indoor—of which man is designed for the former, woman for the latter; man is fitted to travel, to work in the field, to fight, and to be active in public places, while woman is equipped to care for children, train and watch over the servants, store and guard the household goods, and perform other stay-at-home tasks. It is her success at these labors, Ischomachus tells his young wife, that will bring her joy in her marriage: "Be therefore diligent, virtuous, and modest, and give your necessary attendance on me, your children, and your house, and your name shall be honorably esteemed even after your death; for it is not the beauty of your face and shape, but your virtue and goodness, which will bring you honor and esteem which will last forever." Esteem, respect, honor—these are the greatest pleasures she can gain from marriage. If these might seem a threadbare reward to modern woman, they did not to Ischomachus' wife, for according to his own words, she was immediately inspired to begin trying her hand at household management.

In the next long session of instruction, he taught her the orderly arranging and storing of food and goods in the house. "How excellent a thing a regular arrangement of articles is, and how easy it is to find, in a house, a suitable place to put everything!" he rhapsodized after giving her full details. This too, he apparently felt, is an important element of woman's emotional life, for, as he says to Socrates in recounting the instruction he gave her that day: "It seems to be a provision of nature that as it is easier for a well-disposed woman to take care of her children than to neglect them, so it is more pleasing for a right-minded woman to attend to, rather than neglect, her property, which, being her own, affords her gratification." But despite such gratification, generously granted her, there seems to have sprung up in the foolish bosom of Ischomachus' young wife some fugitive desire to be thought ravishing and enchanting, for one day, as he explains to Socrates, he noticed that she had lightened her skin with white lead, touched her cheeks with vermilion, and put on high-heeled shoes. He dealt with her in a gentle, but firm, manner:

"My dear wife," he began, "were we not united that we might have personal intimacy with each other?"

"People say so, at least," she replied.

"I am not better pleased with the color of white lead and red dye than with your own," said Ischomachus, paying her what he conceived to be a loving compliment. He assured her on philosophic grounds that the human body is most beautiful in its natural state; then, rather inconsistently, he argued against a wife's use of cosmetics on the grounds that it could deceive a stranger, but not a husband, since the latter would see her in the morning or in her bath, and know the truth.

"And what in the name of the gods did she answer to those remarks?" asks Socrates.

"Her only answer," says Ischomachus, "was this, that she never afterwards practiced any such art, but took care to appear in a natural and becoming manner." Not being a hard man, however, Ischomachus very kindly offered her some advice on beauty care: she must not sit idle in her room, but preside over the loom, move constantly about the house to watch the servants, and trouble herself to do some of the kneading of dough and the shaking-out and folding of linens. "I assured her," he concludes, "that if she thus exercised herself she would take her food with a better appetite, would enjoy better health, and would assume a more truly excellent complexion. . . . And now, Socrates, be assured my wife regulates her conduct as I taught her."

Whether this impenetrably smug young man was a real person, whether his views are actually those of Socrates, or whether they are those of Xenophon himself, hardly matters; the cloistered, duty-bound, mentally circumscribed Athenian wife of these pages is no figment of satire or of romance, but a composite portrait of the normal, upper-class housewife of Athens, in about 400 B.C. And from other sources one can piece together many details to corroborate and complete the picture shown in *The Economist*. Athenian citizenship was a precious possession of women as well as men, but between the sexes yawned a gulf as great as that between citizen and slave. A boy began to go to school in his seventh year, filling his mind with grammar, poetry, music, arithmetic, legend, and the sports and studies of the gymnasium. By the age of eighteen or nineteen, when he adopted the *chlamys* or man's cloak and swore the oath of loyalty to the State, he had become a gentleman, a warrior, a property-manager, and an amateur philosopher. A girl, in contrast, remained confined to the house from birth to marriage, and learned nothing but a few domestic skills and possibly a little writing. When she reached her teens, her betrothal was arranged by her parents; her consent was not asked, and would have been valueless in any case, since she had hardly ever met or known any young men. Many a girl laid aside her dolls or dedicated them to Artemis only a day or two before her wedding.

The wedding thrust her into the limelight for one day. There was a ritual bath, a careful dressing-up in holiday clothes, and a ceremony at her own house followed by a banquet and libation. Toward evening the groom put her in a bridal chariot and led her home through the streets, while flutists and harp-players made music, and relatives and guests formed a merry procession. At his house the new husband carried her into the bridal chamber and closed the door; outside, the guests chanted *epithalamia* or wedding hymns, the gist of which was that he should attend to business and not fall asleep. By morning, when the bride unveiled herself to her new relatives, her moment of glory was over. Rarely would she again mingle with her husband's friends or go out into the streets, except accompanied by servants; never would she again be celebrated or sung to until she died.

When Pheidias designed the statue of Aphrodite at Elis, dedicated to marriage, he made her with one foot on the shell of a tortoise, wrote Plutarch, to signify that a virtuous woman stayed inside her house and kept quiet. Pericles, the man of his age, once said in a famous funeral speech that "the greatest glory of a woman is to be least talked about by man, whether they are praising you or criticizing you." The seclusion of Athenian women was not quite as complete as that in Oriental harem life: well-born girls marched in the procession in honor of Athena; wives apparently went occasionally to the theater and to a few public festivals; and to judge from vase paintings, women of the poorer classes had to go outside the house to get water from the public wells. But upper-class women sent slaves on all household errands, and could not even do their own shopping. At home, the female quarters (*gynaikonitis*) were physically separated from the men's hall and rooms (*andronitis*); when a husband brought company home to dinner, his wife and daughters were expected to remain unseen. Men sallied forth in the morning and spent their days in public places; when they finally came home at night, it was not to share with an ignorant woman the precious experiences of the day or the subtleties of current politics and warfare, but to go to sleep.

Custom established the distance between them, and the law maintained it. An Athenian female, even though a citizen, could neither make contracts nor incur debts for more than trifling sums. She could not bring actions at law, and at all times had to have a male guardian—either her father, some relative, her husband, or son. Although the law was completely permissive toward male philandering, it prescribed that a woman caught in adultery was not thereafter to attend public sacrifices; if she did, passers-by had the right to maltreat her in any way short of homicide. A husband could "dismiss" or "put away" his wife not only for adultery, but for any other reason, though he had to return the dowry with her. As for his property, though she spent her life caring for it, it went not to her but to his male heirs; for support, after his death, she had to return to her own people. In a famous court oration involving a prostitute who had tried to pass herself off as a married woman, Demosthenes clarified the whole subject of womanhood and marriage for the jury in one sentence: "Mistresses we keep for pleasure, concubines for daily attendance upon our persons, and wives to bear us legitimate children and be our housekeepers." [4]

Having set up such barriers against love within marriage, Greek men found the wedded state distasteful; it was expensive, bothersome, and a hindrance to one's personal freedom. Yet it was unavoidable: a man did need a housekeeper, and it was his duty to the State and to religion to have progeny. He tried to render marriage painless by thorough subjugation of his wife, but only with partial success, for he had to put up with her unless he was

[4] "Against Neaera." This oration is included among Demosthenes' writings in most collections, although its authenticity is uncertain. Scholars generally agree, however, that it dates from his time, is much in his vein, and gives a faithful portrait of the morals of that period.

willing to send her and her dowry back home. Like most overlords, he distrusted and disliked this vassal, and feared every evidence of power on her side.

Down through the centuries have come echoes of that fear, the most familiar of them being the gossipy tales of the terrible wife of that best of all men, Socrates. According to tradition, Xanthippe was a ferocious termagant, who even attacked Socrates physically; she not only drenched him with water during one argument, but once tore the cloak off his back in the market place. Yet these things were minor, compared to the waspishness of her tongue. "How is it," a friend once asked him, "that you do not educate Xanthippe, but are content to have her as your wife, although she is the most ill-trained of all women that are in existence?" "Since I wish to converse and associate with mankind," said the philosopher in his typical mocking way, "I chose this wife, well knowing that if I could learn to endure her, I should easily bear the society of all other people."

As early as the sixth century B.C., the great lawmaker Solon had seriously considered a law—and according to some sources, passed it—making marriage compulsory because it had already become so unpopular that the State was endangered. Similar measures were considered again and again as the problem grew worse, and in Periclean Athens the law actually specified that only married men could become orators or generals. Most men delayed marriage as long as possible, and entered upon it only when they dared no longer avoid it. It is against this background that one can judge the frequent splenetic attacks upon wives and marriage in the creative literature of the era. "He's married, I tell you!" says a character in one for-gotten play. "What's that you say?" replies the other. "He's really married?—but I just left him, alive and well!" Euripides often por-trayed women as adulterous and vicious; Aristophanes lampooned them as drunken, scheming, quarrelsome, and greedy; and after some centuries of this tradition, the Greek poet Palladas summed it up with one of the cruelest epigrams in literature:

> *Marriage brings a man only two happy days:*
> *The day he takes his bride to bed, and the day he lays her*
> *   in her grave.*

The prevailing dislike of marriage was only part of a more gen-eral dislike of womankind. Greek anti-feminism began in the nursery, where naughty children were threatened with bogies—all of which were female—and as they grew up they heard such legends as that of Pandora, source of all human ills, and Helen, cause of the terrible Trojan War. Indeed, it was a cliché of Greek popular thought that there was a woman behind every war. Even philosophers subscribed to much of the general misogyny, though thinking themselves above it. Plato pleaded liberally for equal education and career opportunities for woman in Book Five of the *Republic:* "The gifts of nature," he wrote, "are alike diffused in both; all the pursuits of men are the pursuits of women also." Being a Greek gentleman, however, he could not help adding: "—but in all of them a woman is inferior to a man." Even his famous proposal, in the *Republic*, for a system of communal marriage, superficially seeming to be a liberation of woman from her secluded destiny, is actually no great elevation of her role or status as a love partner; it makes of womankind a mere collective pool of depersonalized fertility, and can be interpreted as the fantasy of a man who has no interest in a close relationship with an individual female.

Sane, sensible Aristotle rejected his teacher's communal-marriage plan, but agreed with him that the male was by nature superior not only in mind and body, but even in the procreative process, on the grounds that semen bears the principle of soul, while female secretions contribute only the material of body. From this and similar considerations, Aristotle arrived at a philosophic principle on married love which nicely rationalized the status quo: because the wife is inferior to her husband, he wrote in the *Nichomachean Ethics*, she ought to love him more than he her; algebraically, this would compensate for their inequality and result in a well-balanced relationship. There is no particular evidence that Greek women agreed with this view.

But what did Greek women actually feel? Did they love their husbands, or hate them, or merely suffer them in boredom? Unfortunately, in the war of the sexes, as in other wars, history is written by the victors; there are no books on love by Greek housewives. We might make a synthesis of their feelings toward men by distilling and collecting samples from the tragedies of Sophocles and Euripides, the scandalous comedies of Aristophanes, and the like; but it would remain unverified and unproven, for all this literature was written by and chiefly for men. The product, in fact, would probably be not so much a reproduction of the attitudes of the real

Greek wife, but of a fiction of the Greek male mind—a phantom shrew, created by him to justify his own hostile and oppressive attitude toward real women.

But we have already seen the objective facts of Greek marriage; in them lies the only reliable answer, and a better guide than the bitter thrusts of creative literature. The Athenian wife had no real contact with any free men except her husband. He was all-important to her, regardless of the inner separateness of their lives. He was her master, the father of her children, the provider for her home. As human beings everywhere tend to feel loyalty and affection for the authorities over them—even when they grumble against and frequently hate those authorities—so Greek wives must have felt a kind of love for their husbands, though it could hardly have been anything that would satisfy the expectations and requirements of women in more recent centuries.

A good objective measurement of the Greek wife's love for her husband is its strength as compared to familial, clan-like ties. A wealth of details concerning Greek marriage, divorce, and property inheritance, some of which we have already seen, make it clear that her ties to her own family always remained far stronger than those to her husband. And this does corroborate a portrait in drama: that of Antigone, in the play by Sophocles, who explains her act of self-sacrifice for her brother by saying that a brother is irreplaceable, though a husband is not—a passage so distasteful to the romantic mind that Goethe once remarked: "I would give a great deal to have an apt philologist prove that it is interpolated and spurious." The Greeks were not similarly offended.

Even more impressive is an instance of the identical sentiment appearing not in drama, but in history; the character in the case is Persian, but her actions were reported with approval by a Greek, Herodotus, in his monumental *History*, as exemplifying noble conduct in a woman. King Darius of Persia, Herodotus related, had convicted one Intaphernes and his kin of conspiring at insurrection, and condemned them all to death. But taking pity on Intaphernes' weeping wife, he sent a messenger to her, who said: "Madam, King Darius gives you one of the prisoners to be reprieved: take which one you choose." Her course was clear. "If the king grants me the life of one only," she said without hesitation, "I choose, above all, my brother." As for Intaphernes, she would weep for him—and let him die.

4

The Descent from Primitivism

❀   ❀

❀

How did it come about that, in the very flowering of this superb civilization, woman was so lowly and unloved? In general, one expects woman's place in a civilized society to be rather better than that in a primitive society, where she is apt to be exploited, treated as property, and subjected to numerous strict taboos. Yet many classicists have claimed that in the Golden Age of Greece, which we have just been visiting, her position was far inferior, both socially and in the hearts of men, to what it had been six to eight centuries earlier in the savage society of the Homeric era. The *Iliad* and *Odyssey* tell of no such extreme seclusion as existed in the time of Pericles, and the women in these epics often exercise considerable influence over their men and over the course of history. Some are shown as archetypes of faithfulness and loyalty. Penelope, who waited twenty wretched years for the return of Odysseus and steadfastly held off a horde of importunate suitors, is the very embodiment of wifely fidelity. In Book Six of the *Iliad*, Andromache and her husband, Hector, are shown to be a devoted and loving couple, and the scene when Hector is about to set out for battle is often cited as evidence of the closeness that could exist in Homeric marriage. Says Andromache:

> When I lose you I might as well be dead. There will be no comfort left, when you have met your doom—nothing but grief.
> . . . You, Hector, are father and mother and brother to me, as well as my beloved husband. Have pity on me now; stay here on the tower; and do not make your boy an orphan and your wife a widow.

Hector replies that he would dishonor himself if he failed to fight the Greek enemy, but adds:

> Deep in my heart I know the day is coming when holy Ilium will be destroyed, with Priam and the people of Priam of the good ashen spear. Yet I am not so much distressed by the thought of what the Trojans will suffer, or Hecabe herself, or King Priam, or all my gallant brothers whom the enemy will fling down in the dust, as by the thought of you, dragged off in tears by some Achaean man-at-arms to slavery.

Certain other ancient legends also show women in a favorable light: the stories of Alcestis, Polyxene, Iphigenia, and others all center about heroines who not only are admirable, but who act with far more freedom and initiative than later Greek women. Literary scholars long racked their brains to find explanations for this perplexing state of affairs. Possibly the most ingenious of them all was Samuel Butler, who, after translating the *Odyssey*, decided that its author had been a woman, and had portrayed society inaccurately, with a feministic bias.

Homer, however, was a very thorough and excellent reporter of folkways, and if one considers in the light of anthropological science the data so liberally strewn through the *Iliad* and *Odyssey*, a rather different conclusion appears.[5] The world that Homer depicted existed about 1300 to 1100 B.C.; if judged by its technology, its social organization, its degree of literacy, and other basic criteria, it was a primitive society about as developed as those of the more advanced American Indians before they came in contact with white men. Woman's place in Homeric society, despite such occasional hints of sentiment as those quoted above, was typically that of the primitive female. She was denied any place at ceremonial banquets, and even the youth Telemachus could tell his mother, Penelope, to leave the banquet hall and return to her proper womanly tasks. Marriages were arranged entirely by men, without the participation or consent of the women. The woman was purchased by her husband, and could be traded, lent, or given away like his other property. She was accumulated in large numbers by the wealthy, and enslaved, abused, or killed on the spot by conquering enemies.

Sexually she had no rights, though her lord had many: Penelope was faithful, but Odysseus was a potent lover who enlivened his tedious travels with many affairs, and though Zeus, chief of the

---

[5] Just such anthropological analyses have been made by sociologist A. G. Keller some decades ago in his book *Homeric Society*, by historian Moses Finley very recently in *The World of Odysseus*, and by others.

gods, boastfully recited to his wife a list of his extramarital triumphs, she dared offer no word of reproach. Above all, between man and woman there was hardly ever the depth, intensity, or quality of feeling that existed between father and son or between male friends. "The poems," wrote Professor Finley, "are rich in such images as this: 'as a father greets his dear son who has come from a distant land in the tenth year'; but there are no similes drawn from a husband's joy in his wife. . . . The meaningful social relationships and the strong personal attachments were sought and found among men."

Nevertheless, even if meaningful relationships and strong attachments were rare between husbands and wives, women in Homeric society were genuinely important to their men, as in all primitive societies. They were food-preparers, makers of clothing, breeders of offspring, nurses to the sick, caretakers of the household and farm during the warriors' absence, and much else. No wonder, then, that they may well have been more active, resourceful, and important than their descendants of six hundred years later; seclusion—and intellectual misogyny—would only come with the emergence of a society wealthy enough to take most of woman's vital functions away from her and leave her nearly useless.

As civilization gradually ripened, long centuries after the barbaric Homeric era of tribal warfare and agrarian economy, the Greek city-states developed both manufacturing and mercantile activities. Finally, after the Greeks threw back the great Persian attacks of the fifth century B.C., Athens emerged as a leading sea power and industrial center. Mines, factories, farms, and other enterprises were profitably operated by slave power. In Attica, the district around and including Athens, there lived some 25,000 citizens and 10,000 free noncitizens; since the average slave cost only two *minae* (about $100 to $200, depending on which decade of the fifth century B.C. one considers), these citizens and freemen lived and prospered by the labors of some 150,000 to 300,000 slaves. Using this great pool of manpower as we use machinery today, Athens passed rapidly from a semi-primitive household economy to an urban economy, and thence to an imperialistic one. Among the results were wealth, leisure, and a great flourishing of art and ideas; but another, and less happy, result was the severe whittling-away of the purposes of family life.

When the home lost its position as the only source of food, clothing, and other essentials, it ceased to be the center of a man's existence and became merely an expensive social obligation. A husband's ties to his wife and household were no longer those of personal survival and close co-operation, but of *noblesse oblige* and absentee overlordship. Women retained their primitive disadvantages, but lost much of their onetime importance; in fact, with leisure, wealth, and slave power at their command, they themselves became enslaved. Meanwhile, as small tribes evolved into the imperialistic city-state, the ancient clanship ties wasted away, leaving Greek men and women with a need to redirect their love feelings and reorganize their deteriorating web of affectional ties. A state is not as warm as a clan, and neither a tyrant nor a democracy fills the gap left by tribal elders.

Affectional ties therefore shifted toward individuals. Greek wives, more closely than ever bound to the home, could partly fill their emotional needs with their children. But Greek men cast about uncertainly, seeking the proper persons with whom to develop a new set of relationships to replace the old ones. Their wives, clearly, were not the answer, since they were totally ignorant of educated ideas, and knew nothing of the richness of Athenian mental and spiritual life. Yet the Greeks enjoyed sex and admired female beauty; their legends, their religion, and their art were full of idealized and highly desirable goddesses, nymphs, and women. Greek men were willing to experiment with a new and more intense relationship to women, if they could find any who offered both gratification to the body and entertainment to the mind.

The Noble Companion

❀   ❀

❀

The hiring of the female as a sexual outlet and a companion was one of the many innovations of city life. According to several ancient authors, the wise Solon himself first established brothels throughout Athens. "You did well for every man, O Solon," exulted one Greek poet. "You, seeing that the State was full of men, young and possessed of all the natural appetites, and wandering in their lusts where they had no business, bought women and in certain spots did place them, ready for all comers." It not only protected wives from philanderers, but was a sound business venture; tradition says that Solon was able to build the temple of Aphrodite Pandemos with the profits.

The supplying of sexual partners later passed into private hands, and became specialized. In the Golden Age and afterwards, there were three categories of hired women. The common prostitutes were called *pornae;* they lived in ordinary brothels, the nature of which was made unmistakable by a wooden or painted phallus near the door. Higher than the *pornae* in the social scale were the *auletrides* or flute-players; these girls were hired out by their teachers or by their masters (many of the girls being slaves) to play, dance, and amuse the men at private dinners. Often they would spend the night, or part of it, with one or more of the dinner guests. The upper-class Greek man had a condescending and mildly contemptuous attitude toward both of these types. He felt no moral loathing for them, but as a man of taste and education he recognized that short-order harlotry was trivial, unaesthetic, and often vulgar.

But at the top level, prostitution was something quite different. In the sixth century B.C., Sappho had first used the word *hetaerae*—

companions—to mean intimate female friends. Much later the word
degenerated to mean prostitutes in general, but during the fifth and
fourth centuries B.C. it was still the dignified label of the high-grade
courtesan. She was often a woman of good blood and Athenian
citizenship, but unlike the usual wellborn girl, she had been carefully trained to be sexually exciting, mentally stimulating, full of
charm and graces, and capable of infatuating intelligent men. The
hetaera lived independently, usually in a house of her own, and en-
tertained such lovers as she chose to admit to it; she might allow a
number of them to pay court to her, or she might for a while become the exclusive companion of one man. Her gown, her hair,
and her make-up were elegant and full of artifice; her table was
artistically set and well spread; her home was a place of beauty and
refuge where a man could pass the time agreeably; and she herself
was a captivating and complex woman. All this gave her a status
vastly higher than that of the housewife. Greek literature of this
period refers again and again to the hetaera as a real friend, a noble
companion, and a woman of golden character, immeasurably superior to the virtuous woman. As the poet Philetaerus remarked: "No
wonder there is a shrine to the Companion everywhere, but nowhere in all Greece is there one to the Wife."

Such was the hetaera; perhaps only a few were quite so ideal and
idealized, but they made up in impact what they lacked in numbers.
In the fifth century B.C., for example, no woman was more influential than Aspasia, a courtesan who learned and practiced her profession in Miletus until about 450 B.C., and then came to Athens.
She is said to have had golden hair, a silvery voice, and a small high-
arched foot, and undoubtedly her physical charms included much
more, of which, unfortunately, there is no record. Her ability to
captivate, however, rested upon the fact that her beauty was allied
to other and more compelling qualities. She was widely read, highly
skilled in speaking, and talented in philosophic discussions. According to some, she gave lectures in her own home on rhetoric and
philosophy, and won such respect for her knowledge and her fine
manners that it is even said some men brought their wives to hear
her speak. (In view of the prevailing feeling about wives, this may
be a doubtful detail.) In the *Menexenus* of Plato, Socrates says that
he studied rhetoric with Aspasia, and that she was responsible for
the training of some of the finest Athenian orators. Pericles himself
was named among them, and a large part of the *Menexenus* con-

sists of Socrates' recollection of a funeral oration which he says was written by Aspasia and delivered by Pericles.

It is a pity that there is no credible record of the first meetings of Pericles and Aspasia; one would like to know if he came to learn rhetoric and stayed to love, or came to dally and was captivated by her mind and soul. Whichever was the case, Pericles and his wife were soon divorced and he brought Aspasia into his own home as his exclusive mistress. From then on she was the uncrowned Queen of Athens. To conservatives, however, she was an irritant, a disgrace, and a danger; they accused her of being a procuress, a schemer, and a malevolent power in politics; it was even said by gossips that the long, dreadful Peloponnesian War was started at her request merely because two of her maidservants were stolen by pranksters from the city of Megara.

Pericles was completely devoted to her, and would have married her except that the law forbade citizens to marry noncitizens. Plutarch wrote that he "loved her with wonderful affection," citing as proof that "every day, both as he went out and as he came in from the market place, he saluted and kissed her." He did much more: he not only willed his fortune to their illegitimate son, but once publicly defended her against malicious charges of impiety, risking his honor and reputation to plead with a jury of fifteen hundred citizens, to whom he appealed even with his tears. The Athenians acquitted her by a handsome vote, and later on even granted citizenship to their son.

A good deal of biographical material was written about other hetaerae in Greek times, but the bulk of it was lost or destroyed in early Christian times. Most of what remains owes its existence, by improbable circumstance, to the abnormal passion of a gastronome of the third century A.D. for collecting quotations. His name was Athenaeus and he lived in Naucratis, in Egypt; almost nothing else is known about him. He wrote an interminable dialogue called *The Deipnosophists* (*The Banquet-table Philosophers*) which is a kind of philosophizing cookbook filled with menus, discussions of various foodstuffs, and advice on table matters. Because Athenaeus could omit nothing that came to hand, it also happens to include a great variety of extraneous discussions and quotations concerning, among other things, hedonism, wars, dirty jokes, literary style, love, women, and courtesans. Athenaeus was probably the least original writer of classic times, and his book is a deadly dull patchwork of quotations from over eight hundred authors. Still, *The Deipnoso-phists* happened to survive, and with it survived scraps and bits of information from scores of works that were otherwise completely lost.

We learn from his quotes, for instance, that like Aspasia, many hetaerae wielded great power over even the highest-placed men. Athenaeus furnishes lists of kings, dictators, and generals who were influenced in state affairs by their mistresses, or married their cour-tesans and made them queens, or passed their thrones on to their bastard sons. Intellectuals, too, sought the companionship of he-taerae. Sophocles, despite his gloomy opinion of love, conceived a sincere passion for a hetaera, Theoris, in his later years and had children by her. Both Plato and Aristotle are said by Greek anec-dotalists to have had favorite courtesans, and the gossip, if doubtful, is not impossible; various hetaerae did study with each of them, and in Athens, as elsewhere, one thing could lead to another. Epicurus, that decent and serious thinker whose name was later wrongly at-tached to philosophies of self-indulgence, lived with Leontion, a courtesan who became learned enough to write a notable attack on certain ideas of the philosopher Theophrastus. The courtesan Gna-thaena, though not so philosophic, was an Emily Post of her time and wrote a treatise on table etiquette, and presumably other he-taerae were similarly intellectual.

Socrates not only studied rhetoric with Aspasia, but when he dis-coursed on higher and nobler forms of love he asserted that he was merely repeating what he had learned from Diotima, a priestess or hetaera at Mantineia. This may be only a literary device, but it probably indicates that he did discuss the subject with her. One may not find this so astonishing, but one *is* rather startled to learn that Socrates could also offer a courtesan practical pointers on tech-nique.[6] Someone had told him of the indescribable beauty of Theo-dota, and he hastened to see her for himself. After praising her beauty, he asked how she could afford such luxurious surroundings, and she replied that her income came from lovers, whereupon Socrates promptly offered her some unsolicited business advice.

"You must not imagine that it is such a simple matter to catch that noble animal, a lover," he said, pointing out that lovers are like

---

[6] What follows rests on the authority of Xenophon (*Memorabilia*, III, xi), who had been a pupil of Socrates and was one of his admirers.

hares, which have to be chased by skilled dogs into the hunter's nets.

"What sort of contrivance should I use, then, in hunting for lovers?" she asked.

"You should get a man, of course, to take the place of the dog," answered the good philosopher; "someone able to track out and discover wealthy amateurs for you; able also to find ways of driving them into your nets." No matter what exegesis one seeks for this, the meaning is plain: Socrates was urging her to use procurers. Nor was this all. He continued at some length, telling her how to excite and gratify her lovers—and not only in terms of intellectual converse.

"You will charm them best," he said, "if you never surrender except when they are sharp-set. You have noticed that the daintiest fare, if served before a man wants it, is apt to seem insipid, while, if he is already sated, it even produces a feeling of nausea. Create a hunger before you bring on your banquet. . . . Seem not to wish to yield. Fly from them—and fly again, until they feel the keen pang of hunger. That is your moment. The gift is the same as when the man did not want it: but wondrous different now its value." Impressed by his technical *expertise*, Theodota asked Socrates to be the agent who would help her net more game; he lightly replied that he was too busy, but that she should call on him if she needed him.

How much of all this actually happened, one cannot be certain, but Xenophon, who included it in his recollections of Socrates, portrayed the philosopher throughout in a fashion that tallies with Plato's portrait of him; one can therefore assume it represents Socrates' attitude, if not a genuine occurrence. It does nothing to enhance our image of the philosopher, but it does show that a better-class hetaera could be on intimate and cordial terms with a man of his stature and serious purpose.

To capture the imagination of philosophers as well as of lesser men, the hetaera did not need to be learned, like Aspasia, Diotima, or Leontion, but she did have to be quick-witted and ready with barbed puns, clever references to popular plays, and allusions (preferably salacious) to famous men. The jokes and quips of courtesans became famous; Machon, a comic poet, even compiled an anthology of them, part of which was preserved by the tireless Athenaeus. Many are puns which do not survive translation, and others are too obscene even for scholars (who translate them as far as Latin, but no further). Even those which labor under neither disadvantage suffer from the effects of time and the sea-crossing. Gnathaena, for instance, was serving to Diphilus, a writer of comedies, wine that had been secretly chilled with snow. When he complimented her on its coldness, she casually answered: "Yes, we always take care to pour into it the prologues of your plays." In her time, and to those who knew Diphilus' lack of emotional intensity, it may have seemed a capital jest.

Whether one can appreciate Machon's examples or not, it is evident that the Greeks considered badinage and sharp wit one of the charms of the hetaerae. They held court, sparred verbally with their suitors, played hard to get, teased, tormented, and frustrated their admirers, and all in all provided them with an experience compounded of intellectual, emotional, and sexual excitement that was vastly more desirable than sex alone; at least, so one would suppose from the market value of the respective commodities. The going price for lying with a common *porna* was two drachmas (about two dollars). Phryne, however, charged at least a mina (roughly one hundred dollars), and sometimes much more. Gnathaena asked one elderly moneybags for a thousand drachmas for one night with her granddaughter, Gnathaenion, and Lais had the effrontery to quote the repulsively ugly Demosthenes a fee of ten thousand drachmas.

That same Phryne, incidentally, reigned supreme as the love queen of Athens about a century after Aspasia's zenith. According to her admirers, she was the most beautiful woman ever seen. Apelles painted her and Praxiteles sculpted her—and both enlisted in the ranks of her lovers. One of Praxiteles' statues of her was even dedicated at Delphi as a religious monument.[7] With a fine feeling for effect, she veiled herself closely when she appeared in public—but disrobed completely in full view of all during the Eleusinian festivals, let down her hair, and waded into the sea to re-create the scene of Aphrodite's birth. Phryne had a sense of humor; she offered to pay for the rebuilding of the wall around Thebes if on it appeared this motto: "Destroyed by Alexander; restored by Phryne, the courtesan." The unamused Thebans refused the boon. At one point in her career, Euthias, an orator, became furious at her for some reason or other, and brought her to trial on charges of impiety. The orator Hypereides defended her, but sensed during his defense

[7] At least eight other hetaerae were similarly honored at various times.

speech that he was making no headway with the judges. He suddenly gambled on a different line of argument: with a dramatic gesture he tore open her clothing and bared her perfect bosom to the judges. In deference to such god-given beauty, they acquitted her.

But if men eagerly fell in love with hetaerae, it was a strange emotion they experienced. Few ever knew the unalloyed satisfaction that Pericles apparently found in Aspasia's company; most felt themselves caught by a passion that was delicious but painful, intoxicating but exasperating. For every word of praise of courtesans, there are two of condemnation. It was inevitable; the relationship was too commercial. Furthermore, a hetaera usually required the support of at least several lovers, and for each of them this meant that his relationship with her had built-in limitations and fatal flaws. And, of course, the drive toward love had to contend with the tradition of contempt of womankind.

The resentment of the hetaerae produced by all this emerged— as it often does in contemporary marriage—in the guise of money troubles. Men scolded hetaerae for their greed and their rapacity. "A courtesan," wrote Antiphanes, a comic poet quoted by Athenaeus, "is a calamity to the man who keeps her; indeed, he rejoices in keeping a mighty pest in the house." Numerous writers told of lovers who were plucked clean and then discarded, and of fine men who blindly squandered their wealth and reputations on insatiable hetaerae. "Not one of the wild beasts is more devastating than a harlot," snarled Anaxilas. Even a whole city might groan under the fiscal weight of love. According to Plutarch (who may have been writing with tongue in scholarly cheek) King Demetrius of Macedon levied on the Athenians a special impost of two hundred and fifty talents (about one and a half million dollars) so that Lamia and her fellow courtesans could buy extra soap.

A vivid impression of the mingled love and hate, adoration and contempt, that men felt for the average hetaera may be gained from a court case of the fourth century B.C. concerning Neaera, whose life story survives in the speech against her written by Demosthenes and known as "Against Neaera." (Her defense is lost; we know only the prosecutor's view of her.) Neaera was accused of living with an Athenian citizen, Stephanus, as his legal wife; she being a noncitizen, this was a serious violation of the law, and severely punishable. The case against her was read to the jury of five hundred and one citizens from Demosthenes' script by one Apollodorus, an enemy of Neaera's husband.

As a young slave girl, Apollodorus told the jurors, Neaera was bought by a procuress in Corinth, trained in the courtesan's arts, and hired out. Two of the clients liked her well enough to buy her outright for thirty minae (three thousand dollars) and share her. Evidently they both felt some sort of friendship for her in addition to lust, for when they were both about to marry, they offered to let her buy her freedom at a reduced price rather than sell her profitably into a brothel.

Neaera put up part of the money herself and got the balance from a young Athenian named Phrynio in return for agreeing to live with him in Athens; she thus advanced herself to the status of free woman and full-time companion to one man. Unfortunately, Phrynio's treatment of her was hardly admirable. As Apollodorus told the jury: "He lived with her in a most indecent and reckless way, took her with him everywhere to dinners, where there was drinking; and she was with him at all his riotous parties, and he had connection with her openly whenever and wherever he pleased, making a display of his privilege to the beholders." Even allowing for the tendency of Athenian orators to exaggerate, Neaera's life as a companion was something less than ideal.

Eventually she ran away to Megara and set herself up as a self-employed hetaera. Stephanus met her there and slept with her; then he offered to bring her back to Athens, pass her off—illegally—as his wife, and claim her bastard children as his own legitimate ones. She accepted the offer with joy. Stephanus, however, was a professional *parasite* (the Greeks were first to use the word) and he soon persuaded her not to waste her talents, but to continue her practice in their home in Athens, while he drove hares into the net. The relationship seems sordid, to say the least. Yet Neaera was no vulgar whore; she must have had great personal charm as well as good looks, for wealthy men paid handsomely to spend time in her presence at the table, as well as in bed. Stephanus and she not only raised their children at home, but even gave her daughter, Phano, a dowry of thirty minae and got her properly married off.

Phano, alas, had learned her mother's ways, and the marriage failed when her husband got wind of her peccadilloes; he not only sent her home, but threatened to sue unless Stephanus forfeited the dowry. Phano came home and went to work with her mother. This, too, sounds rather crass; yet even under these conditions women could inspire feelings of loyalty and affection, for an elderly gentleman who was a lover of both of them voluntarily donated a thousand-drachma dowry to make another marriage possible.

However that might be, Apollodorus was unmoved and unsoftened by it. He pointed out in his summary to the jury that Neaera had been flagrantly guilty of pretending to be a citizen, and worse yet of pretending to be a legitimately married woman; he therefore appealed to the jurors to find her guilty, so as to show the world that "Women who have been carefully and modestly brought up . . . may not be ranked in the same class with one of loose and disgusting manners, who has repeatedly and day after day granted her favors to any number of men that solicited them."

Regrettably, we can never know the ending of the story; there is no record of the outcome of Neaera's trial. But one thing is perfectly clear from the events set forth in Apollodorus' speech, as well as the tone of his final plea: the dominant note in the love of Greek men for hetaerae was ambivalence. Though men were seeking a new love relationship with women, they were deeply influenced and limited by their cultural heritage of misogyny. They were able to love Love completely, but individual women only partly; they hungered for faithful love, but sought to obtain it by gifts, cash, and trickery; they stalked and preyed upon women, and were always dissatisfied with them; and when on rare occasions they actually fell deeply in love, they suffered, quarreled, and regarded it as a dreadful affliction.[8] Athenaeus filled the pages of Book Thirteen of *The Deipnosophists* with quotations to the effect that although moderate love is agreeable, powerful love is a heavy burden, a cause of toil, trouble, and frustration, a type of madness, an overpowering force that robs a man of self-control and wise judgment, a passion that makes the self-controlled man act wildly, a punishment by the gods for arrogance and pride, and so on and on. Elsewhere, Sophocles summarized it thus:

> . . . *Love is not love alone,*
> *But in her name lie many names concealed;*
> *For she is Death, imperishable Force,*
> *Desire unmixed, wild Frenzy, Lamentation.* . . .
>
> Fragment 678

[8] In many ways, this pattern is comparable to that of the adolescent or the emotionally immature adult in our own contemporary culture. One need not brand all Greek love relationships as immature—which would imply an absolute scale of values, apart from cultural context—but the similarities are unmistakable and illuminating.

And so Greek men, in experimenting with a new love relationship to women, were caught in a dilemma from which they could find no escape. Love was either a mere pleasant game, an agreeable diversion, a healthful exercise of body and mind; or it was a tragic madness, an overwhelming force, and a ruinous disease. For if woman were sadly imperfect, how could she merit ideal love, or give it in return?

6

The Love of a Beautiful Boy

❀   ❀

❀

Man was more nearly perfect. It followed, therefore, that he could be a more nearly ideal love object, particularly for men of education and refinement who sought a mingling of minds as part of love. The adolescent boy, with his immature, half-girlish face and body, his unfolding mental powers, and his promise of ultimate manhood, could inspire the Greek man with an emotion still more intense and passionate than that aroused by the hetaera. Far from being a purely genital deviation, it involved refined, aesthetic moods startlingly like those more usually felt by a romantic man for a beautiful young girl. In his *Symposium*, Xenophon described the effect on a group of mature Athenian men when a beautiful boy entered the room. The men were dinner guests at the house of an Athenian gentleman named Callias in 424 B.C., and had all taken their places on the banquet couches when the youth Autolycus entered with his father:

Whoever had then observed what immediately took place would have thought that beauty was naturally something kingly, especially if a person possessed it in conjunction with bashfulness and modesty, as Autolycus possessed it at that time; for in the first place, as a brilliant light, when it appears in the darkness of the night, attracts the eyes of everyone towards it, so the beauty of Autolycus drew upon him the gaze of all on that occasion. . . . Some grew silent, and others composed themselves into a settled kind of attitude. . . . Such as are excited by the gentler influence of Love assume more affection in their looks, sink their voice in greater softness, and manifest in their gestures greater nobleness of soul. . . .

So deeply were they all stirred that when a professional jester entered and spun off a few jokes, he earned not so much as a chuckle, and fell into an acute depression, not realizing the source of their melancholy.

Plato describes similar scenes. His *Charmides* opens with a beautiful boy entering a public building followed by a troop of admirers; as he comes inside, all the men present turn and look at him, deeply affected, and when he sits down on a bench they push and shove to sit next to him until several fall onto the floor. Mature men, one gathers from numerous sources, were often enough in love with other mature men, but the ideal homosexual love affair was thought to be that between a mature man and a youth. The former was the "lover" and played the active (masculine) role, the latter was the "beloved" and played the passive (feminine) role. The outward expressions of the lover's infatuation for the boy were astonishingly parallel to those which, in more recent centuries, have been associated with love for a maiden. The lover made passionate declarations, wrote ardent petitions of devotion, swore solemn oaths, performed foolish errands at the boy's command, and slept all night, cold and miserable, on his doorstep. He blushed when the boy's name was mentioned, bored his friends with incessant praise of the beloved, and became dumb and stupid in the beloved's presence. "I like to see you blushing, Hippothales, and hesitating to tell Socrates the name," says Ctesippus in Plato's *Lysis*, "when, if he were with you but for a very short time, you would have plagued him to death by talking about nothing else." But however romantic the lover's conduct, or complete his success in the wooing, the relationship usually disintegrated when the lad's beard was fully grown (although some said a man could continue to love a boy until the latter was twenty-eight);

the boy himself, having become a mature man, and being discarded as a beloved, ceased to play the passive role and began in turn to stalk and seek out boys to love.[9]

The symptoms of the enamored lover were not inventions of homosexual men, but cultural traditions; fittingly enough, though, they first appeared in Greek literature in the poems of a homosexual woman. She was Sappho, of course, who caused the geographical label "Lesbian" to become a sexual one. Sappho lived in the sixth century B.C. at Mytilene on the Greek island of Lesbos, and ran a sort of finishing school where she taught girls poetry, music, and dancing. She fell madly in love with one after another of them, and expressed her love in delicate, but richly sensuous poems that won her, among later Greeks, the title of "the Tenth Muse." Her sexual preference did not prevent her from having a husband and rearing a daughter, and vengeful males even added to her history the apocryphal yarn that in later life she fell hopelessly in love with Phaon, a boatman, and, being repulsed, flung herself to death from the Leucadian Rock on the island of Leucas—first of the Lover's Leaps in Western tradition.

Sappho wrote a great deal of poetry (about twelve thousand lines, of which only five per cent survived the pious book-burning of Christian zealots), and had an immense influence on subsequent erotic literature. And on life, too: most of the symptoms from which lovers have suffered for nearly twenty-five centuries were first set forth by Sappho, and are perhaps as much a matter of cultural conditioning as of biology. Her most concise statement of the love-sickness syndrome appears in an ode she wrote to one of her favorites when the girl was about to leave her in order to be married.

> *Peer of Gods he seemeth to me, the blissful*
> *Man who sits and gazes at thee before him,*
> *Close beside thee sits, and in silence hears thee*
>   *Silverly speaking,*
> *Laughing love's low laughter. Oh, this, this only*
> *Stirs the troubled heart in my breast to tremble!*

[9] This general picture emerges from such Greek writings as Plato's *Phaedrus*, Xenophon's *Memorabilia* and *Symposium*, Demosthenes' *Erotic Oration*, Plutarch's *Of Love*, and others. It would seem, particularly in view of the reversal of roles at maturity, that Greek homosexuality was not strictly comparable to contemporary homosexuality. The family structure and child-parent relationships were rather different from ours, and it is not surprising, therefore, that Athenian deviation is not altogether explicable in terms of the rejection of masculinity or the too close identification with a mother figure, or in terms of hereditary central nervous system anomalies, congenital influences, and other causes currently thought to account for most homosexuality in contemporary America.

For should I but see thee a little moment,
  Straight is my voice hushed;
Yea, my tongue is broken, and through and through me
'Neath the flesh, impalpable fire runs tingling;
Nothing see mine eyes, and a voice of roaring
  Waves in my ear sounds;
Sweat runs down in rivers, a tremor seizes
All my limbs, and paler than grass in autumn,
Caught by pains of menacing death, I falter,
  Lost in the love-trance.

Ode to Atthis

This is something new, something not to be found in primitive life, poetry, or stories. This is the beginning of Western love; however unlike Sappho's love affairs those of modern men and women may be, the superficial symptoms of infatuation are still the same.

So great was Sappho's authority that Greek physicians accepted her symptom list as a diagnostic aid. About the year 300 B.C., for instance, Antiochus, son of Seleucus, King of Syria, fell secretly and violently in love with his father's young wife. Being an honorable young man, and seeing no hope of happiness, he decided to feign illness and die of starvation. Erasistratus, his physician, recognized the nature of the ailment, but could do nothing without learning who the woman was. As Plutarch tells the tale in his "Life of Demetrius":

> [Erasistratus] took notice that the presence of other women produced no effect upon him; but when Stratonice came, as she often did, alone, or in the company of Seleucus, to see him, he observed in him all Sappho's famous symptoms—his voice faltered, his face flushed up, his eyes glanced stealthily, a sudden sweat broke out on his skin, the beatings of his heart were irregular and violent, and, unable to support the excess of his passion, he would sink into a state of faintness, prostration, and pallor.

Happily, when the physician told all this to Seleucus, that excellent man handed over Stratonice to his son in marriage—making him symptom-free ever after. For such was the nature of love, at least as the Greeks celebrated it: if it culminated in a final and permanent union, the pains—and ecstasies—evaporated.

Homosexual love, with its intrinsic impediments to permanence, fitted the courtship and infatuation pattern perfectly, and ran no danger of permanent union and subsequent disillusion. As it gradually became a national institution, thoughtful Greek men sought to elevate it and justify it as the expression of the highest type of human emotion. Some argued that love between males should remain pure, involving only the mind and emotions, but their rapturous comments on the beauty of boys makes one suspect that such ideal conduct was difficult to maintain. Socrates was one of the few who could do so. Though he confessed to feeling a "flame" within him when he peered inside a youth's cloak, he remained pure. Alcibiades, at his youthful best, once wined and dined Socrates, tried to seduce him, and even slipped into his bed at night, but was astounded to be treated as though by a father. "I thought I had been disgraced," he later said, according to Plato's *Symposium*, "and yet I admired the way this man was made, and his temperance and courage."

Lesser men than Socrates often spoke of boy-love in clearly sensuous terms, praising the sexual satisfaction involved, while some others, relatively few in number, condemned it as degrading, unnatural, and ugly. The law made male prostitution punishable, but said nothing about unpaid voluntary connections. No Dr. Kinsey having been on hand, the frequency of actual sexual contact among Athenian males is unknown, but the literary evidence is clear: emotional liaisons among men were the fashion, nearly all of which involved flirtatious talk, kissing, and embracing, and in the majority of cases this led eventually to full sexual connection.[10]

Pederasty was hardly a Greek invention; it has been known and practiced in most human societies, sometimes widely, sometimes rarely. But in Greece it acquired a veneer of philosophy and was dignified as a superior relationship. And therein lies the reason, not merely the apology, for its prevalence in classic times. Even Aristotle, though he frowned on actual homosexual coition as a "morbid" abnormality, defended at length in his *Nichomachean Ethics* the proposition: "Love and friendship are found most and in their best form between men." Few others felt it necessary to draw so fine a line; they rejected indiscriminate pederasty, but felt that love for a youth of physical and intellectual appeal improved the character of both lover and beloved. Bravery, for instance, was said to result from such love, since both lover and youth would rather die than act cowardly in each other's sight; for this reason the famous

[10] Two major sources of Greek opinion on all this are the *Symposium* of Plato, and the *Symposium* of Xenophon. For summaries of other evidence from Greek writings, see J. Döllinger: *The Gentile and the Jew*, Vol. II, p. 254 et seq., and E. Westermarck: *The Origin and Development of the Moral Ideas*, Vol. II, ch. xliii.

Sacred Band of Thebes, a corps of shock troops, was composed entirely of homosexual pairs. In Sparta every trainee of good character had a mature lover who was a teacher to him and a model of manhood; it was deemed a military asset for them to fight near each other. Aristogeiton and Harmodius, a lover and his beloved, murdered Hipparchus, the tyrant of Athens, in 514 B.C., when he pestered young Harmodius sexually; later Athenians took this to mean that homosexuality was a force for democracy.

At the same banquet, described by Xenophon, where the guests were struck dumb by the beauty of a youth, one handsome young guest made a typical statement as to the beneficial effects of boy-love:

> We beautiful persons, since we produce a certain inspiration in those who are inclined to love, render them more generous with regard to money, fonder of enduring toil and gaining honor in hazardous enterprises, as well as more modest and self-commanding, since they are most bashful in regard to what they desire most. The people who do not choose handsome men for commanders of their troops are mad.

Even those who argued for pure love were apt to admit that the physical side of homosexuality was a good thing, though not the ultimate goal. Plato, for instance, wrote ecstatically of boy-love in his early dialogues; but he built upon it a towering edifice reaching toward spirituality, making love a method of learning the superior reality of abstract ideas. In the *Symposium* he explained that love of a beautiful person enables one to recognize beauty in many persons, and so to extract the concept of beautiful types; likewise the beauty of knowledge in one boy or man leads one to recognize the beauty of all knowledge. Step by step, one can thus proceed to the love of ultimate reality—the pure, universal Ideas of beauty and virtue which, in Platonic metaphysics, are far more real than any individual or object. This early version of what he later developed into the full-flown theory of Ideas (which came to include all mathematical forms, all abstractions, and all generalized concepts) is the original meaning of Platonic love—a meaning which would surely have astonished many of those who have used the term in recent years. (In his later years, Plato changed his mind about some of this, and in Book Eight of his *Laws* condemned homosexual contact altogether as being contrary to nature and productive of intemperate habits and effeminacy.)

Most Greeks, however, criticized boy-love with obvious affection—saying that it was a fleeting kind of joy, that it was so powerful an emotion as to enslave a man, and that boys were cruel and tantalizing toward their lovers. Even these complaints smell somewhat of ink. The preponderance of the evidence indicates that homosexual love provided a considerable measure of intellectual and emotional satisfaction to many upper-class Greek men. But the most difficult aspect of this for modern man to comprehend is that the Greek man, loving a boy, could also enjoy sexual and love relationships with women; in switching from one to the other, he suffered neither from discomfort, guilt feelings, nor potency problems. Moreover, society—including women—accepted all this without hesitation. In the second Idyll of Theocritus, Simaitha, a lovelorn maiden, wonders why Delphis, an athlete, has deserted her bed. Finally an old woman brings her some news:

> After much other gossip she said Delphis was in love;
> But what desire has mastered him, for a woman or a man,
> She was not sure, but knew this only, that he was ever pledging
> His love in cups of unmixed wine, and at last rushed away
> Swearing he'd crown with garlands the threshold of his dear.

Nor does Simaitha care which it is. Performing a magic fire spell, she says:

> O magic wheel, draw hither to my house the man I love.
> Thrice do I pour libation, Goddess, and thrice speak this prayer:
> Whether it be a woman lies beside him, or a man,
> Let such oblivion seize him, as on Dia once, they tell,
> Seized Theseus, when he quite forgot the fair-tressed Ariadne.

She is willing to have him back, in either case. For at that time in history a homosexual was not so much a developmental or biological deviant as a man (or woman) in search of love.[11]

---

[11] Some scholars, particularly those who are homosexual, have said that Greek homosexuality, in view of its social and psychological acceptability, was "normal"; contemporary gay activists make the same claim for present-day homosexuality on broader grounds—that it is a natural, innate part of everyone's psychological structure, is present in all societies, and so on. But even in the societies that have been most tolerant of homosexuality, it has never been the main choice for either men or women, and rarely has been considered as desirable as heterosexual love. This is largely because it reduces the interest and effort put by men and women into being parents and so threatens the survival of society and humankind.

7

The Limits and Fate of Greek Love

Western love began in classic Greece and early established a number of traditions that have never died out; yet in Greece it expressed itself principally as prostitution and sexual deviation. We have seen some of the reasons for this, but possibly the most basic of all was the condition of the Greek conscience.

In recent years, anthropologists have classified societies as "shame cultures" or "guilt cultures," according to their principal way of inducing self-control. In shame cultures, the main pressure toward good conduct comes from fear of public scorn. In guilt cultures, the rules of good conduct are "internalized"—they are absorbed from the parents during childhood, implanted in the unconscious, and form the conscience or the automatic "sense of right and wrong." Homeric society was clearly a shame culture: Homeric warriors did not desire a quiet conscience and a sense of rectitude, but sought public esteem and considered a broken vow or a piece of treachery not reprehensible but admirable—provided it succeeded. And even though the typical Athenian of six centuries later was a highly civilized man and could discuss ethics in a most elevated fashion, he was still much closer to being shame-guided than guilt-guided.[12]

He greatly admired and often cited the example of the dishonest heroes of Homer, and though he considered himself virtuous, he was notoriously tricky in business and crooked in politics. He praised

[12] Professor E. R. Dodds, in *The Greeks and the Irrational*, makes much of the change from Homeric times to the Golden Age, but admits that the internalizing of the rules of conduct and the creation of conscience appeared only late and uncertainly in the Hellenic world (pp. 36–7).

justice before the law, but voted for the thrilling oration rather than the just case. He spoke endlessly of friendship, but defined a friend as one who is useful. He talked of human dignity, but felt not a twinge at ordering a slave tortured to produce evidence for a trial. He swore loyalty to Athens, but easily forgave Alcibiades his treasons in order to borrow his talents.

This shame-guided man, in short, viewed other human beings as objects which either fitted, or failed to fit, his needs; as long as he did not run foul of society, he used them at his pleasure without suffering from guilt feelings. A wife, therefore, was a housekeeper, to be employed as effectively as possible for his own welfare; a courtesan was a pleasure-giving woman, to be enjoyed with as little strain on one's personal life as possible; and a beautiful boy was a delightful thing, to be loved for his body and his inspirational value until he was too mature to be useful any longer.[13] The Greek was not apt to identify his desires or goals in life with those of anyone else, or to subordinate his wishes to theirs; he was principally concerned with the richness of his own experience and the full utilization of his own capacities for enjoyment.

As long as personality remained so structured in the Greek culture, love would not fundamentally change. It did, of course, undergo continual refinement all during the Hellenic era following the Golden Age, but the refinements only devitalized and enfeebled it. Antiseptic shepherdesses and odorless shepherds appeared in love literature and became an enduring blight. In Alexandria, writers introduced into love tales such synthetic types as noble courtesans who sacrificed themselves for true love and passionate virgins who never quite lost their maidenheads, while the ideal male changed from the bearded warrior to milk-white curly-haired Daphnis, half-afraid of love. "A plague is Love, a plague!" groaned a hundred poets, but, strange to say, they seemed to have no fever; the plague had not really infected them. Eros was a naughty boy; life was short and death was long; lovers loved at first sight with never a word spoken. Artificial love-posturing reached what was perhaps a historic high with the epigram-writer Meleager, who produced such fancies as this:

[13] The egocentric nature of the Greek pederast is even sometimes spelled out in the form of blunt complaints by boys that their lovers merely use them for pleasure and give them none in return. See Xenophon: *Symposium*, viii, 21–2.

*Surely it was Love that made Heliodora's fingernail so
   long and sharp:
For does not her lightest scratching pierce me to the heart?*

Sometimes Greek romancers pretended that love was linked with marriage or that lovers wanted to be married, but their tales were always set in a context of make-believe and mythology, with lovers becoming enamored of each other in dreams before ever meeting, or naughty gods playing tricks upon stubborn parents by leading lovers into marriage despite all obstacles. But actually the emotional content of marriage changed little, even though women slowly emerged from total seclusion. Even in the first century A.D., good, decent Plutarch, in the midst of praising conjugal love and giving advice on how to preserve it in his *Conjugal Precepts,* lets us see for a fleeting instant what the relationship was still like:

A young Lacedaemonian bride, being asked by an acquaintance of hers whether she had yet embraced her husband, made answer, No: but that he had embraced her. And after this manner, in my opinion, it behooves every honest woman to behave herself toward her husband.

And so the Greeks, though they invented love, neither connected it with marriage nor endowed it with genuine ethical value, and hence never solved the dilemmas it presented them with. For they found love either a sensuous amusement that faded all too soon, or a god-sent affliction that seemed to last all too long; they yearned for inspiration and found it only in immature, impermanent boyhood, or longed for the love of woman and found it only in the arms of whores.

Chapter III

BREAD AND CIRCUSES,
LOVE AND GAMES

1 Two Views of Pagan Love
2 A Classic Roman Love Affair
3 The Passing of the Old Ideal
4 The *Lex Julia* and Julia:
A Roman Tragedy
5 The Tutor of Love,
and the Textbook of Adultery
6 The Victory of Roman Love
7 Love as Symptom and Disease

I

Two Views of Pagan Love

❀   ❀

❀

Lo, this is she that was the world's delight . . .
Lo, she was thus when her clear limbs enticed
All lips that now grow sad with kissing Christ.
                   Laus Veneris

So speaks Swinburne's Tannhäuser in praise of Venus and of pagan love. Like him, many a modern man longs for the days of Rome, when sensuous pleasure and exuberant sexuality were undiluted by the sense of sin, when Venus was joyously worshipped in temples in every major city of the Empire, and when profane love was as delicious as it was uninhibited. Modern love, an attenuated version of what man once knew, is in contrast a passion tempered by propriety and circumscribed by the mores of the suburb: one can imagine Darby and Joan, but not Antony and Cleopatra, living in Scarsdale, Forest Park, or Pasadena.

But perhaps like Miniver Cheevy, such people sigh for what was not. Love in Rome was often viewed as an exhilarating game, but it had a good deal in common with those other games at which thousands of spectators took delight in seeing one gladiator spill another's intestines onto the Colosseum sands. Love in Rome was lusty, exuberant, and unclouded by the sense of sin, but it was strangely blended with obscenity and hatred; it burned brightest between lovers who quarreled, tormented each other, and were flagrantly unfaithful. Love in Rome was cheerfully lecherous and expertly sensuous, but it was a malign symptom of a wasting ailment—the decomposition of family life, and the over-all enfeeblement of the hardy Roman character. For all its voluptuous appeal, and its healthy appearance of guiltlessness, one can therefore also view

[55]

pagan love as a part of that syndrome of afflictions that resulted in the decline of Roman greatness. A grave charge, indeed; can love ever be so iniquitous and powerful a force in history? Let us look a little closer and see.

2

A Classic Roman Love Affair

❀   ❀

❀

O di et amo"—"I love and I hate": in those three words the greatest lyric poet of Rome epitomized his feelings for the woman in his life and summarized a typical Roman love affair of the first century B.C.

Gaius Valerius Catullus was his name, and he was born in Verona in 87 B.C., of a good family. That is practically all the information Latin historians recorded about him, yet we know him well, for the main events in his life and many of the intimate details of his love affair were recorded by Catullus himself in his poems. Though lyric poetry is, in general, not the most reliable form of social history or biography, the poetry of Catullus is something special. Most of his lyrics make no pretense at fictional invention and show few traces of the conventional terms of literary passion or bookish emotion; furthermore, they are sprinkled with names and allusions to events that correspond to, and are verified by, the reports of other writers on the same people and happenings. Scholars have therefore concluded that Catullus' poems form, in effect, a candid and literal autobiography.

Judging from what he tells of himself, his life was brief and rather uneventful. He came to Rome in his twenties (about 61 B.C.) to make his way in politics, but having an adequate income he chose to spend his time more agreeably, mingling in the patrician and literary circles of the city and playing the role of a poetic dilettante. It was an exciting time to be in Rome, even as a spectator: the city, brilliant and turbulent, was glorying in the Eastern triumphs of Pompey and the early Gallic conquests of Caesar; its people reveled in unwonted luxury, even while the power struggles of the conservatives and the First Triumvirate were destroying republican government. Unmoved by ambition, Catullus took no part in public affairs until he was thirty; then at last he secured an unofficial position as an aide to the provincial governor of Bithynia (northern Turkey). He stayed a year, failed to prosper in the role, and sailed back to Rome; shortly afterwards he died of unrecorded causes in 54 B.C., at the age of thirty-three.

In this brief unremarkable life there was only one experience of importance. When he was perhaps twenty-five years old, Catullus met Clodia, the wife of Caecilius Metellus Celer, governor of the province in which Verona lay. A wellborn lady of the Roman *haut monde*, she was a celebrated beauty and the center of attention of her circle. She was about eight years older than Catullus, but in the very prime of her beauty; her eyes were huge and black, her hands and feet were delicately tapered, her skin was pure white, and her manner was insouciant and provocative. She was the embodiment of sophistication and elegance, and Catullus was instantly infatuated.

Provincial though he was, he knew the customs and the ways of Rome. Such a lady, he was aware, could be pursued by a would-be lover without reproach or disgrace unless he were oafish or indiscreet; indeed, love of someone else's wife was thought far more desirable and more exciting than love of a courtesan or concubine. As a first step in his suit, Catullus translated for her Sappho's *Ode to Atthis*, thereby subtly declaring his feelings. He was able to see her fairly frequently thereafter; in that era the emancipated wives of Roman patricians could go about more or less freely in public, escorted by male friends and servants, and might be surrounded by admirers and hangers-on even in the presence of their husbands. So it was with Catullus; he even wrote that Clodia would scold him or talk to him scornfully in front of her husband so that Metellus would take him to be a youthful nuisance rather than a serious seducer. But Metellus was wrong.

Precisely what took place and in what order can be variously construed by the sequence in which one reads the poems (they were preserved in an arrangement clearly not intended by Catullus himself). According to the most generally received opinion,[1] however, shortly after making the translation of Sappho he was daringly calling her his "girl," thinly disguising her with the name of "Lesbia" because of the Sappho translation, and openly complaining of his pain and his burning desire. He did not have to burn long. Allius, a friend of his, lent Catullus the use of his house, and there he waited in a fever until Clodia came to him alone, a "white goddess" who paused for an endless moment on the threshold before flying into his arms and completing their love. A happy period followed during which no flaw marred the affair. They met again and again, and Catullus wrote exultant boastful poems about their rapturous lovemaking. In his various happy lyrics, he never indicated any troubled thoughts of her husband, or any plans for the future, and his mood was uncomplicated by any philosophic speculations as to the meaning or importance of their love. A typical lyric of this period, as translated by Coleridge, says in part:

> My Lesbia, let us love and live,
> And to the winds, my Lesbia, give
> Each cold restraint, each boding fear
> Of age and all her saws severe.
> Yon sun now posting to the main
> Will set—but 'tis to rise again:—
> But we, when once our mortal light
> Is set, must sleep in endless night!
> Then come, with whom alone I'll live,
> A thousand kisses take and give!
> Another thousand! to the store
> Add hundreds—then a thousand more!
>
> No. 5

All too soon Catullus learned that such love is not quite so simple. Clodia was vain and fickle, and saw no reason not to permit herself the attentions of other men as well, and the provincial youth must have annoyed her when he protested. Judiciously, he struggled to adopt the sophisticated Roman viewpoint: "Although she cannot be content with me alone," he wrote, "I'll bear my lady's rare, discreet adventures, rather than seem to be a nagging busybody." But Metel-

[1] Gilbert Highet, in *Poets in a Landscape*, p. 251, briefly reviews the schol- arly studies on which the usual version of the affair is based.

lus, her husband, died in 59 B.C., leaving Clodia rich and free of the need for caution; from then on her affairs were neither rare nor discreet. Catullus was shaken when she accepted as a lover one of his close friends, Caelius Rufus, and embittered when she began to multiply her lovers almost at random. Soon she was holding feasts and entertainments in her house near the Tiber as openly as any Greek hetaera, and drunkenly lying with any guest who pleased her. Finally she even began to prowl the streets at night, accepting strangers in the darkness of alleyways. Catullus, in a puerile rage, threatened to defame her and to draw red phalli on the walls of her house, as on a brothel. He never could bring himself to do so, of course; what was worse, he could not stop loving her.

But what could he have loved in such a strumpet? Catullus was not explicit about it, but it seems, incredibly enough, that her very debaucheries were a cause of love.

> *Ah, then I loved you, not with passion wild,*
> *But as a father loves a trusted child.*
> *I know you better now, and here confess*
> *I love you more, though I esteem you less.*
> *"How can that be?" you say. Your ways, my dear,*
> *Make love more ardent but less kind, I fear.*
>
> No. 72

It was not the memory of a fine person who had degenerated, but the degenerate herself, whom he loved hopelessly and angrily:

> *I hate and love. You ask, perhaps, how can that be?*
> *I know not, but I feel the agony.*
>
> No. 85

When at last he told himself: "Wretched Catullus, play the fool no more," it was not that he could no longer stomach her, but because she would no longer accept him in her bed.

> *Now she refuses. You then must refuse, you too:*
> *Don't follow when she runs, don't live a poor fool's life.*
>
> No. 8 [2]

How much of his account of the affair was poetic license? How much of the portrait of Clodia's character is merely literary fancy? Not much; perhaps none. For not only did various other Roman writers mention similar details about her, but Catullus' description

---

[2] The poem listed as Number 8 in the traditional jumbled sequence was obviously written late in the course of the affair.

of her was practically duplicated in a Roman courtroom. Caelius Rufus, Catullus' close friend, had apparently broken off his affair with Clodia at his own pleasure rather than at hers, and she, furious for revenge, instigated a prosecution of him in 56 B.C. The counts included charges of lechery and adultery, but rested chiefly on the far graver charges that he had not only defrauded Clodia of money, but attempted to poison her. (Catullus, who would have been horrified and fascinated by the proceedings, was in Bithynia at the time, and had to get the details second hand.)

Caelius' defense counsel was the most distinguished court orator of the day, Cicero himself, who rightly judged that the best defense would be an unsparing attack. His defense speech was no great example of legal reasoning, but a *tour de force* of character destruction through rhetorical technique. "I would attack [Clodia] more vigorously," he told the court, for example, "if I had not a quarrel with her husband—I mean *brother;* I am always making this mistake." The jury and the onlookers must have roared with laughter. Clodia's brother, the radical politician Clodius Pulcher, was a notorious rake who, according to common talk around town, occasionally sampled the delights of his own glamorous sister's bed. The story was well known, and Cicero's "mistake" was sure to be relished by all except the Clodian faction.

Cicero was generous in the use of such sarcasm and insinuation, but toward the end of his speech he became more direct; he summed up Clodia's ways and days (without actually naming her) in one long rhetorical question:

> If any woman, having no husband, has opened her house to the passions of everybody, openly established herself in the way of life of a harlot, and been accustomed to frequent banquets of men to whom she is not related; if she does so in the city, in country-houses, and in that most frequented place, Baiae;[3] if by her gait, her style of dress, and the people who are seen attending her; by the eager glances of her eyes and the freedom of her conversation, by embracing men, by kissing them, at water-parties and sailing-parties and banquets; . . . if in all this she behaves so as to seem a very wanton and lascivious harlot, I ask you whether a young man who has been with her is to be called an "adulterer" —or a lover?[4]

And turning to Clodia a moment later, Cicero said, mockingly:

[3] A near-by summer resort, noted for its dissolute atmosphere.
[4] Cicero: "Pro Caelio," *Orations.*

> You are at liberty to suppose that all I said just now was not said about you.

One can hear, at the distance of two thousand years, the laughter in the courtroom; one can imagine the flushed face and burning eyes of the New Woman, the emancipated Roman lady, the practitioner of pagan love. Caelius was acquitted; history says nothing more of Clodia. Probably she continued her ways until time had stripped her of her charms and cooled her heat.

Yet if she was the most notorious woman of her circle, she was neither unique nor a rarity, but a representative of a trend. That same sickly combination of love and hate that Catullus felt for her —and she for her lovers—was far from unusual; indeed, Roman literature is full of it. Propertius, another autobiographical poet, described his affair with "Cynthia"—a love that could seemingly be kept alive only by the stimulation of particularly dangerous trysts, mutual infidelities, and terrible quarrels. The poet Tibullus doubled the mood by loving two women at the same time, both of whom were worthless, greedy, and hateful. The moralistic Virgil expressed the Roman male's viewpoint in the only love affair he ever wrote about: he had Aeneas abandon Dido in order to carry out his duty and get on with his destiny. Modern readers may weep for Dido and despise Aeneas, but Roman men understood him and enjoyed seeing him victorious over the power of love.

Victory over love—by the avoidance or repudiation of powerful emotions—seems, in fact, to have been the principal alternative in the minds of many Romans to the pain of love-plus-hate. At the very time when Catullus was in the toils of love agony, the philosopher-poet Lucretius was writing his all-encompassing poem, *De Rerum Natura*, in which, among many other things, he gave advice on the rationalistic Epicurean handling of love. Passionate sexual love should be carefully avoided, he said in Book Four; it is habit-forming, causes frenzied and irrational actions, and consumes the lover's strength and wastes his substance. Like Catullus, Lucretius viewed love entirely in terms of sexual activity; unlike Catullus, he considered it a snare and a delusion, a madness in which the lover longs unendurably to have complete union with another body although complete union is forever impossible:

> They cling greedily together and join their watering mouths and draw deep breaths pressing teeth on lips; but all is vanity, for they can rub nothing off thence, nor can they penetrate and

be absorbed body in body (for this they seem sometimes to wish and strive for). . . . At length there is a short pause for a while in the furious burning. Then the same frenzy returns, and once more the madness comes. . . . They can find no device to master the trouble; in such uncertainty do they pine with their secret wound.

And what remedy did this greatest Roman exponent of Epicurean philosophy suggest?—a measured dosage of physical disgust, and a judicious admixture of hatred: the same formula, really, at which poor Catullus arrived willy-nilly. The prudent man turns his thoughts away from love, knowing it to be a disease, said Lucretius; if he feels heat, he chooses to satisfy himself in the easiest connections, undisturbed by emotion. If, nevertheless, some woman begins to affect him with love, he deliberately studies her faults so as to see her plainly. Instead of foolishly admiring her for a delightful disorder, a Junoesque stature, or a sharp and nimble wit, he sees plainly that she is dirty, has sagging breasts, or uses a scolding tongue. He reminds himself, added Lucretius, that even the most beautiful woman does the same things as the ugly woman: she sweats, she eliminates, and she covers up her odors with perfumes. The rational man is not fooled.

It is significant that this excremental refrain, this linking of the loathsome with the lovely, appears not only in philosophizing and satire, but again and again in Roman love literature. Even Catullus—whom Tennyson once called the "tenderest of Roman poets"—set disgusting images next to beautiful ones. He wrote scurrilous poetry about Caesar's pederasty, sneered that one of Clodia's lovers, following an old Spanish custom, washed his teeth with urine, and declared in measured verse that another of her lovers had breath so foul that if he opened his mouth, bystanders would drop dead. And in his farewell poem to Clodia, he views her in thoroughly vulgar, purely genital, terms:

> Give her my goodbye, her and all her lovers,
> Whom she hugs so close to her in their hundreds,
> Loving not one, yet with her constant lusting
>   Leaving their loins limp.

No. 11

That is his final word about love: its most alluring feature is also its most disgusting. *Odi et amo.*

3

The Passing of the Old Ideal

❈ ❈

❈

Times always change, and men always lament the fact. Clodia and the liberated upper-class women of her type seemed glamorous to Catullus, but to conservatives who respected the old traditions they were dangerous revolutionaries.

The Roman woman had once been a figure of strength and moral integrity—a staunch, large-hipped child-bearer, spinner of wool, keeper of the household, and proper mate for the stern, tough, farmer-warrior of the early Republic. They were bound to each other by no such frippery nonsense as romantic preference, but by religious loyalties, clanship ties, and the urgent business of economic and military survival. Without such women, Roman men of the fifth and fourth centuries B.C. could hardly have left home so confidently on their long wars, or so persistently gone about that series of conquests that won them Italy and, in succeeding centuries, the entire Mediterranean, the Middle East, and almost all of Europe. The long-absent fighters demanded that their wives be dutiful and virtuous; they wanted to find neither ruined farms nor bastard sons when they came home. When Tarquinius raped Lucretia, she knew that her virtuous death would cause her husband less sorrow than her soiled life; she stabbed herself, and made him, relatively speaking, happy. But he and his fellow Romans, enraged at the ruling Tarquin clan, drove them out, founded the Republic, and began the conquest of Italy. The whole story is probably legendary, but it summarized ancient Roman morality: the home must be intact, the wife must be spotless, and men must fight, conquer, and die.

In all of Western history there is nothing quite like the patriarchal family of old Rome. It was cemented together by the formidable *patria potestas*, or power of the father. He owned and controlled all family property; priestlike, he directed the worship of family gods; and he himself was godlike in his absolute power to direct or dispose of the lives of his children. The Laws of the Twelve Tables, which date from about 450 B.C., stated that the father had the right during the entire lifetime of his children to imprison them, whip them, keep them to rustic labor in chains, sell them into slavery, or slay them, even though they might have attained to high state offices.

Where the male was drawn in such bold strokes, what was the picture of the female? As in Greece, she was a perpetual minor; even when her father died, she remained under the guardianship of some other male in her family. Marriage merely transferred her from the *patria potestas* of her father into the *manus* (literally into the hands) of her husband, who could then chastise, whip, and correct her as he pleased without external hindrance, put her out at labor like a slave and collect the proceeds, condemn her to death for a capital offense, and even kill her with his own hands if he caught her in adultery.

For all that, the formal law does not tell everything about how men and women treated each other. In actual fact the Roman matron was not a cringing slave, but a self-respecting subject of her lord. In the primitive era she labored alongside him in the fields, and was the nurse and teacher of his children, the provider of his clothing, food, and medicine, and the mainstay of his estate. In the era of expansion she could not, like Athenian wives, pass her time in idle seclusion; her husband might be away for years, conquering Sicily, Carthage, or Gaul, and she had to run things for him until he returned. Ideally she was unsmiling, stern, and hardworking. She considered it a disgrace to have anyone else suckle her children or weave her wool, and prided herself on seriousness, purity, and devotion to duty; lacking only Calvinism, she was the spiritual ancestor of the New England pioneer woman.

After the Punic Wars of the third century B.C. had cleared Carthage from Rome's way, imperialist expansion went ahead rapidly, and the patricians and the equestrians (the middle class) became far wealthier than before. Leisure and a growing taste for civilized refinements brought the affluent to Rome, or enabled them to make their own cities into little replicas of Rome. These upper and middle classes now began to live from the proceeds of wealth, land, and slavery, rather than by working, and there was no longer the need for the family, or for its women, to be what they had been. In addition, fathers were now able to give larger dowries to their daughters, but because they intensely disliked seeing their property pass into the hands of the son-in-law and his family, they began to avoid giving their daughters in *manus* in the older forms of marriage known as *confarreatio* and *coemptio*. Instead they married their daughters off by *usus*, a nonreligious civil marriage in which the girl remained under her father's guardianship. Her husband might enjoy the benefits of her dowry, but could not control it or inherit it; she herself controlled it through her father or through a male business agent. If she found her husband hard to live with, she could divorce him by merely sending him a written notice and return home with her dowry intact.

Conservatives tried to combat the change in woman's rights by turning the clock back. One of the most famous of them was Cato the Elder, an orator, consul, and censor during the second century B.C. In 195 B.C. he predicted disaster if women kept winning new privileges:

> If each of us, citizens, had determined to assert his rights and dignity as a husband with respect to his own spouse, we should have less trouble with the sex as a whole; as it is, our liberty, destroyed at home, is even here in the Forum crushed and trodden under foot. . . . Review all the laws with which your forefathers restrained their license and made them subject to their husbands; even with all these bonds you can scarcely control them. What of this? If you suffer them to seize these bonds one by one and wrench themselves free . . . do you think that you will be able to endure them? The moment they begin to be your equals, they will be your superiors.[5]

But he was sweeping back the tide with a broom; he lost and so did other conservatives, year after year, as woman moved out of the shadow of patriarchal domination. The actual issue in 195 B.C. concerned nothing more serious than the freedom to wear gold ornaments and varicolored garments, but a similar scene was played out a century and a half later, and again the women won—only by then the issue was one of taxation of their property. They had moved far from fighting for mere adornment.

With increasing control of her person and her money value, the Roman wife was changing radically and pre-empting much of the

[5] Livy: *Roman History*, Bk. XXXIV, Secs. ii–iii.

role the hetaera had in Greece. She was reasonably well educated, for as a girl she went to school with her brothers or was tutored at home, learning all the classical subjects and becoming well informed about current affairs. As a woman—if she held with the newer ideas—she moved freely in society, interesting herself in intellectual and social life; she was never sequestered in the home, as in Greece, and she was an ornament of social gatherings. If men jealously kept her out of political office or business life, she could at least seek to entertain herself, and when her husband helped conquer Greece and stole its statues, its plays, its ideas and customs, she found among them love, the best entertainment of all.

Though Roman love was imitative of Greek models, the differences were significant. Pederasty became popular, but remained candidly physical; Roman men had no interest in winning boys through spiritual and mental attraction, but preferred to seduce or buy them and get them into bed without intellectual bother. (Cato was outraged that a pretty boy might be sold for as much as a talent, or more than enough to purchase a farm.) Courtesans became popular, too, though they never captured the imagination of the hardheaded Romans, who preferred their sex unmixed with philosophy or significance. It was an appetite, the satisfying of which was delightful; what else need be said? A fool might let himself be trapped and hurt by it, like Catullus, but a more skillful hedonist would control its intensity by flitting easily from one bed to another. Sighed Horace:

> I am stricken with the heavy dart of Love, yea of Love who seeks to kindle me beyond all others with passion for tender boys and girls. . . . Affection for Lyciscus now enthralls me, he who claims to outdo any woman in tenderness. . . . Stern reproaches of my friends have no power to free me—I can be freed only by another flame, for some other fair maid or slender youth.
>
> *Epode xi*

Were such darts and flames really painful? Not very; reading through the Epodes, one soon senses that the beloved was not really a person, but any person—and not even that, but only an interchangeable set of lips, thighs, and buttocks, all of which served the same purpose.

In any case, Roman love as it emerged in the second and first centuries B.C. involved a variety of possible unions, all of them outside of marriage. The only illegal one was adultery, but up-to-date

Romans favored it above all others, regarding it much as modern man regards cheating on his income-tax return—a zestful wrong-doing that involves no sense of wrong or sin, but only apprehension lest he be caught. Adultery in Rome presented certain problems: there were no decent public lodgings to speak of, daytime trysts involved the danger of recognition, and nighttime trysts meant risky trips around the city alone, without a retinue of torch-bearers and gladiators. The most convenient place was the lady's home, but what peace of mind could a man know in another man's bed? Horace, a nervous fellow, had no moral compunctions against adultery, but objected to it for this very reason:

> A husband may rush back from the country, the door burst open, the dog bark, the house ring through and through with his knocking; the woman, white as a sheet, will leap away, the maid in league with her cry out in terror. . . . With clothes dishevelled and bare of foot I must run off, dreading disaster in purse or person or at least repute.
>
> *Satire i*

Many other upper-class Roman men disagreed. For them adultery was more delicious than whoring or boy-love precisely because of the extra risk; women played the game just as eagerly and with much the same motive. By the end of the first century B.C. adultery had become so fashionable that the ancient tragedy of Helen of Troy took on a new light; Ovid, writing typically upper-class opinions, viewed it thus:

> *Afraid of lonely nights, her spouse away,*
> *Safe in her guest's warm bosom, Helen lay.*
> *What folly, Menelaüs, forth to wend,*
> *Beneath one rooftree leaving wife and friend!* . . .
> *Blameless is Helen, and her lover too:*
> *He did what you or anyone would do.*
> *The means you offered made them misbehave;*
> *What did the wench but take the hint you gave?*
> Ars Amatoria, ii, 359–68

Under the impact of these changes, divorce grew ever more common and marriage came to seem so unimportant that it was broken for any trivial excuse—and in marriage by *usus* all one needed to do was send the spouse an announcement, via a freedman, saying: "*Tuas res tibi agito*"—"Take your things away." One Sempronius Sophus divorced his wife in this way because she went to the games without telling him first, and another man because his wife went onto the street without a veil. Women cast off their husbands for equally insignificant reasons, and men with political ambitions married four or five times in the process of self-advancement. Under such circumstances, child-bearing could hardly seem desirable to women, and the birth rate fell steadily. Abortion and contraception became common among the well-to-do, while the poor, using a cheap but time-honored device, deposited their newborn infants on the nearest dungheap, stairway, or hillside.

If the emotional flavor of the earlier moralistic patriarchy is not altogether agreeable, it is at least understandable to us; but that of the later Republic is so alien that few fictional or dramatic treatments of it have dared to be truthful. How many have ever visualized the great Caesar as a fop, a dandy, and a perfumed homosexual? Yet such he was, at least in his youth. His warm reception at the court of the King of Bithynia won him the nickname of "the Queen of Bithynia," an epithet thrown at him even on the Senate floor in Rome. He wore his clothing with a studied carelessness, kept his body plucked clean of hair, and fussed so endlessly with his thinning locks that Cicero once said: "When I see his hair so carefully arranged and observe him adjusting it with one finger, I cannot imagine that it should enter into such a man's thoughts to subvert the Roman state." [6]

The same man, however, could not only subvert the state, but also become an indefatigable lecher: the historian Suetonius indicated that his conquests included the wives of almost all his close friends, associates, generals, and the heads of state wherever he went. Partly in admiration, partly in resentment, Romans called him *"Omnium mulierum vir et omnium virorum mulier"*—"The husband of every woman and the wife of every man." His four marriages were all made for political or practical reasons; there is no evidence that love was responsible for any of them. He was past fifty and Cleopatra was twenty-one when they met; she deliberately offered him a queen's body for political reasons, and he found her person and her character alluring enough to keep him overtime in Alexandria, but it is doubtful whether the affair involved more than ambition and cunning on her part, and on his the powerful appeal of

[6] These and other seldom-taught details about Caesar were reported by such ancient historians as Suetonius, in his *Julius Caesar*, and Plutarch, in his "Life of Caesar."

having an exotic queen—and so young a one—as his mistress. The woman he was faithful to longest—in his fashion—was Servilia, a matron of a noble family; this affair, in some sense, may have helped undo him, for even in Rome a bastard might hate the man who begot him. Servilia's son, Brutus, was thought to look much like Caesar, and if Suetonius is correct the dying Caesar said to him not "You, too, Brutus?" but "You, too, *my child?*"

The avenger of Caesar's murder, Mark Antony, has for twenty centuries been upheld as the quintessential lover, driven by his passion for Cleopatra to gamble for an empire; the title of Dryden's play summed it up best—*All for Love, or the World Well Lost.* This most loving of lovers was, in actual fact, an unregenerate rake, whose long and gaudy sexual history included a period of adolescent homosexuality as the favorite of a Roman nobleman, youthful debauches with matrons and courtesans, the keeping of a harem of concubines (both male and female) in his house in Rome, and two marriages made for gain and dissolved when no longer gainful.[7] Cleopatra, according to tradition, created in Antony a truly grand passion; yet even while he was most in love with her, he was entirely amenable to the suggestion that he marry Octavia, sister of Octavian, his co-ruler of Rome, so as to create a firm bond between them. The marriage lasted until Antony decided to battle Octavian for the Empire. Then, divorcing the pregnant Octavia by mail, he married Cleopatra, fought Octavian for the world, and lost.

Tradition also says that in defeat he committed suicide after asking Octavian to spare Cleopatra, but that she, spurning Octavian's kindness, clasped the asp to her bosom rather than live without Antony; this too may be as wide of the mark as the usual "facts" of her life. She is always called an Egyptian; in truth, she was half Greek and half Macedonian, with no Egyptian blood whatever. She is said to have been a highly sexed voluptuary, yet there is no evidence from any source that she had any serious love affairs in her life other than those with Julius Caesar and Mark Antony. Even these were very likely somewhat cooler, inwardly speaking, than tradition says. Defying a hundred playwrights and a thousand poets on the basis of little-known Egyptian evidence about her, the learned Dr. W. W. Tarn of Cambridge University wrote in the *Cambridge Ancient History:* "Her two love affairs were undertaken quite deliberately

[7] The unpleasant facts about Antony were given by Cicero in his Second and Sixth Philippics, and by Plutarch in his "Life of Antony."

with the same purpose as all her actions. For the keynote of her character was not sex at all, but ambition." When the world slipped through her hands at Antony's final defeat, she was a woman past her prime and past further scheming for glory. Later ages have romantically imagined that she took the asp up with the same spirit that moved Juliet to snatch Romeo's dagger, but her suicide may actually have had more in common with that of Eva Braun in the bomb shelter under Berlin.

4

The Lex Julia *and Julia:*
A Roman Tragedy

❁   ❁

❁

A significant effort was made to restore family unity and sexual morality to Rome at about this time. It came from a man who, in his youth, gave no promise of becoming a great moralist, but neither did he seem destined to become the wise and all-powerful ruler of the entire civilized Western world. At eighteen he was nothing but a nervous, unprepossessing, somewhat sickly and routinely licentious youth named Octavian, whom Julius Caesar had named as his heir; as the years passed he underwent an astonishing metamorphosis into that calm, judicious, efficient dictator who ruled so well that the Senate granted him the title "Augustus" and made him in fact, if not in name, the first Roman emperor.

The metamorphosis was slow, but marvelously thorough. As a

young man, Octavian had lived the usual life of luxury; as Augustus he preferred simple garments, slept in a plain bed in a cubicle, ate little while his guests gorged themselves, and relaxed from his cares by doing nothing wilder than sailing quietly along the coast. As a youth, trying to inherit the world from Caesar, he ruthlessly exterminated his uncle's assassins and even abandoned his friend Cicero to Antony's blood lust; as the sole ruler of Rome after 30 B.C. (the year in which he finally defeated Antony), he became temperate, magnanimous, and forgiving, and cherished particularly a maxim given him by the philosopher Athenodorus: "Whenever you get angry do not say or do anything before repeating to yourself the twenty-four letters of the alphabet."

In his youth he had the same cavalier attitude toward love and marriage as other modern Romans. Suetonius, that classical scandalmonger, says he may have become his uncle's legal heir by granting the insatiable Julius the enjoyment of his body. Whether this was so or not, he certainly indulged in the usual amount of adultery. He married Antony's stepdaughter in a calculated effort to repair his first quarrel with Antony, but soon divorced her and took on the twice-divorced Scribonia, who bore him a daughter, Julia. In 39 B.C., when he was twenty-five, he fell mightily in love with Livia, compelled her husband to divorce her although she was pregnant, and married her himself as soon as the child had been born.

Since he needed a reconciliation with the aristocratic class at that time, and since Livia belonged to the noble Claudian clan, one might question how sincere his emotions were at the outset. But the marriage actually yielded a warm, mature, and abiding relationship. Augustus was genuinely attached to Livia and remained her devoted husband until his death more than forty years later. His occasional infidelities made no difference; they were routine and trivial, and she kept her peace and loved him just the same. All his life he confided in Livia, consulted her, and shared with her his burdens and his joys. She made him particularly happy by being an exemplar of the classic virtues—beauty, chastity, and devotion to hard work— and yet could mingle easily in glittering Roman society and play a quiet but significant role in affairs of state. Her only failure was that she never bore him any children.

It was a painful failure for Augustus; he wanted to be in every way the example of a good family man to his fellow citizens. Deeply concerned about the changing standards of his time, he read history, pondered long, and decided to restore morality by the force of law. Between 18 B.C. and 9 B.C. Augustus promulgated a series of "Julian Laws" (so named because he was, by adoption, a member of the Julian clan), which have been called the most important social legislation of antiquity.

The crucial law was the *Lex Julia de Adulteriis* which for the first time forbade a husband to kill an adulterous wife, but ordered him, under pain of severe fines, to bring her to court and accuse her. If he did not, her father was required to do so; and if he in turn failed, any right-minded citizen might accuse her, winning part of her property if she were convicted. Adultery, which had been a private wrong, thus became the state's business for the first time. The government was empowered to take away from an adulterous wife half her dowry and a third of her other property; what irritated Roman men even more, they too faced stiff penalties for adulterous connections with married women, though they could still freely use prostitutes. A whole series of other Julian Laws tried to prop up the birth rate of the upper classes: they made bachelors, spinsters, and childless wives ineligible to inherit, granted mothers of three or more children special legal privileges, gave political preference, between equal candidates, to the man with more children, and so on. It was a thoroughly imposing attack.

But although Augustus singlehandedly had brought about the beginning of the Pax Romana and made the civilized world prosperous and happy, he was vanquished on the moral battlefield; his fines and penalties could not genuinely restore disappearing family functions or provide new ones, and thus could not mend the social dissolution that had led to sexual license. To a greater or lesser degree, every one of the Julian Laws was a failure. Some people married merely to fulfill the requirements of his laws, and then were promptly divorced; some others adopted children to qualify for an inheritance and promptly "emancipated" them into the streets; some women gained the advantages of married status by legal unions with eunuchs or freedmen who gave them no trouble. In deference to law, men became discreet—and continued their adulteries; when evasion did not suffice, they challenged Augustus with a storm of protests and by open defiance of the harsher regulations.

Augustus temporized and shifted his tactics. He softened and modified the laws repeatedly, displayed children in his box at the games, gave money to parents of large families, and encouraged

Virgil to sing the praises of farm life in the *Georgics* and of ancient ideals in the *Aeneid*. It was all to no avail. Ten years after the final enactment of the laws in their modified form, they were in disrepair and disesteem. In the next century the historian Tacitus would write them off as a failure, without influence on marriage or fertility. Later emperors added to the laws and stiffened them; they were all equally unsuccessful. It was not legislation that would finally counteract and change the patterns of love and marriage.

To be sure, not all of upper-class or middle-class society was profligate. Augustus' own married life was undoubtedly paralleled in many a conservative home, but decency makes dull reading and historians tend to avoid it. Tombstone inscriptions indicate that there must have been at least some of respectable and enduring unions. One inscription in particular, known as the "Laudatio Turiae" or "Praise of Turia," is noteworthy as a portrait of the good life. On two large marble slabs on a tomb outside Rome was chiseled a lengthy funeral eulogy written by the husband, telling the story of their marriage. It is a long recital of separations and tribulations caused by his fighting on the republican side in the civil wars against Caesar, and later against Antony and Octavian. Finally, however, the wars were over, he was pardoned, and the couple settled down to live in peace and harmony for many years. The wife proved to be barren, and in an excess of generosity offered to divorce her husband so that he might take a fertile bride. "I must confess," he said in his funeral address, "that I was so distressed by your proposal that I almost lost my mind." He made her give up the idea and they lived together, childless and loving, until her death many years later.

It is a touching glimpse of a warm Roman marriage, but it is almost unique. Most other funeral inscriptions are too brief or too traditional in style to be likewise meaningful, and most histories and letters include little similar evidence. Even the widower who wrote the "Laudatio Turiae" observed that long marriages such as his were quite rare. If Augustus personally knew the faithful couple, he must have felt that fate was unbearably ironic; a former enemy lived as Augustus wanted men to live, while Augustus' own daughter symbolized for all Rome the failure of his Julian Laws and his ideals.

Her name was Julia; she was his daughter by Scribonia, and his only child. She grew up in his home, and Augustus personally supervised her upbringing; he saw to it that she was taught to spin and weave, ordered her never to say or do anything that could not be written in the household diary, and forbade her to have meetings or conversations with strangers, even of noble rank and good character. Either in protest against this or against the criticisms of her upright stepmother, Livia, Julia developed an irresistible desire for pleasure and folly. Her first husband having died when she was little more than a child, Augustus married her off, when she was eighteen, to Marcus Vipsanius Agrippa, his faithful deputy, general, and builder of aqueducts, who was by that time wealthy, middle-aged, and tolerant. Julia, in hot-blooded revolt against spinning and weaving, took advantage of this to become the leader of the fast young set, and made her home a center of gay parties and luxurious display.

Like a hetaera of Greece, she developed a sharp and witty tongue. When a conservative friend urged her to avoid luxury, and to imitate the simplicity and frugality of her father, Julia replied: "If he forgets that he is Caesar, I will not forget that I am Caesar's daughter." Livia advised Augustus to chastise her and told him about the rumors of Julia's adulteries. Augustus did chide her (without effect), but as to the stories of adultery, he was reassured by the fact that she dutifully brought forth no less than five children, all resembling her husband. According to rumor, Julia herself had a frank explanation of this flawless record: "I take on passengers," she is supposed to have said, "only when the boat is full."

Agrippa died in 12 B.C. and Julia, a merry widow of twenty-seven, stepped up the pace of her follies at the very time when her father was laboring to complete and to enforce his Julian Laws. The worried Augustus sought to tie her down by marrying her to Livia's son, Tiberius, a dour young Stoic who relished neither her nor her ways. Soon Tiberius found himself in a classically perfect dilemma: the *Lex Julia de Adulteriis* required him to denounce his wife for adultery, yet to do so would be to disgrace his stepfather, its author. He solved the dilemma by resigning his posts and fleeing to Rhodes, where he spent seven years in meditative, self-imposed exile.[8]

Julia meanwhile followed the trail blazed a generation earlier by Catullus' love, Clodia. She went from adventure to adventure, her jaded appetite requiring ever more startling feats of love, and her premature gray hair driving her, in frenzy, to seize all possible pleasure while she might. She seemed impelled by a need to degrade her-

---

[8] His solution was a good one. Many years later, after Julia's sons had died, he was adopted by Augustus, and became his heir and the next Emperor.

self; from love affairs, she moved step by step toward harlotry, and all Rome knew it except Augustus. At last, in 2 B.C. when she was thirty-eight, friends of the self-exiled Tiberius let Augustus know that they would accuse Julia in court if he himself did not. The awakening was horrible. As Seneca recorded the story some decades later:

> Augustus learned that she had been accessible to scores of paramours, that in nocturnal revels she had roamed about the city, that the very Forum and the rostrum from which her father had proposed a law against adultery had been chosen by the daughter for her debaucheries, that she had daily resorted to the statue of Marsyas,[9] and, laying aside the role of adulteress, there sold her favors and sought the right to every indulgence with even unknown paramours.[10]

The aging Emperor was wild with grief and anger; he may have counted the letters of the alphabet, but it did not help. He summarily issued a decree exiling her to the barren island of Pandateria; there she lived in virtual house arrest, expressly denied the use of wine and other comforts and forbidden to have either company or callers except those specifically authorized by himself. Unendurably ashamed, Augustus wrote a letter detailing her crimes and had it read aloud to the Senate, seemingly as self-punishment. He forced one of her lovers to kill himself and banished the others, but even this brought him no relief. For years, whenever Julia's name was mentioned he would sigh and say he wished he had died childless. His accomplishments seemed vain to him, and the order and prosperity he had created were empty victories. Friends urged him to relent and let Julia return to Rome, even Tiberius adding his voice, but Augustus would only reply: "May you, too, be blessed with daughters and wives like her." Merciful and forgiving to many other wrongdoers and enemies, he could never forgive her; perhaps he sensed that she had not merely degraded herself, but used her sexuality as a weapon to strike down her own father.

Augustus eased her exile slightly after five years, by moving her to Rhegium (Reggio), and allowing her the freedom of the city, but there she was forced to remain, and died of tuberculosis at the age of fifty-four after sixteen years of exile. Coincidentally, in that same year her great father also ceased his efforts to remake the soul

[9] A place in the Forum where whores came to offer themselves.
[10] Seneca: *De Beneficiis*, vi, 32.

of man, and died, kissing his faithful wife, Livia. Rome deified and worshiped him, but rejected his ethics; Rome forgot Julia, but adopted hers.

5

The Tutor of Love,
and the Textbook of Adultery

❁   ❁

❁

Ten years after Augustus had exiled his only daughter, the aging, saddened monarch suffered another blow; he learned that Julia's daughter, also named Julia, was leading a life of adultery, heedless of her mother's fate. Once again the storm clouds rumbled and the lightning flashed on Olympus; Julia Minor was banished in A.D. 8 to the tiny island of Trimerus in the Adriatic, and there wasted away until her death twenty years later.

Among her friends was the sophisticated poet Ovid, a middle-aged but frolicsome favorite of the fashionable circles. He had reason to regret being a friend of Julia's, for in that same year he too was plucked up and flung far off to exile in Tomis (modern Constanta) on the southern shore of the Black Sea—a muddy, bitter-cold border town at the margin of the civilized world and a particularly cruel place of exile for an aging, soft-skinned sybarite.

The two banishments were not merely coincidental, but history does not say exactly what Ovid's crime was. He had not been the younger Julia's lover; this seems clear from the veiled remarks he made in the fawning letters of apology he wrote to Augustus, in which he referred to the crime of having "seen" something wrong, but having failed to say anything. Probably, say many scholars, he knew of, or aided in, the details of Julia's adultery. Perhaps he was even present at some wild party where she put on an indecent exhibition. In either case she could have learned her morals and gained her technical proficiency from Ovid's own writings—and therein, it seems, lay the real cause of his banishment.

For among his other works, the poet had written a long instructional poem called *Ars Amatoria*—*The Art of Love*—which was, in essence, the first textbook on methods of flirting, attracting lovers, and consummating adultery. It was no mere piece of vulgar obscenity: Ovid even patterned it (somewhat tongue-in-cheek) along the lines of philosophic and educational treatises, and called himself the "tutor" and "master" of the art of love. Romans agreed; it was said that Ovid had educated his entire generation in the techniques of love, although it would be more accurate to say that he in part educated them, and in part set forth didactically what they were already practicing. One must admire Augustus for withholding his wrath for ten years. Ovid had defiantly written the book in 2 B.C., though the Julian Laws had only recently been completed, and he specifically scoffed at the Emperor's hope of remaking Roman morality in an older style. "Let the past please others," he wrote. "I congratulate myself on being born into this age, whose ways are so congenial to my own." Ten years later, when Ovid played some part in Julia Minor's fall, the Emperor restrained himself no longer.

The tutor of illicit love was born in farming country east of Rome in 43 B.C., a year after Caesar's assassination. His father, a wealthy equestrian, sent Ovid to Rome to learn law, so that he might rise within the government and finally attain senatorial status. Ovid studied the law carefully, and the gay life even more so; he found he preferred the latter, and devoted his life to literature and the pursuit of cultivated amusement. His inherited wealth, his amiable manners, and his wit made him popular in the best circles, and the senatorial clan of the Fabii even gave him his third wife.

But his wives interested him little; he was intrigued by the women he wooed and won for pure sport. In his earliest poems, the *Amores*, he spoke of a lady called Corinna, but in succeeding poems he boastfully revealed that Corinna stood for many, or even any, attractive women. "It is no single she whose beauty calls forth my passion," he ambitiously proclaimed. "No, there are a hundred causes to keep me always in love." He listed the kinds of women he found appealing: modest ones, saucy ones, austere ones, flirtatious ones, literary ones, simple ones, tall ones, short ones— he loved them all, and all equally well. Many years later he would protest he had been speaking only of courtesans, but his own youthful words tell the truth of the matter:

> About my temples go, triumphant bays!
> Conquered Corinna in my bosom lays;
> She whom her husband, guard, and gate, as foes
> (Lest art should win her) firmly did enclose.
> That victory doth chiefly triumph merit,
> Which without bloodshed doth the prey inherit.
> No little ditchëd town, no lowly walls,
> But to my share a captive damsel falls.
>
> Amores, II, xii

When Ovid was forty-one his *Ars Amatoria* appeared. In it, though still lighthearted and laughing, he professorially set forth what he had learned in many years of practice, constructing a detailed guidebook for the playing of an elegant game. And game it was: in his work there is no hint of the genuine misery of Catullus, the studlike activity of Caesar, the psychopathic self-debasement of Julia. All those were extremes of Roman love; Ovid, cynically philosophic, offered a golden mean.

"If anyone among this people knows not the art of loving," he began, "let him read my poem, and having read be skilled in love." First, whom shall the would-be lecher pursue? Not married women; Ovid pretended to be on the side of the law. But this was only lip-service; he was talking about adultery, and made it perfectly clear again and again: "As to men, so also to women is stolen love the most pleasant."

One must first learn where to hunt for quarry, so he first suggested various fashionable public places in Rome. The Circus is particularly useful: the would-be lover can size up the woman first, then take a seat next to her and ask her whose horse is winning; this leads to friendly talk, and the chance to fix her cushion or fan her hot cheek. Now the chase is on. The adept hunter takes time out to befriend her personal maid—a useful ally who can carry messages, whisper his praises to her lady, and tip him off when her lady seems to be in the mood. "You will ask," Ovid said, "whether it profits to seduce the maid herself," for naturally if she is attractive the man will immediately want to do so. A seduced maid will be particularly helpful, out of fear of exposure; but on the whole, Ovid thought it a risky business, and not worth while.

After these early steps, the huntsman begins to use a variety of devices for breaking down the lady's coolness and reserve. They include the writing of flattering and earnest love letters (which must, however, include no learned words or allusions that might make her feel ignorant), intense covert looks and subtle gestures at the games or the secret touching of feet under the banquet table to convey burning desire while escaping the eyes of others, and such aphrodisiac deeds as seizing her cup and drinking greedily from the spot her lips had touched. The lover should hold a parasol for her against the sun, vigorously push aside the crowd when she walks, wait loyally at an appointed place though she fail to show up, and travel through night and storm to do errands that please her. He should be artful and generous with compliments on her gown, her hair, her face, but flattery will succeed best when coupled with some touching evidence of feeling:

> If she appears in her negligé, cry out: "You inflame my passion!"
> Then add in anxious tones: "Take care! You'll catch a cold in
>   this fashion."

Ars, ii, 301–2

None of this will succeed if the lover is not impeccable: he must wear spotless, well-fitting clothes, keep his hair, nails, and nostrils well trimmed, and avoid body odor or halitosis.[2] Curling one's locks or scraping off body hair with pumice stone is too effeminate, but Ovid sanctions the use of tears, which, apparently, are not. The lover should weep, cultivate a pallor, and adopt a look of suffering. When all this finally wins him kisses, he may drop the fragile pose and be a bit more vigorous to gain the rest; she will struggle, for appearance's sake, but will consent. For all women will; it is only a question of the right approach: "Some fish are caught with spears, some are caught with the net, and some are taken by the hook." But all can be taken; and so to bed.

Having captured the quarry, the lover will want to keep her for

---

[2] Ovid also offers such notes on personal hygiene to women as this: "I hardly need warn you to let no rankness as of the goat be beneath your arms, nor your legs be bristling with rough hair" (*Ars*, iii, 193–4).

a while. This is not to be misunderstood as implying fidelity, as
Ovid hastily reassured his reader:

> *Not that I'd doom you to a single flame:*
> *Preserve us! this a wife could hardly claim.*
> *Indulge, but o'er your lapses draw a veil,*
> *Nor of your peccadilloes boast the tale.*
> *Give nought another wench may recognize,*
> *Have no time-table for your gallantries.*
> *Lest any catch you in her favorite stew,*
> *Appoint for each a different rendezvous.*
>
> Ars, ii, 387–94

In this, as in everything else in the *Ars Amatoria*, he has the air of
such a good-natured, well-intentioned rascal that it is hard to dislike
him. He did not write like a pornographer or a calloused thrill-
seeker; indeed, when he discussed sexual positions and techniques,
he so specifically insisted on patience and mutual satisfaction that
he might almost have been writing one of the modern books for
young married couples:

> *Love's climax never should be rushed, I say,*
> *But worked up softly, lingering all the way.*
> *The parts a woman loves to have caressed*
> *Once found, caress, though modesty protest.*
> *You'll see her eyes lit up with trembling gleams,*
> *As sunlight glitters in pellucid streams;*
> *Then plaintive tones and loving murmurs rise*
> *And playful words and softly sounding sighs.*
> *But ne'er must you with fuller sail outpace*
> *Your consort, nor she beat you in the race:*
> *Together reach the goal: 'tis rapture's height*
> *When man and woman in collapse unite.*
>
> Ars, ii, 717–28

But the patience and care of which he wrote were only a matter
of good tactics; the dominant attitude of the *Ars Amatoria* is that
the lover and his beloved are sly predator and wily prey, and the
nature of love is conquest. Despite the honeyed refinement of
Ovidian love, it is frequently given stronger flavor by judicious
infusions of sadism and masochism. An occasional charge of deliberate cruelty or repulse by either partner is, for example, essential to keep its fires burning, and Ovid highly recommended, as particularly delicious, making love to a woman who is in tears. Even
more pertinent is his suggestion that a gladiatorial combat is an ex-

cellent place to feel the first stirrings of passion. Ordinarily, one expects love and sexual excitement to be inhibited and sickened by the sight of cruelty and death; such a thought never occurred to Ovid when he suggested the "melancholy sands" of the Circus as a breeding-ground for tenderness:

> *Love oft in that arena fights a bout,*
> *Then 'tis the looker-on who's counted out.*
> *While chatting, buying a program, shaking hands,*
> *Or wagering on the match intent he stands,*
> *He feels the dart, and groaning 'neath the blow*
> *Himself becomes an item in the show.*
>
> Ars, i, 165–70

Yet the wounds below were real; human beings were stabbing and disemboweling each other, the victor asking the crowd whether to spare the fallen opponent or drive a sword through his throat. And while such games were being played out on the sand, fashionable men and women in the stands laughed to see their agony, munched nuts, plums, and pastries, and fell in "love."

The upright, serious Augustus found the *Ars Amatoria* offensive, but said nothing. But when Ovid was linked with the disgrace of his granddaughter, he could tolerate him no longer, and even ordered the book removed from public libraries. From distant Tomis, Ovid penned innumerable groveling letters. "I assure you," he wrote, "my character differs from my verse; my life is moral, my muse is gay. . . . A book is not an evidence of one's soul." But Augustus was not interested in these protestations; it was the book that had done the harm. Not for nothing did fashionable Romans refer to Ovid as "*praeceptor amoris*"—instructor in love; he had helped flout and wreck the Emperor's effort to restore goodness to society.

No letter ever arrived in Tomis to bid the aging poet bring back his upset stomach, his chilblained hands, and his aching heart. In A.D. 17, after nine years of exile, he died; only his bones returned to the warmth and comfort of Rome. Yet his book lived on, both as an instruction manual and a self-portrait of Roman lovers; like both Julias, the pitiful ex-sybarite was the victor over the emperor-god.

6

The Victory of Roman Love

W ithin my memory," wrote the philosopher Seneca in A.D. 55, "the people in the Forum stabbed Tricho, a Roman equestrian, with their writing-styles because he had flogged his son to death; Augustus Caesar's authority barely rescued him from the indignant hands of fathers no less than of sons." The past was truly dead. In the stabbing of Tricho (who recovered), a symbolic blow was delivered to the *patria potestas* (which did not). Within a few generations, emperors would formally take away most of the powers father nominally retained over their wives and children but almost never used, and would reassign them to courts established by the state. The decline of man's supremacy, foreseen by Cato the Elder in 195 B.C., would effectively be completed during the first century A.D.

During that period, women acquired a number of new legal and social freedoms. By Hadrian's reign (A.D. 117–38) jurists held that the free consent of the female was necessary in marriage; although she still had to use a man as her business agent, she was substantially free to manage her property and to bestow her purse and her hand where she chose. And still, despite their increases in freedom during the century after Augustus' death, Roman women found themselves strangely discontented and insatiable. They vainly sought a new role, a new meaning to femininity to replace the lost one. Some tried being literary and intellectual; some busied themselves with religion, charities, and social events; some were forever having their procurators whisper in their ears about business matters or offer them papers to sign; some preferred to meddle in politics by cajoling and advising the men they slept with or were married to.

Many writings, monuments, and inscriptions attest to all this, but none more vividly than the sixth *Satire* of the poet Juvenal. His account is sensational, exaggerated, and bilious; yet allowing for all that, the types portrayed in it were, by the nature and standards of satire, intended to be easily recognizable to his readers, and hence have some reference to reality. Juvenal reflected his era's uncertainty as to what woman was; in his bewilderment, he knew only that she was terrible. The entire poem, in fact, is simply a catalogue of female faults in the year A.D. 116.

A wife is a tyrant—the more so if her husband is fond or loving. Cruelty is natural to women: they torment their husbands, whip the housekeeper, and enjoy having slaves flogged almost to death. Some women are silly and tedious in their newfangled addictions to religion; others are stupidly susceptible to astrology; still others make themselves ridiculous by donning armor and even taking part in mock combat. Their sexual lusts are disgusting—they prefer slaves, actors, and gladiators; their efforts to sing and play musical instruments are a bore; and their gluttonous eating and drinking are enough to make a man sick. Juvenal described the bibulous woman all too vividly:

> She drains a second pint before she tastes her food, to make her appetite ravenous; then, having washed her stomach, the wine returns in a cascade on the floor—rivers gush over the marble pavement. . . . Her husband, with eyes closed, smothers his rising bile.

But there is something even worse than this:

> And yet that woman is more offensive still who, as soon as she takes her place at the table, praises Virgil, and excuses the suicide of Dido; who matches and compares poets. . . . I hate her who is skilled in antiquarian lore, quotes verses I never knew, and corrects the phrases of her husband as old-fashioned.

Is this the clue? Did the singing, the astrology, and the vomiting really revolt him as such—or was it woman's appropriation of masculine privileges in her efforts to find her new role? One would suspect the latter, for many of the follies he was most aroused by were also committed by men, though he never said a word about that. And what drew his hottest fire was the assumption by women of sexual privilege, once completely the right of the male. Juvenal ranted about immorality—but only that of women; he was furious at their adulteries, but not at their adulterers. Nowadays, he wrote, if a husband scolds his wife for improper conduct, she says to him: "It was agreed that you should do what you pleased, and that I also might have full power to gratify myself. In spite of your outcry, confounding heaven and sea, I am mortal." She insists on her right to seek for diversion, as he does, and to call it love, as he does. Juvenal simply could not stomach this; the time was out of joint, but he knew not how to set it right. He could only be satirical and angry.

Yet if women were much given to adulterous love in Juvenal's time, it was in part because their many other freedoms and activities were little more than dilettantism and play-acting. The Roman woman tried to imitate man, and was not really allowed to. The only women who pursued useful careers came from the lower classes, or were of Greek and other foreign extraction. Highborn Roman women dabbled in literature, but did not become successful writers, and played at politics, but never voted in any senate except the *conventus matronarum*, a mock-congress that debated questions of etiquette and dress. They won financial and legal independence from men, but found themselves in a society which, living parasitically from its provinces, had no useful work for them to do. They imitated men as much as they were allowed to, but gained little sense of importance and little definition of their own value—except in the realm of love.

But their concepts of love were one with the general Roman concept of other pleasures—mere sensation, to be enjoyed until fatigue or boredom set in, and then to be enjoyed again with the help of novelty and change. In the middle of the first century, Seneca wrote a famous description of Roman banqueting:

> The food which their stomachs can scarcely retain is fetched from farthest ocean; they vomit that they may eat, they eat that they may vomit, and they do not deign even to digest the feasts for which they ransack the whole world.

About ten years later, he wrote concerning marriage in terms that are strikingly similar:

> There is not a woman left who is ashamed of being divorced, now that certain high and distinguished ladies count their years not by the number of consuls, but by the number of their hus-

bands; they are divorced in order to marry, and marry in order to be divorced.

Adultery, he said, was the greatest evil of the time, and although he may have exaggerated a bit, he claimed that a woman with only two lovers was, relatively speaking, a paragon of virtue.

In adopting this role, women were less and less interested in playing the role of mother. Among the patrician class, marriages became increasingly infertile. By the early part of the second century A.D., only one of the forty-five great senatorial families that had lived in Rome under Julius Caesar one hundred and sixty-five years earlier was still in existence. A psychological disease was exterminating the former upper class. The equestrians, or middle class, were following their lead: thousands of middle-class tombstone inscriptions were signed not by children of the deceased, but by their freedmen. From the forms of names in first- and second-century epitaphs, scholars have calculated that four-fifths of the population of Rome were emancipated slaves or their offspring—people of non-Roman origin who were filling up the vacuum left by those Romans who, having successfully disentangled sexual pleasure from considerations of permanent union or parenthood, were effectively discontinuing their own species.

Even when they did produce children, most Roman men and women were too lacking in the self-image of parenthood to guide and mold the growing characters of their children. Instead, as Tacitus glumly described it:

> The infant is committed to a Greek chambermaid and a slave or two chosen for the purpose, generally the worst of the whole household train and unfit for any office of trust. From the idle tales and gross absurdities of these people, the tender and uninstructed mind is suffered to receive its earliest impressions. . . . The parents themselves are so far from training their young families to virtue and modesty, that they set them the first examples of luxury and licentiousness.[12]

From parents who cared only for the stimulation of their own nerve endings, children formed their conceptions of Man, of Woman, and of Love, and grew up to repeat the pattern.

Yet there was another side to patrician society; there were still some anachronistic Lucretias, Cornelias, and Turias, and men to match them. At the very time when Juvenal was sourly castigating

[12] Tacitus: "Dialogue Concerning Oratory," Sec. 29.

the world, Pliny the Younger was admiring it and seeing good in it. Caius Plinius Caecilius Secundus, nephew and heir of the Pliny who wrote the famous *Natural History*, found life sweet, mankind decent, and fate kind, an attitude perhaps fortified by the fact that he was one of the wealthiest men of his time. Not content with a brisk legal practice and important governmental duties, he also wrote copiously, and among many other matters expounded upon noble and loving marriages, including his own. In an era of cynicism, he is the principal exponent of sweetness and light, but it is curious that his selection of loving wives seems to hang chiefly upon violent and suicidal acts of loyalty. Whom did he admire and write about?—Paulina, who had Seneca cut her wrists along with his own when Nero ordered him to die; another woman, unnamed, who, seeing an incurable lesion of her husband's genitals, leaped into a lake with him; and Arria, who, when her husband, Paetus, wavered at the Emperor Claudius' order to kill himself, stabbed herself in the breast and handed him the dagger with the words formerly known to every schoolboy: "*Paete, non dolet*"—"It does not hurt, Paetus."

Pliny himself enjoyed the love of a good woman, though she had no need to prove it with a dagger. When he was middle-aged he married his third wife, the young Calpurnia, and his love letters to her are among the very few that exist from antiquity. When he went down to Rome to plead a case and she remained at the country villa, he missed her sorely and wrote how he wandered disconsolately about the empty house. And when Calpurnia took a trip to the coast for her health, he worried continually and begged for word from her:

> As is the way of frightened people, my fancy paints most vividly just those calamities I most earnestly implore Heaven to avert. . . . I pray you, write to me every day and even twice a day; I shall be more easy, at least while I am reading your letters.
>
> (*Letters*, vi, 4)

But aside from a few genuine moments like this, his letters to her are rather artificial, and one gains a far more vivid and credible impression of their relationship from a letter he wrote not to her, but to her aunt, praising the girl:

> She is incomparably discerning, incomparably thrifty, while her love for her husband betokens a chaste nature. Her affection to me has given her a turn to books, and my compositions, which

she takes a pleasure in reading, are continually in her hands. . . . When at any time I recite my works, she sits close at hand, concealed behind a curtain, and greedily overhears my praises. She sings my verses, and sets them to her lyre, with no other master but Love, the best instructor. (*Letters*, iv, 19)

One may wonder whether Pliny's love was not somewhat a literary invention. The style and content of his love letters makes them seem clearly meant for publication; if so, his sentiments may, in part, have been adopted for the benefit of his readers. But to a friend, Fuscus, he described domestic routine at his summer villa in Tuscany, and unwittingly revealed much about his marriage by saying almost nothing about it. He wakes (he wrote), lies abed thinking about the day's writing, and then dictates to his secretary until 10:00 or 11:00 a.m.; then he meditates again for a while out on the terrace. Next he takes a chariot ride alone, followed by a nap, and then by some reading aloud to improve his voice; later he has a rubdown, exercise, and a bath. At supper he finally sees Calpurnia; afterwards he walks in the garden and discusses philosophy and letters—but with his favorite slaves, not his wife. In fact, in this entire recital, she seems no more important than a piece of furniture. "We cannot avoid the conviction," concludes Jerome Carcopino, a scholar of Roman social life, "that, taken all around, it [Pliny's love] was gravely lacking in warmth and intimacy."[13]

And perhaps this was unavoidable, for in the last analysis, Pliny still clung to the remnants of the older concept of marriage—the patriarchal, land-based, economic view. Junius Mauricus, a friend, asked him to help find a match for a kinswoman, and this is what Pliny replied:

You ask me to look out for a husband for your niece. There is no need to look far, for I know a man who might seem to have been provided on purpose. His name is Minicius. He is well-connected, comes from Brescia, which you know to be a good old-fashioned place . . . is a man of active energy and has held high office. . . . His father has ample means, and though perhaps your family is not much concerned on that point, we have to remember that a man's income is one of the prime considerations in the eyes not only of our social system, but of the law. (*Letters*, i, 14)

If sour Juvenal could not see the way to a healthier future, neither could sweet Pliny. He let his wife write, sing, and take an interest in his doings, but he treated her as an unimportant but agreeable

[13] Jerome Carcopino: *Daily Life in Ancient Rome*, p. 89.

household commodity, and viewed marriage in terms that had long since lost their power to bind people and create a stable social order. He was a decent sort of man, but he and Calpurnia, as models, were no more capable than Juvenal of arresting or modifying the course of social deterioration, or restoring the older ways of love.

7

Love as Symptom and Disease

❀   ❀

❀

If Roman voluptuaries accepted the Ovidian concept of love without question, a number of Roman moralists were alarmed by it and considered it responsible for many of the social ills of the Empire. The Christians, moreover, who were beginning to become prominent in the second century, were of the same opinion, and vehemently so. By the fifth century, Saint Augustine and other Christian writers would state flatly that sexual sin was directly responsible for the crumbling away of the Empire, the afflictions of which were interpreted as the punishment visited upon mankind by a wrathful God.

The evidence of comparative anthropology, however, proves that many societies have permitted extramarital sexual activities and love affairs without major damage to themselves. Why, then, were they so hurtful in Rome? The historian need not invoke supernatural explanations. Roman love flourished in the context of the disintegration of family life, and even accelerated it; in that circumstance it produced a problem of utmost seriousness—the voluntary infertility of the native Roman stock. For it was when sex moved outside of marriage and called itself love, while marriage itself lost its values, that the long decline of population began which so worried Augustus, and which he was powerless to check.

By the second century, the Emperor Marcus Aurelius not only had to enroll criminals and gladiators in his army, but had to settle the conquered Marcomanni tribesmen within the Empire as land-holders and require them to supply soldiers to the Roman forces. In the third century, a long period of rebellion and civil war coincided with severe barbarian invasions and a prolonged plague to decrease the Roman population still further, and the prevailing love pattern gave Roman society no chance to recoup its losses. Alexandria gradually lost half its population and other great cities became deserted and ghostly, a large percentage of Roman farms were abandoned for lack of manpower, and later emperors resorted increasingly to the policy of settling conquered barbarians within the borders as farmers and farm-workers. Professor Richard Haywood even argues in his recent study *The Myth of Rome's Fall*, that the dissolution of the Empire was the inevitable result of its absorption of too many people with no cultural loyalty to an imperial structure and no tradition of administrative control over a far-flung society.

But historians differ with the early Christians in assessing the role of love in the overall decline of Rome. To some extent, Roman love was indeed a contributing cause insofar as it produced infertility, but to a far greater extent it was only one painful symptom of a basic disease. What that basic disease was, legions of historians have sought to explain: they have named such factors as the squandering of resources, the indolence of the proletariat, the corruption and greed of the upper classes, the growing political power of the army, and so on; more generally, these are all related to the parasitism, excessive leisure, and purposelessness of imperial Roman life. Whatever the balanced and true explanation, Roman moralists and Christian reformers alike vigorously attacked the symptom, while the disease raged on unmolested and finally killed the patient.

Chapter IV

IT IS BETTER TO MARRY
THAN TO BURN

I

The Dream of Spiritual Marriage

❀   ❀

❀

In the second and third centuries A.D. the Roman Empire, despite its infirmities, still gave the appearance of greatness and glory; indeed, in the great cities life continued to be as sybaritic and elegant as ever, and some of the greatest extravagances of construction and entertainment occurred in this very period. Yet in the midst of these glories, certain citizens were beginning to act in a bizarre and un-Roman fashion: in a world that offered them unprecedented luxuries and pleasures, they were unaccountably attracted to a new religion called Christianity which scorned the former and castigated the latter. Some of the patricians whose philosophy had long been based on the value of power, wealth, and practicality were succumbing to a new philosophy that stressed meekness, poverty, and mysticism. Although they lived in a society that was confirmed in the practice of Ovidian love and the indulgence of desire, they were inexplicably drawn to a faith that denied them the right to worldly love or sensuous enjoyments, and promised them instead a disembodied eternity.

One of these people was a young man named Ammon, who grew up in the latter part of the third century in Alexandria. Despite the buffeting the Empire had taken from civil wars and barbarian attacks for the previous fifty years, that city was still opulent, extravagant, and gorgeous during Ammon's youth; it was the Roman Empire's finest metropolis in the East, and combined the graces and sophistication of Hellenic culture with the pomp and pageantry of Rome. Most of its inhabitants lived just as Alexandrians had for the past two centuries, but a few, including Ammon, had begun to shun luxury and comfort in favor of poverty and pain, and in the very midst of life seemed to long for death.

What Ammon looked like or how he spent his boyhood and youth we do not know; all we are told by historians is that his parents were wealthy, and died when he was young, leaving him in the guardianship of an uncle. He evidently, however, lived in a fine house, was surrounded by servants, and had access to fine food, the baths, the games, the theater, and, of course, women. But Ammon was a Christian, and a devout one; at some point in his youth, taking seriously the words of Saint Paul and the early Fathers of the Church, he decided to remain chaste and to prepare himself for eternity.

The uncle held no such somber views, however, and having selected a proper bride for Ammon, he forced the youth to submit to a wedding. It was celebrated in the traditional Hellenic fashion by a joyous gathering of both families, followed by the usual banquet and then the procession to the nuptial chamber. Here the friends and relatives undoubtedly uttered all the worn amiable jokes, wished the bridegroom well with hearty platitudes, and finally left the two alone. Ammon closed and bolted the door, and turned to his bride, who was lying on the nuptial couch. There followed a remarkable scene, according to the account given by the fifth-century ecclesiastical historian, Socrates Scholasticus:

> He took a book containing the epistles of the apostles and read to his wife Paul's Epistle to the Corinthians, explaining to her the apostle's admonitions to married persons. [*1 Corinthians* vii: 1–9 are the particularly relevant verses, and include such crucial ideas as: "It is good for a man not to touch a woman. Nevertheless, to avoid fornication, let every man have his own wife, and let every woman have her own husband. . . . I would that all men were even as I myself. . . . I say therefore to the unmarried and widows, it is good for them if they abide even as I. But if they cannot contain, let them marry: for it is better to marry than to burn."] Adducing many external considerations besides, he descanted on the inconveniences and discomforts attending matrimonial intercourse, the pangs of child-bearing, and the trouble and anxiety connected with rearing a family. He contrasted with all this the advantages of chastity; described the liberty and immaculate purity of a life of continence; and affirmed that virginity places persons in the nearest relation to the Deity.[1]

[1] Socrates: *Ecclesiastical History*, iv, 23. The story was also told, with minor variations, by another fifth-century historian, Palladius, in his *Historia Lausiaca*, 8.

Ammon's young bride—her name was not recorded by Socrates—listened to this harangue with what very likely began as astonishment, but, according to the historian, ended as conviction. She and Ammon forthwith purified their marital union by jointly renouncing the world and taking a vow of celibacy. The last laugh was on the wedding guests.

The young couple lived as brother and sister, devoting themselves to contemplation and to the adoration of God, but after a while they realized that their life in Alexandria, surrounded as it was with fleshly comforts, was out of keeping with their aims. Abandoning all comforts, they moved south of Alexandria to Mount Nitria in the Egyptian desert country, installed themselves there in a rude hut, and took up an ascetic existence. Yet Ammon's wife, considering their way of life, found even this still too close to worldly ways. "It is unsuitable," she said to him one day, "for you who practice chastity to look upon a woman in so confined a dwelling; if it is agreeable to you, let us live apart." Ammon thought it a meritorious suggestion; they lived thenceforth in two huts, near enough for occasional visits, and observed identical rules of self-mortification, using neither oil nor wine, eating nothing but dry bread and water, and often fasting one, two, or three days at a time.

Even so, Ammon sensed that temptation lay always in wait for him. Considering that the sight of his own body involved danger, he took a resolve never to remove his clothing. "It becomes not a monk," he said, "to see even his own person exposed." Once he wished to cross a river, but was as unwilling to get his clothes wet as to remove them. In this dilemma, he besought the help of God; if one may believe the devout historian, He must not have considered the matter beneath His notice, for an angel promptly appeared, picked Ammon up, and deposited him on the other side, both dry and virtuous.

The fame of Ammon and his wife spread rapidly; not only did five thousand monks (according to the possibly wishful estimate of Palladius) gather about them within a few years to emulate their asceticism, but continent marriage became a Christian dream for several centuries thereafter. If it was never dominant statistically, it surely was intellectually. For centuries, while Christianity struggled against the flesh, continent marriage was praised as the highest form of union between man and woman. Genuine data do not exist, but innumerable allusions to cases of continent marriage appear in the patristic writings and ecclesiastical histories; even if we allow for the adverse effect of piety upon accuracy, it would seem that it existed with some frequency and was talked about to the point of obsession.

To be sure, one may doubt that many of the reported cases were altogether successful; even those ecclesiastics who most praise continent marriage admit its fragility, and tell of instances of failure. Saint Jerome, writing from Palestine in A.D. 408 to a wealthy young man named Rusticus in one of the outlying provinces, revealed just such a story. "Your former wife," he said, "who is now your sister and fellow servant in Christ, has told me that, acting on the apostolic precept, you and she lived apart by consent that you might give yourselves to prayer, but that after a time your feet sank beneath you as if resting on water and indeed—to speak plainly— gave way altogether." For Rusticus and his wife had moved together again and sunk back into wedded pollution; then, overwhelmed by a sense of guilt, the wife journeyed to Palestine to do penance, while Rusticus promised to follow as soon as he could settle his affairs, which were in tangled condition due to a threatened barbarian invasion. Time passed, but he did not arrive. So Jerome wrote him, urging him to come, but whether he ever did is not known; he may have feared the misery of continent marriage as much as life under barbarian masters. Yet even though Rusticus failed in his attempt to lead this purified kind of married life, the very fact that he and his wife tried to do so indicates the power of the new ideal; had he and his wife lived two centuries earlier, they would have regarded any such notion with derision and incredulity.

For several centuries—those very centuries when the once-firm structure of the Empire was weakening, and at last disintegrating— continent marriage was celebrated by Christians as a state scarcely less noble than dedicated celibacy; it seemed, indeed, to be one form of Christian reaction to the doom and destruction that first lowered, and then broke, upon the Roman world. Cases of it were reported and celebrated throughout the disintegrating Empire from its most civilized redoubts to its lost colonies, from indolent, decadent Alexandria to semibarbaric Gaul.

It was from Gaul, in fact, that there came one tale of continent marriage that sounded a new and important theme—that of chaste romance. Gregory, Bishop of Tours in the sixth century, told in Book One of his *History of the Franks* the story of Injuriosus, a wealthy young man of senatorial rank who had lived in Auvergne in southern Gaul in the early part of the previous century. Though the Visigothic invasions had disturbed and disrupted life in many parts of the Western Empire, Auvergne was relatively tranquil, and Injuriosus lived in a fine mansion, as befitted a Roman patrician, and got his income from his vast inherited domains. When he reached manhood, he paid a sizable price to obtain a bride of good senatorial stock, and married her. But when they retired that evening, his bride turned her face to the wall as soon as she got into bed, and began weeping bitterly. Injuriosus gently asked why she was crying. According to Bishop Gregory, she explained: "I had resolved to keep my poor body for Christ, pure from the contact of man. But woe is me, who am in such wise forsaken of Him that I availed not to carry out my desire." In place of unfading roses, she added, there would now be disfigurement and corruption. Would that she had died as a child! She abhorred the things of this world, including—for she was specific about it—Injuriosus' fine mansion and great estate.

The young man replied mildly that she was, like him, an only child, and that both their families would be made happy by the continuation of each line. This appeal fell flat; the world and its vanities, she argued at considerable length, were worthless, and the only real bliss lay in the eternal life. Injuriosus, having listened to her long harangue, at last found himself strangely freed of his desires and uplifted in spirit. "Through thy sweetest eloquence," he said, "eternal light hath shone upon me, as it were a mighty radiance." To her great delight, he thereupon vowed to abstain from fleshly desires; husband and wife then made a solemn pact of virginity, clasped hands, and at once fell asleep peacefully.

For many years they slept chastely in the same bed and led a good life, managing their property and serving God. When both of them died, the servants built tombs for them against different walls of the building, but in the middle of the night the tombs moved together until they rested side by side. "Which thing shows," concluded Gregory, "that when two are united in heaven, the tomb that holds their bodies buried may not keep them asunder. The people of that place have chosen to call these twain 'The Two Lovers' until this day." He was much impressed, as always, by a physical miracle; the modern reader may think the emotional miracle by far more impressive.

Even stranger than continent marriage was a somewhat similar arrangement between men and women known as spiritual marriage that existed in the early days of the Church. Unmarried virgins known as *agapetae* (from the Greek, *agape*, spiritual love) would become spiritual sisters or spiritual wives (the two terms being used almost interchangeably) of the clergy, with whom they lived in household intimacy. Their relationship ostensibly involved no unchastity, but they had not even the tie of marriage to excuse them from sin in case their feet (to borrow Jerome's phrase) were to sink beneath them. The agapetae must have been numerous and widespread from the second through the sixth century. Tertullian and Hermas, among other early writers, praised them; what is more significant, such ecclesiastical writers as Irenaeus, Jerome, Saint John Chrysostom, Epiphanius, and Eusebius all complained about them, and, at least from the historian's point of view, one complaint is better evidence of their prevalence than ten hosannahs.

Many of the religious leaders and sects which permitted agapetae and spiritual marriage later came to be regarded as heretical. Perhaps the Church was wise to recognize that the arrangement would fail in the long run. Only in a disintegrating society, when men and women were transfigured by their search for an eternal and better world, might they be able to maintain such a relationship; and even then it was often suspect. Paul of Samosata, Bishop of Antioch at the end of the third century, was sharply scolded by a group of fellow bishops for having two "blooming and beautiful" spiritual sisters who traveled everywhere with him. Other heretical clerics such as Alexander the Montanist and Apelles the Marcionite maintained companionships they claimed were pure, but the orthodox doubted the wisdom of their efforts and the truth of their claims. Since the orthodox destroyed the writings of most of the heretics, one can hardly come to an impartial conclusion on the question.

But agapetae were also found within unimpeachably correct churches as well. No diaries or letters of these women or their male friends have survived, but one can glean some vivid details about the companionship from the outraged polemics of the righteous. "From what source has this plague of 'dearly beloved sisters' found its way into the church?" fumed Jerome in A.D. 408. "They live in the same house with their male friends; they occupy the same room, often the same bed; yet they call us suspicious if we think that anything is wrong." The early Christians were, after all, Romans; they tried to carry out the tenets of a new faith within a framework of old customs. Even a celibate cleric and his spiritual sister might still wear senatorial garments and live in a mansion; similarly their sexual patterns might be a composite of old and new, confusing to observers and themselves alike. In the search for chastity, for instance, they evidently arrived at a kind of compromise that consisted of intimate love play stopping short of actual sexual connection; such is the picture one gets from a troubled letter written in A.D. 249 by Cyprian, Bishop of Carthage, to a fellow church-leader who had consulted him on the subject.

We have read, dearest brother, your letter which you sent to Paconius, our brother, asking and desiring us to write again to you and say what we thought of those virgins who, after having once determined to continue in that condition and firmly to maintain their continency, have afterwards been found to have remained in the same bed side by side with men (of whom you say that one is a deacon); and yet that the same virgins declare that they are chaste. . . . We must interfere at once with such as these, that they may be separated while yet they can be separated in innocence, because by and by they will have become firmly joined by a guilty conscience. . . .

And do not let any of them think to defend herself by saying that she may be examined and proven a virgin, for both the hands and the eyes of the midwives are often deceived, and even if she be found to be a virgin in that particular in which a woman may be so, yet she may have sinned in some other part of her body which may be corrupted and yet cannot be examined. Assuredly the mere lying together, the mere embracing, the very talking together, and the act of kissing, and the disgraceful and foul slumber of two persons lying together, how much of dishonor and crime does it confess! [2]

Some of the more earnest practitioners of this relationship considered that great merit lay in this "trial of chastity," and sought to expose themselves to the maximum of temptation so as to gain virtue by resisting it. According to the legend recorded by a medieval scholiast, a certain Irish holy man of the sixth century named Scuthin always slept in bed with two beautiful virgins. When Saint Brendan the Navigator chided him for taking such risks, Scuthin challenged him to prove himself equally capable of virtue. Brendan tried it and managed to resist temptation; he found himself, however, quite unable to sleep, and cut the experiment short.

[2] Cyprian: *Epistle lxi* in the Ante-Nicene Library edition; same as *Epistle iv* in Oxford edition.

By diligent opposition, the Church slowly eradicated agapetism. It persisted longest in monastic life; in the Irish Church, for instance, monks and nuns shared monastic houses until late in the sixth century. "They did not scorn to administer and live together with women," wrote an old ecclesiastical historian, "because being founded upon the rock, they did not fear the wind of temptation." But the Church felt the rock could stand some buttressing, and the practice was condemned by the sixth-century Irish Rules and Penitentials. In Spain, three separate synods in A.D. 589, 590, and 633 recognized the inability of conscience permanently to master such temptation, and ordered the housekeepers and female companions of the clergy to be sold as slaves. As for the central Church itself, from the Council of Nicaea on (A.D. 325), the clergy were forbidden to have women in their houses; the custom must have been difficult to stamp out, for the penalties grew ever stricter as time passed. Leontius, Bishop of Antioch, gave the only convincing answer to those who doubted that a man and his agapeta could be wholly blameless: faced with an order to rid himself of his female companion, he castrated himself and kept her. It was not an answer most men cared to give.

2

The Sources of Asceticism

At first it seems incredible that asceticism should so rapidly have become the ideal of a large part of Hellenistic and Roman society, since the love and sex patterns of those cultures had been firmly and completely established in the other direction for many centuries. Everyone knows how long and painfully the Christians fought to evangelize the pagan world; everyone is familiar with the repeated persecutions by which that world fought back and expressed both horror and detestation of the new religion; and yet it gradually and inexorably captured the loyalty of a large segment of the population, and with the conversion of the Emperor Constantine in A.D. 323 became effectively the dominant state religion, its ascetic ideal being progressively embodied in law and rigorously enforced. In view of that protracted and difficult struggle against social ideals so unlike those of Christianity, one wonders why asceticism had so powerful an appeal and so inexorably conquered the violently resisting Romans.

The answer is bound up with the whole question of the victory of Christianity, a subject beyond the scope of this book. Yet within the area of love itself, the triumph of asceticism is neither as surprising nor as paradoxical as it first seems. Pagan eroticism had, over the centuries, worn itself down in excess and over-refinement, producing a jaded appetite and weariness on a national scale; meanwhile, the disintegration of family life had left people without a satisfying system of affectional ties, and with a disturbing feeling of isolation and emotional frustration. These matters were obviously bound up with sexual practices, and when the Roman world still knew of Christ only that He had been a minor Jewish troublemaker, certain pagan philosophers had already begun to argue in favor of sexual restraint and even asceticism. Musonius Rufus, a first-century philosopher, held that sexual acts outside marriage were impermissible, and Apollonius of Tyana argued that even married love was impure. Precursors of Neoplatonism such as the Stoics took Plato's doctrine of Ideas and paralleled his metaphysics with an ethic in which flesh and the world were held to be transient and impure, while spirituality and ideality were timeless and good. (Saint Paul himself was deeply influenced by this early Neoplatonism, and so were many Church Fathers, both heretical and orthodox.) Meanwhile, among the non-Christian pagans there also appeared in the second century a popular religious-philosophic movement known as Gnosticism, mystical in nature, which stressed the need for salvation from sins, and relied on the intervention of a savior.

By the third century, many Stoics and Neoplatonists lived and acted much like Christians, even though not believing in the Christain God. Even when Julian the Apostate succeeded to the throne of the Eastern Empire in 361, bringing to a temporary end the reign of Christian emperors, there was no real change in palace life or official attitudes. True, Julian had deserted Christianity in favor of paganism, and during his short reign strove to reopen the pagan temples and revive the glories of Greek philosophy; yet he lived in celibacy after his wife died, ate food as plain as any monk's, wore his beard uncut and full of lice, and shunned soft beds, the theater, and the races. The Christians never rejoiced at having Julian on the throne, but he was no great threat to them after all.

The most glamorous woman of the age was Hypatia, the beautiful and brilliant lecturer in philosophy at the Alexandrian Museum. Students from far lands came to study with her; many ended by falling in love with her. Although Christian monks finally murdered her, they might better have reverenced her for her attitude toward the body. As lovely as she was, Hypatia chose to remain a virgin, and when one student professed his passionate love for her, she hoisted her dress to the waist and contemptuously said: "This, young man, is what you are in love with, and not anything beautiful."

The Christian influence on love and sex life was not, therefore, so much a revolution as an alliance with sympathetic forces. A growing current of asceticism and antifeminism had already manifested itself within pagan society in the Hellenic part of the Empire as early as the time of Christ. By the third century these trends had become far stronger, and were accompanied by an increasing cynicism and weariness that affected the Western Empire as well as the Eastern, maturing into widespread soul-sickness by the time of the major fifth-century invasions.

It was within this context that Christian morality made such notable conquests and so effectively displaced the traditional Greco-Roman patterns of sexuality. In a society in which asceticism was already so powerfully on the increase, the Jewish Old Testament seemed to offer an excellent explanation of the source of evil and a thorough justification of antifeminism and celibacy. The primal transgression of man against God, it said, was instigated by woman, resulted in the creation of the sense of sexual shame, and brought about the permanent misery of mankind. God Himself explicitly stated that a permanent antagonism would thenceforth exist between the sexes. "I will greatly multiply thy sorrow and thy conception," He told Eve. "In sorrow shalt thou bring forth children;

and thy desire shall be to thy husband, and he shall rule over thee." To Adam He said: "Because thou hast hearkened unto the voice of thy wife, and hast eaten of the tree, of which I commanded thee, saying, Thou shalt not eat of it: cursed is the ground for thy sake; in sorrow shalt thou eat of it all the days of thy life" (*Genesis* iii: 16–17).

Yet the connection between sex and the Fall, which so intrigued and even obsessed the early Christians, had not really been central to the thinking of the Jews. Men in the Old Testament were patriarchal and powerful, and often guiltlessly enjoyed the services of several wives and concubines (as, for instance, Jacob, in *Genesis* xxix). Women were sometimes portrayed as scolding or conniving, but more often as loyal, diligent, and devoted (as was Abigail, in *Samuel* xxv, or the good wife delineated in *Proverbs* xxxi: 10–31). Even when women were portrayed as an aggravation to man, they were not said to have caused the pollution or corruption of his soul. And though the Jews, unlike the pagans around them, were sternly opposed to whoredom, adultery, fornication, and all forms of sodomy and homosexuality, their attitude towards sex within marriage was essentially lusty. The *Song of Solomon* is far from the only case in point; there are countless passages which refer to "laying with," "begetting," or "going in unto" without the faintest overtone of sin or dirtiness.[3]

It was not until Paul was carrying out his mission in the first century that the Temptation, Original Sin and Fall began to seem the central tragedy of mankind, or that Eve's guilt appeared so great as to justify woman's subordination in life. The earlier Jews had considered marriage and procreation a holy duty, looked down on childlessness, and even excluded castrates or eunuchs from their congregations (*Deuteronomy* xxiii: 1); in contrast, Christ—though His strictures against easy divorce seemed to indicate concern for family integrity—spoke approvingly of those "which have made themselves eunuchs for the kingdom of heaven's sake."[4] Paul went

---

[3] *Leviticus* xv:16–24 does prescribe ritual purification for the "uncleanliness" resulting from intercourse, but if this is read in context (the chapter also deals with several forms of nonsexual uncleanliness), it assumes no great significance.

[4] The quote is from *Matthew* xix:12. It is now generally agreed that He meant voluntary abstinence rather than actual castration, but early Christians interpreted His words in both senses. Thousands mutilated themselves in the early centuries (Origen being the most famous case), but the Church slowly concluded that this was absolutely impermissible, and forbade it.

further, urging all men to be abstinent if they could; and a little more than a generation after Paul's death, the author of *Revelation* saw, in chapter fourteen of his vision, 144,000 virginal men who had never been "defiled" with women, standing next to the Lamb on Sion.

Within the next two centuries, Christianity developed a fanatical fixation about the glory of virginity, the evilness of woman, the foulness of sexual connection, and the spiritual merit of denying the flesh and repudiating love. To be sure, these were not the only concerns of Christianity, which also warred against the riches, selfishness, war, usury, and cruelty of the Roman world. Yet even these evils were always linked with sexual sin; in *Revelation* and much other early Christian writing, for instance, the terms "fornication," "lust," and "whoredom" were used symbolically to refer to any and all sins against God. So essential did asceticism seem to the early Church that when a maverick monk named Jovinian came to Rome in A.D. 385 to argue that marriage was superior to celibacy, he drew the concentrated fire of the Church's top thinkers and writers, and Pope Siricius personally excommunicated him for heresy and blasphemy. Bishop Gregory of Nyssa and other Christian thinkers, facing the thorny question of how Adam and Eve—had they never sinned—could have blamelessly obeyed God's injunction to produce offspring, laboriously concocted theories about a "mode of transient generation" by which they could have reproduced more or less like pollinating plants, without contact or pleasure.

Although sin was equated with love of man for woman, the love of man for man was attacked with particular ferocity. The Council of Elvira denied pederasts communion even *in extremis*. Constantius and Constans, sons of the Emperor Constantine, made homosexuality a capital offense, and the Emperor Valentinian borrowed in the name of Christianity a technique of its persecutors and burned homosexuals at the stake. Why all this? Possibly because homosexuality was an indulgence in pleasure without the excuse of child-getting; this made it not merely sin, but heresy.

Yet whatever methods Christianity finally employed, it was not really by legal sanctions that it managed to create in a happy mankind an overwhelming sense of guilt and the equating of sexual love with transgression against God. If these attitudes became dominant, it was because they coincided with and expressed larger, more pervasive social forces. And those were the changes in the Empire itself—the erosion and deterioration of a once impregnable world. From the middle of the second century on, the Empire was almost continually under barbarian attack. At first the barbarians were thrown back, although the imperial mechanism creaked and groaned ominously under the strain. Then during the third century, a series of civil wars, plagues, and Teutonic invasions greatly strained and weakened the economy, and caused genuine alarm about the condition of the imperial defenses and growing pessimism about the future. The fourth century saw some respite from some of these pressures, but no improvement in the Empire's basic internal problems—the abandonment of farms, the decline of commerce, the falling birth rate, and other indices of social necrosis. Fear and gloom lay always close behind the façade of gaiety and splendor; Rome was brilliant still, but the firm earth shook, and men trembled to see the Empire changing and perhaps dying.

Even Christians, their thoughts directed toward the eternal world, and their personal affections more engaged by the intense family-like society of the early Church than that of the Empire, wept for Rome. When it fell in A.D. 410 for the first time, taken by Alaric the Goth, even that most ardent evangelist, Saint Jerome, wrote from Bethlehem: "Who would have believed that Rome, victorious so oft over the universe, would at length crumble to pieces? . . . In vain I try to distract myself from the sight by turning to my books; I cannot fix my thoughts on them." A little more than a century later, when the process of disintegration had gone much further, Pope Gregory was in still deeper despair. "Everywhere we see mourning and hear groans," he wrote. "Cities are destroyed, strong places are cast down, the fields are depopulated, and the land is become desert. . . . Moreover, the scourge of God's justice resteth not, because men's guilty deeds have not been corrected, even under this scourge."

There *was* evil on earth, and people hungered for an explanation and a justification of it; the angry God of Christianity furnished better ones than the philosophies of even the most ascetic pagans. While imperial armies, once invincible, now sometimes lost their battles, and while emperors temporized and let barbarians into the Empire unchallenged, men and women made sense of their fears and miseries by calling themselves the very source of evil. To do so was to find a way one could deal with it personally. Voluntary suffering and self-denial would earn spiritual credit and pay off, in part, a

debt that would be due eventually. In this process of propitiating
the Deity by self-denial, it was inevitable that the love life of mature
adults, being the most intense of all satisfactions, should be the most
severely attacked.[5]

3

The Struggle against Lust

❀   ❀

❀

I n the latter half of the fourth century, enthusiasts reported, per-
    haps with more zeal than accuracy, that in Egypt alone at least
twenty-two thousand men and women had quit civilized communities to lead monastic and ascetic lives in the desert along the upper
Nile. Some lived in huts or caves, but the more devout preferred
dry wells, the deserted dens of beasts, and tombs. Most refrained
altogether from washing, and prized their crusted, malodorous
state. A monk named Arsenius wove palm leaves, and refused to
change the nauseous water in which he steeped them year after year,
so as to add stench to his other discomforts; the monk Macarius ate
nothing but raw desert herbs for seven years; and the monk Besarion
did not lie down while sleeping for forty years. The most famous
was Saint Simeon Stylites, who, it is often pointed out, spent thirty
years on top of a sixty-foot pillar; it is less often mentioned (though
equally true) that he also accumulated spiritual credit by allowing
himself to become a mass of clotted and ulcerated filth, and that he

---

[5] The Roman-Christian experience
was far from unique; many other peoples have tried to propitiate angry gods
by sexual self-denial. See Havelock Ellis: *Sex in Relation to Society*, pp.
1415–17.

bound a rope around his waist so tightly as to produce a maggot-infested putrefaction. Worms filled his bed, and fell from him as he walked; sometimes he replaced them, saying: "Eat what God has given you!"

All this seems a long way from love, but it was not. In the *Verba Seniorum*, a collection of anecdotes and maxims of the desert fathers, a young monk tormented by sexual daydreams asks a wise old monk: "I entreat thee to explain to me how thou hast never been harried by lust." The old man replies: "Since the time that I became a monk I have never given myself my fill of bread, nor of water, nor of sleep, and tormenting myself with appetite for these things whereby we are fed, I was not suffered to feel the stings of lust." To judge by other accounts in this ancient work, few other monks were so easily able to be rid of their desires; they endured the same penances, but suffered continually from sexual fantasies. Indeed, it becomes clear as one reads these scores of brief tales that the monks had no genuine wish to be free of tormenting desire; their heroism and spiritual satisfaction lay in defeating the powerful urge, and without it their desert life would have been hollow and meaningless.

For these practitioners of asexuality were, in fact, more totally preoccupied with sex than any pagan debauchee. They credited themselves with immense concupiscence and very fragile will power; not by thought, but by desperate deeds, did they stay pure. In lower Egypt, according to the *Verba Seniorum* again, a prostitute hired by some practical jokers tried to seduce one desert-dwelling solitary by coming to his cell at evening, weeping that she was lost, and pleading fear of the wild animals. The monk let her in, and was immediately seized by overpowering desire. Realizing the gravity of his situation, he lit the lamp and held a finger in the flame, "and when it burnt and scorched he felt it not, for the flame of lust that was in him." Nevertheless it kept him busy; by morning all his fingers were gone, but he was still pure.[6]

The intensity and obsessiveness of such temptations are nowhere more vividly recorded than in a letter written by Saint Jerome to a

[6] Many other celibate men also possessed—or thought they possessed—extraordinary strength of desire. In sixth-century Italy a priest took orders, and parted from his wife although he loved her. Forty years later, when he lay in a coma, dying of ague, his aged wife visited him and bent over his bed. "In great fervor of spirit," noted Pope Gregory the Great in his fourth *Dialogue*, "he burst out, saying: 'Get thee away, woman, a little fire is yet left; take away the straw!'" What non-celibate man could claim as much?

female follower, recalling for her his own desert sufferings of A.D. 375. It is an awesome confession of the struggle against lust.

> How often when I was living in the desert and the solitude that affords hermits a savage dwelling-place, parched by a burning sun, how often did I fancy myself amid the pleasures of Rome! I sought solitude because I was filled with bitterness. Sackcloth disfigured my misshapen limbs, and my skin had become by neglect as black as an Ethiopian's. . . . Yet I, who from fear of hell had consigned myself to that prison where I had no other companions but scorpions and wild beasts, fancied myself amongst bevies of dancing maidens. My face was pale and my frame chilled with fasting; yet my mind was burning with the cravings of desire, and the fires of lust flared up from my flesh that was as that of a corpse. So, helpless, I used to lie at the feet of Christ, watering them with my tears, wiping them with my hair, struggling to subdue my rebellious flesh with seven days' fasting.[7]

Again and again that same thinly disguised note of inflamed eroticism appears in the writings of the holy men. Among the several biographies of saints written in the fourth century, that of Saint Mary the harlot exemplifies, even better than the more familiar story of Thaïs, the strong brew of sex and piety on which the early monks became intoxicated. In a desert region near Edessa in Mesopotamia (modern Iraq), a girl, Mary, was brought up by her uncle, Abraham, a devout Christian solitary, whose entire contact with her took place through a tiny aperture between the two rooms of their hut. When Mary was a beautiful girl of twenty, a stranger lured her into opening her door to him, and promptly defiled her. In shame she fled to the city of Assos and became a harlot in an inn. The grief-stricken Abraham sought her for two years and finally learned where she was. Dressing his aged body in military disguise so that Mary would not take flight, he pretended to be a client and roundly praised her charms before her and the innkeeper. They drank wine together and she fondled him; then he gave the innkeeper a gold piece and said: "Now, friend, make us a right good supper, so that I may make merry with the lass, for I am come a long way for love of her." After the supper Mary enticed him to her room, and locked the door. He sat on her bed, and she knelt before him, smiling, and began to pull off his shoes; not until then did he reveal his identity. This, of course, brought on the predictable sequence of tears, repentance, and forgiveness; they then made their

---

[7] Saint Jerome: *Epistle xxii* (to Eustochium), 7.

escape, fled the city, and returned to the old happy life in their twin cells. The ending is moral, but the tale itself is dangerous stuff: it skirts hard by the forbidden heights, the blasphemous act, the incestuous abomination.[8]

The struggle against lust produced an explosive state of mind; the personality could be held together only by the tenacious cement of irrationality. The desert fathers saw and worked little miracles every day. In themselves, these sound harmless enough, but the same intellectual orientation could lead further, and did; not by mere coincidence, it was a towering figure of asceticism, Tertullian, whose formula for finding the truth of Christianity was *Credo quia absurdum* (I believe because it is absurd), while Pope Gregory— later sainted and called "the Great"—burned the Palatine library because he considered it a hindrance to Bible study. Asceticism led thus to intolerance, obscurantism, and overt aggressiveness. The ascetic was not content to master himself; inevitably his route led him to try to master other men's flesh, and their minds as well.

His greatest assault was launched against the female half of humanity. He constantly dinned in her ear such words as: "She [woman] was created as a helpmate for her husband, yet brought only ruin upon him," and: "You are the gate of hell, the unsealer of that forbidden tree, the first deserter of the divine law." [9] A bishop soberly offered for debate at the Council of Mâcon in A.D. 585 the proposition that woman did not even have a mortal soul, but after earnest discussion the Council decided she did. In the opinion of some Fathers of the Church, however, heaven would be spared the indignity of ever having women on the scene, for at the Resurrection they would, by God's grace, become sexless.

A second ascetic attack on woman was to desert her. Continent marriage itself was a form of partial desertion; in addition, literally thousands of marriages were completely broken up because of the earnest desire of the husband (or occasionally the wife) to lead a dedicated life. Saint Abraham (the uncle of Saint Mary the harlot) and Saint Alexis both fled from their brides on their wedding nights; Saint Nilus persuaded his wife to permit him to leave her and their children in order to live on Sinai; and Saint Melania talked her husband into letting her go seek a monastic life. But these are only

[8] Saint Ephraem of Edessa: "Life of Saint Mary the Harlot," *Vitae Patrum*, I.

[9] Clement of Alexandria: *Paedagogus*, iii, 2; Tertullian: *De Cultu Faeminarum*, i, 1.

names and events, and tell us nothing of the feelings of the people behind them. What was the actual emotional condition of these zealots? What feelings could make a man fly from marriage and love as though they were a loathsome infection?

In A.D. 370, when Saint John Chrysostom, the greatest orator and writer of the Eastern Church, was still a young man, his friend Theodore fell in love with a maiden named Hermione and made plans to marry her. Chrysostom salvaged him for celibacy by writing him an impassioned letter which changed his mind completely, and of which this is a significant segment:

> The groundwork of this corporeal beauty is nothing else but phlegm and blood and humor and bile, and the fluid of masticated food. . . . If you consider what is stored up inside those beautiful eyes, and that straight nose, and the mouth and cheeks, you will affirm the well-shaped body to be nothing else than a whited sepulchre. . . . Moreover, when you see a rag with any of these things on it, such as phlegm, or spittle, you cannot bear to touch it even with the tips of your fingers, nay you cannot endure looking at it; are you then in a flutter of excitement about the storehouses and repositories of these things?[10]

This attitude was translated into doctrine in diverse ways. Montanus and his followers advocated the separation of husbands and wives, the adherents of Tatian the Syrian attributed the invention of marriage to the devil himself, and comparable views were held by Marcionites, Basilidians, Saturninians, Gnostics, Manicheans, and other early Christian and semi-Christian sects.[11] Eventually the Catholic Church labeled them all heretical; yet the Church itself incorporated much of the same point of view in its own doctrines. In the writings of the Fathers of the Church nothing is more highly praised than celibacy, while marriage is only grudgingly permitted. For over seven centuries the Church waged a bitter fight to impose celibacy on its clergy, and finally won; at the same time, monasticism for each sex grew from a few tiny communities to a vast organized institution throughout Europe. So profoundly was the orientation against all sexuality built into the Church that many centuries later, even under the attacks of Protestantism, the Catholic Church did not retreat; rather, the Council of Trent in 1563 went one step further and finally condemned with anathema the

[10] Chrysostom: "Letters to Theodore," i, 14.

[11] The Gnostics, referred to above as a non-Christian sect, became increasingly allied to Christianity as time passed.

doctrine that the married state was as good as, or superior to, celibacy.

The third and worst attack on woman consisted of convincing her to renounce her own sexuality and all it meant as lover, wife, and mother. Nearly every great writer and preacher of the early Church wrote voluminously in praise of virginity. Among female martyrs, the favorites were virgins who preferred burning pitch, the rack, and the hot iron, to sexual intercourse. Such virginity was said to have miraculous powers; typically, when a hungry lion was turned loose upon Thecla in the arena, he stopped short and then licked her feet in humble admiration of her purity.

The most notable exponent of virginity and cultivator of saved women was the gifted Saint Jerome, who so graphically described his own torments in the desert. After receiving a thorough education in Rome and spending several years in the desert, he entered the priesthood and became secretary to Pope Damasus. Still affecting the brown robe of an anchorite, he spent much time winning to the holy life a number of wealthy Roman women, whom he persuaded to live in dirt, tears, and austerity in the midst of luxury and self-indulgence. From his many letters of guidance and encouragement to them, one can extract a dismal picture of the only way of life a Christian woman could, at that time, pursue with self-respect and dignity. Its absolute prerequisite was the renunciation of sexual pleasure —virginity for the unsoiled, self-denial for those who had already sinned. To one of his virgins, a young woman named Eustochium, he wrote a letter in A.D. 384 that became a classic description of the Christian virgin's life.[12] "I need not speak of the drawbacks of marriage," he began—but then immediately listed them in full: pregnancy, the crying of infants, the torment caused by a rival, the household chores, and so on. "I praise marriage," he added piously, "but only because it gives me virgins. I gather the rose from the thorns, the gold from the earth, the pearl from the shell."

He told Eustochium, in commendably specific terms, how to remain a virgin and avoid all temptation and danger. She must shun wine as though it were poison, and eat only the simplest and smallest meals, for "the rumbling of our intestines . . . the emptiness of our stomach . . . [and] the inflammation of our lungs . . . [are] the only way of preserving chastity." She must not visit wealthy

[12] Jerome: *Epistle xxii.*

homes or look upon the ways of luxury. She should read much, fast
often, wear the meanest clothes, remain at home, and weep for her
sins every night. Yet she must not be vain in her sufferings or
publicly display her devotion: "Do not lower your voice on purpose, as though you were worn out by fasting; nor yet lean upon a
friend's shoulder, imitating the gait of one who is completely exhausted." Yet, wonder of wonders, for all her self-denial she will
still have a love life of sorts—the only one a decent woman may
have:

> Let the seclusion of your own chamber ever guard you; ever let
> the Bridegroom sport with you within. If you pray, you are speaking
> to your Spouse: if you read, He is speaking to you. When sleep falls
> on you, He will come behind the wall and will put His hand through
> the hole in the door and will touch your belly. And you will awake
> and rise up and cry: "I am sick with love." And you will hear Him
> answer: "A garden inclosed is my sister, my spouse, a spring shut up,
> a fountain sealed."[13]

4

The Transformation of Marriage

Only a small percentage of Christians actually succeeded in
sublimating their drives and leading lives of abstinence; the
rest continued to lust and love, fornicate and marry. But all these
activities were undergoing major changes in form and in spirit, and
none more so than marriage. And since love seems so full of

[13] The Biblical echoes are from the *Song of Solomon*, iv:12, and v:2, 4.

paradoxes, perhaps we should not wonder that Christianity affected marriage in two seemingly irreconcilable ways: it at once ennobled it and debased it, strengthened it and poisoned it.

The Christians criticized and fought against the wanton customs of marriage and divorce that had long existed in the Roman Empire, but their own beliefs and practices long remained unformulated, and were crystallized only in the course of several centuries. The process was slow partly because of the immense discrepancy between long-established Roman habits and Christian doctrines—and even, to be truthful, because of internal quarrels as to what Christ Himself had thought about divorce. (In *Matthew* xix:9 He recognized "fornication"—the word means "adultery" in Biblical usage —as grounds for divorce, but in *Mark* x:11–12 He recognized no grounds whatever.) For centuries it was held by some Christians that a second marriage was equal to adultery; others would allow two but not three, others three but not four, and so on. But after the conversion of the Emperor Constantine the trend was unmistakable: civil divorce regulations grew ever tighter, and religious opinion became ever more strict. Gradually marriage came under clerical domination. By the fifth century it was rare for any wedding not to include an ecclesiastical benediction, and the notion that marriage was a sacrament—a holy act, not dissoluble by private or personal wish—steadily gained ground, although it was not authoritatively defined until the Middle Ages. The sixth-century Code of Justinian (which was chiefly effective in the still-flourishing Eastern Empire but influenced the West during the brief period of Justinian's reconquest of Italy) made divorce almost impossible and listed adultery as a capital offense; simultaneously, however, it revoked the ancient penalties placed by Augustus against celibacy and childlessness. Marriage, in short, had become indissoluble, but sexual self-denial stood above all else as the ethical way of life.

When Italy was again inundated by the Lombards, beginning in A.D. 568, the Code of Justinian ceased to be enforced, and Italy's connections with the Emperor in the East were effectively ended. Western Christianity, cut off from continued imperial influence, faced the difficult task of adapting itself to, and amalgamating itself with, the primitive customs of the Teutonic tribes. This retarded the progress of its moral ideas for some centuries, but in the end they prevailed: Roman monogamy became the pattern in the barbarian lands, thoroughly modified by Christianity into a serious lifetime contract made under religious auspices and not to be dissolved lightly, if at all.

Most authorities agree that this was a major contribution to the sexual and marital life of Western man. But since life is rarely simple and history seldom logical, Christianity also worked in precisely the opposite direction: it both reversed the partial emancipation of woman and thrust her firmly back under male domination. Oriental, Jewish, and barbarian ideas were mingled and fused with the Christian contempt for women; the concept of the wife was that of an inferior and sinful creature who should be confined, dominated, and chastised according to need—a viewpoint which contradicted, but coexisted with, the vaguely romantic ideals of continent marriage.

"What cause have you for appearing in public in excessive grandeur?" wrote Tertullian, scolding wives for putting on fine clothes and jewels. "You have no reason to appear in public except such as is serious. . . . Submit your heads to your husbands, and you will be enough adorned. Busy your hands with spinning; keep your feet at home; and you will please better than by arraying yourselves in gold." The *Apostolic Constitutions* of the fourth century summed up the early Christian view of woman's place in marriage: "O wife, next after the Almighty . . . and after His beloved Son, our Lord Jesus Christ . . . do thou fear thy husband and reverence him, pleasing him alone, rendering thyself acceptable to him in the several affairs of life. . . . Ye wives, be subject to your own husbands, and have them in esteem, and serve them with love and fear, as holy Sarah honored Abraham. For she could not endure to call him by his name, but called him Lord. . . ."

But this was only part of the change; the Church Fathers invaded the very marriage bed with their ukases, exhortations, and pronouncements. In his *Paedagogus* (in effect, a third-century Christian version of Xenophon's *Economist*), Clement of Alexandria told married people when it was permissible to lie with each other —not during the day or even after coming back from the market place, for such times should be devoted to reading or praying, but only after supper. Even then, married love-making would remain sinless only if delight were confined and restrained. The moral man is required to practice self-control, he warned, but there is no self-control in enjoying something intensely pleasurable. Two centuries later, when the evils of the world were much more advanced, Jerome restated the point in far harsher terms:

It is disgraceful to love another man's wife at all, or one's own too much. A wise man ought to love his wife with judgment, not with passion. Let a man govern his voluptuous impulses, and not rush headlong into intercourse. . . . He who too ardently loves his own wife is an adulterer.

He went even further: each experience of marital intercourse, he argued, constituted a temporary separation from the holy spirit, for such was the nature of sexual love—even within marriage—that just after it neither prayer nor communion was possible.

This startling doctrine became Church dogma. The seventh-century *Penitential* of Archbishop Theodore of Canterbury (a manual for priests) set down what must even then have been an old established rule in the Western Church: "Those who are joined together in matrimony should abstain from cohabitation three nights before receiving communion." The Church had made marriage a holy act—and yet considered this part of it an unholy, almost abominable, lapse from grace. The resulting frame of mind in which man and wife embraced each other was surreptitious, hasty, and guilt-ridden—somewhat, says Bertrand Russell, like drinking during the Prohibition.

No personal confessions of those blighted intimacies remain, but a good idea of their emotional content can be gained, inferentially, from the tone in which Tertullian, one of the great married clerics, addressed his own wife in a letter. Though Tertullian turned away from the Catholic Church in his later years and headed the Montanist sect in Africa, he was the first truly great Church writer of the West. Born about A.D. 160, the son of a Roman centurion of Carthage, he received an excellent classical education both there and in Rome itself, in the latter of which he then practiced law. In his early forties Tertullian underwent conversion to Christianity, returned to Carthage, married a Christian woman, and became a presbyter. Using his immense rhetorical powers, he began to turn out a veritable flood of influential writings on Christianity; it has even been said that Christian literature in the West sprang from him full-grown. When he was about forty-seven, he wrote his wife a long letter on marriage and widowhood which became one of the standard Christian tracts on these subjects, and which is particularly intriguing for the tantalizing glimpses it gives of his relationship to his wife.

"I have thought it meet, my best beloved fellow servant in the

Lord," he began, "even from this early period to provide for the course you must pursue after my departure from the world, if I shall be called before you." Tertullian directed her not to remarry, likening second marriage to outright adultery. Widowhood was God's call to sexual abstinence; he explained at great length that though marriage is permissible, God would much prefer that men and women practice celibacy. A widow is really getting a chance to please God. In any case, if Tertullian did die first, he wanted his wife not to grieve, for his death would be only the early ending of an enslavement to a disgusting condition which, under any conditions, they would have to give up to enter heaven:

> To Christians, after their departure from the world, no restoration of marriage is promised in the day of resurrection, translated as they will be into the condition and sanctity of angels. . . . There will at that day be no resumption of voluptuous disgrace between us. No such frivolities, no such impurities, does God promise to His servants.[14]

It is one of the most remarkable consolations ever addressed by any man to his wife.

To most Romans this must have seemed thoroughly demented, but harmless. It was then only A.D. 202; the Empire still seemed to flourish on all sides, in Carthage, Spain, Italy, Gaul, and of course in the East. It was but three generations since Hadrian had finished beautifying Rome, and only one generation since the reign of the benevolent Stoic, Marcus Aurelius. Plotinus, the greatest of the pagan Neoplatonists, was still unborn, the vast Baths of Caracalla were yet unbuilt, the sensual excesses of Elagabalus were not even dreamed of. Tertullian must have seemed a foolish fanatic, who would soon be forgotten. As it turned out, his was the voice of the future. By him, and by Saint Paul—the source of so much of his thinking—morals and love would be influenced for many generations; indeed, he and Paul would still speak within the consciences of many people in the twentieth century.

[14] Tertullian: "Ad Uxorem," i, 1–3.

5

Saint Augustine: The Victory of Guilt

❀   ❀

❀

Far more influential even than Tertullian was a man who, living two centuries later, saw the first fall of Rome and became the first definitive voice of the medieval mind. He was Saint Augustine, nominally only the Bishop of Hippo, a small African seaport,[15] but in actual fact a master theologian who exerted an immense influence on all of Christendom by pouring forth a flood of brilliant commentaries and speculations which were multiplied by copyists and carried throughout the Empire by messengers. Augustine wrote two hundred and thirty major works, many hundreds of letters, and a vast quantity of sermons; engaged in protracted warfare with Donatists, Manicheans, and Pelagians (all of whom considered themselves good Christians, and all of whose doctrines he considered pernicious); and elaborated upon every major Christian theological idea, including original sin, free will, election, predestination, monism, idealism, the state of grace, salvation, the Trinity, and the nature of the sacraments. "Theology in Western Christianity," a scholar has said, "has been a series of footnotes to Augustine."

With most of this we are only tangentially concerned; what interests us directly is that Augustine's *Confessions* are the first autobiography in Western literature, and contain an intimate record of the love life of a man who has profoundly affected other love lives for more than fifteen hundred years.

He was born in A.D. 354 in Tagaste, a minor city in Numidia, North Africa, where his father was a sort of local magistrate. Ac-

[15] At that time, in Africa, the term "bishop" meant something roughly equivalent to parish priest.

cording to Augustine's evaluation of his parents, Patricius, his father, was a quick-tempered, domineering, and unfaithful man who wanted his son to be a pagan; Monica, his mother, was submissive, meek, and virtuous, but fanatically determined to make her son a Christian. The struggle for Augustine's soul was fought on more than one battleground.

Augustine received a good schooling at Madaura and later at Carthage, and proved to be an excellent pupil; even so, he found time in his teens to be a monstrously wicked young fellow.

> And what was it that I delighted in, but to love, and be beloved? but I kept not the measure of love, of mind to mind, friendship's bright boundary; but out of the muddy concupiscence of the flesh, and the bubblings of youth, mists fumed up which beclouded and overcast my heart. . . . I was tossed about, and wasted, and dissipated, and I boiled over in my fornications.

This is how Augustine saw his youth many years later; yet the facts he himself scattered throughout the *Confessions* oddly bely the continual self-accusations of dissipation. For when he was seventeen, he moved to Carthage to continue his studies, and there acquired a young concubine (whose name he never recorded), to whom he was completely faithful for the next fifteen years, and who bore him a son he reared and cherished, calling him Adeodatus, or gift of God. It is hardly a picture of moral abandonment.

Yet if it felt so to Augustine, it may have been because the short, thin, rather feeble youth was already struggling to resolve his own feelings about his manhood, pulled one way by the pleas of his mother to avoid fornication and adultery, and the other way by his desire to emulate his virile pagan father. The Oedipal conflict was, in his case, perfectly aligned with the conflict between the dying order and the new one. "In effect," wrote Dr. Charles Kligerman of the Chicago Institute for Psychoanalysis in a recent study of the *Confessions*, "Monica demanded that Augustine relinquish sexuality in favor of the Church, which meant, at an unconscious level, that he should belong to her forever . . . but the events at the time show vividly how desperately he struggled for his manhood."

In Carthage, Augustine became a successful professor of rhetoric; meanwhile, in his own continuing search for truth, he allied himself with the Manicheans, but remained unbaptized. At twentynine he decided to move to Rome, and when his mother tearfully begged him either to remain or to take her along, he lied about the departure date, left her praying in a dockside chapel, and sailed without her. Dr. Kligerman interprets both the choice of a heretical sect and the escape by ship as desperate efforts by Augustine to resist his mother's attack on his sexuality, for she, now widowed, daily wept and prayed for his salvation, and was gradually gaining control over him.

After teaching in Rome for a year, Augustine won the post of public professor of rhetoric in Milan. There he heard Ambrose lecture, was deeply moved, and grew a little closer to Catholicism; there, too, Monica eventually found him, moved in with him, and took over control of his house. She convinced Augustine that at last he must make a proper marriage, and selected for him a twelve-year-old child whom he would not be able to wed for two years; meanwhile, however, she used the betrothal as a potent argument for ousting his faithful mistress from the household. Augustine spinelessly agreed to this heartless act, although it apparently caused him genuine pain:

> My concubine was torn from my side as a hindrance to my marriage; my heart which clave unto her was torn and wounded and bleeding. And she returned to Africa, vowing unto Thee never to know any other man, leaving with me my son by her.

This admission of affection seems real, but Augustine hastened to disparage it, claiming that it had been nothing much but sexual need after all, as proven by his actions a few weeks later:

> Not being so much a lover of marriage as a slave to lust, I procured another, though no wife, that so by the servitude of an enduring custom the disease of my soul might be kept up and carried on in its vigor or even augmented, into the dominion of marriage.

Yet he felt more wretched than ever, desperately wanting what he desperately wished to avoid. "Give me chastity," he prayed, "but not yet."

In the summer of 386, when he was thirty-two, he was sitting one day, "soul-sick and tormented," in the garden with his friend, the celibate youth Alypius. Suddenly Augustine was seized by a paroxysm of weeping and fled to the end of the garden; there, after a while, he heard a childlike voice saying: "Take up and read; take up and read." He seized a copy of the writings of Paul and opened it at random, finding the words: "Not in rioting and drunk-

enness, not in chambering and wantonness, not in strife and envying: but put ye on the Lord Jesus Christ, and make not provision
for the flesh, in concupiscence." At once his heavy soul-sickness
disappeared, and he felt joyous, serene, and certain. He hastened
back to tell Alypius, who read on in the passage and found the
sentence: "Him that is weak in the faith, receive." They went in-
doors together and informed Monica they were ready to be baptized; hearing this, wrote Augustine, "she leaps for joy, and triumpheth, and blesseth Thee." It is no wonder the psychoanalyst
finds the *Confessions* so rewarding and revealing; the single word
"triumpheth" is worth chapters.

On Easter Sunday, 387, Augustine, Adeodatus, and Alypius were
baptized by Ambrose, with Monica standing proudly by. The *Confessions* say nothing more of the second mistress or the fiancée;
all of Augustine's conflicts, on all fronts, had been resolved. He
gave up the comfortable Roman life not long afterwards and returned to Africa, where he founded a religious community of celibate men—the Augustinian order, oldest monastic fraternity of the
West. In 396 he was chosen Bishop of Hippo and remained in that
post for thirty-four years until his death, sending out from that
minor post words that shaped the future of the Christian world.

The outcome of the struggle between love and asceticism in him
was embodied in many of the doctrines he gave to Christianity.
Trying to solve the dreadful question as to where evil came from,
in a world made by a good God, Augustine reasoned that although
man does have a free will, it is permanently inclined to choose the
bad by an indelible stain of original sin. Original sin included not
just Adam's and Eve's specific defiance of God, but their concupiscence, or sensuous desire. Though Augustine did not invent the
idea of original sin, it was he who first held that it attached to virgins, to celibates, and even to newborn infants; he argued that
since parentage and new life come about only by means of the
pleasurable sexual act, all flesh is inherently depraved, and all mankind is necessarily a "mass of perdition."

Some of Augustine's opponents protested that in effect he had
denied the sanctity of marriage by so coloring it with depravity,
and he tried to rebut the charge. "Marriage and fornication are
not two evils, the second of which is worse," he wrote, "but marriage and continence are two goods, the second of which is better."
Yet he belied his own words, for he also argued that the earlier in

life a married couple could begin to refrain from intercourse with each other, the better they would seem in God's eyes, and he repeatedly maintained that the evil of lust—even married lust—was justified only when it had the sole and immediate aim of begetting children. In brief, Augustine set up a permanent barrier between personal affection and sexual expression, and gave formal theological structure to the confused ideal of continent marriage and asexual love. The Oedipal conflict had at last been enshrined in a religion, and enlarged into a lifelong struggle for salvation.

Most revealing of all is Augustine's attempt to figure out how children might have been purely propagated, had Adam and Eve remained free of original sin. Augustine devoted many chapters of *The City of God*, his magnum opus, to solving this problem. He started by candidly agreeing that the sexual act "is the keenest of all pleasures on the level of sensation. . . . At the crisis of excitement, it practically paralyzes all power of deliberate thought." The flesh takes command over man, defying his will as he defied the will of God. Augustine was by then so used to ascetic thinking that he simply took it for granted that any good and reasonable person "would prefer, if this were possible, to beget his children without suffering this passion." And in Eden it would have been possible: "Even if there had been no sin in the Garden, there would still have been marriages worthy of that blessed place and . . . lovely babies would have flowered from a love uncankered by lust."

How would this have been achieved? The imagination balks at the task, Augustine admitted. But he would not shirk his duty; he would try to portray as best he could the method of propagation in Eden.

> In Paradise, then, generative seed would have been sown by the husband and the wife would have conceived . . . by deliberate choice and not by uncontrollable lust. After all, it is not only our hands and fingers, feet and toes, made up of joints and bones that we move at will, but we can also control the flexing and stiffening of muscles and nerves. . . . Some people . . . can make their ears move, either one at a time or both together. . . . There are individuals who can make musical notes issue from the rear of their anatomy, so that you would think they were singing. I knew a man myself who could raise beads of perspiration at will. . . . Human organs, without the excitement of lust, could have obeyed [the] human will for all the purposes of parenthood. . . . At a time when there was no unruly lust to excite the

organs of generation and when all that was needed was done by deliberate choice, the seminal flow could have reached the womb with as little rupture of the hymen and by the same vaginal ducts as is at present the case, in reverse, with the menstrual flux. . . . Perhaps these matters are somewhat too delicate for further discussion.[16]

It is an astonishing piece of fantasy, scarcely surpassed by the myths of primitive men, or the hallucinations of schizophrenic ones.

6

The Dark Ages of Love

It is the latter part of the sixth century. Mighty Rome has been repeatedly ravaged and looted. Her people have died off or slunk away to country towns and semi-fortified villages not so attractive to the endless armies. Where once half a million to a million people lived in imperial magnificence, perhaps fifty thousand now exist in a deserted city whose great buildings are burned ruins, whose streets are filling with rubble and growing over with grass, whose aqueducts are broken, whose ancient swamps, long drained, are filling again with stinking ooze, and whose once-glorious Senate has finally ceased to meet because it cannot muster enough qualified men to make a showing. The Eastern Empire has lost all but the merest toehold on southern Italy, and Western Europe is committed to going its own way: breaking down into semi-barbaric kingdoms, dukedoms, towns, and manors, forgetting how to read or write,

[16] *City of God*, Bk. xiv, Ch. 24 and 26.

and abandoning the hygiene, science, and culture of the Romans for the myths, terrors, and tribal customs of the Germans.

Infinitely complex, infinitely painful is the fusion of the rotting Roman sophistication with the vigorous primitive cultures of the Franks, Normans, Goths, Burgundians, and others. The result is what history calls the Dark Ages—A.D. 600 to A.D. 1100 will do as well as any dates for it—out of which the emergence of medieval feudalism will look like the very dawning of day; and just as learning, health, economics, and government are on a semi-primitive level during the Dark Ages, so too are love and morals.

The Roman Christians had dissociated love from sex, the former being God's business, the latter being the Devil's. The Teutonic savages were unwilling to accept ascetic ideals at first; they could agree that sexual activity was mere lust, but saw nothing bad in that fact, and no reason to refrain from it. Their earthy sexuality might have been given sophistication or refinement by contact with Periclean Greece, but gained only a base and gloomy coloring from Christian Rome. For some centuries, Teutonic sexuality was not so much inhibited by Christianity, as soured by it; what had been unromantic and lusty became unromantic and ugly. The sex life of the Dark Ages was grossly sensual, harsh, and sinful—with penance easily and cynically performed as often as required.

Few accounts exist of the loves of real men and women in this period, but occasional scraps remain, embedded in histories of wars and dynasties, which tease the imagination and grant us a tantalizing instant of vision. One such scrap can be found in the *History of the Franks,* where Gregory of Tours mentions some details in the private life of Lothar (Clotaire) I, King of Gaul. In the middle of the sixth century, Lothar married a lady named Ingund and, wrote Gregory, "loved her with all his heart." What, precisely, did that phrase mean to Lothar, or to Bishop Gregory who wrote it down? We read on, and learn. Shortly after their marriage, Ingund told Lothar that she was well pleased to have been chosen for his bed, and had only one favor to ask of her husband: he should find a good husband for her sister, Aregund. Lothar, listening to her praises of Aregund, found himself instantly inflamed; he traveled to the sister's domain, married her, and then returned to explain things. "I sought a man wealthy and of good wit whom I might give to thy sister," he told Ingund, "but I found none better than myself. Know, therefore, that I have taken her to wife, which I believe will not displease thee." "Let my lord do that which seemeth good in his sight," replied Ingund, "only let his handmaid live in the enjoyment of his favor." Seven hundred years' worth of gains by Roman women had thus been wiped out; woman was once again a useful, desirable, domesticated animal, and love was much as it had been in the days of the primitive Homeric warriors who either fought over captive women or gave them to each other as presents.

Two centuries after Lothar, the mighty Charlemagne briefly reconquered an empire in the West and almost rescued Europe from the barbaric doldrums. By the standards of the eighth century, he was both learned and enlightened, and he adored women. He could hardly get enough of them, in fact; he married four times, had five known mistresses, and indulged in a multitude of brief encounters. He was patriarchally fond of his six daughters and ordered them not to marry so that they might remain in his household; this was not due to paternal jealousy, however, for when at times one or another grew suspiciously fat and retired to give birth, he indulgently smiled and accepted the situation. In short, for all that he was crowned Emperor of Rome by Pope Leo III and tried to play the part of a second Augustus, he too was still basically a Frankish chieftain.

Gradually, however, the persistent clerics, laying heavily about them with their ascetic doctrines, changed things. The primitive customs did not suddenly alter, but they took on the color and odor of sin. From the top of society to the bottom, men heard themselves and their actions described in the same harsh terms Saint Boniface used in 756, when he wrote a letter of bitter castigation to King Ethelbald of England, saying in part:

> Your contempt for lawful matrimony, were it for chastity's sake, would be laudable; but since you wallow in luxury and even in adultery with nuns, it is disgraceful and damnable. . . . We have heard that almost all the nobles of the Mercian kingdom, following your example, desert their lawful wives and live in guilty intercourse with adulteresses and nuns.

Perhaps things were not quite as bad as all that; the only literate people from the sixth century to the thirteenth were clerics, trained to see the Devil lurking in every shadow, and we have no one else's evidence. Nevertheless the emotional tone of the Dark Ages is unmistakable. What had been a guiltless habit became a guilty one;

appetite was renamed lust; men and women did not all become ascetic, but learned to be ashamed of what they did.

The status of woman resulted from a blending of Church and Teutonic views. Woman became, once again, a piece of property, and lost her status as a real person in the eyes of the law. A Kentish law of the early seventh century stated that "If a man forcibly carries off a maiden, he shall pay fifty shillings to her owner and afterwards buy from the owner his consent." The Franks excluded women from the courts, barred them from the inheritance of certain ancestral lands, and even kept them out of family councils. Adultery in a wife was punishable by death; for men there was no penalty whatever.[17] Free-born women required the consent of their parents, and later of their overlords, to marry, and eventually women became attached to land, both person and title going as a package to purchase military loyalty. What women thought of the disposal of their persons was of no consequence; Charlemagne, that light in the darkness and admirer of women, is said by legend to have married off in one mass ceremony all the widows of his barons, killed in the war in Spain, to young noblemen of his own choice.

Even the clergy, who were supposed to rise above the sordid lusts of ordinary men, clearly showed the effects of the fusion of barbarian morality and ascetic values. Though Eastern anchorites and despairing Romans had been capable of renouncing the flesh, the clergy of the Dark Ages lacked any such sophisticated character. The more the Church fought against clerical marriage, the more the clergy turned to simple concubinage. Bishop Boniface and the Venerable Bede in the eighth century, Bishop Ratherius of Verona in the tenth century, and scores of others have left their written complaints about the widespread failure of the clergy to live up to the celibate ideal. A canon in England specifically ordered that the property of dead priests should go to their churches and not, even by testament, to their concubines; another canon said, in part: "Let not sons be instituted in their fathers' benefices, unless someone succeed between them." These conditions were

[17] In a well-known passage, Tacitus praised Teutonic morality early in the second century A.D. But the conduct he admired was neither moralistic nor ascetic; it restricted woman's sexual freedom because it gave man a property-right in his wife, and this typically primitive idea appealed to the Roman historian since it harked back to the early days of the Republic.

common until the Lateran Council of 1059 and the decrees of Pope Gregory VII in 1074 inaugurated an all-out fight; even so, it took three more centuries before it was won.

Meanwhile, the papacy itself had been the scandal of Christendom all through the tenth and half of the eleventh century. In 904, Marozia, daughter of a high official of the papal palace, got her lover made Pope (Sergius III); her mother secured the job in 914 for *her* lover (John X); and in later years Marozia's son and grandson took their turns, the latter being the notorious Pope John XII, who was tried before an ecclesiastical council and charged by his own cardinals with incest, and adultery with his father's concubine. This spectacle continued with only brief interruptions until the middle of the eleventh century, when Pope Leo IX began a thorough reform of the Church.

The reform coincided with other notable changes in Western civilization: the emergence of medieval culture, of knighthood, of feudal chivalry—and the discovery of a new meaning to love.

7

The Heart's Paradox

The influence of Christianity upon love and marriage is thus an impossible tangle of opposites—purification and contamination, the rebuilding of the family and the total flight from the family, the glorification of one woman and the condemnation of womankind. But the paradoxical is not meaningless, for it is a reflection of a basic mechanism of human personality; in the human heart paradox has its equivalent in the form of the paired and warring drives of love and hate, selfishness and altruism, submissiveness and rebelliousness. It is, in a word, ambivalence—the ability to feel two ways about one thing: the most perplexing, best-hidden, and most pervasive aspect of human nature.

Christianity accentuated ambivalence in the area of love far beyond any previous social system. Formerly, men and women accepted sex as a human appetite, considered love a pastime and sometimes a torment, and viewed marriage as an inescapable social duty. They had some conflicting feelings about each, but not too many, and consequently felt at ease about taking their several satisfactions jointly or separately. Christianity forbade the separate gratification of the desires for sex, love, and marriage, but made it impossible to enjoy them together. Sex became so sinful and disgusting that even within marriage, as an act allowed by God, it seemed shameful and more ignoble than elimination. Men and women hungered for it and hated the hunger, enjoyed it and felt guilty for the enjoyment. Marriage itself was the only state in which the body's yearnings could legitimately be satisfied, and through which God's commandment to be fruitful was realizable, yet it was expressly said to be an inferior condition, and one suited for weaklings. The more elevated emotions of love, since they could hardly be linked with the shameful act of sex, were limited to the painful and dangerous artifice of continent marriage. An ever-larger fraction of the European population, unable to find any tolerable solution to these dilemmas, voluntarily deprived themselves of sex and marriage, and fled to a celibate life in monasteries and convents; there they could love God, the saints, and the Pope without complications.

Saint Augustine epitomized the Christian conflicts in a single terrible sentence: "Through a woman we were sent to destruction; through a woman salvation was sent to us." In comparison, the *"odi et amo"* of Catullus looks almost puerile, and the inner conflicts of Greek men concerning women seem like childish make-believe. Yet paradox has the final word, after all: out of ambivalence, out of sexual restraint, out of the virgin-mother image of woman, man would first fashion that new notion of romantic love that has seemed so enormously valuable to him ever since.

Chapter V

THE CREATION OF THE ROMANTIC IDEAL

1 Courtly Love: A Game That
Became a Reality

2 The Service of Woman

3 The New Love in Theory
and Practice

4 A New Plant Grows in an Odd Soil

5 The Founders and Exponents

6 Courtly Love in the Court of Love

7 The Spread of the New Doctrine

8 The Outcome of Courtly Love

I

Courtly Love:
A Game That Became a Reality

❀   ❀

❀

Toward the end of the eleventh century A.D., a handful of poets and noblemen in southern France concocted a set of love sentiments most of which had no precedent in Western civilization, and out of them constructed a new and quite original relationship between man and woman known as *l'amour courtois*, or courtly love. *Cortezia, courtesie,* or *Frauendienst,* as it is also called, began as a game and a literary conceit, but unexpectedly grew into a social philosophy that shaped the manners and morals of the West. It started as a playful exercise in flattery, but became a spiritual force guiding the flatterers; it was first a private sport of the feudal aristocracy, but became finally the ideal of the middle classes; and with wonderfully consistent inconsistency, it exalted at one and the same time adultery and chastity, duplicity and faithfulness, self-indulgence and austerity, suffering and delight. Although satirists have slain and buried it in the tinsel costume of all its follies a thousand times over, it has not stayed interred for one night, and men and women throughout the Western world still live by and take for granted a number of its principal concepts.

Scholars, historians, and religionists, according to their special bents and personalities, have interpreted it in startlingly diverse ways. Some have seen it as a mere passing foolishness and an amusement of the aristocracy; others have found it a diabolically clever disguise of the undying Manichean heresy.[1] Some have

[1] The Manichean sect, which became particularly prominent beginning in the third century A.D., was one of those semi-Oriental religions which became closely allied to early Christianity, but was finally stigmatized as heretical by the Catholic Church; see chapter four. Augustine, it will be recalled, was a Manichean before becoming a Christian.

viewed it as a quaint but unimportant chapter in social history; others as a poisonous ethic that has corrupted morals and marriage ever since; and still others as the origin of modern romantic love and a huge forward stride in human relationships that has set our millennium and our part of the world permanently apart from the Western past and the Oriental present.

2

The Service of Woman

On Sunday, April 25, A.D. 1227, crowds gathered at every crossing along a road on the Italian mainland near Venice, to watch an extraordinary procession pass by. It had been thoroughly advertised in advance by a messenger bearing an open letter to all the knights of Lombardy, Austria, and Bohemia. The letter stated that on April 24 the goddess Venus would arise from the sea near Venice and start the next day to travel north to Bohemia, breaking lances with every warrior who would meet her in the lists. Whoever tilted with her would gain a gold ring and great honor with ladies; whoever failed to meet her would henceforth be shunned by all lovely ladies; and whoever first unhorsed her would win all the horses of her retinue.

The cavalcade of the putative deity, when it finally hove into view, was worth the wait. First there slowly rode by a dozen squires, extravagantly dressed in white; then came two maids-in-waiting, also gorgeously got up, followed in turn by half a dozen musicians, festively sawing and blowing away; finally there appeared on a luxuriously caparisoned horse a husky man-sized figure, attired in an outrageously ornate white gown, a heavy veil, a pearl headdress, and waist-length pearl-bedecked braids. Even in the credulous Middle Ages, none but fools and louts supposed this to be a real goddess, nor even a real woman; indeed, it was an open secret, not particularly meant to be kept, that inside the finery, the pearls, and the braids, was none other than Ulrich von Lichtenstein, knight-errant, jouster of great prowess, *Minnesinger* of some talent, and devoted admirer of an unnamed lady for whose love he was undertaking this superb, arduous, and all but impossible task. The curious poor watched and cheered, noblemen saluted gravely, the ladies, informed by gossip of Venus' real identity, hastened to kiss him warmly at every halt, and impatient knights-at-arms sent their men to him with invitations to combat.

Ulrich accepted every challenge, and by his own reckoning (which may, of course, represent some degree of hyperbole), broke the incredible total of three hundred and seven lances as he fought his way to Vienna in the course of the next five weeks. In those combats, he succeeded in unhorsing four of his opponents, and was never himself unhorsed. It was a notable performance; throughout the world of Austrian chivalry his name and fame spread greatly, and lords and ladies spoke admiringly at many a dinner table of the magnitude of the love that could have inspired such service and produced such a record of performance in the lists. And what was the purpose of these immense exertions and this very considerable expenditure? To win for Ulrich the unutterable joy of being allowed to see and speak to the nameless lady face to face, and possibly be favored with a kiss.

To understand this singular state of affairs, let us learn something of Ulrich's life up to that point. He had been born about A.D. 1200 in the hilly, fertile Austrian province of Steiermark, or Styria. His father must have been a member of the lesser nobility, for although Ulrich never possessed any great titles or vast fiefs, he grew up within castle walls, was knighted after a suitable apprenticeship, and led an active life in the service of his feudal overlords. His signature on certain existing documents indicates that for his successes as a knight-errant and jouster, he eventually won the position of high steward of Steiermark, and later on also became a marshal and a justice of the province. At the height of his fortune he owned not only the castle of Lichtenstein, from which he took

his name, but two others and considerable land. According to a
fairly recent scholarly German monograph, these and other documentary details indicate that he was a reasonably clever, energetic,
and purposeful medieval politician and landowner.

But of all this Ulrich never bothered to say anything in his
autobiography, which is the principal source of information on his
life. It runs to a wearying thirty thousand lines of narrative verse
plus numerous added lyric poems, which is surely room enough for
everything, but he devoted it entirely to the only subject that
seemed important to him—courtly love. Its very title is the story
of his life: *Frauendienst*, or the service of woman. *Frauendienst*,
dictated by the illiterate knight in later life to a scribe, is not a work
of fiction, even though the aging man-at-arms may have yielded to
the delights of exaggeration or been tricked by the distortions of
memory. Nor is it a work of satire, though *Don Quixote de la
Mancha*, not written until more than three centuries later, could
have been directly patterned upon it. *Frauendienst* is one man's
personal testimony—the actual record of his life as he lived it
under the domination of courtly love.

When he was a mere lad of five, says Ulrich, he first heard older
boys saying that true honor and happiness could come only through
serving a noble and lovely woman; he was deeply impressed, and
began to shape his childish thoughts in that direction. Even at that
tender age it was perfectly clear to him that such service, the key-
stone of courtly love, could be undertaken only for a woman one
could never marry. True love had to be clandestine, bittersweet,
and beset by endless difficulties and frustrations; by virtue of all
this, it was spiritually uplifting, and made a knight a better man and
a greater warrior.

The subject evidently dominated the thoughts of the boy, for by
the age of twelve he put away childish things and consciously chose
as the lady of his heart a princess. In every way, it was a perfect
choice: she was far too highborn for him, considerably older than
himself, and, of course, already married. He became a page in her
court, and conscientiously cultivated his feelings of love until they
commanded his whole being. He adored her in total secrecy, and
trembled (inconspicuously) in her presence. When he saw her
hands touch the petals of flowers he had secretly placed where she
would see them, he was all but in a faint. And when she washed
her hands before dinner, young Ulrich would sometimes filch the

basin, smuggle it off to his room, and there reverently drink the dirty water.

Five years of this went by; his love affair progressed no further, however, since being totally unworthy of the lady he dared not even tell her of his feelings. At the age of seventeen he therefore took himself off to the court of the Margrave Henry of Austria, to raise his status; there he studied knightly skills for five more years, and at last was made a knight in 1222, during the wedding festival of the Duke of Saxony. By a marvelous coincidence, his ladylove, whom he had not seen but religiously dreamed of during those years, was one of the guests at the wedding, and the very sight of her so moved him that he immediately took a secret vow to devote his newly won knighthood to serving her. This decision filled him with melancholy and with painful longings, a condition which apparently made him very happy.

That summer, feverish and flushed with his infatuation, he roamed the countryside fighting in numerous tourneys and winning many victories, all of which he ascribed to the mighty force of love within him. At last, having compiled an impressive record, and feeling worthy to offer the lady the tribute of his devotion, he persuaded a niece of his to call on her and privately tell her of his desire to be an acknowledged but distant, respectful admirer of hers; he even got his niece to learn and sing for the Princess a song he had written (Ulrich was already a competent *Minnesinger*—the German equivalent of the troubadour—as were many young noblemen of breeding).

The heartless lady, unmoved by his ten years of silent devotion and his recent feats of valor, sent back a cruel and pointed reply: she considered him presumptuous, was scornfully critical of the high-flown language of his quite inappropriate offer, and for good measure, took the trouble to let him know he was too ugly to be considered even in the role of a very distant admirer. For it seems (and the lady was specific) that the unhappy young knight had a harelip. Undaunted—perhaps even inspired by this obvious proof that she had actually noticed him—Ulrich promptly undertook a journey to a famous surgeon and had his lip repaired. Considering the techniques of medieval surgery, this must have been both excruciatingly painful and quite dangerous; indeed, he lay feverish on a sickbed for six weeks. News of this, plus a new song he wrote for her, softened the lady's heart, and she sent word that he might attend a riding party and enjoy the rare privilege of speaking with her for a moment, if the opportunity should arise. And it did, once, when he had the chance to help her down from her horse, and could have uttered a sentence or two of devotion; unfortunately he was tongue-tied by her nearness and could say nothing. The lovely lady, considerably put out, whispered to him that he was a fraud, and gracefully indicated her displeasure by ripping out a forelock of his hair as she dismounted.

Not in the least angered by this, Ulrich reappeared the next day, this time found his voice, and humbly begged her to permit him to be her secret knight and to allow him to fight for her and love her. She accepted his service, but under the very minimum conditions, granting him no "favor" whatever—neither embrace, kiss, nor word of promise, and not so much as a ribbon to carry in his bosom. Ulrich, nevertheless, was filled with joy and thankfulness for her kindness, and sallied forth, tilting about the countryside with anyone who would break a lance with him, and composing many a song to his ladylove, which his secretary set down for him since writing was not a knightly accomplishment. The messages and letters that passed between him and the Princess at this time conveyed, in the one direction, his endless, burning, worshipful feelings and, in the other direction, her condescension, coldness, and criticism. But this was exactly what was expected of her in the situation, and he found each new blow a delicious pain; it even sounds somewhat as though a large part of his pleasure lay in observing his own noble constancy under duress. If so, he must have had a thoroughly agreeable time for the next three years.

At the end of that period, Ulrich petitioned her forthrightly through a go-between to grant him her love, at least verbally, in return for his faithful adoration and service. The Princess not only sharply rebuked the go-between for Ulrich's unseemly persistency, but expressed her scorn that Ulrich had falsely spoken of losing a finger fighting for love of her. Actually, he had suffered a finger wound which healed, but an incorrect report had reached her. When the go-between related her scornful message, Ulrich paled for a moment, then resolutely drew out a sharp knife and ordered his friend to hack off the finger at one blow. This done, the knight had an artisan make a green velvet case in which the finger was held by gold clasps, and sent her the mounted digit as a keepsake, together with a special poem about the matter. Deeply impressed by this evidence of her power over him, she returned word that she would look at the finger every day from thenceforth, a message which, incidentally, he received as he did all other communiqués from her—on his knees, with bowed head and folded hands.

Determined now to earn her love by some stupendous feat, Ulrich conceived the scheme of the jousting-trip from Venice to Bohemia in the disguise of Venus. He went to Venice and there had seamstresses make a dozen white gowns to his own measurements; meanwhile he sent off a messenger with the open letter announcing the event. The northward march began on schedule on April 25, and concluded five weeks later, during which time Ulrich shattered an average of eight lances every day, made the notable record already mentioned, and acquired great glory and honor, all in the cause of love and for the sake of the Princess he so faithfully adored.

All this being so, it comes as something of a shock when one reads Ulrich's own statement that in the midst of this triumphal *Venusreise* he stopped off for three days to visit his wife and children. For the fact is that this lovesick Galahad, this kissless wonder, this dauntless knight-errant, had long had a wife to lie with when he had the urge, and a family to live with when he felt lonely. He himself speaks of his affection (but not his love) for his wife; to love her would have been improper and almost unthinkable. Like the other men of his class and time, Ulrich considered marriage a phase of feudal business-management, since it consisted basically of the joining of lands, the cementing of loyalties, and the production of heirs and future defenders. But the purifying, ennobling rapture of love for an ideal woman—what had that to do with details of crops and cattle, fleas and fireplaces, serfs and swamp drainage? Yet, though true love was impossible between husband and wife, without it a man was valueless. Ulrich could therefore unashamedly visit his wife during his grand tour, proud of what he had been doing and certain that if she knew of it, she too was proud, because *Frauendienst* made her husband nobler and finer.[2]

Having completed his epochal feat of love service, Ulrich waited for his reward, and at long last it came: the Princess sent word that

---

[2] Ladies, too, were increased in value by being loved. In a fictional counterpart of Ulrich's relations with his wife, a lady in an old Provençal romance, reproached by her husband for having a lover, proudly replies: "My lord, you have no dishonor on that account, for he is a noble baron, upright and expert in arms, namely, Roland, the nephew of King Charles." (*Gesta Karoli Magni ad Carcassonam et Narbonam*, p. 139)

he might visit her. Yet he was to expect no warm welcome; she specified that he must come in the disguise of a leper and take his place among lepers who would be visiting her to beg for alms. But of course this monstrous indignity fazed the faithful Ulrich not in the least; nor did he falter when she knowingly let him, disguised in his rags, spend that night in a ditch in the rain; nor was he outraged when the next night he was finally allowed to climb a rope up the castle wall to her chamber, only to find it lit by a hundred tapers and staffed by eight maids-in-waiting who hovered about her where she lay in bed. Though Ulrich pleaded urgently that they all be sent out, she continued to be coyly proper, and when she began to see that this patient fellow really was getting stubborn at last, she told him that to earn the favor he would have to prove his obedience by wading in a near-by lake. She herself assisted him out the window—and then, bending to kiss him, let loose the rope, tumbling Ulrich to the ground, or perhaps into a stinking moat. (It is worth remembering at this point that this painful incident was not recorded by any enemy or satirist of Ulrich, but by himself, his purpose being to make clear the extent of his suffering for love and his fidelity in the face of trials.)

Even such torments cannot go on forever. The cruel Princess next ordered Ulrich to go on a crusade in her service, but when she learned that he joyfully and obediently received the direct command from her, she suddenly relented, bade him rather stay at home near to her, and finally granted him her love. What an outpouring of thankful verse then! What a spate of shattered lances, dented helmets, broken blades, humbled opponents! For having won her love, Ulrich was puissant, magnificent, impregnable; this was the height of his career as a knight. Regrettably, it is not clear in the *Frauendienst* just which of her favors she so tardily vouchsafed after nearly a decade and a half, but in the light of other contemporary documents concerning the customs of courtly love, one can be fairly sure that she permitted him the kiss and the embrace, and perhaps even the right to caress her, naked, in bed; but if she gave him the final reward at all, it was probably on extremely rare occasions. For sexual outlet was not really the point of all this. Ulrich had not been laboring nearly fifteen years for so ordinary a commodity; his real reward had always been in his suffering, striving, and yearning.

The proof of this is that it took him nearly fifteen years to win her love and to become idyllically happy—but that condition, once achieved, lasted only a brief two years. For at the end of that time, the Princess wounded him in some fashion so cruel that he could not bring himself to name it, even long after. Perhaps she had accepted the service of some other knight, or even granted her love to another; what is probably more to the point, Ulrich's quest had ended when he won her, and in the peculiar psychology of courtly love, most of the magic had vanished with the pain. Whatever the cause of his break with her, at any rate, he formally quitted her service after all the years of loyalty, wrote a series of bitter songs against womankind, and permitted his affair and his break with her to become a matter of aristocratic gossip.

But for him the absence of love was an intolerable spiritual impoverishment. Soon he discovered another perfect lady; in her service he made another mighty tour, this time in the get-up of King Arthur; the new lady, too, eventually granted her love and was a source of increasing spiritual power. And then she, in turn—well, let us be brief about it: Ulrich continued this kind of thing for most of his long life. Even in his reflective years, looking back with perspective on all of it, he could write of his harelip, his torn-out forelock, his chopped-off finger, his transvestite mumming, his leper's rags, his tumble into the moat, all in a tone of self-admiration. For, to the end, he considered that love, the finest thing in his life, had made him a true Christian and a model knight.

The New Love in Theory and Practice

❀   ❀

❀

Admittedly, Ulrich's case is an extreme one; yet its very exaggerations serve to highlight the originality of the beliefs embodied in *l'amour courtois*. Whether many other real persons acted out these beliefs in as extreme a form as Ulrich is doubtful, but it is perfectly certain that nobles of France, Germany, Italy, and other countries spoke and wrote eloquently of them, and listened raptly to countless poems and romances based upon them. Many stalwart French fighting men, long accustomed to take what they wanted by warfare and to consider women little better than serfs, were beginning to think that a man should act reverent, stupefied, and suppliant before the all-perfect lady of his heart. Hundreds of songs written by these lords and sung by their hired *jongleurs* (or *Singerlein* in Germany) echoed the theme sounded by Bernard de Ventadour, one of the most notable twelfth-century troubadours:

> *I stand in my lady's sight*
> *In deep devotion;*
> *Approach her with folded hands*
> *In sweet emotion;*
> *Dumbly adoring her,*
> *Humbly imploring her.*

In the resounding vaulted chambers of hundreds of baronial castles, ladies and gentlemen were beginning to enjoy the reading aloud or reciting of long verse romances after dinner, telling the legends of King Arthur, of Charlemagne, and of Greece and Rome. The actions of the knights in these romances, though fanciful, are indicative of what twelfth-century lords and ladies were interested in. They bore somewhat the same relationship to history as do our modern historical novels; one can learn more about the 1940's from *Forever Amber* than about the eighteenth century, and more about the twelfth century from Arthurian romance than about King Arthur.

When, in medieval romances, the Count de Nevers faints dead away at the mere sound of his lady's name or Parsifal falls into a love swoon of several months' duration, we need not suppose such things really happened to knights under the influence of courtly love; what does intrigue us is that such representations of knightly conduct seemed neither objectionable nor laughable to the real lords who loved real ladies. Whether fiction followed life, or life patterned itself upon fiction, sometimes they were fairly close to each other. The troubadour Peire Vidal was being autobiographical when he wrote of the extremity to which love had driven him: in his misery he had dressed himself in a wolf's skin and lived for some time in the woods like a beast.

Less bizarre, yet perhaps just as significant, was the change in manners coming first over the medieval noblemen of France and then those of adjacent nations. Rather suddenly—in a mere handful of years—these fierce semi-primitive chieftains had begun to culti-vate the arts of singing, dancing, and composing, in order to please the ladies of their courts. They put on finer clothing, started to use handkerchiefs, and began to bathe more often; they practiced gen-teel discourse and sophisticated argumentation; and they took love vows in secret (though the secrets were discreetly told) and squan-dered both money and health on endless jousts and harrowing pilgrimages designed to gain merit in their ladies' eyes. By dint of such continued "service," plus unswerving fidelity and thorough self-abasement, they traveled the long course of love, rising slowly from the initial stage of the mere aspirant to love (*fegnedor*) to that of the suppliant (*precador*), the recognized suitor (*entende-dor*) and finally the accepted lover (*drut*).

Yet even in the final stage the behavior of the lover and his lady was, by most standards, curious, if not altogether improbable. For they were very likely to indulge repeatedly in protracted sessions of sex play, unclothed and in bed, without yielding to the imperious drive toward completion. This seems a trying undertaking for mature men and women, and at first one may wonder if he has misread or misunderstood the evidence; but the many testimonials that remain as to the existence of the practice of *amor purus*, or "pure love," make it very clear that adult, healthy, normally sexed lords and ladies frequently, and perhaps most of the time, managed to limit themselves to this kind of dalliance in their courtly love affairs—and considered it a finer form of love than the completed act. "He knows little or nothing of the service of women who wishes to possess his lady entirely," wrote the troubadour Daude de Pradas, and scores of rhapsodists of *l'amour courtois* scorned the culmination of the sex act as "false love" while extolling as "true love" the "pure" kissing, touching, fondling, and naked contact of the lovers.

Some students of the subject have doubted that such conduct could be, and have assumed that the relationships of the troubadours and their ladies were generally completely adulterous. Even on literary grounds, one might disagree with them; there is an almost endless amount of praise of looking upon the body of the beloved, or holding her, or touching her, but there is practically never any expression, even implicitly, of the ideas of satisfaction, climax, or weary peacefulness. On the basis of circumstantial evidence, too, one might doubt that the relationship was fully consummated most of the time; although bastardy was quite common in the Middle Ages (nine per cent of the villeins of a typical English manor in the time of Edward III were known bastards), references to children born of courtly love affairs are practically nonexistent both in romance and in historical writing. But above all we can believe that this curious sexual pattern did exist, for it, at least, was one part of courtly love that was not quite new; it had had a precursor in the form of the spiritual marriage experiments of the early Christian centuries and the agapetae cults of the heretical sects. Those mutations of sexual behavior were the result of the violent separation of love from sex in the teachings of the early Church. When the lusty Frankish barbarians overran the Empire, they resisted the ascetic influence for centuries, but it was perhaps inevitable that in time they should yield to it too. Out of the same teachings, therefore, a sexually inhibited form of love again appeared in the eleventh century, this time richly surrounded by sentiments and observances which coalesced into a coherent new relationship.[3]

[3] Many scholars, however, have assumed that courtly love almost always involved sexual consummation; see, for instance, Robert Briffault: *The Mothers*, Vol. III, pp. 474–5. But the bulk of medieval writing on the matter says

And it *was* a new thing in Western history. The relationship of the agapetae and their spiritual brothers had been innocent of the theory that moral and ethical improvement was the major purpose of being in love. Among the troubadours, however, ceaseless desire, unending yearning, and unsatisfied passion were thought to illuminate and elevate the character. "No man is of value without love," said our dumbly adoring, humbly imploring troubadour, Bernard de Ventadour, and many a man who could ride all day without fatigue, fight in armor for hours, or spend two years in going to Jerusalem for his soul's good, was able in all seriousness to kneel before his lady and thank her for having made him a better knight and Christian by causing him suffering and rarely fulfilled desire. One could overstress the role of *amor purus;* even those who believed in it and preached it sometimes admitted that lovers might easily lapse into "false love" unless they consciously thought of the higher values. But whatever the extent of such lapses, pure love was the ideal many professed to believe in, and which they were impelled to follow as best they could.

Such emotions and practices could thrive only on separation and denial; they were wholly inappropriate for, and unsuited to, the intimacies and necessities of married life. And since lust and love could not be combined in the same person, marriage inherited only lust, and was totally denied the possibility of love. Not surprisingly, therefore, the high arbiter of courtly love—Marie, the Countess of Champagne—issued the following proclamation to all interested persons in the year 1174:

> We declare and we hold as firmly established that love cannot exert its powers between two people who are married to each other. For lovers give each other everything freely, under no compulsion of necessity, but married people are in duty bound

otherwise, and so important a source as the *Tractatus de Amore* of Andreas Capellanus (see below, pp. 156–61) refers to "mixed love" (consummated love) as a dangerous practice into which some slip, but which most of the judicious carefully avoid. G. R. Taylor has summarized evidence against consummation in *Sex in History*, pp. 87–93. Even Father Alexander J. Denomy, a Jesuit scholar who has analyzed troubadour love as a grossly sensual heresy, concluded from painstaking study that "it was a love that yearned for, and at times was rewarded by, the solace of every delight of the beloved except physical possession of her by intercourse . . . [namely] the delights of kissing and embracing, the sight of the beloved's nudity and the touching and lying beside her nude body." ("Fin' Amors," *Mediæval Studies*, Vol. VII (1945), p. 139f).

to give in to each other's desires and deny themselves to each other in nothing.[4]

All in all, courtly love, as it appeared during the first century or so of its existence, was a human relationship with only the faintest of precedents in Western culture. Plato, Ovid, and Saint Augustine, though they might have recognized traces of the loves they knew, would all have been astonished and even mystified by it. Only in Greece had love been even vaguely allied to the ennoblement of character—but there the relationship was a special type of latent or overt homosexuality. Only in Rome had secrecy and adultery been so systematically studied and practiced—but there it was purely for sensual pleasure, without the faintest coloring of real "service" or praise of purity. Only among the early Christians had the emphasis on sexual restraint and pure love appeared—but there it was without any admixture of the adoration of woman, the abasement of man before her, or the theory that in suffering, desire, and doled-out dalliance there was Christian virtue. *L'amour courtois* borrowed and blended components from the past, yet was something distinctly new in the history of love.

---

[4] Quoted by Andreas in *Tractatus de Amore*, Bk. One, Ch. vi, Seventh Dialogue.

4

A New Plant Grows in an Odd Soil

❀   ❀

❀

In many ways, it would seem as though there could have been no less propitious time and place for romantic love to appear than France of the late eleventh century. When Charlemagne's brief monarchy had disintegrated, Western Europe had been plunged into two centuries of semi-barbarian warfare; out of this chaos the feudal hierarchy had only begun to emerge. Despite vows of fealty and vassalage, petty nobles were still constantly warring upon one another without pretext other than the bald hope of gain. Though powerful rulers began to limit the right of private baronial warfare, fighting and hunting remained the basic interests of the noblemen. They accepted tourneys in place of actual combat, but even these long continued to be bloody and ferocious affairs. Such men would hardly seem to have been candidates for gentle emotions and silent suffering.

Noblemen and ladies alike still used their fingers at the table (the fork being unknown), and they customarily wiped their knives on the bread and their hands on the tablecloth. For lack of dinner dishes, they ate their meat on trenchers (large thick slabs of bread), which they flung under the table afterwards, together with the leftovers, to quarreling dogs. The bones and dog dung remained there undisturbed; even in the fourteenth century an Italian artist, describing the making of fine plaster for frescoes, advised his readers to begin by collecting the oldest and driest chicken bones lying about the floor. Castles were being built in somewhat lighter and grander style than in the Dark Ages, but carpets were nearly unknown and the rushes sometimes strewn over the floor in the homes of minor lordlings were changed only when, after collecting

spittle, vomit, and the urine of dogs for a number of months, they
began to smell intolerable.

The Franks had always regarded woman as a useful piece of
property, and protected her accordingly; in the ninth century, the
penalty called for by the *Leges Alamannorum* for killing a free,
mature woman was the payment of six hundred *solidi* to her master, while if she were a young unskilled girl the price was only two
hundred *solidi*. Such an evaluation of woman was clearly far removed from the spirit of chivalry. Similarly, clerical writers of the
canon law had long given husbands express permission to beat their
wives, and civil law often followed suit. A notable thirteenth-
century statute of the town of Villefranche in Gascony granted
every man the right to beat his wife, "provided death does not
ensue." A woman's word could not be admitted in court because of
her "frailty," she could not represent herself in any legal action,
and her husband assumed full authority over the property she
owned at the time of marriage. Divorce was, until later centuries,
simple enough for a husband discontented with her personality or
the yield of her lands; whatever his real reasons for wanting to be
rid of her, he had only to "discover" that he and she had a single
great-great-grandparent in common (a relationship known in canon
law as "consanguinity in the fourth degree") in order to cast her
off with Church approval and marry more profitably elsewhere.

Despite the gradual influence of Christianity, the early Middle
Ages were an unthinkably crude era—not as licentious as Ovidian
Rome, but infinitely more vulgar. Noblemen considered that they
had a natural right to ravish any peasant woman they happened to
meet in a lonely spot, and did so without compunction or hindrance. Prostitution was so candidly accepted that many European
towns and cities legalized it under municipal supervision. The *jus
primae noctis* theoretically entitled the lord of a manor to deflower
the bride of a vassal, and scattered but reliable reports indicate that
this custom was actually practiced in several European countries,
even in the period when chivalry was becoming the guiding philosophy of the aristocracy. For the chivalrous could also be thoroughly boorish: on the first crusade of the pure-souled King
Louis IX (who later became Saint Louis), the King's barons openly
set up brothels around his royal tent. So could the pious: in 1311
even the Vatican, according to Durand, Bishop of Mende, permitted
brothels to operate near by for a consideration. Possibly the ulti-

mate in blasphemous lewdness is an incident referred to by the knight, Geoffrey de La Tour Landry, who claimed to know of people fornicating within the very walls of a church.

Teutonic primitivism in sexual matters was made still harsher by the teachings of ascetic clerics. Traditionally the clergy were woman-haters, and as the Church slowly succeeded in enforcing priestly celibacy, their misogyny became ever more virulent. Preachers systematically thundered at woman from the pulpit, a typical medieval sermon containing endless fulminations of this type:

> In the woman wantonly adorned to capture souls, the garland upon her head is as a single coal or firebrand of Hell to kindle men with that fire. . . . In a single day, by her dancing or her perambulation through the town, she inflames with the fire of her lust perhaps twenty of those who behold her, damning the souls God has created and redeemed at such a cost.[5]

The Church considered marriage a precious sacrament and stoutly defended it, but by the Middle Ages, Jerome's statement that "he who too ardently loves his own wife is an adulterer" had become the general ecclesiastical opinion. Confessors' manuals and penitentials ordered that marital sexual connection be performed only in one position, and not at all during penance, or on Sundays, Wednesdays, and Fridays, or during a number of holiday seasons; indeed, all sexual intercourse within marriage, except when specifically undertaken in order to beget a child, was considered by confessors a venial offense.

Yet it was out of this unlikely compost of feudal barbarism, male domination, and religious asceticism that courtly love suddenly burst into flower. Scholars have long wondered why and unearthed many answers, most of them not individually very satisfying. Some, for instance, have stressed the role of socio-economic factors. They point out that the increasing leisure and wealth of the nobility gave them time to develop love as an amusement; more particularly, the marriage system and the suppression of private war made for a large number of propertyless younger sons who had a great deal of time to idle away at the courts of powerful nobles, and who were inevitably attracted to the women they themselves had been unable

[5] From a sermon by a fourteenth-century English preacher named John Bromyard, quoted in G. R. Owst: *Literature and Pulpit in Medieval England,* p. 392f.

to win in marriage. Yet by itself this explanation is clearly insufficient; though economic conditions might have allowed time and place for adulterous amusement, why should it have been endowed with such ethical and philosophic value—and why should it have put such emphasis on incompletion and technical chastity?

The worship of Mary has often been suggested as an answer. Though churchmen regarded woman as the primal temptress, theologians were beginning to title Mary "Mother of God" in the fourth century, and thereafter slowly but inevitably deified her. By the eleventh century, Mariolatry was creating an ideal image— sacred Mary, as opposed to profane Eve—that may have prepared men for a new feeling about women. Troubadours, indeed, often addressed their ladies as "Madonna," and even Saint Bernard de Clairvaux, the great monastic reformer and a bitter foe of courtly love, made God Himself sound like a mooning knight-errant. In a sermon on the Annunciation, Bernard portrayed God asking Mary if she wanted to have a child by the Holy Ghost. "He, the King and Lord of all things," said Bernard, "waits for the word of your consent, by means of which He has proposed to save the world, inasmuch as He has approved of your graces. He whom in silence you have pleased, you will please still more by speech, since He cries to you from heaven: O fairest among women, let me hear thy voice. If then thou doest this, He will cause thee to see our salvation." Yet for all the similarities between Mary-worship and troubadour love, the former reached its high point some time *after* the appearance of troubadour love, and it is hard to know which influenced which the more; one might suspect that both stemmed from, and were twin effects of, some still more fundamental causes.

Others have explained courtly love as a heresy in disguise. In the very area of southwestern France where troubadour love began, a type of deviant Christianity became popular during the eleventh century, its principal body of adherents being known to history as the Albigenses. The Albigenses were dualists who thought the world of the flesh was evil, and ruled by Satan, while God ruled only the world of the spirit, which was good. Logically enough, they placed great value on abstaining from procreation, which would only make more creatures for the Devil's domain. Many of them therefore gave up sex relations with their wives; they thus plainly resembled the Manicheans and those other early heretical

Christians who had practiced spiritual marriage and praised the chaste love of the agapetae. Certain scholars therefore say that courtly love, with its idealization of chaste love and its disinterest in procreation, was only a poetic disguise for the Manichean heresy.

But the Manichean attitudes toward sex, love, and celibacy were really very close to those held by the Catholic Church itself at various times. Furthermore, courtly love was just as appealing to the orthodox as it was to the heretical; the French armies which made a bloody crusade into Provence at the behest of Pope Innocent III were led by knights of unshakable loyalty to Rome—but they too had been captivated by courtly love, and saw nothing heretical in it. Throughout Europe, in fact, courtly love rapidly caught on among the unimpeachably orthodox without subverting their religion.

Evidently, there were still deeper forces at work. And in fact they had been implicit in early Christianity, which established the diametrical opposition between sexuality and love. For it is true in all monogamous family life that children must repress the sexual impulses they feel toward the parents they love; but it was early Christianity that made a philosophy of the situation and turned it into a life-long problem, rather than a problem of childhood alone.

It was, in sum, an institutionalized incest-fear, setting up nearly impassable barriers between sexual desire and the emotions of love, which made simultaneously for the ill-concealed voluptuousness of Mary-worship and the partial impotence of *amor purus*, and which led men to treat women as chattel and sexual beasts of burden and at the same time regard them as goddesses and sovereign rulers. But powerful as the incest-fear was, it successfully produced the pattern of courtly love only when many other forces coincided and contributed their shaping and enriching influences. Courtly love *did* catch on first by no mere coincidence in a heretic-dominated area of France with a tradition of chaste love, and appropriately enough offered the orthodox a genteel way to defy the misogynist clergy. It undoubtedly drew upon the growing cult of Mary-worship, borrowing its moods, its mystical transports, and its emphasis on humble supplication. It spread and throve wherever feudal order had emerged from barbarian chaos, for feudalism provided both leisure and wealth enough to permit the new game and make it welcome; moreover, it ideally met the need of that society to find duties which would refine and tame men's manners. Finally, it also met the unsatisfied need of individuals for affection—the result of a marriage system which took no account of love.

All in all, despite the barbaric past, the residuum of primitivism, and the ascetic tradition of Christianity, it would seem that the unpromising ground had actually been fertile; it had needed only someone to plant the seed.

5

The Founders and Exponents

Guilhem was his name: William IX, Duke of Aquitaine and Count of Poitou, born in 1071, and first of the troubadours. When one puts aside all speculations about the origins of courtly love, there remains the concrete fact that the first of the new-style love lyrics, and manners to match, were the creation of William, and seemingly from that single point of origin set a fashion which swept through Provence where he maintained his court, and went on later to conquer Europe. Lyricist or no, this was no mincing rhymester; William was a powerful ruler, and a full-blooded, fierce, independent warrior. He became the feudal overlord of nearly a third of France when he was scarcely more than a boy, and ran it well enough. He went along on the First Crusade and played an active part in its trials and fierce battles. At home he defied and flouted mighty churchmen in matters political and social, protected the Albigenses in his domain, was excommunicated for his unyielding spirit, and long refused to yield to the Church.

One day he happened to meet the Bishop of Poitiers and demanded absolution, threatening otherwise to kill him; the Bishop offered his neck and told him to strike, but William, intractable as ever, changed his mind. "No," he said irritably, "I do not love you well enough to send you straight to Paradise."

Despite his arrogance and belligerence, he was in many ways the model for all future courtly lovers. According to an old Provençal chronicle: "The Count of Poitou was one of the most courteous men in the world, and a great deceiver of ladies; and he was a brave knight and had much to do with love affairs; and he knew well how to sing and make verses." So there it is: abruptly and without evident preparation, courtly love had begun. From William, the fashion of flattering and celebrating one's ladylove in delicate verse spread rapidly throughout the castles and courts of southern France. Probably thousands of knights followed suit, for despite the fragmentary remains of medieval literature, we know the names of four hundred and sixty troubadours and possess twenty-five hundred of their poems. Many were minor nobles, but there were even several kings among them, of whom Richard Coeur de Lion, great-grandson of William IX, was the best-known.

Though William was said to be "a great deceiver of the ladies," he paid lip service to fidelity and spirituality, and courtly lovers after him seized upon and emphasized these aspects of the new manners. Many of the troubadours dwelt at length on the sensuous aspects of *amor purus*, but others exaggerated the ascetic element in the relationship until love assumed an extremely rarefied form. Within a few years, the troubadour Gaucelm Faidit could tell his lady: "Nor kiss I ask, nor sweet embraces, lest I were blaspheming," and Sordello, an Italian who lived and wrote as a Provençal, could set down this extraordinary love sentiment:

> *Thus, lady, I commend to thee*
> *My fate and life, thy faithful squire;*
> *I'd rather die in misery*
> *Than have thee stoop to my desire.*

But whether the lady was totally untouchable, or whether she could be touched within specified bounds, courtly love as practiced by the troubadours remained a matter of devotion to an almost inanimate object; the lady was an inert, icon-like figure, and one cannot find in Provençal writing anything about what she said, felt, or did. She simply was loved. When the new idea spread to northern France, however, it became allied to chivalry—the social and military philosophy of feudal knighthood—and the knight lover, instead of limiting his adoration to self-humbling verses, began also to perform deeds and services called for by his lady. She thus ceased to be a graven image for worship and started to enter into the process; she became an actual participant in an interaction of personalities. Courtly love acquired elements of mutuality and reciprocity, and very likely this was one major reason for the mysterious appeal it so clearly exerted from then on.

In 1122, when middle-aged William's ideas were already flourishing among the Provençal nobility, his granddaughter Eleanor was born. It was her fortune to become one of the most famous and powerful of medieval women and, among many other accomplishments, bring courtly love from Provence to the royal courts of both France and England and help it grow from a literary fad into a seriously practiced way of life. Oddly enough, although Eleanor was ideally fitted for this task, she did the chief work of propagandizing for courtly love when she was a disillusioned middle-aged woman and the mother of ten royal children. Perhaps a love that could, in many cases, remain chaste and purely verbal was well suited to her circumstances.

When Eleanor was fifteen and already thoroughly imbued with troubadour ideas, her father, the son of William IX, died; the young girl thereupon became Countess of Poitou and Duchess of Aquitaine, and thus the major marriage prize in Western Europe. Her feudal overlord, Louis the Fat, King of France, instantly dispatched southwards his son and heir apparent, a seventeen-year-old youth named Louis Capet, to wed her. Eleanor had nothing to say about this, since it was King Louis's undeniable legal right to dispose of her in marriage; in any case, she understood perfectly that marriage was an instrument of political policy, and that love was no consideration.

Two weeks after the marriage, Louis the Fat died, and the teen-aged girl found herself the Queen of France. It was the beginning of a long, turbulent, and unique life. She struggled to bring some of the poetry and charm of her ancestral home into the drab royal court at Paris, but her husband was a sober, religious youth who was uninterested in these matters and pious beyond all expectation; Eleanor later remarked that she had married a king only to find him a monk. When Louis decided to go on the Second Crusade in

1147, the bored young Queen accompanied him on the long ter-rible expedition in order to see new sights and escape the tedious routines of Paris. She saw more than he expected her to. In By-zantium, where they remained for a while, she was overcome by admiration for the sensuous, indulgent way of life the Eastern Christians practiced, and chroniclers alleged later that during the crusade she began the first of many amours. Some even said, im-probable as it seems, that she made love to the great Saladin, arch-enemy of all Christians. But a rather more likely story holds that she fell in love with her uncle, Raymond, Prince of Antioch, at whose Syrian court the French royal party rested and recouped its forces after a military disaster in Asia Minor. King Louis, belatedly realizing this, suddenly seized his own wife prisoner and spirited her hastily out of the city under guard. After prolonged adventures and misadventures they came back to Paris, but by 1152 Louis was ready to let her go her own way, for in fifteen years of marriage she had provided him with only two daughters and no sons. They were divorced on the excuse of consanguinity, under an agreement which returned to Eleanor her lands and titles and made her Louis's loyal vassal instead of his disloyal wife.

So thin was that loyalty, however, that within two months she married young Henry Plantagenet, Duke of Normandy, eleven years her junior, and Louis's most dangerous political rival in north-ern France. Faced by this threatening alignment of Normandy and Aquitaine, Louis promptly invaded Normandy, only to be beaten back by Henry and his men. This safely accomplished, Henry left Eleanor in charge at his castle at Angers, in Anjou, while he went to England to press his own claims to that throne.

Eleanor, now relatively free to lead that kind of life she had long dreamed of, gathered knights, ladies, and poets around her and began to create an elegant court. Among the poets who soon paid homage to the thirty-year-old Duchess was Bernard de Venta-dour himself, imported by Eleanor from his Provençal homeland. "She had understanding in matters of valor and honor," says an old chronicler, "and cared for a song of praise; and the songs of Ber-nard pleased her; she received and welcomed him cordially. He was a long time in her court and he fell in love with her and she with him." One cannot judge how intimate or complete the relationship between the poet and the beautiful young Duchess became, but Henry, probably hearing about it, soon summoned her away to

London, and she left Bernard behind—very likely at Henry's order. He had been putting his time and energies to good use, meanwhile, for in 1154, on the death of King Stephen, he became Henry II, King of England. Eleanor thus became a queen, at the age of thirty-two, for the second time in her life. Again she introduced her new fashions and ideas into a royal court, and apparently had considerable success; so one may conclude from the fact that within five years of her coronation, John of Salisbury, a scholastic philosopher, devoted a whole book to the follies and extravagances of courtiers in London.

For the next fifteen years Eleanor led a busy life; the times were filled with complex power-struggles among Henry of England, Louis of France, their various insubordinate vassals, and the lords of the Church. Also filling her time was the almost nonstop production of Henry's children—eight in fifteen years. This output indicated no love between the King and Queen; their personal relations had long since progressed from a workable partnership toward unendurable mutual dislike, particularly when Henry built a retreat for his mistress, Rosamond Clifford, and openly flaunted his affair to the shame of the Queen. In 1169 or 1170 Henry sought to end their strife. He divided the succession to his lands among his sons, and allowed Eleanor to retire to her own county of Poitou, in control of her former French domains; their second son, Richard, who went with her, was guaranteed the eventual inheritance of both Aquitaine and Poitou.

At this time Eleanor was still under fifty. Despite her many *accouchements*, she was said to be still beautiful, and her death-effigy in the abbey at Fontevrault, near Le Mans, shows a woman of graceful figure, with a straight fine nose, an oval face, and a full ripe mouth. She had seen much of the world in high places, and possessed poise and learning unusual for her time. Mistress of her own affairs, she chose the recently enlarged castle at Poitiers as her official seat, and gathered around herself there a brilliant new court, thronged with poets, philosophers, and young knights and ladies who came to learn the ways of wit, courtesy, and graciousness. To this court, too, came her own daughter, Marie, the Countess of Champagne (the child of Eleanor's first marriage to Louis of France), to be in effect *maîtresse d'école* to the court and the principal tutor of the new manners and morals. Music and games, chivalry and knight-errantry, dialectic and love-making, table manners and courtesy, literature and philosophy, were all part of the way of life demonstrated by Eleanor and Marie to a culture-thirsty retinue of young lords and ladies who came here from northern France, England, and even from the farthest of Eleanor's own southern domains.

Among the methods Eleanor and Marie employed to teach the concepts of courtly love was a formal piece of play-acting known as the "Court of Love." In mock-legal proceedings, an anonymous lover or his lady—speaking through representatives—could present a complaint or defense in a disputed question of love behavior. Hearing the case and handing down the decision might be a single judge—a great lady such as Eleanor herself—or an entire panel of noble ladies acting as a jury. This idea may have come from Provence and Gascogny where, a few years earlier, debates on the new manners were an exciting after-dinner amusement. But in the hands of Eleanor and Marie, such debates became more than after-dinner talk; they grew to be a semi-serious pedagogical device for perfecting the new relationships, codifying and clarifying them, and promulgating them among the nobility at Poitiers.

And it is even possible that the Court of Love at Poitiers had greater stature than this: it may have been a pseudo-legal hall of justice where pronouncements on love questions were seriously sought and honestly obeyed. But whether it really was this, or simply an artful way to examine a growing code of behavior, there is one significant fact about it: men and women met in the Court of Love on terms of mutual respect to explore the propriety, the ethics, and the aesthetics of their relationships to each other. This is the importance of the Court of Love, and a measure of the profound alteration beginning to take place, at the top level of European society, in the kind of feelings existing between the sexes.[6]

[6] Whether the Court of Love actually considered cases and exercised quasi-judicial powers is a question that has vexed generations of scholars. At first they accepted the medieval evidence at face value; later they rejected it completely and considered all Courts of Love a fictional device used by poets. Today there is a tenable middle ground held by such scholars as Amy Kelly, the most recent and thorough student of Eleanor's life and times. The above and succeeding sections generally follow the viewpoint expressed in chapter fifteen of her book, *Eleanor of Aquitaine and the Four Kings.*

6

Courtly Love in the Court of Love

❉ ❉

❉

There are scores of fictional and poetic representations of the Court of Love, but happily for the historian, one man who lived in Eleanor's castle at Poitiers observed the Court of Love in session there and later wrote a more-or-less reportorial account of what he had seen. He was a cleric named André; later he became the chaplain at Countess Marie's court at Troyes, and is known to history by the way he then signed his name and title: *Andreas Capellanus*, i.e., André the chaplain. At Marie's urging Andreas wrote a *Tractatus de Amore et de Amoris Remedio* (*Treatise on Love and Its Remedy*), the only straightforward exposition of the theory and practice of courtly love which exists from that period.[7] From the title and the overall structure, it is clear that Andreas thought of himself as the twelfth-century equivalent of Ovid, whose mantle he expected the book to drape around his shoulders. If it seems strange that a clergyman should undertake so secular a work, that only indicates the astonishing ambivalence inherent in medieval man and the ability of the orthodox to hold seemingly heretical beliefs; a medieval chaplain of the Church of Rome could believe both in the Church and in profane love without too great a sense of strain.

To judge from his side remarks in the *Tractatus*, Andreas was a vain, shallow, and yet likable man. His learning is inconsiderable, his quotations from classic writers are often secondhand and inaccurate, and his arguments have none of the wit of his master, Ovid. But there is something disarming about his simple egotism when he

[7] This is one of several medieval titles for the work, which is also sometimes called in English *The Art of Courtly Love*.

calls himself "Andreas the Lover," and says without false modesty: "We consider ourselves very expert in the art of love." This he excuses in himself by pointing out that, though the clergy should refrain from sin, hardly any are actually able to do so. In fact, he spends quite some time trying to prove that clerics are better lovers than knights because they are more prudent and have better judgment. Nevertheless, Andreas admits that no clergyman can win high Church honors if it is known that he indulges in love, so, after spending most of his space explaining and extolling it, he hastily adds a brief and unconvincing retraction of the whole thing. The gist of it is that to win greater recompense from God for refraining from love, one must first know all about it. Andreas was no fool: later manuscript copies of his book call him "chaplain of the royal court," from which it would appear that his retraction cleared the way for his advancement from Troyes to Paris.[8]

For all the limitations of Andreas's character, his *Tractatus* has been called by Robert Bossuat, a French scholar, one of those rare works which "explain the secret of a civilization." The greater part of it consists of specimen dialogues between lords and ladies of differing rank, showing the arguments they might be expected to use with each other in requesting love on the one hand, and specifying the service that will earn it on the other hand. But the actual forms of argument and speechmaking are much less interesting than the insight we get into the emotional content and the actual practices of courtly love. For this, like Ovid's book, is no fictional dream or poetic exaggeration, but a guidebook; this is a manual of sound advice on how people should, and did, practice courtly love.

And it is all here, in somewhat more down-to-earth form than we find it in the poets, but here nevertheless. The unswerving loyalty of a lover to his beloved; the emphasis on pleasing habits, courteous conduct, and personal attractiveness; the subservience, in the courtship stages, of the man to the woman; the gentleness and considerateness required in actual love-making; the spiritual benefits of being in love; the techniques of *amor purus* and the dangers of "mixed love" (love that proceeds to consummation); and, behind the tedious talkiness of the arguments, some brief indications of mutuality and reciprocity in the entire process:—all this is documented, blueprinted, and reported from real life. We might

---

[8] It is also true that he was only further imitating Ovid, who placed after his *Ars Amatoria* a *Remedia*.

have supposed from the poems and romances that they existed, but now we know.

Andreas thought he was emulating Ovid, but the difference between them is extraordinary. The *Tractatus* is always dead serious; the *Ars Amatoria* was always amused. The Roman spoofed at the exaggerated effects of infatuation and urged men to simulate them in order to succeed at seduction. Andreas never dreams of spoofing; love is an earnest and virtuous exercise of the soul, and simulated passion is unthinkable, sincerity being a *sine qua non*. Andreas shows the woman not as the prey, but the predator, and man not the conqueror, but the conquered; as for the nature of the conquest, Ovid was candidly and plainly speaking of intercourse, the sooner achieved the better, while Andreas carefully and specifically urged his readers to control their lusts, and avoid the completion of the process. The change that has come about is enormous—and Andreas does not seem especially aware of it.

Nothing in Andreas's book makes such absorbing reading as the brief section on the Court of Love (Book II, Chapter VII). Andreas tells us that as many as sixty ladies formed the panel on one important case; in others, individual opinions were rendered by Queen Eleanor, Countess Marie, Countess Isabelle of Flanders, Countess Ermengarde of Narbonne, and so on. Most likely they convened in the large ceremonial hall that had recently been added to the castle at Poitiers. The ladies sat on a dais, while the courtiers assembled on the stone benches lining the walls. Advocates for the anonymous plaintiff and defendant would present their arguments, and the ladies would then ponder the case and pronounce judgment on it.

Andreas cites a total of twenty-one such cases, probably a sampling of those he had seen. The complex mores of courtly love are caught with astonishing sharpness in these little abstracts. Here, for instance, is one complete case just as Andreas records it:

A certain knight loved his lady beyond all measure and enjoyed her full embrace, but she did not love him with equal ardor. He sought to leave her, but she, desiring to retain him in his former status, opposed his wish. In this affair the Countess gave this response: "It is considered very unseemly for a woman to seek to be loved and yet to refuse to love. It is silly for anybody disrespectfully to ask of others what she herself wholly refuses to give to others."

The knight's vows of fidelity, in other words, would not permit him to desert his cold mistress without her permission, but the Countess Marie denied that the mistress had a right to such consideration because of the one-way nature of the affair. The wording of Marie's dictum is somewhat airy, yet it clearly means to say that love should not be an unequal relationship, but an interplay of mutual emotion; for the twelfth century, this was a daring and even a radical idea.

Some of the cases, to be sure, are seemingly so artificial that we cannot easily project ourselves into the situations or take them seriously. A knight presented this complaint in court: his lady had been vowed to another, but gave him the promise of her love if she ever lost her present lover; later on she married her lover, whereupon the knight demanded she make good her promise, since marriage cancelled her lover's status. Adele, Queen of France, heard the case; she ruled that since love cannot exist between husband and wife, the lady had indeed lost her love and hence must honor her vow to give her love to the plaintiff. It seems like an empty charade; one wonders what kind of love could be summoned up by edict in this fashion. And yet there is something interesting and fresh even here: this equality, this responsibility of each party to carry out the promises of love, is something drastically different from the domination-submission pattern of medieval marriage.

Another lord wanted to prove the constancy of his lady by asking her for permission to make love to another woman. A month later he returned and told her he had only been testing her, and had not actually been unfaithful to her. At that point she angrily rejected his love, out of pique and disbelief. He appealed to the Court, claiming no wrongdoing. Queen Eleanor herself made the following pronouncement:

> We know that it comes from the nature of love that those who are in love often falsely pretend that they desire new embraces, that they may the better test the faith and constancy of their co-lover. Therefore a woman sins against the nature of love itself if she keeps back her embraces from her lover on that account or forbids him her love, unless she has clear evidence that he has been unfaithful to her.

Such pranks and tests seem rather juvenile and game-like; yet games often provide the pattern by which one learns about, and prepares for, the real world. Is it possible, then, that behind the

foolish details of this case there was a twelfth-century man who
seriously sought loyalty and devotion in a love relationship, but
tried to make certain of it by a childish means?

And even with its background of secrecy and adultery, the growing code of courtly love was developing values that would seem
fully applicable to legitimate relationships. In one case a knight who
was totally lacking in chivalric virtues asked a lady's love, and she
granted him the hope of it if he became a worthy knight. This
apparently stiffened his spine, improved his manners, and added to
his general manliness, with the result, as Andreas noted, that "by
her teaching she developed in this lover so good a character that
she gave him a kiss and an embrace and through her he was brought
to the highest excellence of conduct." At this point, unhappily, he
became enamoured of another and perhaps less demanding lady,
and abandoned the first. She complained to the Court, asking the
return of her rightful property. The Countess of Flanders ruled
that the first lady had a right to reclaim her lover, since "she has a
just and reasonable claim upon a man whom she, by working with
him, had made worthy, after he had been worthless." Andreas wrote
nothing more about this case, but is it not evident that the courtiers
and the ladies of the Court of Love were trying to define loyalty
and responsibility? Is it not possible that beneath the artificiality of
the mock judgment there is a plea for love that is not mere amusement, love that endures despite disappointments and errors, love
that achieves value by considering the loved one's desires as well
as one's own?

Finally, Andreas codified the thirty-one basic rules of courtly
love, which were the foundation of "law" upon which the cases
had been tried, and upon which all other rules, forms, and manners
must be based. Some of them reflect simply the conflict of adultery
with the marriage system:

> When made public, love rarely endures.
> The easy attainment of love makes it of little value; difficulty of
>   attainment makes it prized.

Others seem merely like the vacuous play-acting of idle nitwits:

> He who is not jealous cannot love.
> Every lover regularly turns pale in the presence of his beloved.
> A slight presumption causes a lover to suspect his beloved.

But certain others have a quaint, if unsophisticated, sound of seriousness, and a hint that conscience is entering into love relationships:

> That which a lover takes against the will of his beloved has no relish.
>
> A true lover does not desire to embrace in love anyone except his beloved.
>
> A true lover considers nothing good except what he thinks will please his beloved.

No doubt many of the important lords of the twelfth century were too busy to spend their time in castle halls playing at love, and too proud to reshape their ideas of right and wrong to this tamed and civilized pattern. No doubt the admiring young noblemen, the subsidized and hired troubadours and trouvères—and Andreas too —were acting in earnest only in part, and in part pretending to emotions they did not altogether feel. No doubt, finally, the ladies of the court were in part dreaming aloud of a vague ideal not genuinely possible in their own time. But in part, says Amy Kelly, they were doing more—they were attempting to "rationalize a conduct that [had] outburst the rigid feudal scheme for women." The *Tractatus* was not just a guidebook to a complex amusement; it was the manifesto of an emotional revolution.

The Spread of the New Doctrine

❧   ❧

❧

The gay civilized life at Poitiers lasted only four years and then came to a sudden halt. Eleanor, ever a meddler in politics, had been intriguing with powerful French lords on behalf of her sons, Richard and Geoffrey; this posed a threat to Henry II, her estranged husband, who thereupon crossed the channel and swept down upon Poitiers in the spring of 1174. He routed her court and captured Eleanor herself on the road, fleeing in man's disguise, but failed to catch his own sons, who escaped and sought asylum with the King of France. Eleanor was hauled off to England and imprisoned in various castles for fifteen years until Henry's death. Even then the dauntless woman was not done. She acted as regent of England while the King, her son, Richard Coeur de Lion, was off crusading; she went to Austria to ransom him after his capture; and she remained endlessly busied by the continuing struggle between the Plantagenets and the Capets. Not until 1204, at the age of 83, did she finally give over; since then she has lain in the abbey at Fontevrault alngside Henry, the husband who used her, shamed her, imprisoned her, and who broke up the one perfectly happy period of her life.

Meanwhile, courtly love was not snuffed out with Eleanor's imprisonment. When the court at Poitiers was broken up, Marie of Champagne, Eleanor's daughter, returned to her own court at Troyes, county seat of Champagne, and there re-established just such a circle and such practices as Eleanor had sponsored. And she did much more—she patronized writers who would explain the system of courtly love and spread it to the rest of the civilized Western world. One of her writers was Andreas, and it was at her court, and at her request, that he wrote the *Tractatus*. And here Marie also caused the code of courtly love to be embodied in a work of romance that had immense influence and became the very master pattern after which all future stories of knights in courtly vassalage to ladies were modeled. Although it is only a romantic fiction, its purpose is avowedly didactic, and it had as great an importance as the *Tractatus* in conveying instruction in the new form of love throughout Europe.

The author of the romance was the most important poet of medieval France, but almost nothing is known of him except his first name, Chrétien, to which he added the further identification "de Troyes" to show that he was Marie's resident versifier. His work, *Le Chevalier de la Charrette* (*The Knight of the Wagon*), was a story of Lancelot and Guinevere, and one of the first long romances in French to use the newly popular Arthurian legendary background. So great was its success that long romantic narratives rapidly became the reigning literary style, displacing troubadour lyrics and acting for centuries as the chief vehicles of ideals and sentiments among the ruling class.

Marie had not only directed Chrétien to write it, but quite specifically told him how to make it a demonstration of courtly love. Chrétien had to obey, though he seems not to have approved, for he tried to wash his hands of the results by saying in the prologue: "Matter and meaning of it the Countess gives and delivers unto him; and he undertakes to direct his thinking so that he may add nothing to it except his own effort and understanding." [9] And no wonder Chrétien was uncomfortable; he was attributing to a noble lord a host of actions that violated or conflicted with feudal masculine beliefs. Lancelot, for instance, starts out to rescue Guinevere, but loses his horse. Along comes a tumbril of a type used to carry common criminals, and the dwarf driving it offers Lancelot a ride. Though it was a dishonor to a mighty lord to ride in such a wagon, the power of love and lady's service conquers, and Lancelot climbs in. Later, after Lancelot has found Guinevere and is about to fight in a tournament for her, she secretly commands him to show his obedience by letting himself be unhorsed again and feigning cowardice and fear in combat; he does all this to her order. And though

[9] Chrétien was over-generous in so crediting her; Lancelot had already appeared in other writings which Chrétien probably had seen. But in none of them was he Guinevere's illicit lover; this innovation, plus some of the details of Lancelot's service, may have been Marie's contribution.

a knight's proper business might seem to be war, the increase of his land, the service of justice and the Church, and the like, Lancelot has little to do with such matters, except as they happen to fall in with his ceaseless efforts to please Guinevere.

For thousands of lines he and she undergo suffering and misery, perform noble deeds, enjoy trysts and meetings, concoct artful ruses to deceive the rest of society, and triumph over all mundane obstacles to their illicit love. It is the archetypal story of knightly service in the name of love. It is the fiction upon which men like Ulrich patterned their real lives. Similar ideas and actions, carried throughout Europe by the irresistible appeal of the Arthurian legends, would appear for centuries, elaborated, varied and reshaped in hundreds of different ways. They would be told and retold by historians and *Meistersinger* alike; they would preoccupy Chaucer and obsess Sir Thomas Malory; they would be allegorized by Edmund Spenser and ridiculed by Cervantes; they would be blended with the burning religiosity of the Grail legends and diluted by the endless dull details of sentimental romances. They would appear in forms as diverse and far-flung as as Dante's *Commedia*, Rousseau's *Nouvelle Héloïse*, and the operas of Richard Wagner. The seed sown by William IX, Duke of Aquitaine, and carried north by his granddaughter Eleanor, would indeed flourish.

The growth of courtly love between 1100 and 1400 is indicated by a remarkable production of romances, poems, and didactic works dealing with its ideas, but there are even better proofs of its influence scattered throughout the pages of history and the chronicles of men's lives. To begin with, various medieval historians recorded public celebrations in honor of love which would have been unimaginable before the days of Eleanor of Aquitaine. The Florentine historian Villani, for instance, gives us this glimpse of thirteenth-century upper-class life:

> In June of the year 1283, at the festival of St. John in Florence
> . . . a social union was formed, composed of a thousand people
> who, all clad in white, called themselves the Servants of Love.
> They arranged a succession of sports, merrymakings, and dances
> with ladies; nobles and bourgeois marched to the sound of trumpets and music in wild delight to and fro, and held festive banquets at midday and at night. This Court of Love lasted nearly
> two months, and it was the finest and most famous that had ever
> been held in Florence, or in all Tuscany.[1]

[1] K. Vossler: *Medieval Culture*, Vol. I, p. 323.

The last phrase reveals that the collective celebration of love in this elaborate fashion was not uncommon. As for mock-legal trials of love suits, they continued, and we find them recorded as late as 1389, when King Juan of Aragon and his wife held hearings before a Court of Love in Barcelona, using the *Tractatus* as a textbook.

But as early as 1159 the English scholastic, John of Salisbury, painted a picture in a work called *Polycraticus* of what to him was the newly degenerate society all around him. He complained that young knights were "sleeping until daylight," "postponing honorable duties to fornication," and becoming far too fond of "the cithern, the lyre, the tambourine and the note of the organ at the banquet." He regretted the passing of roughhewn warriors and scolded the new-style courtiers for showing no marks of duty on them; "bristling beard and hardened skin," he lamented, "are now in disrepute as being unmeet for works of wantonness."

Was this really widespread? Even if one makes liberal allowance for the fault-finding habitual with spiritual leaders, the details he gave are convincingly realistic. And he specifically added that this was not confined to petty lordlings, but that the infection had attacked even the mighty and the proud: "The singing of love songs in the presence of men of eminence was once considered in bad taste, but now it is considered praiseworthy for men of greater eminence to sing and play love songs which they themselves with greater propriety call *stulticinia*, follies."

So it was no limited fad, but a spreading habit; moreover it was no mere affectation of new manners, but a major motivation in life and a force shaping character. In 1409 a biographer of the heroic fighter and statesman, Jean le Meingre, le Maréchal Bouciquaut, wrote his life story expressly to demonstrate that chivalry and courtly love were guiding lights of the Maréchal's entire life. Another chronicler, writing the life of Duke Louis of Bourbon, pithily summed up the two sources of the Duke's sterling character as follows: "He was a very amorous knight, first towards God and then towards all ladies and highborn girls." Jean Froissart, a leading chronicler of fourteenth-century chivalry, likewise recorded the acceptance of courtly love ideals by many of the historical figures of whom he wrote, and took for granted the beneficial effects on their character.

Even the literature that scorns, criticizes, or ridicules courtly love—and there is plenty of it—indicates by its very intensity the

appeal and threat of the new ideas. Geoffrey de La Tour Landry, a
fourteenth-century knight of Angers, wrote a curious book whose
purpose, he said, was "to teach my daughters the conventions of
love"; actually, it is a series of admonitions against straying from
strict virtue, and so carefully did he point out the pitfalls and
temptations of love talk, kissing, and the like, that it is perfectly
clear courtly love had become a dominant fashion, and one that
worried a conservative father.

Beyond being a danger to the chastity of girls, courtly love also
looked subversive to many, since it tended to mock religion and
the marriage system, and to loose the controls that both of them
exerted on society. The ladies of the Court of Love at Poitiers, and
Andreas Capellanus after them, had specifically discredited marriage and extolled adulterous love instead. Troubadours, in ad-
dressing their ladies as "Madonna," trod dangerously close to impropriety, and Aucassin, in the tale of Aucassin and Nicolette,
bluntly said he would prefer hell with his beloved to heaven without her. Chrétien de Troyes, finally, had the temerity to portray
Lancelot coming to Guinevere's room, spending some hours in bed
with her in "agreeable and sweet sport," and then bowing and
genuflecting at her door as he leaves, precisely as if before a shrine.
The code of courtly love had become practically blasphemous, and
churchmen were bound to fear and fight it. Saint Thomas tried to
combat *amor purus* by specifying that to kiss or touch a woman
with delight, even without completing the act of fornication, was
to commit a mortal sin, and confessors' handbooks listed specific
questions designed to uncover the practices of courtly sex play. In
1277 the Bishop of Paris condemned the entire *Tractatus* of
Andreas; in one century, the merry chaplain's codification of love
had ceased to be a permissible piece of folly, and been reassessed as
an instrument of heresy and social disorder.

The more conservative feudal noblemen likewise often disliked
and resented the notions of *l'amour courtois*. When the Countess
of Flanders returned to her own city of Arras after the court at
Poitiers had been dispersed, she brought with her a taste for the
fashions she had seen; one of her husband's vassals obligingly sighed
and mooned, Poitiers-fashion, in her presence, but Count Philip, her
husband, had no stomach for it and ordered the fellow to be
beaten half-dead and then suspended head downward in a sewer.
King Henry II may even have seized Eleanor and dissolved the

court of Poitiers partly because of what he sensed to be pernicious and dangerous doctrines coming out of that gay gathering.

Malicious satirical writings mocking courtly love were subsidized and enjoyed by high-ranking noblemen, and gained in popularity along with courtly romance itself. About the year 1237, for instance, the poet Guillaume de Lorris began a work called *Le Roman de la Rose;* it was intended as an extravagant tribute to courtly love, but Guillaume died and left only 4,266 lines finished. Forty years later the poet Jean de Meung completed it by adding another 18,000 lines—but these were filled with cynicism, ribaldry, and satire. The poem ends with the victory of the God of Love, but this is mere pretense; Jean was transparently contemptuous of women and romance, and what had started out as a super-romantic poem ended by being alloyed with frivolity and cynicism. It could hardly have become the most famous single poem of the Middle Ages had there not been so great a desire for levity and reassuring cynicism about the whole subject of noble love.

For throughout medieval society, even as courtly love was making its greatest gains, the symptoms of the ancient ambivalence toward sex and love were becoming ever more distinct. The "quarrel of women"—the pro-and-con discussion of courtly love, and of the excellence or vileness of the female sex—was growing in volume and intensity from the eleventh century to the fourteenth, and would become still more violent in the Renaissance. While poets and knights were celebrating the beauty and the spotless purity of their ladies, there existed simultaneously a contrasting hunger for bawdiness and vulgarity. Pious volumes and books of spiritual edification were often decorated with crudely sexual, and even excremental, illustrations; even church decorations embodied these themes in the frankest way. (And why not? Even so revered a Father of the Church as Augustine, expressing his lowly opinion of the procreative process, had said forthrightly: "We are born between feces and urine.") In direct opposition to the refinement of the courtly romances and lyrics, there was an undiminished, and perhaps increased, market for vulgarity in literature; one might point, merely by way of example, to the ribald Goliardic poems of the wandering medieval scholars, and to the bawdy sexuality, somewhat later on, of Boccaccio's *Decameron* and such fabliaux as Chaucer's "Miller's Tale." More ominously, during the 1300's there began to appear a new and spreading interest in witchcraft, and a growing belief in the evil powers of women who had formed pacts with Satan—an explanation of womankind totally at odds with that of courtly love.

The dilemma of medieval love therefore offered two alternatives —courtly love, with its tantalizing and often incomplete sexual expression, or loveless fornication, with its ugliness and weight of sin. The more men tried to ally noble and ethical qualities to love, the wider grew that split, and the more outlandish grew their concept of love itself. One of the most extreme forms of adaptation to the ambivalent fear of love lay in the direction pointed out earlier by those Provençal poets who had fervently begged their ladies not to grant them sexual favors under any conditions. Not only did this bizarre attitude not die out after the crusade against the Albigenses, but it came to have great historical importance. In the thirteenth century, the Tuscan poets of Italy seized upon the theme and intensified it, finding in it a way to obey Saint Thomas, to emulate Plato, and yet to preserve something of the worship of sensuous beauty in woman that they found in troubadour poetry. They were living exemplars of the ambivalent human soul: they sought sexual outlet in marriage and in brothels, but adored ladies for years at a time without even letting them know about it, and were content to love without even desiring so much as a kiss, certain that they were the better for it.

The most famous and influential example of this is Dante's celebrated love for Beatrice. In the *Vita Nuova* he tells how he first saw her in the year 1274, when he was only nine years old, and immediately began to worship her with a pure and inspiring love. He never spoke one word to her, and scarcely hoped to; he made no efforts to meet her and saw her only at rare intervals. As for intimacies, even to think of them would have been totally impossible. Beatrice was perfect, goddess-like, and a source of spiritual guidance, rather than a flesh-and-blood female.

Actually, Dante had come to the point where he was no longer concerned with exploring the nature of human love; he was interested in divine love, as revealed through human experience. Beatrice was really only an instrument through which he felt uplifted and inspired to seek the divine heights; in the *Commedia*, it is therefore Beatrice's spirit that guides Dante to Paradise. This, in a general way, is the kind of evaluation literary scholars have given to Dante's love for Beatrice. To the psychologist or the historian of love, however, there is something else to be said. Dante did love Beatrice (he *says* so) though she neither knew of, enjoyed, nor was influenced by his distant worship. His writing on the subject of his love, whatever religious implications or value it had, was taken by his contemporaries and by subsequent generations down to the Victorian period to be a true picture of how man and woman should love each other.[11] It will not do to argue that Dante merely used Beatrice as a symbolic way to explore divine love: she was nearly all the love he was capable of feeling for actual woman. He had a wife and several mistresses, but in all his writing he said practically nothing about them; the impulse toward love was directed toward his remote ideal, and for the other women in his life there remained only the gratefulness he felt for their seeing to his sexual needs and his household requirements. His wife and mistresses might have had much to say about what it was like to share so sublime a lover with a hypothetical ideal; unfortunately for the history of love, they left us not a word.

[11] As late as 1884, Violet Paget ("Vernon Lee"), a British scholar and essayist, wrote that Dante had made sexual desire "burn clear towards heaven," and purified it of lust; this, she held, could even benefit marriage: "If the old lust-fattened evil of the world is to diminish rather than to increase, why then every love . . . should tend, to the utmost possibility, to resemble that love of the 'Vita Nuova.' " (*Euphorion*, Vol. II, p. 205)

8

The Outcome of Courtly Love

It began as a game, but it ended as a way of life. Yet "ended" is not the right word; it has never ended since the eleventh century, for its influence has been paramount in Western love ever since—minimized at some times, emphasized at others, absent from none.

But attitudes toward the influence of courtly love have ranged, for eight centuries, from complete approval to total condemnation. We will see, as we proceed, how various succeeding centuries continued and modified the romantic tradition, and how many a generation has considered that love was heightened and purified by the troubadour influence, and particularly by the contribution of Dante. A contrary view exists, however. The Swiss scholar, Denis de Rougemont, maintains that courtly love was bad to begin with and worse in its development; he holds that it has exerted a wholly baleful influence by making Western man believe that to love means to be mastered by emotion, overcome by it, powerless, unhappy, and tragic because of it. "Why does Western Man wish to suffer this passion which lacerates him and which all his common sense rejects?" he asks, and answers: because it represents a repressed longing for death. He sees the kind of love immortalized in the lives of Héloïse and Abélard and the legend of Tristan and Iseult as having cast upon love a permanent blight—the desire for passion, suffering, and death. Some psychiatrically oriented writers have even seen in these same love stories clear allegories of the medieval incest-fixation: when one loved where one lusted, the guilt feelings that resulted could only produce a desire for the ultimate punishment. Tristan had to die, for did he not both adore Iseult and possess her rapturously?

But we have already so often seen unexpected and incongruous values within any one variety of love that we might well look for them here too. Consider the elements that courtly love introduced for the first time into the emotional relationships between men and women. For one thing, it brought into them tenderness and gentleness, exaggerated and sometimes absurd in form, but important nevertheless. It operated within a framework of adultery, yet it stressed as never before the importance of the fidelity of one man and one woman, each to each. It expressed itself via the artificialities of love debates and Courts of Love, but introduced the revolutionary notions that love must be a genuinely mutual relationship, involving respect and admiration. Perhaps all this only proves the incestuous overtones of *l'amour courtois,* since all of it is copied from good parent-child relationships; whether so or not, love which incorporated these elements has proved to have an undying and unkillable appeal ever since, despite the great changes in manners, religion, and social structure. And since few courtly lovers desexualized their feelings as thoroughly as Dante, it was courtly love through which erotic or semi-erotic emotions began to be wedded to moral achievement. "Oh, what a wonderful thing is love," exulted Andreas, "which makes a man shine with so many virtues and teaches everyone, no matter who he is, so many good traits of character!"

Those who, like de Rougemont, claim that courtly love and the romantic ideal damaged marriage have ignored the fact that medieval marriage was no joining of personalities, no merging of desires; it was a master-and-servant, owner-and-property connection. Until woman's status was drastically altered in society, the marriage relationship would hardly become more emotionally satisfying. And it was courtly love, with all its shortcomings, absurdities, and neurotic components, that began to change the position of women. By the end of the fourteenth century, says the historian Sidney Painter, "woman had edged her way into the mind of feudal man and had elevated and enlarged her place in society as he recognized it. No longer was she merely a child-bearer and lust-satisfier—she was the inspirer of progress." In short, by still another of those paradoxes that occur so often in the history of love, the adulterous flirtation and illicit infatuations of the Middle Ages were the very instrument that began to enhance woman's status, and hence eventually to alter marriage. But before all that could happen, man would have to solve the major problem of love: he would have to decide whether woman was really a madonna of heaven, or a witch serving Satan, or possibly a bit of each.

Chapter VI

THE LADY AND THE WITCH

The Flame of Love,
and the Flame of the Stake

In the three centuries after the death of Eleanor of Aquitaine, the European world acquired a very different look. Cities swelled and spilled out over their medieval walls. Commerce and manufacturing flourished, and princes learned to befriend the bankers and merchants who financed their wars and intrigues. Gunpowder made castle walls obsolete, and printing did the same thing to medieval obscurantism. Scholars, poets, and courtiers reveled in their rediscovery of Cicero, Plato, and Sappho, and the arts became consciously imitative of ancient classic models rather than the Gothic and Christian ones of recent centuries. By 1500 the bright sunlight of the Renaissance shone over Italy and was beginning to reach the North, dispelling the fogs and glooms, and dissolving demons and dungeons like so much morning mist—or so we often think.

The past, however, is no such insubstantial vapor, and its shadows tend to persist. In the Renaissance, one of the longest of them was still cast by the figure of Saint Augustine. It was eleven centuries since he had said: "Through a woman we were sent to destruction; through a woman salvation was restored to us," but at the end of the fifteenth century his dictum seemed even more compelling than ever. The concept of woman had gradually become completely dualistic: she was not Woman—she was either Lady or Witch, Blessed Virgin or sinful Eve, object of adoration or vessel of abominable lust.

In the year 1507, for instance, at the ducal palace in Urbino, a group of elegant lords and ladies spent four spring evenings de-

bating the manners, ideals, and love life proper for courtly persons.
Their comments, later set down by one of them, became the very
gospel of aristocratic conduct. One of the nobles present apotheo-
sized the Lady as follows:

> Who does not know that without women we can feel no con-
> tent or satisfaction throughout this life of ours, which but for
> them would be rude and devoid of all sweetness and more savage
> than that of wild beasts? . . . [They] alone banish from our
> hearts all vile and base thoughts, vexations, miseries, and turbid
> melancholies. . . . It is impossible for vileness ever again to rule
> in a man's heart where once the flame of love has entered.[1]

It is still the voice of the twelfth century, speaking through the lips
of the sixteenth century. And even though the nobleman does not
frown too darkly on actual sexual union, he refuses (like any Provençal troubadour) to suppose that it is in any way the product of
woman's desires. Instead, it is due entirely to seduction by the male:

> What day, what hour, ever passes that the persecuted girl is not
> besought by the lover with money, gifts, and all things that must
> please her? When can she ever go to her window, but she shall
> always see her persistent lover pass, silent in word, but with eyes
> that speak, with sad and languid face, with those burning sighs,
> often with most abundant tears? . . . What wonder is it if . . .
> [she] is finally brought to love him by continual wearing (as
> water wears the hardest marble), and, conquered by this passion,
> contents him?

Renaissance noblemen not only idealized beauty in woman, as had
their medieval predecessors, but having rediscovered in Plato arguments that made Beauty identical with the Good, they viewed it
with quasi-religious awe. A Polish ambassador, upon being presented to the striking Queen of Navarre, stated in heartfelt terms:
"Never do I wish to see such beauty again. Willingly would I do as
do the Turks, pilgrims to Mecca, where the sepulchre of their
prophet, Mahomet is . . . [who] burn their eyes out with hot
irons, saying that nothing more could be seen as fine, and therefore
they would see nothing."

Yet at the very same time, other men in Western Europe were
studying, applying, and imitating the words of another immensely
influential book dealing with women—a manual of witchcraft
which had been written near the close of the fifteenth century, at

---

[1] Castiglione: *The Courtier*, Bk. III.

the request of the Pope. Its authors were two German Dominican theologians, but their opinions were not wholly derived from bookish studies; as Inquisitors for northern Germany, they had personally interrogated hundreds of women. Their conclusions about the sex were unmarred by qualifications or hesitation:

> A woman is beautiful to look upon, contaminating to the touch, and deadly to keep . . . a foe to friendship . . . a necessary evil, a natural temptation . . . a domestic danger . . . an evil of nature, painted with fair colors . . . a liar by nature. . . . [She] seethes with anger and impatience in her whole soul. . . . There is no wrath above the wrath of a woman. . . . Since [women] are feebler both in mind and body, it is not surprising that they should come under the spell of witchcraft [more than men]. . . . A woman is more carnal than a man. . . . All witchcraft comes from carnal lust, which is in women insatiable.[2]

Like the courtier, the Inquisitors had an explanation for consummated love affairs, but they reversed the roles of hunter and hunted:

> These women satisfy their filthy lusts not only in themselves, but even in the mighty ones of the age, of whatever sort and condition, causing by all sorts of witchcraft the death of their souls through the excessive infatuation of carnal love.

Their reaction to female charms was rather different from that of the Polish ambassador: making no talk of blinding themselves in ecstasy, they preferred to hoist women aloft by the thumbs, twist ropes around their heads, hammer needles under their fingernails, and pour boiling oil on their feet, in the devout hope of eliciting confessions of iniquities. Even after a suspect confessed her abominations, the pious investigators were wary of her physical seductiveness; to protect the judge, they caused her to be shaved bare at the head and crotch, and dragged backwards into court naked, so her eyes could not bewitch him.

It is an astonishing fact that the schism in men's feelings about women appeared to be most extreme not in the early Christian era nor in the Middle Ages, but during that golden Renaissance that we think of as almost modern, almost enlightened. The burning of witches was never more prevalent than at the very time when woman was being glorified by Botticelli, Giorgione, and Titian. Love and sexual feelings had become hopelessly entangled in the struggle between medieval religion and Renaissance humanism, be-

[2] Sprenger and Kramer: *Malleus Maleficarum*, Pt. I, Quest. 6.

tween the power of the Pope and the power of the emerging nations of the West. Caught in this intense struggle, sexual neurosis
might look like satanic skulduggery and lead to the stake, while
romantic love could become an issue over which a king might break
his ancient ties to Rome.

2

The Courtier in Love —
A Two-dimensional Portrait

✸   ✸

✸

At the beginning of the sixteenth century, there was no more
civilized court in Italy than that of Guidobaldo di Montefeltro, Duke of Urbino. Guidobaldo's tiny principality, nestled on
the slopes of the Appenines in north-central Italy, was prosperous,
well-administered, and peaceful, and his father, Federico, having
ruled it excellently for forty years, had left a legacy of love for the
Montefeltro name. Guidobaldo should have been a happy man, but
he was not. Gaunt and fragile, he tried like other Renaissance
princes to be both a warrior and a man of culture, but was able to
succeed only at the second; his feeble body had been plagued by
various ills from his earliest teens, and by twenty was crippled by
gout. Nor was this his severest affliction. At sixteen he had married
Elizabetta Gonzaga, the gentle, gracious young sister of the Marquis of Mantua, and almost at once discovered himself to be impotent.

Fortunately, the young Duke and his Duchess were steeped in the literary traditions of Dante and Petrarch, both of whom had exalted the disembodied form of courtly love. Moreover, the young couple were also students of Neoplatonism, which provided such love with a properly classical rationale.[3] Guidobaldo and his young wife therefore comforted themselves with lofty discussions on the superiority of chaste love, and Elizabetta showed him a devotion and loyalty that would have honored any marriage. In 1502, for instance, when Duke Guidobaldo was thirty, the treacherous Caesar Borgia made a surprise descent upon Urbino while the Duke's artillery was away helping Caesar's father, Pope Alexander VI. Guidobaldo and Elizabetta fled, and Caesar added Urbino to the Pope's possessions. Seeking to stabilize the conquest, the Pope then offered Elizabetta an annulment and a potent French husband, while Caesar Borgia added the promise of a pension. Though she was living on Venetian charity in ignominious exile with her ailing husband, Elizabetta refused all. In 1503 malaria killed the Pope. Caesar Borgia's power swiftly crumbled, the people of Urbino drove out his soldiers, and the Duke and his faithful Duchess were joyfully welcomed back. They celebrated their happiness by surrounding themselves with the leading poets, painters, musicians, and writers of Italy, and conducting endless discussions about life, ethics, manners, poetry, and love.

All these topics, as examined and demonstrated at Urbino, were talked about throughout Western Europe, and the ways of Urbino were diligently copied; wherever wealth had made for increased leisure, and the concentration of power had produced important capital cities and princely courts, such things were becoming all-important. It was expected that every lord and lady would know Latin and a touch of Greek, be able to write sonnets and compose a tune, and discourse gracefully on philosophers, gods, and lovers. The medieval trouvères, jesters, and jugglers, entertaining in dank baronial halls, were succeeded by chamber orchestras, troupes of players, and elegant banquets, presented in well-lighted palaces which had glazed windows and hence were often warm and comfortable.

Courtiers and merchants alike bought and avidly studied large

---

[3] Neoplatonism of the Renaissance was a Christian reinterpretation of Plato's doctrines, and not identical with the philosophic-religious system called Neoplatonism which arose in Alexandria in the third century (see chapter four, p. 101). In the present chapter, the terms "Platonic," "Platonizing," etc. will be understood as referring neither to the original Platonic doctrines nor to Alexandrian Neoplatonism, but to Renaissance Neoplatonism.

numbers of "courtesy books" in which the manners of gentlemen were set forth in detail, although to the modern age some of the subject matter seems curiously elementary. One of the most famous courtesy books (the *Galateo* of Giovanni della Casa, first published in 1559) advised, for instance, against yawning, sneezing, scratching in public, smelling someone else's meat, or making bad puns.[4] Though the economic basis of feudalism and feudal warfare had largely disappeared, there was a keen renewal of interest in the romantic aspects of chivalry. Tourneys became popular again and were more splendid than ever in the sixteenth century, even though armored knight and wooden lance were nearing obsolesence and jousting had lost much of its military and political importance. Above all, the courtiers cultivated the art of *bel parlare*, or fine conversation, and practiced it immoderately: the poet Bembo told of a single discussion of love that lasted for three days. Extensive lists of love questions, the raw materials of such heroic exercises, were published continuously from the fourteenth to the seventeenth century and contained such fertile problems as these: Can a man love more than one woman at a time? Is love noblest which never possesses the body of the beloved in any way, or is the kiss permissible? Which is more agreeable—to speak to the beloved without seeing her, or see her without being able to speak to her? (By 1566 a French writer was able to fill sixteen pages with his discussion of the latter question.)

Such were the principal leisure distractions of Renaissance courts, of which the one at Urbino was a leading example. Among the noblemen attached to that court was Baldassare Castiglione, a gentle, meditative, well-born young man from Mantua, who had entered Guidobaldo's service first in 1503 as a soldier, remained to serve him also as ambassador and court intellectual, and soon became deeply enamored of the Duchess. Luckily, he too could attune himself to Platonic love, and although he wrote sonnets to her and was fairly outspoken in his admiration, he lived for many years in blameless amity with her and Duke Guidobaldo in what seemed to him the best of all possible worlds.

[4] If such advice seems unnecessary, it is worth noting that as late as 1611 an English traveler remarked with astonishment upon an Italian custom he had seen nowhere else in Europe: they used forks at the table while cutting meat off the main joint. "The reason of this curiosity is," he explained, "because the Italian cannot by any means endure to have his dish touched with fingers, seeing all men's fingers are not alike clean." (Thomas Coryat: *Coryats Crudities,* 1611)

That world, he felt, should be preserved and offered as a model to all other men, and he did so in the form of a book entitled *The Courtier*, which is an account of four evenings of conversation among several dozen lords and ladies at Urbino in March 1507.[5] One can assume that much of the wording is of Castiglione's own invention, but the people named were all real and the opinions of several key speakers tally with what they themselves wrote in other books. *The Courtier*, though no stenographic transcript, is therefore very likely a faithful portrayal of what was actually said at Urbino, either during that four-day series of talks or at other times. As a clear exposition of aristocratic ideals, it was immensely influential, and was translated into French, German, and Spanish. In England it was considered required reading for every gentleman. One Italian lady, as she lay dying, recited not a prayer, but favorite passages from *The Courtier*.

A large part of *The Courtier* deals with the characteristics of the ideal gentleman. He must, of course, be of aristocratic birth. He must be learned in the classics, and possess both literary and conversational style. Arms are his true profession, but in order not to become brutalized, he must cultivate refinement; the book therefore intimately inquires into his clothing, his grammar, his manners, and even the types of practical jokes he plays on others. The ideal court lady is likewise anatomized; significantly, she is not at all the remote, rarely approached goddess of medieval troubadour lyrics, but a real person who must be witty, well read, active in social gatherings, skilled in writing and conversation, and capable of handling worldly and political matters.

The most important segments of the book are concerned with Renaissance concepts of love, courtship, and sexual conduct. Many of the statements, like the quotations from *The Courtier* with which this chapter began, are essentially repetitions of the principles of courtly love somewhat modified in flavor by the passage of time, but throughout the book there is also a strong overlay of Platonism, a distinctly new element. The fundamental theme is that love is the source of all sweetness and moral virtue, since it leads men to concentrate on beauty, and beauty leads the mind toward the contemplation of divinity. It was therefore clear that the lover and the

---

[5] Castiglione wrote that he himself had not been present and was only repeating what he had been told, but the dates of some of his letters prove the opposite; the statement is a graceful pretext for omitting himself from the dialogue. His manners were always impeccable.

lady had to see and converse with each other frequently (there would be none of those interminable medieval quests away from the lady in the name of serving her), but their love, to be finest and most ennobling, had to remain chaste and free of actual physical union. Although they would talk of love a great deal, it was up to the lady to preserve their purity by refusing to let the talk heat her blood. Giuliano de' Medici (the third son of Lorenzo, and brother of the later Pope Leo X), explained how a lady should handle this, and it is reasonable to suppose that he was really portraying the Duchess Elizabetta herself.

> If the gentleman shall be pert . . . she will give him such an-swer that he may clearly understand he is causing her annoyance. Again, if he shall be discreet and use modest phrases and words of love covertly . . . the lady will feign not to understand and will apply his words in another sense, always modestly trying to change the subject. . . . If, again, the talk is such that she can-not feign not to understand, she will take it all as a jest, pretend-ing to be aware that it is said to her more out of compliment to her than because it is true, depreciating her merits and ascribing the praises that he gives her to the gentleman's courtesy.

One may wonder whether this bloodless feinting was intended to go on indefinitely. Lord Giuliano was quite clear on that point:

> I would have her yield her lover nothing but her spirit; nor ever let her show him any clear sign of love (either by words or by gestures or by any other means) by which he may be sure of it.

What intrigued this particular assemblage of Renaissance cour-tiers and ladies was not sexual conquest, but the prolonging of chaste raptures and exaltations, the artful playing of conversational games, the indulging in purified courtship. But they did not con-sider this a mere amusement or trivial pastime; philosophy dignified it with a high and worthy goal, without the tiresome mechanics of good deeds or knightly service. Pietro Bembo, a poet and minor cleric who later became a cardinal, made the definitive closing speech on love in *The Courtier*, eloquently expounding the Platonic theory of chaste love in terms compared to which even the medieval talk of *amor purus* seems almost hot-blooded and sensual: [6]

> Beauty seen in bodies and especially faces . . . is an effluence of divine goodness. Beauty is good, and hence true love of beauty

---

[6] The ultimate origin of his ideas was, of course, Plato's *Symposium*, though Bembo's Renaissance mind reinter-preted what he said there and ignored the homosexual context. See above, chapter two, p. 47.

is most good and holy . . . but whoever thinks to enjoy the beauty by possessing the body deceives himself, and is moved, not by true perception through reasonable choice, but by false opinion through sensual appetite. . . .

The true courtier who wishes to possess beauty in a perfect and lasting way (Bembo continued), and who uses it as a guide along the ascent toward divinity, permits himself only the two least fleshly senses—sight and sound. He enjoys seeing his lady's beauty, her grace, her actions; he revels in the sweetness of her voice and the concord of her words. Using these perceptions of beauty in one body, he strives step by step to learn to love the beauty of human nature; thence he proceeds to the recognition of the beauty of the universal intellect.

Let us, then, direct all the thoughts and forces of our soul to this most sacred light, which shows us the way to heaven. . . . Let us lay aside the passions wherewith we were clothed at our fall, and by the stairway that bears the shadow of sensual beauty on the lowest step, let us mount to the lofty mansion where dwells the heavenly, lovely and true beauty, which lies hidden in the inmost secret recesses of God.

With this, the fourth evening of discussions at Urbino in March 1507 was concluded; there was really nothing more anyone could say.

Such theorizing about love was especially welcome at Urbino, in view of the Duke's sexual difficulty, but it also became highly fashionable at courts throughout Western Europe. Neoplatonism gave a pleasant classical dignity and a philosophic aura to the pure love that had been invented in Provence, developed in Poitiers, and perfected by Dante and Petrarch; it offered the Renaissance humanists a way to blend the highest pagan thinking with their own version of Christianity. For the most part, they studiously ignored the fact that Plato thought of the first step toward the divine as the love not of a woman, but of a beautiful boy.

For some men, Platonic love seems to have been entirely satisfying. Castiglione himself, despite his mother's pleas that he should marry and perpetuate the line, remained a pure-minded bachelor at Urbino for nearly a dozen years. During the latter eight of them Elizabetta was a widow, but there is no hint of impropriety between her and Castiglione. She was at least six years older than he, a semi-invalid with a heavy pale face and listless eyes, but perhaps that has nothing to do with it; he might have remained pure in any case.

In 1516 Pope Leo X deposed Guidobaldo's nephew from the ducal throne and put one of his own on it instead. Castiglione had to leave, and returned at last to Mantua where, when nearly forty, he faced up to his familial responsibility and married a teen-aged girl. To his great surprise, he found considerable happiness in marriage and learned that he could love in a new way, quite unlike that he had thus far practiced. But his happiness lasted only a few years, for his young wife died after bearing their third child. Castiglione turned back to his long-neglected manuscript and thrust aside the meaning of his recent experiences; the finished form of *The Courtier*, published at last in 1528 after circulating privately for some time, reflected only the ideas expressed at Urbino and nothing learned in his actual marriage. For him, the make-believe was important, after all, and reality was not.

3

The Courtier in Love —
A Three-dimensional Portrait

C astiglione's portrait of Platonic love in the year 1507 is, really, only a silhouette—a simplified and idealized likeness, drawn from life in a court with a special problem. Platonic love of the Urbino variety was a highly fashionable subject of discussion in the other courts of Western Europe, but most men and many women were not completely attuned to the ascetic and spiritualized form of love. They strove to be Platonic, but often satisfied the hunger of the flesh in shameful places and with lowly persons; they talked Platonism and sometimes practiced *amor purus* with their Platonic loves—and sometimes lost their grip on Platonism altogether.

Many clues indicate that the ancient separation of sex from love still dominated the emotions of Renaissance men. To a considerable extent, they were able to love ladies purely while seeking their relief elsewhere. Petrarch himself, the best-known of pure lovers and the pattern upon which Italian men, and then French and English ones, modeled themselves, had shown just the same clear-cut schism in his feelings. He had grown up a couple of centuries earlier, when Dante was still alive, and had been deeply influenced by Dante's love for Beatrice. Following this lead, Petrarch had a famous long-range love affair with a lady he called Laura; his sonnets on the subject set the mode for centuries, and like him countless lovers admired their ladies from a distance, wrote poems to them, sighed, wept, and prayed for the tiniest favor. The real Laura, meanwhile, sturdily bore her husband eleven children, none of them Petrarch's; he would never have dreamed of real intimacy. On the side, however, he took a mistress while writing his sonnets, and sired two bastards before abandoning both sex and Platonic love in favor of scholarly studies. Any number of later Petrarchans followed the same route, up to but not including the final abandonment.

But as in the time of Andreas, many of those who professed spiritual love were tantalized by desire, and drawn on to experiment, sometimes gingerly, sometimes zestfully, with the physical embodiment of their love. Sometimes we gather this indirectly, as when a writer scoffs at Platonic-Petrarchan posturing for going on too long and being too prissy. One Melchiorre Zoppio, writing a *Treatise of Love* in 1587, portrayed a pale and sighing youth standing before the bed of his ladylove, who asks what troubles him. "Only what you see, that you should wish me well," he says.

"I do," she answers.

"And that you know I wish the same to you."

"I know it."

"And that you hold it dear."

"I hold it dear. Do you wish anything else?"

"Only that you wish me well and know that I wish you the same."

Having had about enough of this, the lady finally says: "Since you wish me well and I wish the same to you, leave me to sleep by myself as I will leave you to sleep by yourself. Good night." And she rolls over. Such love, Zoppio said, is really only friendship; true love should end in embraces—"and most lovers will be found of the same opinion."

Yet this is only an imagined scene, and Zoppio may have been indulging in some wishful thinking. Although a good deal of true love undoubtedly ended in embraces of one sort or another, it is also true that the double standard kept many ladies pure out of fear of the consequences. Some of the great ladies of the Renaissance, for whom men felt celebrated Platonic affections, remained perfectly virtuous and found in Platonic love an intellectual and emotional recompense for their husbands' erring masculine ways.

Such motives may explain why Platonic love was so important in the life of Marguerite of Navarre, sister of King Francis I, who preached it to French courtiers and ladies for thirty years in the early part of the sixteenth century. Married for political reasons at seventeen, she could find nothing to love in her first husband; her second, Henri, titular King of Navarre, was eleven years younger than she, and treated her amiably but with little pretense at fidelity. Marguerite, as the arbiter of fashion and leading female intellectual of the court of King Francis, and later as the co-ruler of her husband's courts at Nérac and Pau in southwestern France, diligently encouraged and fostered Platonic love discussions and customs among the courtiers, poets, intellectuals, and mystics who gathered about her. She also encouraged the practice in a personal fashion: nearly a dozen men are said to have been in love with her, and she loved them all in return, sincerely, intensely, and chastely. It was the safe course for a lady, and one that neatly complemented the dominant male view of woman as either a hallowed saint or vulgar sinner.

But at all levels of Platonism, including the most rarefied and elevated, Renaissance men and women candidly recognized the less exalted practices of love and sex that existed side-by-side with professedly divine love, and were not in the least shocked by the contrast. Marguerite's own brother had the morals and tastes of a stud bull, but she never found fault with him for it, and though she was the champion of spiritual love, she willingly befriended his various unspiritual mistresses. All around her she saw and heard stories of licentious and vulgar conduct, and though her own habits were so exemplary, she found the opposite amusing and put much of her laughter into the *Heptameron*, a collection of seventy-two tales she wrote in frank emulation of Boccaccio. The Abbé Brantôme, a dilettante historian of the latter part of the century, claimed that a key existed to the stories, identifying its scapegrace characters as real persons; if so, French morals were no better in the sixteenth century than in the twelfth. But whether the Abbé was right or not, it is astonishing that Marguerite, a sweet, intelligent, inspiring, and religious queen, could permit herself to write stories as bawdy and ribald as any in the *Decameron*.

Some of them, to be sure, contain lofty Platonic sentiments. "No man loveth God," says one of her characters, "who hath not loved with a perfect love one of His creatures." But side by side with this are stories of bed-partners switched in the dark, incestuous mix-ups, insatiable priests, and cuckolded husbands. One is hard put to know just how the most Platonic lady in France felt about these unedifying yarns or the persons in them. Evidently, along with her intense Platonism she had an equally intense feeling for vulgarity and brazenness—a Renaissance combination that is often called refreshing frankness or healthful realism by those who like to view the past with nostalgia and longing. "What!" exclaims one of Marguerite's characters, "you mean that if no one is advised thereof, all things are lawful to lovers?" "In good faith," is the typically Renaissance answer, "there is but one crime I have seen punished, and that is folly; for your murderers, thieves, and adulterers are neither overtaken of justice nor blamed of men, if they be but as crafty as they are wicked."

Such candor contrasted oddly with the sublime ethics of Platonism, but in the same way, Renaissance men could exhibit both an ultra-refined adoration of female beauty, and a startling frankness about sexual functions and marriage. In Italy, men charged with impotence by neglected wives had the legal right, as late as the sixteenth century, to disprove the allegation before witnesses either in a brothel or at home. Vincenzo Gonzaga, Duke of Mantua, is said to have so proved himself in the presence of a group of ambassadors and dignitaries of the Church. At the very time when Bembo and others were penning tributes to woman as the first step of the stairway to divinity, King Henry VII of England sent three gentlemen of his court to study the young Queen of Naples, widow of

Ferdinand II, as a possible match for himself. Some of the points on
the detailed directive he gave them are wonderfully enlightening:

> *Item*, specially to mark the favor of her visage, whether she be
> painted or not, and whether it be fat or lean, sharp or round.
>
> *Item*, to mark well the fashion of her nose and the height and
> breadth of her forehead.
>
> *Item*, to mark her breast and paps, whether they be big or small.
>
> *Item*, to approach as near her mouth as they honestly may, to
> the intent that they may feel the condition of her breath, whether
> it be sweet or not.
>
> *Item*, . . . [to] make inquisition and ensearch what land or
> livelihood the said young queen hath or shall have after the
> decease of her mother.[7]

The young woman was apparently satisfactory on all counts except
the last, but it was the most important; Henry VII, neither Pla-
tonist nor hot-blooded youth, decided to remain a widower.

For in the earlier part of the Renaissance, marriage was treated
with utter candor—not only as to its physical aspects but its financial ones. Love, Platonic or otherwise, was neither the basis for
making a marriage, nor any essential part of it, once made. As it had
been for many centuries, marriage was still fundamentally a genetic
device, with household and welfare functions among the lower
classes, and economic and political values for the propertied classes
and the aristocrats. Throughout Renaissance Europe the principal
questions asked by parents of both the girl and the boy concerned
dowry, income, and property guarantees. Marriage was a financial
transaction and a lifelong business; raptures and adorations would
either be hurtful to it, or simply perish in its mundane soil. "I would
not counsel ye to marry her with whom thou hast been in amours
withal," wrote Juan Luis Vives, the leading educator of the early
sixteenth century.

But few had the chance to try illicit amours before marriage,
and so they tried them afterwards; most marriages took place when
the girl was between fourteen and sixteen, and the boy but little
more, while many children and even infants were espoused in
church ceremonies at the desire of parents who had struck a bargain.
Such an espousal was effectively a marriage, for though it had to
be ratified by actual marriage later on, only a few of the children,
when they grew up, dared to appeal for a release from the contract.
In 1477, Anna Sforza, aged three, was affianced to Alfonso d'Este;

---

[7] *Historia Regis Henrici Septimi*, p. 223–39.

she walked in the ceremony, but he, being newborn, had to be carried by a chamberlain. Not only the mighty arranged such marriages for benefit. A study made of the records of the English diocese of Chester in the middle of the sixteenth century shows a number of similar marriages among the children of obscure burghers. John Somerford and Jane Brerton, three and two years old respectively, were held in arms by adults who spoke the words of the ceremony for them. In another such espousal, John Rigmardon, aged three, was coaxed by a priest to repeat the matrimonial vows aloud; halfway through, the child said he would do no more, to which the priest replied: "You must speak a little more, and then go play you."

Though many an economic marriage may have resulted in some degree of affection, the feelings were apt to remain strongly colored by the money value of each partner. Messer Donati Velluti, a fourteenth-century Italian gentleman, wrote in his diary these telltale phrases: "Bice, my first wife, was a little woman and not pretty, but sagacious, good, kindly, well-mannered, and full of every virtue. . . . She lived with me in blessed peace and got me favor, honor, and possessions enough." The effect of money considerations on the emotional aspects of courtship is revealed still more clearly in several of the Paston Letters, a wonderful collection of the papers of a family of well-to-do gentry in fifteenth-century England. John Paston, a younger son, wrote to his older brother, Sir John, in July 1474, concerning certain prospects for his marriage:

> Right worshipful sir, I recommend me to you, praying you to remember, before ye depart out of London, to speak with the wife of Harry Eberton, the draper, and to inform her that I am proffered a marriage in London which is worth 600 mark and better. . . . If so be that Mistress Eberton will deal with me, ye should not conclude in the other place,[8] even though Eberton would not give so much with Mistress Elizabeth, his daughter, as I might have with the other, for such fantasy as I have in the said Mistress Elizabeth Eberton.[9]

But fantasy did not impress the Ebertons, for John Paston had too little property of his own; and probably for the same reason, the deal in "the other place" also fell through. Three years later, still single, he met and wooed Margery Brews, daughter of a Sir Thomas Brews, and apparently managed to inspire some tender

[8] He was at the same time dickering for the daughter of someone named Stockton.

[9] *Paston Letters,* Vol. III, no. 739.

sentiments in the girl. But a message of hers to him mingles fiscal and tender sentiments in a fashion never seen in anthologies of love letters:

> Right worshipful and well beloved Valentine . . . ye be pur-
> posed to come to Topcroft in short time . . . to have a conclusion
> of the matter between my father and you; I would be most glad
> of any creature alive if the matter might grow to effect. . . .
> [If not] then should I be much more sorry and full of heaviness.
> And as for myself, I have done and understood all in the matter
> that I can or may, as God knoweth; and I let you plainly under-
> stand that my father will no more money part with in that behalf
> but an hundred £ and fifty marks, which is right far from the ac-
> complishment of your desire. Wherefore, if that ye could be con-
> tent with that good, and my poor person, I would be the merriest
> maiden on ground.[1]

Happily John Paston saw the light and the marriage took place on those terms; it is also possible that he may have been influenced by the fact that still another marriage prospect his older brother was looking into for him had just proven fruitless.

For all these reasons—the continuing schism between noble love and sexual function, the financial involvements of upper-class mar-riage, the medieval tradition that placed romance outside marriage, and the preciosity of the Neoplatonic conception of love—the average Renaissance husband looked upon his wife with eyes which appraised rather than adored. Yet he was equally capable of look-ing with adoration elsewhere, for although Platonic love was only a pose for some people, the qualities it praised in the Lady were real and existed in many Renaissance women. Vittoria Colonna, Lucrezia Borgia, Catherine de' Medici, Beatrice d'Este, Margaret More, Mary Stuart, Queen Elizabeth—history is studded with their names. And there were even more whose names are practically forgotten, but who still live in remote bits of biography. Here, for instance, is a vignette written in the seventeenth century, limning a typical six-teenth-century virago,[2] Elizabeth Nevill, daughter of Baron Lati-mer:

> . . . Prodigious parts for a woman. I have heard my father's
> mother say that she had Chaucer at her fingers' ends. A great
> politician; great wit and spirit, but revengeful. Knew how to
> manage her estate as well as any man; understood jewels as well

---

[1] Ibid., no. 784.
[2] A woman who was a man's equal; in the Renaissance, a term conveying only admiration.

as any jeweler. Very beautiful, but only short-sighted. To obtain pardons for her sons she married Sir Edmund Carey, cousin-german to Queen Elizabeth, but kept him to hard meat.[3]

Even courtesans occasionally managed to capture something of the intellectual glamor and high status the Renaissance Lady had attained outside her marriage. This was particularly true in Rome, where the glittering papal court was nearly devoid of married ladies. The courtesan Imperia was celebrated by a hundred poets and honored with burial in the chapel of San Gregoria. Tullia d'Aragona's salon was crowded with philosophers, courtiers, and cardinals, and no one laughed when she wrote a book praising Platonic love. Guglielmo, Duke of Mantua, was honored rather than embarrassed when Veronica Franco dedicated a book of verses to him.

These latter details are reminiscent of the hey-day of the hetaera in the Athens of Pericles. Yet except in the cities of Rome and Venice, the high-grade courtesan was not particularly important in the Renaissance, and neither was the homosexual lover. For although both of them could offer sexual satisfaction, when it came to the rich spiritual and emotional content that love had acquired they were simply no match for the Lady.

[3] John Aubrey: *Brief Lives,* p. 42.

4

The Minions of Satan

❀   ❀

❀

Meanwhile, another version of woman—the Witch—had simultaneously been taking clear and frightening shape in Western Europe. So novel and distinct was this phenomenon that churchmen and inquisitors concluded a new race of malefactors, not heretofore known, had appeared on earth. Prior to the fourteenth century, according to their studies, blighted crops, storms, diseased cattle, and deformed children had been the work principally of male sorcerers and devils; now, inexplicably, the Inquisitors found these and other forms of *maleficium* (evil-doing) being performed chiefly by women. At the same time it appeared to them that *maleficium* had become dominated by sexual matters. The most common deeds of witches were the stealing of semen from sleeping men, the causing of impotence, sterility, and miscarriages, and the afflicting of the private parts with diseases and deformities. This being so, nightmares, dreams of forbidden activities, sexual reveries, and waning powers all began to assume a new and more terrifying aspect; they were the work of Satan, carried out by his new hordes of female vassals.

All this was in sharp contrast to the earlier Church attitude. Even though Saint Augustine and other Church Fathers had written about the existence of succubi, or evil female spirits, the Church had long discouraged the belief that the average woman could voluntarily join the legions of the Devil and be granted magical powers. The Synod of Paderborn stated in 785 that such a belief was in itself a deception produced by the Devil, and set the death penalty for anyone who burned a woman on the grounds that she was a witch. Charlemagne confirmed this ordinance. Various councils and canons from the ninth to the thirteenth century commanded bishops to combat the popular belief in witchcraft, and stated that witches' night journeys and marvelous powers were pure illusion.

Then the change came. Beginning in the 1300's, the belief in witchcraft spread rather rapidly through the clergy, particularly in Germany, France, and the Lowlands, and news and reports of cases reached all ranks of society in Western Europe. A series of papal pronouncements and bulls starting in the early 1300's advised ecclesiastical courts on the activities of witches and urge their extermination. Theologians wrote impassioned appeals to the public, and preachers terrified their congregations with lectures on the dangers and symptoms of witchcraft. By 1400, civil courts began to recognize that actual copulation with the Devil was not only possible, but should be cause for capital punishment, since it constituted the ratification of the witch's pact with Satan. By 1450 it had become accepted dogma that witches could fly by night. Witch trials and burnings grew increasingly common even in the most civilized centers of Western Europe; Catholics and Lutherans, Inquisitors and humanists, accepted them as a normal facet of life, and those few who raised their voices against the mania were at once accused of being in league with the Devil himself.[4]

And is this dismal aspect of Renaissance life a part of the history of love? Alas, yes. Many centuries earlier, as we have seen, the separation of woman into two aspects was becoming a reality in the mind and life of Christian man. By the Middle Ages, his conflicting feelings about woman had finally caused him to decompose his notion of her into two clearly opposed halves—the all-good, tender, passionless goddess (the Virgin-Mother, and the Lady of the troubadours), and the evil-doing, seductive, lascivious sorceress (Eve, and all sinful or physically desirable women).

But why should this dichotomy have become intensified just as men's minds were turning toward worldliness, rationalism, and the rediscovery of joyousness? Why should the Witch have flourished in the same soil as the Renaissance Lady? The subject is extremely complex; let us be content merely to note a few suggestions. Courtly love, as we saw in the previous chapter, was somewhat of

[4] The change from the early Church attitude to the later one is documented in J. Hansen: *Zauberwahn, Inquisition und Hexenprozess im Mittlelalter;* Henry C. Lea: *History of the Inquisi-* *tion of the Middle Ages;* Ernest Jones: *On the Nightmare;* G. R. Taylor: *Sex in History;* Lynn Thorndike: *History of Magic and Experimental Science;* and others.

a disturbing force, running counter to feudal patriarchalism and Catholic ideology; it had already met opposition and occasionally found itself linked with heresy. But all this was before the real trouble arose. For it was the Renaissance, and the concomitant social, economic, and intellectual changes in European society, that seriously disturbed the equilibrium of the Church and upset the stability of the order it had long maintained. Sensing its own illness, the Church began to fight back without clearly knowing what was ailing it; it hazily saw all the new influences as one common enemy, and identified heresy, nationalism, humanism, and Renaissance love as one interconnected plot.

The two views of women became standards of the two sides in the impending conflict. Cultured courtiers saw women as ladies, the clergy and the poor still saw them as nuisances or worse; humanists were interested in love, theologians in sin. But economics and geography cut across these alignments: in Italy, where there was no doubt about the Pope's powers and control, witchcraft hysteria took hold for the most part only in a few Alpine valleys; in northern Europe, where economic development was making for dissatisfaction with Vatican control and the Pope's power was in danger, Inquisitors were inclined to see spooks and witches everywhere.

The most important document about the witches of northern Europe was written by two men who not only saw them, but interrogated, tortured, and burned them, and wrote down their findings for the good of mankind. The two were Jacob Sprenger and Henry Kramer, Dominican brothers and professors of sacred theology at the University of Cologne in the latter half of the fifteenth century. Both were Germans, but about their family backgrounds, personal appearance, or habits and tastes, we know nothing; we know only that for many years both of them were active Inquisitors in Germany (Sprenger was named to the task by Pope Sixtus IV in 1475, and Kramer was named later as his associate), and that they traveled widely in Germany, took part in many trials, and were unsparing of their own energies in pursuing their important work.

After some years, Sprenger and Kramer appealed to Pope Innocent VIII to help them overcome the opposition and reluctance of local clerics and princes to aid them in their efforts. In December 1484, Innocent issued a famous bull, *Summis Desiderantes Affectibus*. "It has indeed lately come to Our ears," began the Pope, "that in some parts of northern Germany . . . many persons of both sexes [5] . . . have abandoned themselves to devils, incubi, and succubi." Having done so, they have obtained magical powers, he said, by which they have been producing stillbirths, killing calves, destroying crops, causing disease, creating impotence, and doing other sundry acts of *maleficium*. The Pope said he was shocked that Inquisitors Sprenger and Kramer had not received co-operation from some lay people and clerics; indeed some of these people had even brazenly denied that witchcraft was being practiced within their provinces. His Holiness decreed that Sprenger and Kramer should proceed without let or hindrance, and that all persons in all towns and provinces of northern Germany should aid them.

Armed with the Bull, which gave a crucial stimulus to the witch-hunting movement, Sprenger and Kramer intensified their activities and their research, and reaped a rich harvest of burnings. Within three years they were able to produce a monumental study of witchcraft they called *Malleus Maleficarum* (*The Witches' Hammer*—i.e., a hammer to strike witches with). Officially endorsed by the University of Cologne and avidly studied throughout Western Europe, it was scarcely ever out of print for the next two centuries. It went through nineteen separate editions by the eighteenth century, inspired the publishing of scores of similar works in other languages, and influenced the direction and content of nightmares, neuroses, accusations, trials, and burnings for at least two hundred years.

From actual testimony of witnesses and confessed witches, Sprenger and Kramer had learned that, by means of their incantations and brews, evil-doing women could summon plagues of locusts to destroy a harvest or bring a hailstorm to ruin it, make men impotent or women frigid, induce abortions or dry up a mother's milk. They could see at a distance, fly at night, and leave a duplicate body behind to fool people; sometimes they could turn themselves into cats or other creatures; some of them turned men into animals and kept them at hard labor; and some kidnapped children, and roasted and ate them.

But the dominant concern of the *Malleus Maleficarum* was with the sexual problems caused by witches—principally infertility, impotence, nocturnal emissions or sexual dreams, painful coitus, nymphomania and satyriasis, and the like. Sprenger and Kramer were

[5] Sprenger and Kramer later corrected this impartiality by amassing evidence to show that the great bulk of acts of witchcraft was done by women.

such good reporters that despite their attribution of these and other ailments to supernatural causes, their descriptions often permit the modern doctor to make an unequivocal diagnosis of psychosexual disorder. A typical case is that of a woman with a phantom pregnancy which seemed real in every way, but was only the result, they said, of a quantity of wind in the bowel; modern doctors immediately recognize the ailment, but diagnose it as a form of conversion hysteria, probably due to an intense, frustrated desire to conceive, rather than a digestive disturbance. Also very likely of neurotic origin was such a case as that of the young man on whom an angry witch cast a "glamor" (a type of spell) which made it seem to him as though his penis had disappeared from his body; even the Inquisitors pointed out that it had not really come off, and that this was only an illusion she had created.

Impotence was a problem of deep concern to the Inquisitors, and they recorded some case histories with almost journalistic flair. A count living in the diocese of Strasburg had enjoyed an illicit relationship with a mistress, but broke it off in order to marry a young noblewoman. On the wedding night, he found himself completely impotent with his wife. This distressing condition continued unchanged for three years, until one day the Count happened to meet his old mistress as he was walking in the streets of Metz on business. For old times sake, he stopped to chat with her. She asked after his health; he smiled and lied, saying that it was fine. Seeming a bit surprised, she asked about his wife and then about his children; he said his wife was fine, and they already had three splendid children. Her perplexity and distress were obvious, and the Count asked: "Why, my dear, do you make such careful inquiries? I am sure that you congratulate me on my happiness." "Certainly I congratulate you," she said, "but curse that old woman who said she would bewitch your body so you could not have connection with your wife!" She told him in detail how she had paid to have a pot containing bewitched objects placed in his well. "But see," she concluded, "it is all in vain, and I am glad!" The Count hurried home, drained the well, and burned the contents of the pot, and according to Professors Sprenger and Kramer he immediately recovered his virility and consummated his marriage.

The Inquisitors explained at length why witchcraft was far more common among women than among men. Basically, woman is a weak, inferior creature; moreover, she is afflicted with insatiable carnal lust. This makes her easy prey to the advances of the Devil, who offers to satisfy her desires. "It is common to all [witches] to practice carnal copulation with devils," they stated; indeed, only after doing so with Satan himself, in person, did each witch gain her extraordinary powers.

The sexual union with Satan took place during the travesty of Christian Mass known as the Witches' Sabbath. The first report that such a ceremony existed was made in 1335 at a witch trial in Toulouse; prior to that, it was unheard of, but in the century after it, the Witches' Sabbath became a central feature of the trials. The details that gradually accumulated were so vivid and thorough that at least one recent scholar has maintained that in late medieval and Renaissance times, there must have been a widespread pagan religion whose adherents worshipped a horned deity, met in "covens" or clans, and practiced orgiastic rites. But in the opinion of several eminent psychiatrists who have intensively and independently studied the evidence, the descriptions of the Witches' Sabbath bear the unmistakable characteristics of abnormal sexual fantasies, which the celibate Inquisitors eagerly, even hungrily, seized upon and accepted as objectively real.[6]

Certainly, there was an ample cultural tradition on which, whether they realized it or not, both inquisitors and suspects could draw in piecing together their versions of the wicked celebration. In earlier medieval times, the inferior clergy in many European countries had practiced an annual New Year's revel called the Feast of Fools which was basically a vulgar burlesque, full of genial nose-thumbing at all moral and religious standards. Although various popes criticised its excesses, the Feast of Fools was allowed to continue because of its great popularity; both clergy and townspeople found in it a welcome temporary release of pent-up feelings and restrained emotions. In 1445, members of the Faculty of Theology at the University of Paris described it as follows:

> Priests and clerks may be seen wearing masks and monstrous visages at the hours of office. They dance in the choir dressed as women, panders, or minstrels. They sing wanton songs. They eat black puddings at the horn of the altar while the celebrant is saying Mass. They play at dice there. . . . Finally they drive about the town and its theatres in shabby traps and carts, and

[6] Ernest Jones: *On the Nightmare,* pp. 203–6, 210–12, 226; Gregory Zilboorg: *Medical Man and Witch during the Renaissance,* pp. 144–6; Walter Bromberg: *The Mind of Man,* p. 51.

rouse the laughter of their fellows and the bystanders in infamous performances with indecent gestures and verses scurrilous and unchaste.[7]

From such materials, it was easy for theologians and suspects alike to construct a picture of the Witches' Sabbath that became clearer with each passing decade.[8] In general, it would start with a summons blown on a trumpet that only witches could hear. They would gather at night, riding through the air to some remote glen or ruin. There the ceremony began with a long formal processional of witches, both male and female; at last the Devil appeared in a cloud of stinking smoke, and each witch paid him homage by kissing his buttocks or "filthy parts." A burlesque of Christian ritual followed, in which the most beautiful witch present was baptised in the Devil's urine while he made the sign of the Cross backwards with his left hand; then she lay prone while the host was prepared, her bare buttocks being the altar and the dough being composed of feces, menstrual blood, urine, and the like. After the entire coven completed the Black Mass by eating the host, the orgy began; during this part the Devil personally had connection with each witch in turn, while the rest continuously performed a lascivious dance.

The neurotic element of the Witches' Sabbath revelations is nowhere more obvious than in the frequent claims that sexual relations with the Devil, so eagerly sought by the witches, were at the same time horribly painful, a fantasy which, Dr. Ernest Jones has pointed out, is characteristic of many guilt-laden anxiety dreams. Hundreds of witnesses testified that witches howled in pain during the process and came away bleeding. Jeanette d'Abache, a thirteen-year-old girl, swore that the Devil's penis was covered with fish scales which wounded his partner with each movement. Other girls and women supplied different but equally frightening details.

Like these witnesses, the investigators saw things they unconsciously both wanted and feared to see. In examining a suspect, they would strip her naked and closely scrutinize her whole body

[7] The document is quoted in E. K. Chambers: *The Medieval Stage*, Vol. I, p. 294.

[8] The *Malleus Maleficarum* itself spent relatively little time on it, but fuller descriptions were given in such other Renaissance witch-studies as: J. Bodin: *De la Démomanie des Sorciers* (1593); P. de Lancre: *Tableau de l'Inconstance des Mauvais Anges et Dé-* mons (1612); James VI (King James I of England): *Daemonologie* (1597); etc. What follows is a synthesis of these and other Renaissance sources, as made by Jones, op. cit., Bromberg, op. cit., and M. Garcon and J. Vinchon: *The Devil*.

e Alexander VI, for instance, who followed Innocent VIII,
ughly admired the female of the species; he surrounded him-
ith them, had a twenty-year liaison with Vanozza de' Catanei
ore him four children, and in his aging years acquired a teen-
blonde mistress named Giulia Farnese. Nevertheless he felt no
unctions about writing new bulls on witch-hunting to add to
fect of Innocent's *Summis Desiderantes Affectibus*.

manists were supposedly liberated persons, relatively free
medieval superstitions. Pico della Mirandola, a precocious
who flared briefly across the philosophic sky during the
ficates of Innocent and Alexander, wrote and argued in favor
emperate, liberal, and emancipated religion made up of the
arts of all religions; but he also stated that he personally knew
riest who, for forty years, had been having relations with a
bus named Hermeline, and another who for thirty years had
demon mistress named Fiorina.

manists, furthermore, were generally fond of life, literature,
earned women, and Sir Thomas More, the outstanding English
nist in the early sixteenth century, had an appropriately warm
life, educated his daughters excellently, and envisioned in his
ia a communist state in which women might even be priests,
riests might marry. It is confusing, therefore, to learn that he
wrote deeply devotional works, wore a hair shirt under his
ing for a long time, and believed implicitly in the actuality of
craft. He loved his wife and daughters, but in a thoroughly
ashioned, patriarchal way. Sir William Roper called on him
one morning to propose he marry one or the other of More's
hters. More ushered Roper into the room where the girls were
asleep and whipped the covers off them; both lay on their
s, their smocks up under their armpits, but awoke and rolled
in a pretty confusion. "I have seen both sides," said Sir William,
ied; then he patted the older girl on the rump and announced:
u art mine." One must presume that since this method of mate
tion was Sir Thomas More's own idea, it seemed perfectly ade-
e to him.

rhaps no one included in his own person so many of the con-
ctions of the age as Henry VIII of England—scholar and
ot, lover and hater of women, enemy of the Pope and of
in Luther. Without reviewing Henry's well-known history
, we must still pause to note one or two aspects of his love life

for the Devil's mark. Finding none, th
body, particularly the genitals, with sh
poking repeatedly in the effort to locate
supposedly a telltale sign of a witch. G
they sought, but only after long and sati
not, incidentally, consider that such proc

Such was the spirit promulgated by th
its offspring. According to an officer
Paramo, writing in 1554, the Holy Offi
least thirty thousand witches in the pre
save for which the world would have b
had been sanctioned by popes who thems
and court ladies of Italy, but saw witches
ern Germany. So it was that the Renaissa
Urbino and the Witch at Cologne, and p
across Europe in the complex struggles of t

5

Crosscurrents and Con

❀ ❀

❀

At this point, one can construct a beautiful
to wit: the Lady was perfected by th
spirit and the Witch by the reactionary med
was the ideal of the aristocrats and the rich
seen by the clergy and the poor; the one w
liberals, the other as seen by defenders of th
simply too neat, too pat, too comfortable; it m
beings are not that logical and consistent.

which spell out the remarkable change of the era and the equally remarkable persistence of old ways of thought.

Literature has done little for Henry; few people remember that he was a wonderfully handsome golden-haired youth who excelled at tennis and jousting and adored the study of the classics. These graces disappeared in the later and more dramatic part of his life; the image that remains is that of a fat, irascible tyrant, immensely vain, repulsive of person, and coldly capable of beheading his friends (including More) and two of his six wives. Love, its frustrations, and its ailments, played a large part in the metamorphosis.

In 1509 the youthful Henry had married his late brother's widow, Catherine of Aragon. She was six years older than he, and only moderately attractive; but Henry took her as his Queen because he felt, first, a due regard for treaty obligations with Spain, and second, a sense of obedience to his dying father's wish. Gallantly, however, the young King wore his own wife's favors in the lists, linked their initials on his sleeve, and poetically proclaimed his devotion to her. For a few years, the marriage seemed to go along well enough, but it had been made primarily for state reasons and Catherine was unable to fulfil the most important state function of all: she could not produce a live son. Whether she could or not, he was not tied to her emotionally in any fashion that made him faithful, and after several years of marriage he began to dally with various mistresses for amusement. He found amusement and something more—a continuing illness, probably syphilis, that slowly ruined his body, sapped his potency, and helped bring about the shocking change in his character.

When he was thirty-six, Henry's eye was caught by the fresh charm and winning insouciance of Anne Boleyn, a lady of the court; for the first time, he was genuinely infatuated. As everyone knows, he belabored Pope Clement VII with demands for an annulment of his marriage to Catherine on canonical grounds; the Pope dawdled and temporized until Henry eventually broke all ties with Rome and became head of a nationalized English Church; and Henry got his divorce at last from compliant English clerics, and married Anne.

Was it all for love? Historians say that Henry had been thinking of an annulment long before the infatuation began in 1527, because of the clear political value of having a son to whom he could pass on the throne. But not any woman would do. Cardinal Wolsey had a French princess in mind for whom, he thought, the Pope might grant Henry an annulment; Henry wanted no one but Anne. Cardinal Campeggio, the papal legate who sat on the annulment proceedings with Wolsey in 1528, was astonished. "He sees nothing, he thinks of nothing but his Anne," he wrote to the Pope. "He cannot be without her for an hour, and it moves one to pity to see how the King's life, the stability and downfall of the whole country, hang upon this one question."

The point is that Henry VIII wanted love and wanted a son, and sought to have them in the same place; otherwise his need for a male heir and the Pope's obstinacy might not have made history. Even more remarkable is the fact that although Anne Boleyn slowly and judiciously parceled out her favors to the King, she could not withhold them long enough to insure marriage—and yet he married her. In one of Henry's early letters to her he speaks of "the pang of absence" and "the hope of your unchangeable affection." Because Anne, though not a virgin, skillfully held back, Henry was soon writing: "Assuring you that henceforward my heart shall be dedicated to you alone, with a strong desire that my body could be also thus dedicated." A while later he is saying: "I trust within a while to enjoy that which I have so long longed for. . . . I think it long since I kissed you." After nearly two years, toward the end of 1528, matters had come very slowly to the following state:

> Mine own sweetheart, this shall be to advertise you of the great ellingness[9] that I find here since your departing, for I ensure you, me thinketh the time longer since your departing now last than I was wont to do a whole fortnight. . . . Wishing myself (specially an evening) in my sweetheart's arms, whose pretty duckies I trust shortly to kiss; written with the hand of him that was, is, and shall be yours by his will,
>
> H.R.

Henry wrote only one more letter, though he did not marry Anne until January 1533; from this, and the fact that he and she had adjoining apartments in Greenwich, it seems fair to conclude that she had not been able to hold the line for six years. Yet the striking fact is that Henry, having bedded Anne, still wanted her to be his wife, and forced his quarrel with the Pope until the break was past mending and Anne was Queen. The example had immense force; marriage for love became a living issue in England, and since most men faced far smaller obstacles than Henry had surmounted, it seemed a not-impossible idea after all.

[9] Loneliness

But Henry was both kinds of Renaissance man, where woman was concerned. In less than three years of marriage, he wearied of Anne's temper and her incessant demands, and when she failed to produce a son, and his own declining sexual powers infuriated him, he began to re-evaluate his whole romance; it even seemed to him sometimes that he had been seduced into marriage by the dark machinations of witchcraft (after all, did Anne not have a rudimentary sixth finger on her left hand?). He might have chosen this charge as his avenue to freedom, but possibly because waning potency bred jealous thoughts he turned instead to suspicions of misconduct and obtained evidence of it, if a confession extracted by torture deserves that name.[10] Anne and five supposed lovers of hers lost their lives. Six years later Henry passed a law making it a felony to practice conjurations or sorcery, including any such acts as would "provoke a person to unlawful love." Perhaps that was his final opinion of the whole question.

---

[10] In addition to the tortured witness, a number of toadies swore to improbable evidence, saying what they knew Henry wanted to hear. Sixteen persons testified to Anne's incest with her brother, George Boleyn, swearing that they had all clearly and at the same time seen her "alluring him with her tongue in the said George's mouth and the said George's tongue in hers." (Indictment of May 15, 1536)

6

The Quarrel Shows Signs of a Reconciliation

❀   ❀

❀

In 1558 Anne Boleyn's daughter, Elizabeth, ascended the throne; the child of love triumphed after all. In Elizabeth—virago of viragoes, virgin and lover, humanist and autocrat, queen and woman —the Renaissance Lady had reached her ultimate exemplar. Yet even in her presence, Bishop John Aylmer could still sound the ancient theme of woman's dual nature—with his emphasis being on the evil side. "Women are of two sorts," he intoned from the pulpit one day, duly deferring to the omnipotent woman sitting before him. "Some of them are wiser, better learned, discreeter, and more constant than a number of men." Then he gathered his energies, filled his lungs, and thundered:

> But another and a worse sort of them, and the most part, are fond, foolish, wanton, flibbergibs, tatlers, triflers, wavering, witless, without council, feeble, careless, rash, proud, dainty, nice, tale-bearers, eavesdroppers, rumor-raisers, evil-tongued, worse-minded, and in every way doltified with the dregs of the Devil's dunghill.

Queen Elizabeth probably smiled at Bishop's Aylmer's fulminations, knowing them to be the saber-rattling of an obsolescent warrior. For although the "argument of women" reached its greatest volume in the sixteenth century, it seemed to mean less than it said. Woman's status was changing and people had to talk and think about it, but even as the quarrel waxed loudest, it lost some of its genuine virulence. In 1541, for instance, an all-inclusive anti-female diatribe

called *The Schoolhouse of Women* had been written by a hack journal-
ist named Edward Gosynhill. It drew several stinging profemale
replies of which the first, printed in 1542 and entitled *The Praise of
All Women*, was written by none other than Gosynhill himself.
Writing about women, pro or con, was in other words already less a
matter of conviction than of good business. In the 1560's a writer
named Pyrrye even published *The Praise and Dispraise of Women*,
trying to be sure of capturing the entire market. The tone of pamphlets on the subject remained intemperate,[11] but that was characteristic of all Elizabethan pamphleteering; actually, the ambivalence of men's feelings about women began, little by little, to be
somewhat of a pose and not so much of an agonizing reality. Evidently something was happening to the dualist view of women; a
process of fusion was beginning, and her two aspects were starting
tentatively to merge.

Occasional signs and hints of a fusion had appeared even earlier
in Italy. Pinturicchio painted Giulia Farnese, Pope Alexander's
mistress, on the walls of a Vatican chamber and surrounded her
with angels; Palma Vecchio painted a courtesan as Saint Barbara;
Filippo Lippi had his own mistress model for none other than the
Blessed Virgin. Was it blasphemy? Or did these men no longer find
it impossible to see both aspects in one and the same person? Pietro
Bembo, who had delivered the ultimate speech on Platonic love in
Castiglione's *The Courtier*, became papal secretary in Rome some
time after the Urbino conversations, and took to Roman ways;
when he was fifty, he acquired a mistress, Donna Morosina, a lady
of Venetian origin. Far from keeping his sexual functions separate
from his high concept of love, Bembo proceeded to develop a
tender attachment to her and had three sons by her. When she
died, the aging cleric wrote to a friend in terms quite remote from
his former brand of love talk:

> I have lost the dearest heart in the world, a heart which tenderly
> watched over my life, which loved it and sustained it neglectful
> of its own; a heart so much the master of itself, so disdainful of
> vain embellishments and adornments, of silk and gold, of jewels
> and treasures of price, that it was content with the single and
> (so she assured me) supreme joy of the love I bore it. This heart,
> moreover, had for vesture the softest, gracefulest, daintiest of

---

[11] A very successful 1615 pamphlet was typically entitled: *The Arraignment of Lewd, Idle, Froward and Unconstant Women*, and one of the replies was: *The Worming of a Mad Dog, or A Sop for Cerberus, the Gaoler of Hell.*

limbs; it had at its service pleasant features, and the sweetest, most graciously endowed form that I have ever met with in this country. I cannot forbear lamenting.

Bembo, being in orders, had been unable to marry the lady during their long friendship, but elsewhere Platonists were beginning to introduce even wedlock into their thinking. In a work on Platonic love first written in about 1540, an Italian writer named Alessandro Piccolomini stated: "Love is a reciprocity of soul and has a different end and obeys different laws from marriage. Hence one should not take the loved one to wife." By the time he rewrote his book twenty years later, he had changed his mind and argued that Platonic love is not a separate entity but a prelude and accompaniment to marriage, inspiring the highest feelings, creating the desire for the joining of lives and bodies, and sweetening and purifying the sex act. Perhaps Piccolomini had merely grown practical; more likely, he had sensed and given voice to a new direction in human relationships.

At the same time, there began to appear in anecdotal historical writings of the time various stories in which the romantic impulse culminated in marriage. In their raw form, lacking the transfiguring treatment given love stories by the dramatist, they are often tedious and pedestrian—but perfectly believable. In 1554, for instance, a handsome Florentine youth named Ludovico di Neri Capponi fell in love with a girl named Maddalena Vellori. Maddalena's stepfather, who had married her mother for her wealth, hastily tried to marry the girl to his own son, while at the very same time, the Medici Duke of Florence, Cosimo I, tried to appropriate the heiress for one of his own favorites. The imperiled Maddalena fled to a convent while her mother pleaded, plotted, and maneuvered to change the Duke's mind. After many routine incidents, Cosimo agreed to talk to each of the lovers separately. Each pleaded ardently for the right to marry where love called, and Maddalena, on her knees, swore she would rather die than marry anyone but Ludovico. Disturbed and confused, the Duke finally laid aside his seignorial privileges, dismissed the stepfather's suit, and gave the lovers their will. It is hardly a great narrative, but it is a clear sign of changing attitudes.[12]

Against this background, we can be somewhat more certain that romantic marriage, as sometimes portrayed in the imaginative literature of the era, had a counterpart in reality. Two famous examples

[12] G. E. Saltini: *Tragedie Medice e Domestiche, Narrate Sui Documenti*, pp. 8–31.

are worth mentioning—Spenser's *Faërie Queene*, Books III and IV
of which are an allegory of the defeat of courtly love and its re-
placement by romantic marriage; and Shakespeare's *Romeo and
Juliet*, which is essentially a tale of Renaissance love, with marriage
as its goal, frustrated by old-fashioned familial and political traditions.

Shakespeare, to be sure, took another stand on the husband-wife
relationship in *The Taming of the Shrew*, and Spenser's allegory is
muddy at best. But Spenser was less ambiguous elsewhere. One of
his shorter poetical pieces is an enraptured tribute to a young lady,
in which, like any good courtly lover, he praises her beauty, admires
her soul, and pants for the shelter of night:

> *Ah when will this long weary day have end,*
> *And lend me leave to come unto my love?*
> *How slowly do the hours their numbers spend?*
> *How slowly does sad Time his feathers move? . . .*
>
> *Now welcome night, thou night so long expected,*
> *That long day's labor does at last defray,*
> *And all my cares, which cruel love collected,*
> *Hast summed in one, and cancelled for aye:*
> *Spread thy broad wing over my love and me,*
> *That no man may us see.*

But totally unlike the courtly lover, he concludes with a prayer for
plentiful offspring—for the lady in question was Elizabeth Boyle,
his fiancée, and the poem ("Epithalamion") was a bridal hymn,
written before their wedding but published a year after it. The distance from Castiglione is immense, though less than a century has
passed; one can hardly visualize an ideal Italian courtier printing a
love song to his wife.

Not only were aristocrats and intellectuals beginning to think
about the allying of romance and marriage, but so was a much
larger group, soon to become important in history. The slowly
growing middle classes had long been envious of the romantic love
conduct of the nobility, but since the average bourgeois and his wife
could afford neither the time nor money for extramarital courtly
love affairs, they had traditionally frowned upon it and used Christian morals as the justification of their views. But romantic ideals
blended with marriage were something the middle class not only
could accept, but secretly hungered for. The prosaic domestic-
conduct books of the middle class therefore began to reveal signs of

a change from the mid-sixteenth century on. Writer after writer, for instance, discussed whether marriages should be arranged by the parents or by the personal inclination of the young people; even though many writers still held out for the former, it is obvious from the amount of talk that they were dealing with a perplexing situation and an unsettling new phenomenon. Roger Ascham, tutor to Elizabeth when she was a princess, observed it with alarm just prior to 1570:

> Our time is so far from that old discipline and obedience as now, not only young gentlemen, but even very young girls dare without all fear though not without open shame, where they list and how they list marry themselves in spite of father, mother, God, good order, and all.

The subject was hashed and rehashed endlessly, for it had become genuinely important. Shakespeare might please the ancient prejudices of men by having Petruchio tame Kate—yet in the very same play he held Kate's father up to ridicule for auctioning off Bianca to the highest bidder.

The middle class yearned to emulate the love-making manners of the courtiers, but always in a purified and moral context. In 1632, for instance, an unknown scribbler wrote a handbook of amorous conversations entitled *Cupid's School*, from which the uncouth could learn the refined manner of love-making, and at least in the preface the author managed to sound like a properly devilish fellow:

> He that thinks to win affection by telling a maid in plain terms that he loves her is much deceived, for when she hears you begin so plainly, she will start back from you, and think you to be some ignorant Corydon that know not Cupid's language; when on the contrary, he that can deliver his mind in amorous words doth seem to keep the keys of their maidenheads, of which he can take possession when he list.

But it was all only a bourgeois affectation of sin, without seriously sinful intention; each and every specimen dialogue in *Cupid's School* was directed specifically toward convincing maidens to yield to respectable matrimony.

More important still, the many books advising men on the proper control and management of wives were increasingly filled with statements to the effect that man and wife should not be tied to each other only as co-workers and begetters of offspring, but ought to experience with each other companionship, friendship, and the tender, intense, delights of passion just as lovers do. A work on marriage written in 1604, as typical as it is forgettable, stated the matter in limping verse:

> *Marriage is God's indenture which he draws*
> *'Twixt man and woman: 'tis life's obligation;*
> *It is love's pillar: this the chain of laws;*
> *'Tis the good evil, the bitter delectation.*
>
> *Wedlock's hell is when the husband throws*
> *His frowns, his brawls, his curses and his blows,*
> *On his wife's head: yet spends the amorous charms*
> *Of smiles and kisses in a strumpet's arms.*

And thus within the very century when lady-worship and witch-burning reached their greatest intensity, a partial rapprochement of the two attitudes became evident. The Renaissance enlightenment, with its pagan echoes, had made sex seem not so sinful and disgusting after all; men and women could therefore begin to associate it with love. But sex and love combined might have meant only adultery; instead, it began to imply, or at least infiltrate into, marriage. In addition to the reasons for this which we have already seen, there was one other of major importance—the changing nature of family life. In the Middle Ages, most noblemen and many merchants had regarded the family as a kind of depot at which one stopped occasionally to pick up fresh gear and to deposit one's seed. But in the Renaissance, aristocrats spent less time in petty skirmishings and more in cities and princely courts, while merchants were able to transact business by letter and bank draft, and could insure their goods with no need to defend them in person. In both cases, men spent more time in or near their homes, and the selection of a desirable and well-matched mate assumed new importance. A tiny clue tells much of the new emotional significance of marriage: late in the sixteenth century we find, for the first time, the suggestion that young married couples should live apart in a dwelling of their own.

All this may make one suppose that something like modern marriage was beginning to appear by the year 1600. Like it, but not *very* like it. Although the status of the wife as a human being and love object was rising, her status as a legal person remained little better than in the Middle Ages. Her identity was submerged in that of her husband when she married him; he had the right to make all contracts for her, to bring suit or to plead, and to run her affairs in every way. The law's position was summed up in the apothegm: "Husband and wife are one, and the husband is the one." Wife-beating was still a husband's legal right, against which the wife had no redress, according to an English legal manual for women published in 1632. Some lawyers maintained otherwise, but the domestic-conduct books and pulpit orations so continually criticized wife-beating that it must have been common.

Even more important, along with her growing value as a companion and a love partner, the wife was still thought of as an economic acquisition—not only a worker and manager, but one who brought property with her. In England, in the sixteenth and seventeenth centuries, a woman's personal belongings (money, furniture, linens, and the like) still became the *absolute* property of the husband at marriage, and he did not have to pass them on to her designated heirs. As for dowry, though that did pass to her heirs, the husband used and enjoyed it during her lifetime; if she died first, he could continue to use her land until his own death. The law in other Western countries, though varying in details, was generally similar.

The romantic value of a bride did not mix any too well with her cash value, though Renaissance men made continuous efforts to blend the two. In the legal manual for women just cited, the anonymous seventeenth-century author quaintly opined that the dowry "is the condiments of love. . . . Good meats are the better for sauce; venison craveth wine, and wedlock hath certain condiments, which come best in season at the wooing time." But as long as a man thought of his wife as a bringer of dowry and a preserver of his wealth, the generous ardor of the lover was apt to be held in check by the critical scrutiny of the economist. Even so romantic a figure as Sir Walter Raleigh, a good lover and later a good husband, urged his son to love his wife—and to put limits upon that love:

> Have therefore ever more care that thou be beloved of thy wife rather than thyself besotted on her; and thou shalt judge of her love by these two observations: first, if thou perceive she have a care of thy estate, and exercise herself therein; the other, if she study to please thee, and be sweet to thee in conversation without thy instruction, for love needs no teaching.

Yet having duly noted all this, we can still agree that between the early and the later phases of the Renaissance, a notable change had begun to show itself. As the power of medieval repressions abated, men began hesitantly to see women as complex creatures who united within themselves both good and bad attributes. If a real woman was somewhat less divine than the Lady, she was also considerably less vile than the Witch. Men could begin to feel the emotions of affectional love where they also felt animal heat, and to envision in the ideal wife the qualities that produced both.

7

"A Wise Man and Lusty" Marries a Courtesan

❀　　❀

❀

Just how far things had gone in the direction of uniting the sundered aspects of love by the early seventeenth century can best be seen in the form of a famous (and, in its own time, infamous) love affair of the period. Sir Kenelm Digby, the hero of the piece, was born in 1603. The son of a conspirator executed for his part in the Gunpowder Plot of 1605, he grew up despite the stain to be a splendid specimen of the cavalier—handsome, swashbuckling, and learned; a poet, a fashion plate, and a philosopher; a man as willing to brawl for honor's sake as to spend long nights at chemical experiments. In his youth, Digby met and was infatuated by Venetia Stanley, a girl of adequate, though unimportant, family. When his intentions toward her became too serious, he was shipped off to Europe. Digby himself later wrote that his affair with her was broken off because of old disagreements between his family and hers, and that he went to the Continent to forget his woes; it seems more likely, from other historical evidence, that Venetia was already known to have been seduced by one or two wealthy noblemen, and that Digby's mother sent him away to break up the unfortunate attachment.[13] In Europe he heard that she had moved to London and become the mistress of several important men; he suffered, hated her, and sought to forget.

He returned to London three years later in 1623 and almost at once saw her by accident, riding past in her carriage, elegant, utterly lovely with her oval face, delicate coloring, and rich dark hair, and yet strangely sad of countenance. Overcome and softened by the sight, he called upon her and paid his respects. It was a highly successful reunion; each greeted the other with quivering politeness, and their warmth rapidly grew as they told each other of the events of the intervening years. When Digby hesitantly mentioned the ugly rumors he had heard, Venetia was able to explain them all away and made him thoroughly happy by convincing him of her virtue, or so he says; the subject is somewhat confused, since he concluded that first reunion by making an all-out attempt to seduce her. Venetia wisely repelled him and he fell more in love than ever.

Nevertheless his friends and his mother soon told him that Venetia was generally thought to be the favorite of the Earl of Dorset and to have had one or two children by him; she was also said to entertain and receive support from several other noblemen. In Digby's mind all was bewilderment. Considering himself to be hopelessly in love, he tried to believe in her purity, but somewhat inconsistently he bribed the servants to let him into her house one morning while she was asleep and crawled into her bed stark naked. The excellent Venetia awoke and drove him away with maidenly indignation; Digby's love thereupon became boundless, and despite the strong opposition of his friends and his mother, he determined to marry her.[14]

That, at least, is what he wrote; actually, he must have known that the rumors were based on fact. Perhaps it made no difference to him; he is said to have remarked on various occasions: "A wise man, and lusty, can make an honest woman out of a brothel-house." Pos-

[13] Digby wrote an autobiography which he called *Loose Fantasies*, first published in 1827 as *Private Memoirs of Sir Kenelm Digby*. In it he used pseudonyms for all persons, and altered some of the facts so as to put the best complexion on the affair. Other sources of information, however, have enabled literary historians to identify the principals, and to spot the improvements on truth; see Notes.

[14] This and certain other incidents were expurgated from the 1827 edition, but were published in 1932 in E. W. Bligh's *Sir Kenelm Digby and his Venetia*, pp. 285–300.

sibly he was also fortified by financial considerations; shortly before
he decided Venetia was good enough to marry, she had put up her
jewels as security and made him a very considerable loan. Later in
the century John Aubrey, the writer of brief biographies, recorded
a story that the Earl of Dorset, who had settled £500 per annum
on Venetia, cut it off when Digby married her and that Digby
promptly sued him for it. In actual fact, Dorset died before the wedding; probably what happened was that he earlier cut off some sti-
pend when he saw Digby replacing him, and Digby pestered him
about it. It would seem highly likely that Digby knew exactly what
Venetia was, and that his friends knew he knew. Perhaps the final
clue is a statement of Digby's, in his autobiography, that a woman's
honor does not consist in chastity alone, and that in some cases it is
justifiable for a man to consent to his wife's pollution.

In any case, Sir Kenelm married Venetia in 1625, and from then
on no scandal attached to their name or way of life; she bore him
three sons and a daughter, conducted herself as an admirable wife,
and there is reason to think they were well satisfied with each other.
Such notables as Ben Jonson and Thomas Carew were frequent visitors at their home, and Jonson paid tribute to her sterling qualities in
verse. After eight years of marriage, she died of a sudden illness.
Digby was nearly unhinged by grief; he immersed himself for a time
in chemical studies at Gresham College in London, and what with
his long mourning cloak, untidy beard, and piercing eyes, assumed
the look of a latter-day alchemist. He eventually recovered from his
depression, but remained an eccentric the rest of his life, dabbling in
politics, conniving with Cromwell (although a Catholic) during the
Civil War, playing at chemistry, and writing several inconsequen-
tial books.

The love story of Sir Kenelm Digby and Venetia Stanley is a curious one, blurred by the distortions in his autobiography and somewhat self-consciously modeled upon patterns of fiction and drama.
Yet its basic outlines are clear enough. If the affair hardly represents
the usual or the ideal concept of love and marriage in the early seventeenth century in England—for few men were able to fuse the
Lady and the Witch to such an extent as Digby—it is nevertheless a
valuable bench mark: it was no fiction, but a real love affair, with a
not very pure woman, that led to a happy marriage. Much talked
about in its own time, it would have seemed impossible and even unthinkable only a century or two earlier.

Chapter VII
THE IMPURITANS

I

Puritanism Revisited

❊   ❊

❊

The Puritans, as everyone knows, were against love; indeed, the very word Puritanism has long been used as a synonym for disapproval of sexual passions, of sensuous enjoyment, and of all but the most circumspect emotions of love. Let us eavesdrop across the centuries for a moment, and hear how these formidable and depressing people spoke.

It is a rainy Sunday in London, in the spring of 1620; we take our seats, in imagination, in the church at Rotherhithe to hear the eminent Puritan preacher Thomas Gataker. His sermon today is upon marriage; at the moment he is discussing marriage-by-arrangement versus marriage-for-love. We listen, and wonder if we have got into the wrong church or the wrong century, for this pious sober-sides is saying things that are sentimental and even romantic—and linking them to heaven:

> As there is no affection more forcible [than love], so there is none freer from force and compulsion. The very offer of enforcement turneth it oft into hatred. . . . Things fall out many times so unexpectedly, such strong liking taken to some [one] suddenly not once thought on before, and such strange alienation of affections where there hath been much laboring to link them . . . that even a natural man's dim eye may easily see and discern a more special providence of God oft carrying things in these cases.

The words have a Puritan seasoning but their substance is almost neo-pagan, for it was a Greek conceit that love was a gift—or curse —given by the gods, holding mortals helpless in its power. What has this to do with Puritanism? Let us leave the church and look further.

[217]

We move on, and stop at a bookstall in St. Paul's Churchyard, in
the year 1642. London is noisy and bustling as usual, but not far outside it armies are fighting; the opposition between King Charles
and Parliament, between the aristocratic way of life and the middle
class, has finally come to bloodshed. Love, though not the crucial issue, is at stake too; the fashionable Neoplatonism, the love literature,
and the amours of the courtiers are all abominable to the Round-
heads, who have vowed to uproot them from English life. The Puritans, it is clear, are the enemies of love. We pick up a brand-new
book called *Matrimonial Honor* by Daniel Rogers, the son of a notable Puritan preacher and himself one of the same, and flip through
it; we find not one, not a dozen, but two hundred rhapsodical pages
on love. A typical sentence strikes the eye:

> Husbands and wives should be as two sweet friends, bred under
> one constellation, tempered by an influence from heaven, whereof
> neither can give any great reason save that mercy and providence
> first made them so, and then made their match.

All very well, but what does Pastor Rogers think of the physical
side of love? Is it a disgusting necessity, a shameful weakness of the
flesh? We turn the pages, and find the answer; here is a passage in
which he says that "marriage love" is "a sweet compound" of spiritual affection and carnal attraction, and that this blend of the two is
the "vital spirit and heart blood" of wedlock. Can this really be a
Puritan speaking?

Thoughtfully replacing the book, we decide to search for the
real, undiluted Puritans, and whisk ourselves across the Atlantic to
the colony of Massachusetts in the 1670's. Surely in this harsh, grim-
faced theocracy, the desires of the flesh have been put in their proper
place; at the very least, those weak mortals who yield to pleasure
must suffer the inner hellfire of guilt and remorse for their sins. In
a small comfortless courtroom, the Justices of the Middlesex Court
are seated in hearing on a bastardy case, and a clerk is about to read
aloud a letter that had been written by the unwed mother. Let us
steal in and listen:

> Dear Love, I remember my love to you, hoping your welfare,
> and I hope to embrace thee, but now I write to you to let you
> know that I am [with] a child by you, and I will either kill it or
> lay it to another and you shall have no blame at all, for I have had
> many children and none [of their fathers] have [to support] none
> of them.

In some confusion, we seek reassurance in a visit to that bulwark of probity, good, gray Judge Samuel Sewall, who nearly thirty years ago sat on the trial of the Salem witches, and whose record of devoted service to the Puritan ideal is unsurpassed. We hurry to him on an October evening in 1720, unmindful of the fact that Judge Sewall, now a widower, is paying a social call upon Widow Winthrop. We approach the drawing room, but pause in alarm; the Judge is acting more like a Cavalier than a Roundhead. Having stolen a kiss a few nights ago, he is getting still bolder tonight; at the moment he is holding Mrs. Winthrop's hand and saying: "Will you acquit me of rudeness, Madam, if I draw off your glove?" The lady archly asks why he need draw it off, and he replies in handsome, if rather homespun, fashion: " 'Tis great odds, Madam, between handling a dead goat and a living lady." The widow tries to blush, the glove comes off, and we depart hurriedly to return to our own times and reconsider our notions about the Puritans.[1]

2

The Anti-Augustinian

❀   ❀

❀

Protestants like to think of the Reformation as a progressive outgrowth and enlargement of the Renaissance; Catholics prefer to think of it as a reactionary repudiation of the Renaissance and a retrogression from it. In order for us to see the Puritans whole, we

[1] The several quotations in this section come, respectively, from: Thomas Gataker: *A Good Wife God's Gift— A Marriage Sermon;* Daniel Rogers: *Matrimonial Honor* (1642), pp. 200 and 151; a letter in the files of the Middlesex Court, quoted in *The New England Quarterly*, Dec. 1942, p. 602; and Samuel Sewall: *Diary*, Oct. 11, 1720 (Vol. III, p. 267).

must first agree to an awkward assumption: namely, that the Reformation was both things. Historians may simplify, but history itself is always complex.

The Renaissance, for instance, had unfolded and blossomed in the good earth of increased trade and accumulating wealth, yet the Catholic Church, so closely identified with it and so prone to adopt its luxuries, still taught Aquinas's view that pursuing money beyond one's bare needs was "sinful covetousness," and continued to treat business as a somewhat shameful activity. The Reformation, which likewise flourished in that same soil, praised financial effort, removed the stigma from the charging of interest, and regarded business success as a sign of God's special blessing—yet the Protestants disapproved of the very luxuries that their new wealth could buy them. The Renaissance revival of learning weakened the hold of medieval theology on men's minds, but although the Reformation was indebted to this, in its revolution against Rome it rejected much of the enlightened thinking of the time, immersed itself once more in theology, and temporarily disrupted university education. The Reformation broke up the antiquated feudal systems of economics, politics, and religion, but in the process also destroyed much of the beauty, the joy of living, and the rationalism that had lately come into Western life.

The Protestants' feelings about sex and love were similarly complicated and contradictory. They devalued celibacy, praised marriage without qualification, and argued that marital sex was wholesome and free of taint; nevertheless they continued to examine, condemn, and execute witches very much as the inquisitors had, often exhibiting in these activities the same morbid sexual fantasies. In 1597, after eighty years of liberalizing Reformation influence, the Protestant King of Scotland, James VI, could still personally inform his subjects and the world at large that the Devil, in order to leave his mark on witches, "doth lick them with his tongue in some privy part of their body," and a century later in Salem, Massachusetts, a jury of Puritan women would still eagerly jab pins into the genitals of one Bridget Bishop, ostensibly by way of searching for a telltale dead spot or Devil's mark.

No man was a more bewildering mixture of the liberal and the reactionary than the first reformer, Dr. Martin Luther himself. Often he spoke like one who had come to liberate the body altogether from guilt-induced asceticism: "If our Lord God may make excellent large pike and good Rhenish wine," he said, "I may very well venture to eat and drink. Thou mayest enjoy every pleasure in the world that is not sinful." He lustily and vigorously battled against the Catholic tradition of asceticism, and specifically prescribed small doses of deliberate enjoyment as the best antidote for temptation:

> Satan has so spoiled and besmirched our nature that we don't want to let ourselves be comforted. Therefore, whoever feels such devilish thoughts and is tempted by them, I advise to drive them out quickly—think of something merry, take a good drink, play, and amuse yourself.

Yet Luther often spoke like a monk of the despairing early Christian centuries. "We are the children of wrath," he maintained, "and all our works, intentions, and thoughts are nothing at all in the balance against our sins." "Works"—including gifts to the Church—could not buy one's way out; faith alone could save, but God allowed few that salvation and most would burn for their sins. God, said Luther, "seems to delight in the tortures of the wretched." [2]

In the course of his long fight against the Catholic Church, Luther often found himself confronted by the Devil in person, and many times argued violently with him and fought against his subtle temptations. As improbable as it seems, however, those struggles were marked less by weeping and suffering than by a mood of healthful exertion and an exuberant appetite for vulgarity. Everyone knows that Luther once flung an inkhorn at the Devil, but it is more indicative of his peasantlike sense of humor that he specifically advised throwing a handful of dung in the Devil's face, or breaking wind at him, or even saying to him, as Luther himself once did: "Lick my ass!" (On that particular occasion, Luther noted with gratification: "He said no more. A good way of getting rid of him!")

Luther found in sex an ideal weapon in his war against Rome. He early sanctioned the marriage of priests and hotly argued that celibacy had been invented by the Devil as a source of sin; after a while he advanced to the radical view that marriage was not a sacrament at all, but a civil matter, subject to city and state regulations rather

---

[2] In contrast, Friar Johann Tetzel, whose peddling of papal indulgences angered Luther into posting his ninety-five theses on the church door, had an almost jolly view of sin, and is said to have offered to relieve sinners of their burdens with the following cheerful formula:
As soon as cash in the coffer rings,
The soul from purgatory's fire springs.

than to canon law; and still later in life (1532) he held that Christ had probably committed adultery with Mary Magdalene and other women so as to partake fully of the nature of man.[3]

But to arrive at such a point of view had been no easy matter for him. The son of a stern German peasant who became a miner, Luther was brought up under harsh Teutonic discipline. Both parents beat him mercilessly for small boyish errors, gave him a vivid sense of his own wickedness, and filled his head with medieval notions of demons, witches, and miracles. When he went away to school, a natural zestfulness asserted itself, and he sang, played the lute, and learned to love good company. But he had not resolved his inner conflicts, and during a thunderstorm one day in 1505 when he was a twenty-two-year-old law student, he was struck with terror at the thought of death and decided he had received a warning from God; he abandoned the study of law forthwith and entered the Augustinian Eremite cloister in Erfurt. There he fasted, prayed, and so strictly observed the ascetic regime of his order that he very nearly killed himself. After a while, he learned to moderate his austerities, became a priest and an instructor in the Augustinian monastery at Wittenberg, and slowly attained a degree of clerical stature. In October 1517, when he challenged anyone to debate his ninety-five theses on the nature of sin, contrition, forgiveness, and the inefficacy of bought indulgences, he still considered himself a devout Catholic and completely loyal to the Pope. Carried away by forces beyond his imagining, within the next several years Luther was inevitably led into open defiance of the Pope's direct orders, was excommunicated and branded heretic, stood before Emperor Charles V and the Diet at Worms and defended his position, and saw the Reformation he had touched off sweep across Northern Europe like a grass fire.

Under the immense pressure of these events, Luther came to defend (somewhat reluctantly at first) the breaking of monastic vows and the marriages of priests, and in 1521 he wrote that the sexual impulse was both natural and irrepressible. Yet not until another four years had passed did he himself marry, and even then the event was produced neither by romance nor by urgent desire. In 1525, Luther, then forty-two, recommended to a group of nuns that they leave their convent and helped them find husbands. Katharina von Bora, a woman of twenty-six, was the last of the lot; Luther tried

---

[3] This last startling statement appears in Luther's *Table-Talk* (*Tischreden* 1472, Weimar ed.).

to pair her off, but the proposal fell through and she was forced to go to work as a domestic. Meanwhile the Peasants' War was raging, threatening the entire Reformation. It occurred to Luther that the war was the Devil's attack on him, and to spite the Devil—and only incidentally to solve Katharina's problem—he married her.

Enthusiasts have sometimes said that Luther was carried away by her beauty, but her portrait belies the story. She was buxom, strongly made, and distinctly lumpish of feature—no Iseult, nor even an avant-garde Anne Boleyn. By no means in love when he married, Luther was soon plagued with misgivings and feared that his marriage had cost him the respect of some of his followers; then, happily, he saw that this was only more of Satan's work, and accepted his marriage cheerfully. After a year he wrote to a friend: "My Käte . . . is well and, by God's grace, is submissive to me, obedient in all things, and more agreeable than I had dared to hope." Not only was she agreeable, but productive, useful, and efficient; she ran the farm, bore Luther six children, fed and housed all of them plus eleven of his nieces and nephews (luckily, their home was the many-roomed former Augustinian monastery at Wittenberg, by then emptied of monks), and did all this on the modest salary paid Luther by the Elector Frederick of Saxony.

As the years passed, Luther saw his wife in many lights—and always with blithe inconsistency. After half a dozen years of marriage, he once said in an expansive mood: "My wife is more precious to me than the Kingdom of France and all the treasures of Venice," but the following year he sourly grumbled: "Get you a wife and then your mind, however fuzzy it is, will become straight as a ribbon; it will be reduced to one idea: Do and think as *she* wishes." Like a mooning young swain, he could say: "I love my Käte, and know that I love her more than she loves me," and like a henpecked husband, he could say: "If I were to marry again I would carve myself an obedient wife out of stone, for to find one of flesh and blood is not conceivable."

Luther evidently found the sexual side of marriage satisfactory, for having experienced it he continued to argue that sexual love was as natural and necessary as eating; he retained the medieval notion that it was somehow sinful, but felt that within marriage "God covers the sin," leaving the act untainted. But if he had no qualms about married sex, he was hardly ecstatic. "Had God consulted me about it," he said in one of his many dinner-table pronunciamentos,

"I should have advised Him to continue the generation of the species by fashioning human beings out of clay, as Adam was made."

Luther loved his Käte, but he had very firm old-fashioned ideas about woman's role in life. Every woman, he said, should—like Käte—be a good housewife and mother. "Take women from their housewifery and they are good for nothing," he remarked, ignoring the evidence of the Renaissance ladies even then shining in all their glory in Italy, though not in Wittenberg. Woman's proper sphere was the bearing of children and the providing of household comforts to her husband, to whom she should be meekly obedient; a husband was a fool who, because of love, let her rule the household, but he should be gentle and considerate, recognizing that she was but a frail vessel. This consciously biblical attitude fitted Luther's theological position; even more to the point, it was ideally suited to the habits and needs of the very class to which Protestantism appealed for other reasons.

Through Luther's personal life and public actions, most of the major attitudes of the Reformation toward women and love were clearly, if contradictorily, established. Little remained of the Renaissance idealization of woman or of exaggerated and gallant courting. Not only was the average Protestant a more practical and businesslike person, inclined to prefer Old Testament patriarchalism, but he regarded the elegant courtier's religion of beauty with suspicion and fear as something typically Roman. But as for sexual frigidity, repression of sensuous enjoyments, or the prudish avoidance of biological facts, these had been no part of Luther's make-up and were not inherent in Protestantism. They appeared, rather, only among the extremist factions of those who followed him.

3

The Bluenoses

❁   ❁

❁

If Luther was inherently genial but chronically inconsistent, John Calvin, a young Frenchman he inspired, was inherently dour, and chronically consistent. Calvin wrote his epochal work, the *Institutes of the Christian Religion*, when he was only twenty-six, and never changed his mind on any salient point; in it, he rigorously drew together all the most severe elements of the Old Testament, the patristic writings, and Lutheranism, and derived from them by selection and extension a ferocious theology built upon total human depravity, the implacable wrath of God with man, and the concepts of absolute predestination, the election of the very few, and the certain damnation of all the rest.

Had Calvin been a happier or healthier man, Puritanism might never have been puritanical, and the thinking of the Genevans, the Dutch, the Scotch, the English, and the Americans ever since might have been different. Historians reassure us that it is not so, and that larger forces were responsible for the rise of Calvinism: his democratic, primitive church structure appealed even more to the bourgeoisie than Lutheranism, which was controlled by princelings; his disapproval of frivolity and luxury was ideally suited to the temperament of those whose aim was to work and accumulate; and so on. Yet it may be that trivial forces also have mighty effects. Unlike Luther, Calvin did not enjoy playing the lute or flute, eating broiled fish, or downing a flagon of beer; unlike Luther, he was small and thin, dyspeptic and ailing, intense and unhumorous. Conceivably, the ascetic and repressive features that mark Puritanism at its unloveliest and have given it a bad name owe as much to one man's glandular shortcomings as to the social goals of the bourgeoisie.

Calvin was born at Noyon, in Picardy, in 1509. His father, a law-yer, wanted the boy to be learned, and from the first Calvin proved an excellent student. For unknown reasons (possibly because he grew up under a harsh stepmother), he was so censorious and mor-alistic even in his boyhood—and so excellent at Latin—that fellow students called him "the accusative case." He studied law and the classics as earnestly as though seeking his salvation, poring over his books until midnight and arising with the dawn to begin again. Headaches, indigestion, and fits of anger plagued him, but he would not slacken his efforts. Later on he added to these ailments ulcers, stones, and pulmonary tuberculosis; it is little wonder he could con-sider life of no value and God a pitiless tyrant.

In 1532, when Calvin was a budding humanist scholar of twenty-three, he happened to read some of the sermons of that bold ex-monk Martin Luther and underwent a conversion. Almost at once he saw his destiny and, mustering all his learning and his legal train-ing, began to write his epochal study of the original nature of the Christian Church and the Catholic additions to it; the result, the *In-stitutes*, was a blueprint for a neo-biblical, primitive Christian life. A year after it was published, Calvin became an evangelizing Protes-tant preacher in the city of Geneva, and there, already famous at twenty-seven, he began to play a role in the affairs of that city which eventually made him its virtual dictator. In its developed form, the government of Geneva became a model theocracy: the Council (civil government) chose a Consistory or Presbytery (reli-gious government) of five pastors and twelve elders, which was given dictatorial powers over the religious observances and morality of every citizen. Calvin, as head of the Consistory, was thus, in ef-fect, a complete dictator of morals, and his views on sex, love, and other pleasures became the code by which Genevans lived for the next century.

The most depressing features of that code are familiar to every-one who has read any history. It was punishable by fine or imprison-ment to sing, to dance at weddings, to curse, to serve too many dishes at dinner, or to wear clothes of too extravagant a cut. Plays were banned, jewelry and other adornments discouraged, and ele-gant hair-styles made grounds for jailing.[4] Sexual transgressions,

---

[4] Probably echoing Luther, Calvin had written: "We are nowhere forbid-den to laugh, or to be satisfied with food . . . or to be delighted with mu-sic, or to drink wine." (*Institutes*, III, xix, 9) Nevertheless, in one two-year period, 414 people were prosecuted for crimes such as singing or wearing ex-

however, were something else again—they merited as severe punishments as heresy: fornication was cause for exile, and adultery deserved death, sometimes by drowning, sometimes by beheading. Some sinful Genevans actually met such fates, although many sexual offenders were let off with steep fines and jail sentences. Even legitimate love was astringently regulated. Engagements were limited to six weeks' duration, for one did not dally or play at romance, but got down to cases. Having done so, if either the bride or groom arrived late for the wedding, they were to be sent away again; there would be no nonsense in Geneva. As for the wedding itself, it would be grave, correct, and simple; the law expressly forbade revelry, minstrelsy, dancing, or the use of tambourines.

What kind of person could cram such regulations down the throats of ordinary human beings by the force of his personality and his arguments? His portrait shows a middle-aged man with a thin intent face, domed forehead, and penetrating eyes. We can read into it genius, tremendous drive, a terrible persuasiveness, but we cannot easily imagine his personal feelings. Unlike Saint Augustine he left no intimate record of his inner torments and sufferings over sex and love; the scanty details given by his contemporaries leave room for many interpretations.

Calvin had been a bachelor, and almost certainly celibate, until the age of thirty-one; he left no word as to whether he suffered temptations and lusts in all this period of youth, and perhaps in itself that is a valuable clue. During a brief period of exile from Geneva (1538–41), he lived in Strasbourg, was minister to a small church, and took in boarders. Finding this burdensome, he asked friends to find him a wife, and provided us with one clue to his nature when he specified: "I am none of those insane lovers who, when once smitten with the fine figure of a woman, embrace also her faults. This only is the beauty which allures me, if she be chaste, obliging, not fastidious, economical, patient, and careful for my health." A poor widow named Idelette de Bure filled this bill of particulars, and he married her in 1540. She served him faithfully until her death nine years later; Calvin wrote kindly words about her after she was gone, but remained a widower thereafter.

Some light is shed, too, by his official statements on married love. Like the Catholics before him, Calvin spoke of marriage as having

travagant clothing. Calvin said, however, that he wanted his people to be happy, and encouraged them to play quoits.

two main functions: the production of offspring and the remedying
of incontinence. Like the most antifeminist of the early Fathers of
the Church, he had nothing to say about its involving companionship, affection, passion, or adoration. He condoned married sex, and
in fact insisted on it (in Geneva a woman could sue for divorce if
her husband became impotent); but he was obsessed by the subject
of adultery and defined it so broadly as to include even immodest
gestures or words. Both attitudes, it would seem, could logically
grow out of the same conception of sexual love as a purely animal
activity.

Like many another reformer before him, this first Puritan was
quite sure that his actions would make people good; like others before him, he overestimated their wish to be good. Although various
visitors remarked that Geneva was orderly, decent, and sober, the
records of the Council show that beneath the surface of that rigidly
conformist life, much was going on: how else can one explain the
numerous entries relating to illegitimate children, abandoned infants,
forced marriages, and death sentences? (Ironically, even a stepdaughter and a son-in-law of Calvin himself were condemned for
adultery.) He must have known of these shortcomings; to some extent he comforted himself and his followers with the thought that
almighty God had sent syphilis to earth to punish those who escaped
the law.

Few men are of so stern and severe a character, but surprisingly
enough Calvin's ideas and practices took hold in a number of countries of northern Europe; in each, the more extreme and dogmatic
leaders of Calvinist thought were responsible for giving Puritanism
a name for intolerance, hard-working asceticism, and lovelessness.
If most Puritans and Puritan life in general were quite unlike the
ideal of Calvinism, it is nevertheless true that many of the vocal and
identifiable Puritans did sound almost inhumanly joyless to the Renaissance peoples all around them.

In England, from whence American Puritanism sprang, the movement was at first diffuse and moderate in character. In part it consisted of extreme Calvinists inspired by John Knox, who had made
Scotland over along more or less Genevan lines by the 1560's; in
part it consisted of a variety of Englishmen still within the conservative official Church of England who disagreed with certain forms
and ceremonies reminiscent of Catholicism, and wished to "purify"
it of them. (As one witty preacher later said about the Church of

England: "King Henry the Eight brake the Pope's neck, but bruised not the least finger of Popery.") But the Puritan label rapidly acquired a Calvinist flavor and became a term of opprobrium. "I find many that are called Puritans," noted Owen Feltham several decades later, "yet few or none that will own the name. Whereof the reason sure is this, that 'tis for the most part held a name of infamy."

The English Puritans grew increasingly Calvinistic and severe as the cleavage widened between the aristocracy and the middle class, between the Renaissance tradition and the Reformation zeal. All during Elizabeth's reign and the Shakespearean era, Puritan critics of the stage, the court, and upper-class life were growing ever more outspoken. Elizabeth's successor, James I, thought to quiet the Puritans by persecuting them, but only drew them together; in a still worse blunder, he drove some of them to emigrate to New England beginning in 1620 and thus made them the inheritors of the New World. In the reign of Charles I the schism in English life continued to widen; the King and Parliament were locked in a struggle over the King's rights of taxation and certain other powers, with the Puritan elements aligning themselves against the royal party. The Anglicans at court so loved ritual and pageant as to seem practically Catholic to their opponents in Parliament; coincidentally, the growing licentiousness and dissoluteness of the courtiers, who affected Neoplatonic words but practiced wantonness, gave the extremists among the Puritans an excellent target.

In the autumn of 1642 King Charles and the Commons finally took to the field to settle the issues between them; by 1646 Puritanism of the Calvinist variety was triumphant, and by 1649 Charles lost his head. Like Calvin, the extremists closed the theaters, enforced church attendance, passed strict laws limiting the elegance of clothing, and made fornication punishable by three months' imprisonment, and adultery by death. But it was one thing to pass such laws and another to make them work in England, where there had been so long a time for Renaissance ideas to become absorbed into the culture. English juries and justices, for example, even when Puritan in sentiment, felt little sympathy with the harsh laws against sexual misconduct, and very few persons were actually convicted; by 1657, in fact, the law had become practically inoperative.

In any case, the extreme Calvinist measures were soon swept into oblivion, for in 1660 the Commonwealth government disintegrated and Charles II, son of the beheaded king, was summoned home from

France. Meanwhile, however, thoroughgoing Calvinism was getting a far better trial in New England; there the Cavalier influence was negligible, and the terms of the charter maintained the Calvinist theocracy in power from 1629 until 1691.[5] It is there that we may see Puritanism at its severest, except for Geneva and Scotland. Even though some of the "Blue Laws" of Massachusetts and Connecticut never existed (having been concocted by an unfriendly historian in 1781 and perpetuated by the unwary ever since), it is perfectly true that there were numerous restrictions on smoking, drinking, gaming, Sunday amusements, fancy clothing, and unchaperoned meetings of the unmarried. No Puritan church had an organ ("the Devil's bagpipe"), sermons ran two to three hours long, and tithing men switched those who fell asleep or let their attention stray. A New England gentleman could attend a funeral and seriously say afterwards, that it had been "an awful, yet pleasing, treat."

Public whippings, brandings, and duckings were handed out for such offenses as riotous conduct or scolding. Sexual offenses were treated more strictly: prior to 1650, adultery was a capital offense in Massachusetts, and some adulterers are known to have been actually executed. After 1650 the law required less—or was it more? —in the form of a whipping and the lifelong wearing of the scarlet letter. Repression of pleasures in general, and of sexual pleasure in particular, undoubtedly played a part in the two outbreaks of witchcraft hysteria in New England; the earlier one began in 1647 and resulted in the execution of fourteen witches in Massachusetts and Connecticut, while the Salem frenzy of 1692 brought about the execution of twenty persons and two dogs.

Yet to sense the leaden atmosphere of Puritan life at its most oppressive, we need to step into a real home. It is January 13, 1696, and this is the house of good Judge Samuel Sewall in Boston. His young daughter Elizabeth, who has recently heard a sermon on the text: "Ye shall seek me and shall die in your sins," has been dejected and sorrowful all day. The family finishes eating, and then, as Judge Sewall later noted in his diary, "a little after dinner she burst out into an amazing cry, which caused all the family to cry too." Mrs. Sewall questions the girl and at last the reason comes out: the child "was afraid she should go to Hell, her sins were not pardoned." Such a spell of childhood terror was not unique. Seven years earlier

[5] The charter expired in 1684, but the new non-theocratic charter was not granted until 1691, after some interim uncertainties.

Judge Sewall had lectured his ten-year-old son Sam one day on the need to prepare for death, and afterwards noted disconsolately: "He seemed not much to mind, eating an apple." But Sam did mind, for later, when saying his prayers, "he burst out into a bitter cry and said he was afraid he should die. I prayed with him and read scriptures comforting against death, as 'O Death, where is thy sting,' etc." [6]

And that is the stern, bloodless portrait of Puritanism that hangs in the hall of historical caricature. But like all caricature, it is incomplete and exaggerated; moreover, this particular one is far from a good likeness. All the things we have described were true of Calvinist Puritanism, but like the Neoplatonism of Castiglione's friends at Urbino, it was a faith more sworn by than lived by, a goal men and women could not quite reach. A complete and realistic portrait of the early Puritan would have a stern expression thinly masking two ill-controlled moods: one of mischief, and the other of romance.

4

The Puritan as Sinner

To redraw the portrait so as to make it more than caricature, let us use as our model not England, for there Puritan control was brief, the country was divided in sentiment, and the records of morality under the Commonwealth are fragmentary; instead let us draw it from life in New England, where the ideals of the Puritan churches were the law of the land for nearly three quarters of a

[6] *Diary*, Jan. 13, 1696 and Jan. 12, 1689.

century, where the population was almost entirely Puritan, and where documentary materials are relatively abundant.

The easiest thing to observe about a man is his clothing; yet even in so obvious a thing the caricature differs significantly from the reality. It is commonly believed that Puritans all dressed in drab-hued clothing of a plain, functional cut, and certainly they appear so in countless statues, murals, and book illustrations. But Puritan Governor John Winthrop knew better. In his *History of New England* he reported that in 1638 a court had directed the elders of all churches to curb extravagant dress, but Puritan dandies defiantly continued to sport ruffles, capes, and roses and silver buckles on their shoes. The next year a law was passed expressly forbidding these follies; it, too, must have been ineffective, for other laws continued to be passed on the same matter again and again.

Many a seventeenth-century preacher heaped verbal fire upon those New England men and women who affected wigs and periwigs, and by 1675 a law was passed banning such follies; yet periwigs gained ground and in 1685 Judge Sewall noted in his diary with evident annoyance that two people just received into the Church wore wigs. By the end of the century many men and women were wearing them without prosecution; in 1704 Judge Sewall scolded a young man who had just cut off his hair and taken to a wig, but it was a personal scolding, not an official one, and had no effect. After the turn of the century still more outrageous finery could be found in Boston and elsewhere—slashed sleeves, fine gloves, lace, jewelry, satin doublets, and the like. If most Puritan dress in the early years was somewhat dull, it was as much due to pioneer frugality as religious conviction; as conditions improved, the basic instinct to preen re-emerged.

Even before the close of the seventeenth century, Boston had its first fencing-master and soon afterwards several New England towns had granted licenses to dancing-masters. Though children sometimes wept for fear of God and death, there were toys and dolls on sale in shops in Boston and Salem. In a number of homes there were guitars, virginals, and celli; the picture of the Puritan family spending all its leisure studying the Word is, like all partisan propaganda, thoroughly untrustworthy. Still more surprising, the court and church records of early New England are filled with case histories of men and women who gamed, swore, fought, and got drunk—but who were Puritans.

So, too, with the practice of sex and love. If one but looks into the faded, crumbling archives of county courts and of churches, he may catch momentary glimpses of normally libidinous, moderately sinful men and women caught and made immortal not by poetry or art, but by a line or two of legal jargon. Here, for instance, is one John Smith of Medfield, Massachusetts, leaving his wife and going off about 1670, brash as you please, to live with Patience Rawlins; the Suffolk County Court purifies him with thirty lashes and a fine of £10, and orders him home. Here are Elizabeth Wheeler and Joanna Pierce both being severely admonished for sitting in the laps of men other than their husbands. Mrs. Edmond Maddock is charged with sitting up late by the fireside with two male friends while her husband is asleep. A Mr. Clark is ordered by a court to stop keeping company with Mrs. Freeman, "concerning whom there is a strong suspicion of incontinency." Abigail Bush of Westfield, a shrewish young woman, is censured in church in 1697 for using bad language about her elderly father's remarriage: to wit, she has said that his new wife is "as hot as a bitch." Can this be a Puritan woman speaking, and can she really be describing another Massachusetts female in the year 1697? But conditions in Connecticut are no better. In 1660, Jacob Minline and Sarah Tuttle of New Haven are summoned to court for an offense described in fond detail: in the presence of others these shameless people "sat down together, his arm being about her, and her arm upon his shoulder or about his neck; and he kissed her and she kissed him, or they kissed one another, continuing in this posture about half an hour." The court fined and scolded Miss Tuttle with a strangely honorable term of condemnation—it found her to be a "bold virgin." [7]

The very wording of the laws which thus interfered with private conduct is often an excellent indication of the real state of affairs. The legislators of Massachusetts, for instance, unwittingly documented an all-but-forgotten aspect of Puritan life when they set down in 1647 the justification of a new law to control and regulate courting: "It is a common practice in divers places," they explained, "for young men irregularly and disorderly to watch all advantages for their evil purposes, to insinuate [themselves] into the affections of young maidens, by coming to them in places and seasons un-

[7] These and many similar cases have been extracted from church and court records by Professor Henry W. Lawrence in *The Not-Quite-Puritans;* Edmund S. Morgan in "The Puritans and Sex" (*The New England Quarterly,* Vol. 15, Dec. 1942); and Emil Oberholzer in *Delinquent Saints.*

known to their parents. . . ." And so they made a law; but eight
years later the General Court noted with alarm an increase in fornication, and still three years later remarked on the large number of
bastards in the colony. In Plymouth Colony, similar controls had
had a similar lack of success; Governor William Bradford, recording in his *History of the Plymouth Plantation* a veritable epidemic
of sexual misdemeanors in 1642, speculated for a moment along surprisingly advanced lines:

> It may be in this case as it is with waters when their streams
> are stopped or dammed up; when they get passage they flow with
> more violence, and make more noise and disturbance, than when
> they are suffered to run quietly in their own channels.

And for all the emphasis on the sinfulness of fornication and adultery, the early Puritans were definitely not against sex as such. Not
only did they breed large families and take pride in so doing, but
their spiritual leaders praised married sex and roundly condemned
the "Popish conceit of the excellency of virginity." The congregations themselves acted from the same point of view. At the First
Church of Boston, for instance, the congregation considered action
against one James Mattock for several offenses, one of them being,
of all things, sexual abstinence. Mattock, it appeared, had denied his
wife conjugal relations for two years on the grounds that he was
punishing himself for his sins; the congregation voted that this was
unnatural and unchristian, and expelled him from membership in the
church.

It was only sex outside of marriage that the early Puritans attacked. The churches, punishing more sinners than the courts, employed a public form of confession far more painful than the Catholic confessional they had repudiated. Church elders would investi-
gate allegations of fornication, adultery, or other serious sins, and
require the accused, if guilty, to make a written confession which
was read aloud to the congregation on Sunday. The congregation
would then vote to accept it, restoring the member to grace, or to
reject it, leading to suspension or excommunication from membership. All this sounds revoltingly autocratic and severe to the modern
mind. But Dr. Emil Oberholzer, a diligent historian, recently read
all the 1,242 confessions of fornication, or reports of such confessions, that exist in church records from 1620 to 1839, and concluded
that what is most remarkable about them is how unremarkable they
seemed to the Puritans; the vast majority were recorded in a per-

fectly matter-of-fact manner without comment, as though they were nothing but routine business.[8]

The 1,242 confessions are not a valid reckoning of the incidence of illicit love-making in New England, but only a small sampling. For one thing, only those who got caught had to confess; for another, many of the church records are missing or imperfect. Yet there *is* one exceedingly important statistic to be gleaned from these records. Dr. Oberholzer tabulated by type all disciplinary cases of every sort mentioned in the records of the Massachusetts churches he visited, and discovered that a plurality of them concerned fornication. It was, in other words, the most prevalent and most popular sin in Puritan New England.

5

The Puritan as Lover

❀ ❀

❀

If it is somewhat surprising to learn that Puritans could be so impure, it is still more so to find that some of them were tenderly romantic, and that both English and Colonial Puritanism absorbed various love concepts from the Renaissance tradition.

It is true, of course, that English Puritans were opposed to the dandified worship of beauty and the adulterous follies of the court

[8] Op. cit., p. 150. Another indication of that attitude can be found in the civil law in Plymouth where, under the Revised Statutes of 1671, fornication was conceded to be a fairly natural impulse; at least, one may so interpret the fact that ordinary fornicators were fined £10, but if engaged to each other at the time (which would ostensibly heighten the impulse and decrease the inhibitions), were fined only half as much.

of Charles I; it is true furthermore that much of what they said
about love was a justification of marriage along patriarchal biblical
lines. They lavished an enormous amount of rhetoric, via pulpit and
printing press, on the justification of the God-appointed subordination of woman to man. A fair sample of the mood of such writing is
this brief passage from William Whately's *The Bride-Bush* (1617):
"Whosoever therefore doth desire to be a good wife, or to live comfortably, let her set down this conclusion within her soul: Mine husband is my superior, my better; he hath authority and rule over me,
nature hath given it to him . . . [and] God hath given it to him."
For via family and congregation, the Puritans desperately sought to
shore up the changing and shifting society of their time. William
Gouge, who wrote a full seven hundred pages entitled *Of Domesti-
cal Duties,* linked housekeeping with divinity: he set forth a theo-
cratic pecking order that ran from child to mother, and thence to
husband, magistrate, king, and God. "A family is a little church
and a little commonwealth," he stated, "a school wherein the first
principles and grounds of government and subjection are learned."

But the Puritan idea of the patriarchy was quite different from
that of earlier systems of female subordination. Unlike Greek wives,
Puritan women were supposed to be good companions to their husbands; unlike early Christian and medieval wives, they were not
subordinated because of their vileness and frailties, but because of
their adaptation to child-rearing and home-making. Puritan writers
stressed the importance of emotional harmony between man and
wife, and Gouge wrote that they should be closer and more nearly
attuned to each other than to any other people on earth. Whately
sounded practical and unromantic when he advised young men to
pick and choose carefully, weighing the health, wealth, skills, position, and temperament of various girls; but once he got beyond the
subject of courting and into marriage, he slipped into another vein:
"For him to think her not only more comely, handsome, beautiful,
but also more loving, more dutiful, more submissive, more trusty,
than perhaps she is . . . by looking through the spectacles of love
. . . is doubtless a praiseworthy blindness." A Puritan view, this—
yet indebted ultimately, to the medieval troubadors and to Castiglione, for no Western people before the eleventh century had said
that man should unrealistically exaggerate the excellence of his beloved.

The romantic elements in a Puritan love affair can best be illustrated by the story of Lucy Apsley and John Hutchinson, an account of which is contained in Mrs. Hutchinson's *Memoirs of Colonel Hutchinson*. Lucy Apsley was born in 1620 in the Tower of London, of which her father, a faithful servant of the Crown, was then lieutenant-governor (Puritans were not all boorish tradesmen and ink-stained merchants). The Apsley home life was a blend of pious and worldly influences. At one time young Lucy had eight tutors—several teaching her languages, music, and writing to make a gentlewoman of her, others teaching her needlework, sums, and other housewifely skills. From her parents she acquired a serious moral outlook and used to deliver childish lectures on good conduct to the maidservants, but at the same time she read omnivorously, and enjoyed nothing better than romances and love poems.

In 1637, when the Apsleys had a house at Richmond, near London, a handsome youth named John Hutchinson was spending the summer in Richmond with friends. He was the son of a country squire and mingled easily in aristocratic company, but like his Puritan father he was serious, studious, and moral. During the summer, Hutchinson happened to visit the Apsley home at a time when seventeen-year-old Lucy was in London; while there he saw some of her Latin books, asked what sort of girl took such interest in learning, and was deeply intrigued by what he heard. The young ladies of Richmond told him, with much artful giggling, that Lucy was studious, conceited, and dull, but the more they mocked, the faster his pulses beat. One evening someone played a song Lucy had written, and young Hutchinson said he would simply have to meet so gifted a lady. "Sir," answered a gallant youth, "she is of such a humor she will not be acquainted with any of mankind. . . . She shuns the conversation of men as the plague." Tristan never felt the magic potion take more violent effect than did John Hutchinson.

Evidently it showed, for several days later his friends took the trouble to play a practical joke on him. They arranged for word to be brought during dinner that Lucy had been married in London. The results were noteworthy: young Hutchinson, though he had not yet met her nor even seen her picture, turned pale, broke into a sweat, and nearly got sick at the table. Excusing himself, he fled to his room and sank into a depression, wondering how such a thing could have happened to him.

Lucy soon returned from her trip to London, the joke was exposed, and Hutchinson finally met her. She was struck by his good looks, quiet manners, and serious personality; for his part, he found her earnestness and her disregard for feminine frills and manners quite lovable. Best of all, he did not worship her in the foppish courtly style, but stood ready to guide and command: "Never was there a passion more ardent and less idolatrous," wrote Lucy many years later. "He loved her better than his life, with inexpressible tenderness and kindness . . . [but never] suffered the intrusion of such a dotage as should blind him from marking her imperfections" —which, she adds, he patiently and gently corrected. (If Hutchinson had heard of William Whately's *Bride-Bush*, he failed to see the need for "praiseworthy blindness.")

After six weeks of courtship (almost all of which consisted of walking in the garden and discussing intellectual matters), they were ready. Friends met to conclude arrangements—and that same day Lucy fell ill with smallpox. Then, indeed, was Hutchinson put to the test. He passed it nobly, insisting on marrying her as soon as possible even though, as Lucy wrote, "all who saw her were affrighted to look on her." Lucy reported that her deformed face gradually improved and that she regained all her beauty; we would like to believe it was so. Whether it was or not, they succeeded in having a warm, solid, rewarding marriage for the next twenty-five years.

Hutchinson devoted his time to his estate, and to the study of divinity; gradually he became involved in the Puritan cause and during the Civil Wars was a colonel in the Puritan army, a member of Commons, and one of the judges who signed the death sentence of Charles I. After the Restoration, he was arrested as a regicide, and died while in prison. Lucy Hutchinson wrote her memoir to moderate her grief and preserve her love, and we may be thankful she did; no other such intimate Puritan autobiography exists from that period.

The courtships of less well-to-do and less well-educated Puritans were not so perfumed with learning and rather more influenced by the immediate domestic values to be gained by the union. This was particularly true in colonial New England, where each man urgently needed a wife to satisfy many imperative needs—clothing, food, medical care, companionship, sex, and, not least of all, status.[9]

[9] In many a New England town the bachelor was suspect. Hartford taxed bachelors twenty shillings a week for living alone, and Massachusetts and Plymouth permitted them to live only in homes approved by the selectmen, who kept them under constant surveillance.

It was common for a man to meet a girl, appraise her, propose to her, and publish the banns all within a few weeks or less. In 1675, Thomas Walley, living in a town some distance from Boston, decided to go to Boston as soon as spring came in order to find a wife. Just then some friends mentioned to him that a Mrs. Clark had moved to town and was available. Walley hustled off and called upon her without ceremony, and within a day or two they had agreed to wed. Walley was much relieved, and wrote to his friend, John Cotton: "God hath sent me a wife home to me and saved me the labor of a tedious journey."

Yet one can exaggerate the extent of such primitivism. Even in New England, seventeenth-century Puritans far more frequently were servants of Eros than either their religion or the hard necessities of colonial life would lead one to suppose. The wonderful diary of Judge Sewall is full of vignettes of human beings who, though they do not resemble the inhibited, self-torturing Puritans of Hawthorne's novels, nor exhibit the sweetly Victorian ways Longfellow ascribed to John Alden and Priscilla Mullens, have the merit of being real and genuine. Timothy Dwight, for instance, a young servant in the house of Samuel Sewall's father, fell down in a frenzy one day in 1676, kicking and banging the floor, and talking incoherently even after being put to bed. Sewall's father questioned him when he grew calm. The youth would say only that he had a reprobate nature and was spiritually disturbed, but the younger Sewall observed the case more closely and recorded what he saw:

> Notwithstanding all this semblance (and much more than is written) of compunction for sin, 'tis to be feared that his trouble arose from a maid whom he passionately loved: for that when Mr. Dwight and his master had agreed to let him go to her, he eftsoons grew well.

One of the better-known Puritan love letters, written by the Reverend Michael Wigglesworth to a Mrs. Avery in 1691, is often cited as evidence of the arid and unemotional nature of Puritan relationships. It lists, for instance, ten logical reasons why she should marry him, Point Three being: "I have not been led hereunto by fancy (as too many are in like cases) but by sound reason and judgment." Yet the evidence is unfair; Wigglesworth was sixty at the time, and elderly people, even in romantic times, have often had to make practical arrangements. Moreover, as evidence it can be used for the other

side—for perhaps the real clue lies in the Reverend's statement that
he is not led by fancy *"as too many are in like cases."*

What the modern person may especially dislike in Puritan love
letters is the now-unfashionable mixture of romance and righteous-
ness. Yet if one carefully analyzes that mixture, he must at least admit that the original Puritan was not altogether frigid; he simply
felt, or tried to feel, that the love of God came first, and that of
woman right afterwards. The opening sentence of a letter from Edward Taylor, a minister in Westfield, to his fiancée may have a distinctly unpleasant flavor for the contemporary palate:

> My Dove, I send you not my heart, for that I trust is sent to
> Heaven long since, and unless it hath woefully deceived me, it
> hath not taken up its lodgings in anyone's bosom this side of the
> Royal City of the Great King.

But Taylor went on to praise conjugal love in orotund tones above
all others on earth and to say that the only limit on it is that it must
be subordinate to God's glory. One cannot be sure whether the
young lady was flattered or irritated, but since she probably had different vision from ours, she could perhaps see through the fog of
piety and perceive the minister's meaning.

Often, too, God won first place in men's affections only by a narrow margin. The wife of one Thomas Shepard nearly died in child-
birth; when she had passed the crisis, Shepard stopped to reflect on
the experience, and commented thoughtfully in his diary:

> As the affliction was very bitter, so did the Lord teach me much
> by it, and I had need of it for I began to grow secretly proud and
> full of sensuality, delighting my soul in my dear wife more than
> in my God whom I had promised better unto.

Many another man, not so providentially warned, very likely found
mortal love sweetest of all and delighted himself in it as much as
any Renaissance courtier, even though the circumstances and the
coloring of it were so very different.

Finally, it is worth noting that even that Devil-wrestler, that
soother of demon-possessed girls, that champion of a dying theocracy, Cotton Mather himself, once suffered from a painful romantic
yearning for a slightly tarnished young lady. God won, but nearly
at the cost of Mather's reason. This strange episode is not what one
thinks of when Mather's name is mentioned: what comes to mind,
rather, are the less amiable recollections—Mather preaching against

plays, card games, and Christmas festivities; indulging in fasts and
bouts of weeping, and telling of his visions from the pulpit of his
Second Church in Boston; portraying for his flock the way to
Heaven as a wilderness filled with fiery flying serpents, dens of
lions, and droves of devils; helping to ignite the fires of the Salem
witchcraft hysteria of 1692 by "investigating" supernatural phenomena and publishing several credulous reports on possession by
demons and other matters; and proudly writing the official, self-
satisfied report of the Salem trials under the title, *Wonders of the
Invisible World*. By all these things one may know Mather, and by
a very tiny detail one may know him still better: one day, having
just relieved himself, he pondered what a great deal of time he had
wasted in life in all his evacuations—time that might be put to God's
use—and quite seriously wrote down a resolve "to make it an opportunity of shaping in my mind some holy, noble, divine thought
. . . that may leave upon my spirit some further tincture of piety."

Yet even this man wept and suffered for love, and confided his
agonies to his diary. It began in December 1702, when Mather's
wife died, leaving him with a brood of nine children. Mather was
still only thirty-eight, physically attractive, and at the height of his
career. Shortly he began to receive notes from a "young gentlewoman" (he never named her in the diary), who offered sympathy,
and asked to call on him. Early in February, 1703, she first came to
his study, a handsome girl a little over twenty, well educated, and
with considerable wit. But she had not come to be witty. According to Mather's account of the meeting, she forthrightly spoke of
having always admired him; now that he was a widower, she felt
herself free to "confess herself charmed with my person to such a
degree that she could not but break in upon me with her most importunate requests that I would make her mine. . . . I was in a
great strait, how to treat so polite a gentlewoman." He offered her
a number of discouraging facts, including the probable opposition
of his congregation, but she was undaunted, and by the time she
left Mather was half entranced, half fearful. "I know she has been
a very airy person," he wrote. "What snares may be laying for me,
I know not."

The snares soon became evident: her airiness had won her a
somewhat doubtful reputation, yet at the same time Mather felt
himself deeply attracted. "I am in the greatest straits imaginable,"
he jotted in his diary on February 12. "Nature itself causes in me

a mighty tenderness for a person so very amiable." Nevertheless, he wrote her a note asking her to leave off lest the strain of it kill him (he used that very word). "Yet such was my flexible tenderness," he added less than a week later, "as to be conquered by the importunities of several[10] to allow some further interviews."

By March 6, however, Mather began to perceive the Prince of Darkness beginning to meddle in the affair, hoping to wreck his ministry.

> There is a noise, and a mighty noise it is, made about the town. . . . Satan has raised an horrid storm of reproach upon me, both for my earliness in courting a gentlewoman, and especially for my courting of a person whom they generally apprehend so disagreeable to my character. . . . My spirit is excessively broken.

Concluding that his congregation would never accept his marriage to someone young, saucy, and possibly tarnished, he decided after an agonizing soul-struggle to follow duty and break off the affair, but suffered intensely from the decision.

> I set myself to make unto the Lord Jesus Christ a sacrifice. . . . I struck my knife into the heart of my sacrifice by a letter to her mother. . . . Should I tell in how many forms the Devil has assaulted me, it would strike my friends with horror. Sometimes temptations to impurities; and sometimes to blasphemy and atheism and the abandonment of all religion as a mere delusion; and sometimes to self-destruction itself. These, even these, O miserable Mather, do follow thee with an astonishing fury.

The girl herself seems to have been just as upset, but she and her mother doggedly continued the suit, even going to see his father, Increase Mather. By late spring, however, Cotton Mather discovered that a suitable young widow, Mrs. Elizabeth Hubbard, lived only two houses away, and he called upon her. In a single evening he appraised her as being agreeable, civil, appropriate, and full of veneration for himself. "I see," he wrote in his diary that night, "she will be a great gift of Heaven unto me." When the "young gentlewoman" heard of this new interest, she was outraged and threatened to cause the minister public embarrassment or disgrace, but nothing came of her threats. In August he married the widow Hubbard, having by then come to regard her as "a most lovely creature and such a gift of Heaven to me and mine that the sense thereof

[10] Her mother and, probably, friends.

. . . dissolves me into tears of joy." We may as well believe him, since he is the only source of evidence on the matter.

The point of the story, in any event, is perfectly plain: even if one wishes Mather had had the courage to follow his heart and marry the saucy young thing, the affair and his feelings about it thoroughly belie the accepted image of the Puritan with his stony heart, his ice-cold blood, his repressed and unuttered desires. Even this Devil-fighting fanatic was capable of feeling both heat and tenderness; as for keeping quiet, that was the furthest thing of all from his character. He published four hundred and fifty titles in his lifetime, and his desires, far from being unutterable, were to him another excellent source of literary and hortatory material.

6

"Hail Wedded Love"

No survey of Puritan love would be complete without a look at the central figure of seventeenth-century Puritanism—John Milton, the man whose personality, thoughts, and writings are the perfect expression of that movement.

It has long been fashionable to praise Milton's poetry and to dispraise his personality, to admire his technique and dislike his content. Studious, unsmiling, virtuous, and devoid of winning graces, he is genuinely difficult to like. Samuel Johnson called him "an acrimonious and surly republican," and most critics and historians have thought him tough-minded, unsociable, egotistical and priggish. As for his feelings about love, Robert Graves wrote a novel showing

Milton as an abominably tyrannical husband, and a contemporary scholar referred to him, typically, as "a sore, angry, intolerant, and arrogant critic of women." All this is certainly true, but it is not all there is to say. If he was priggish and virtuous, he also expressed a completely healthy view of sex—at least of married sex; and if he was not a very loving husband, it may be because his expectations of married love had been excessively idealistic and romantic.

Milton, born in 1608, was from early youth a studious and serious boy. Partly this was the result of his father's special efforts, for the elder Milton, a scrivener (a writer of legal contracts and a money-lender), had literary ambitions for his son. Partly, too, it fitted in with the fact that young Milton was physically slight and somewhat retarded in bodily maturation ("I do notice a certain belatedness in me," he once observed.) At Cambridge, his smooth-cheeked imma-turity and his dislike of bawdy talk or sexual adventures led some students to nickname him "the Lady." "Why do I seem to them too little of a man?" Milton later complained; then, contemptuous of their inferior morals, he answered the question: ". . . Perhaps be-cause I have never showed my virility in the way these brothellers do."

During his early manhood, Milton wrote a handful of exquisite poems which abound in ravishingly sensuous imagery, but these were a triumph of art over personal habits. Charles Diodati, his closest friend during his college years, once gently scolded Milton for his cloistered ways in a letter:

> Why do you despise the gifts of nature? Why inexcusably per-sist in hanging over books and studies all day and all night? Live, laugh, make the most of youth and the hours; and cease studying the zeals and recreations and indolences of the wise men of old, wearing yourself out the while. . . . Farewell, and be joyous.

Diodati's mood intrigued Milton, and sometimes he would write as though he were considering taking the advice to heart:

> *Alas! what boots it with uncessant care*
> *To tend the homely shepherd's trade,*
> *And strictly meditate the thankless Muse?*
> *Were it not better done as others use,*
> *To sport with Amaryllis in the shade,*
> *Or with the tangles of Neaera's hair?*
>   Lycidas, 64–9.

But it was all talk. John Milton, Puritan and puritanical, and dedicated to becoming a great poet, sported in no shades and tangled no girl's hair. To the best of anyone's knowledge, he lived in complete chastity; as for romance, he felt love only twice before his marriage —once for an unknown girl he saw for a fleeting moment in a London crowd, and once for an Italian lady with whom, in Petrarchan fashion, his connection was limited to the writing of some sonnets. Yet he had no intention of spending his life in bachelor chastity, and industriously read about married life, expecting it some day to yield him a very special kind of human relationship.

In the summer of 1642, when Milton was thirty-three and deeply involved in writing polemic tracts on behalf of the Puritan cause, he went to Oxfordshire on vacation and visited the Powells, a family he had known for some years. Mary Powell, who had been only a child when last he had seen her, was now a blooming girl of sixteen. Some June madness came upon him, and when his month's vacation was over, he brought her home to his house in London as his wife.

It was an astonishingly poor choice. The Civil War was imminent and the Powells were Royalists. Milton, furthermore, was a quiet, settled man, dedicated to scholarly studies, while Mary was a mere girl, high-spirited, ignorant of learning, and unable to appreciate his poetic aims. Great love and great understanding on his part might have made the marriage work, but in the emotional dealings between man and woman Milton was still an unfledged adolescent. He expected everything in her, and found almost nothing. Even the long-deferred pleasure of physical love was soured for him by the boredom, the shallowness, and the petty bickering of the marriage; later he referred to sexual connection under such conditions as "a displeasing and forced remedy against the sting of a bruit desire."

The situation must have been as painful for Mary as for him. Within a few weeks she asked Milton for permission to visit her family for the balance of the summer. Probably he hoped the separation would ease the tension and let them start afresh, for he agreed, but set Michaelmas, in September, as the date of her return. In late August, however King Charles unfurled his royal banner at Nottingham and rallied his army. Oxford became his headquarters, and the Powells found themselves in the very thick of events. Only great love could have brought Mary back to her scholarly Puritan husband under such circumstances; not surprisingly, she made no attempt to do so. Milton wrote letters asking her to return, but she ignored them; he sent a messenger, who was brusquely turned away from the Powell home. But why did Milton want her back at all? Because even if he had chosen ill, it was his only chance. The divorce law of England consisted of the conservative canon law of the official Church of England. Milton, who wanted love, could not get rid of one wife for another, and would not seek love outside marriage; he therefore longed to try again with his adolescent wife, and being rebuffed again and again, grew bitter and full of hate.

A year after Mary had left, he published what was in part the product of this experience—a forty-two-page pamphlet addressed to Parliament and entitled *The Doctrine and Discipline of Divorce*—to which, within the next two and a half years, he added three more similar tracts. His aim in all of them was plain: he urged the Puritan Parliament to revoke canon law, authorize divorce on the radical ground of "contrariety of mind," and "with one gentle stroking to wipe away ten thousand tears out of the life of man."

The divorce tracts are full of bilious hatred for woman, yet they rest upon an idealistic, quasi-romantic concept of married love, as magnified by the imagination of an unusually chaste, inexperienced, and serious man. Milton distinguished between two kinds of sexual expression—a noble one, growing out of a beautiful and natural desire, and the other a venomous burning, incontinent and vulgar, which he equated with illicit love or with lustful connection between a husband and wife who do not love each other. Chaste and puritanical though he was, Milton insisted that the former kind of sex was natural and healthful. For normal persons to remain unmarried in the effort to attain continence was, he said, "a diabolic sin" and he held the Catholic views on celibacy to be the work of the very Antichrist.

But the most important goal of marriage, he argued, was not sexual outlet; there was a higher goal—loving "conversation" (i.e., loving companionship). Milton even reinterpreted Saint Paul; when the Apostle said that it was better to marry than to burn, the word "burn" must have referred not to sexual desire, he said, but to a "pure and more inbred desire" to join with "a fit and conversing soul"—this was "that rational burning that marriage is to remedy." Half religious, half humanistic, Milton took not an anti-sexual, but a supra-sexual view of married love:

> Conjugal love [arises] from a mutual fitness to the final causes of
> wedlock: help and society in religious, civil, and domestic conversa-
> tion, which includes as an inferior end the fulfilling of natural desire
> and specifical increase. . . . God, in the first ordaining of marriage,
> taught us to what end he did it . . . [namely] to comfort and re-
> fresh [man] against the evil of solitary life, not mentioning the pur-
> pose of generation till afterwards. . . . He who affirms adultery to
> be the highest breach affirms the bed to be the highest [goal] of
> marriage, which is in truth a gross and boorish opinion.

Repeatedly he stressed the importance of nonsexual factors in love,
and sometimes his personal experience shows through:

> For all the wariness can be used, it may yet befall a discreet man to
> be mistaken in his choice. . . . Who knows not that the bashful
> muteness of a virgin may oft-times hide all the unliveliness and
> natural sloth which is really unfit for conversation?

From all this, Milton derived the sweeping conclusion that divorce should be granted where there was a deep-seated inability of
a man and wife to be happy together. The just ground of divorce,
he wrote in a famous sentence, is "indisposition, unfitness, or contrariety of mind, arising from a cause in nature unchangeable, hindering and ever likely to hinder the main benefits of conjugal society, which are solace and peace."[11]

But the divorce tracts were not merely an outlet for Milton's
personal unhappiness; the postulates on which they rested had all
been expressly contained in the earlier writings of Puritan divines.
Milton, being a deep thinker and a tormented man, simply carried
them to their logical extreme. It was a profound shock to him,
therefore, when various Puritans preached against his views, wrote
stinging answers to his tracts, and sometimes even labeled him a
heretic. Parliament did far worse: it ignored his recommendations
completely. Years later, when Cromwell became Lord Protector,
the divorce law was modified, but scarcely a tenth of the way
toward Milton's position.[12]

Long before Cromwell's changes, however, Milton was no longer
an abandoned husband. The King's cause had suffered a mortal
blow at the battle of Naseby on June 14, 1645; the Powell family,

[11] The sentence is from *Doctrine and Discipline of Divorce*, as are most of the quotations
and opinions cited above; some, however,
are from *Tetrachordon*, another of the divorce
tracts.

[12] The "Barebones" Parliament of 1655
gave civil magistrates the power to grant divorce, but only on the usual limited Calvinist grounds—desertion, impotence, or adultery.

tacking desperately, sent Mary down to London to a relative of
Milton's, who stationed her in a side room one day when Milton
was expected. He came and was unwittingly steered into the room
where he suddenly found her on her knees before him, weeping
and begging for pardon. A passage in *Paradise Lost* seems almost to
be his memory of this very scene:

> *She ended weeping, and her lowly plight,*
> *Immoveable till peace obtained from fault*
> *Acknowledged and deplored, in Adam wrought*
> *Commiseration. . . .*
> *As one disarmed, his anger all he lost,*
> *And thus with peaceful words upraised her soon.*
>
> (X, 937–46)

Life is usually a little less than poetic; a nephew of Milton's wrote
that Milton softened only after considerable talking and urging by
friends and relatives who were also present. But in the end he
relented, and Mary returned to his home after a three-year absence.

One aspect of their marriage functioned at least adequately, for
Mary produced four children in the next seven years. But time had
neither made her better-suited to him, nor him more flexible and
undemanding. He wrote no more on the divorce question, but he
felt neither joy nor fulfilment in his marriage. Less than two years
after Mary returned, he wrote to Carlo Dati, a dear friend, as follows:

> Those whom the mere necessity of neighborhood, or some-
> thing else of useless kind, has closely conjoined to me . . . sit
> daily in my company, weary me, nay, by Heaven, all but plague
> me to death whenever they are jointly in the humor for it. . . .
> Those whom habit, disposition, studies, had so handsomely made
> my friends, are now almost denied me. . . . I have to live well-
> nigh in a perpetual solitude.

Mary died in 1652, leaving Milton with three living children. He
was by then Latin Secretary to the Council of State, a job which involved his writing official letters and papers for the Puritan government. Having children to rear, and official chores to perform, and
having, furthermore, become completely blind in 1652, Milton cast
about for another wife and remarried in 1657. This second wife
died in a year, and he married once more in 1663, his third wife
caring for him until his own death eleven years later. Very little is
known about either of these later marriages except that they were

matters of absolute necessity to Milton—and both worked, albeit in a fashion different from that of his early expectations.

During his third marriage Milton completed and published *Paradise Lost*, the noblest effort of the Puritan movement to sum up its cultural and religious philosophy. Though the Commonwealth had foundered, Puritanism was a continuing force in English and colonial life, and *Paradise Lost* was long a favorite work with the humbly pious, who took Milton's portrayal of Adam and Eve almost as a doctrinal guide to the relationships between the sexes. Though in part it surely reflects Milton's personality, it is still more an expression of the Puritan tradition and a guide to Puritan conduct. It perfectly summarizes in a few lines the improbable Puritan compound of romanticism, sensuousness, and pious patriarchalism:

> . . . *Both*
> *Not equal, as their sex not equal, seemed;*
> *For contemplation he and valor formed,*
> *For softness she and sweet attractive grace;*
> *He for God only, she for God in him.*
> *His fair large front and eye sublime declared*
> *Absolute rule.* . . .
> (IV, 295–301)

The happy pair had neither doubt nor guilt in their love-making; conjugal sex was beautiful and pure:

> . . . *Into their inmost bower*
> *Handed they went; and, eased the putting off*
> *These troublesome disguises which we wear,*
> *Straight side by side were laid; nor turned, I ween,*
> *Adam from his fair spouse; nor Eve the rites*
> *Mysterious of connubial love refused.* . . .
> *Hail wedded love, mysterious law, true source*
> *Of human offspring, sole propriety*
> *In paradise of all things common else!*
> *By thee adulterous lust was driven from men.* . . .
> (IV, 738–53)

When Eve ate the apple, Adam followed suit not so much to gain forbidden knowledge, but for love of Eve, saying:

> . . . *With thee*
> *Certain my resolution is to die:*
> *How can I live without thee! how forego*

Thy sweet converse and love so dearly joined,
To live again in these wild woods forlorn!
                                    (IX, 904–10)

Eve, being woman above all else, was so flattered that she referred
to Adam's impending Original Sin as a "glorious trial of exceeding
love."

   Adam ate, and he and Eve were then overwhelmed by a new kind
of desire—hot, lascivious, and guilty. Milton thus precisely denied
the entire view of Saint Augustine. Concupiscence did not cause
Original Sin, but was its result; sexual union was not the product of
eating the apple, but existed prior to it and was blighted by it. But
in Milton's view, Adam and Eve then recovered the purity of
wedded love after a bitter quarrel during which Adam bade Eve
go from him, and she, repenting of her ways, begged forgiveness
and reassumed that fitting subservience the laying-aside of which
had caused their Fall:

> *Forsake me not thus, Adam! witness heaven*
> *What love sincere and reverence in my heart*
> *I bear thee, and unwitting have offended,*
> *Unhappily deceived; thy suppliant*
> *I beg, and clasp thy knees. . . .*
>   *Both have sinned, but thou*
> *Against God only; I against God and thee. . . .*
>   (X, 914–931)

It is, after all, just a masculine daydream; but it is also the kind of
advice Puritan parents gave to their daughters, assuring them that in
such dulcet female accents lay the secret of lasting love.

The Meaning of "Puritanical"

What, then, did the Reformation and in particular its Puritan outgrowth, do to love?

The feminists of two generations ago (and less) were inclined to see it as a retrogression to stern patriarchalism, a dethroning of woman from her status as Lady to the lesser one of housekeeper, and a blighting of love by repression and joyless piety. There is some truth in all this, but much distortion and omission; though Puritans shunned amorous verse, high-flown compliments, and the elegant techniques of adulterous upper-class flirtation, they borrowed some of the ideals of romantic love, accepted the normality of sex and tried to fuse the two within marriage.

Nevertheless they seemed dismal, joyless people to their contemporaries. In part, they had turned their backs upon the enlightened mood of the Renaissance. In part, they came mostly of a class which valued money more than leisure, and success more than culture. In part, they were reformers who threw out the baby with the bath water, for while repudiating both Neoplatonism and illicit love, they flung away much of the magic, tenderness, and intimacy of romantic tradition. It took a Puritan (William Gouge), writing in 1622, to soberly urge wives not to use terms of endearment upon their husbands, specifically cautioning them against such unseemly familiarities as *sweet, sweeting, heart, sweetheart, love, joy, dear, duck, chick,* and *pigsnie* (*sic*); none of these would do, and neither would the first name or nickname. The only proper way for a woman to address her mate was *Husband*.

Yet in some practical ways, woman's status continued to improve under Puritanism. In Puritan New England a woman whose hus-

[251]

band beat her could win legal separation, and sometimes divorce; in the Southern colonies, where the influence was Anglican and Cavalier, the law made no such provision. In Salem, in 1682, a man named Daniel Ela was fined forty shillings for having told his wife in front of neighbors that "she was none of his wife, she was but his servant." Property rights and inheritance laws continued to improve slowly in woman's favor. Marriage in Protestant countries (except for England) became in general a civil contract, and divorce with the right of remarriage was established firmly, if on limited grounds. And finally, if early Puritans were collectively intolerant of love and sex outside of marriage, they were all in favor of both within it.

How can all this be equated with the standard image of Puritanism? Perhaps the discrepancy lies in the fact that the picture of early Puritanism has been distorted by the later phenomena that took its name. Seventeenth-century Puritanism was tight-lipped, severe, and pious, but it was simultaneously frank, strongly sexed, and somewhat romantic. Except for the extreme forms of Calvinism, it was as much an offshoot of the Renaissance as a reaction against it. The frigidity and neuroses associated with Puritanism belong to a much later date: hellfire-and-brimstone sermons reached their zenith in the middle of the eighteenth century, and the suffocating prudishness of the Victorians came in the middle of the nineteenth.

Modern men and women often speak of struggling to free themselves from their "Puritanical" background, but they misunderstand the tradition they have inherited; it is really the nineteenth-century emphasis on respectability and gentility they are speaking of. Actually, the early Puritan was rather close to modern man in many of his attitudes toward adultery, sexual enjoyment, love, and marriage. Milton hailed wedded love in a spirit much like our own; like many another prophet, however, he was too far ahead of his time, and died in a world that seemed increasingly to scorn the ideals he believed in.

Chapter VIII

THE CONTACT OF TWO EPIDERMISES

Love Becomes Ridiculous

❀   ❀

❀

Love, Jonathan Swift earnestly assured a young lady who was about to be married, is a "ridiculous passion which hath no being but in play-books and romances." It was the year 1723, and most people of wit and good breeding throughout Europe were of a similar opinion; it was the Age of Reason, and love had fallen into disrepute among the upper classes and the intellectuals—the very people who had made so much of it ever since William, Duke of Aquitaine, wrote his first troubadour songs six centuries earlier.

There was good reason for the change. By the middle of the seventeenth century, the religious and philosophical wars between Catholicism and the Reformation had exhausted Europe and ended in the only possible solution: hostile toleration. Intellectual Europeans were disillusioned and disenchanted with the several traditions of the Middle Ages, the Renaissance, and the Reformation, and sought instead a new, calm, humane philosophy that would be more stable and productive of well-being. They turned away from emotion, authority, and the past, seeking to base a way of life on reason, the individual, and the present. Theology and metaphysics yielded to mathematics and physics, and it was in all seriousness rather than in a spirit of satire that Alexander Pope wrote:

> *Nature and Nature's laws lay hid in night:*
> *God said,* Let Newton be! *and all was light.*

Along with so much else, the romantic, suffering, idealizing way of love seemed to them merely another superstitious folly of the infancy of mankind. The loutish sons and pious daughters of tradesmen and the lower classes might still indulge in this and other "enthusiasms," but the educated aristocracy and upper-middle-class

men and women scorned to be enslaved by emotion. They chose to
consider love a matter of natural sexual desire, a normal hunger
that should be gratified whenever convenient—with suitable style,
perhaps, but certainly without any barbarous exaltations or nonsense about ethical values.

Rationalists not only put these principles into practice, but were
dismayingly lucid and outspoken about them, and perhaps it was for
this sin above all others that succeeding generations condemned
them. Giuseppe Parini, an Italian poet, defined love in terms free of
all romantic nonsense simply as "the satisfaction of desire in noble
liberty"; the Comte de Buffon, a naturalist, said acerbly: "There is
nothing good in love but the physical part"; and the sarcastic wit,
Sebastien Chamfort, uttering the ultimate rationalist word on the
subject, said that love was but "the contact of two epidermises, and
the exchange of two fantasies." Little wonder that later generations
disapproved: one can forgive a mute sinner, but not an articulate
one.

Yet the Age of Reason, despite its contempt for emotion and its
insistence that man's intellect should govern his actions, was obsessed with love, or rather with that special variant of it called
"gallantry"—a socially required, intricate, ritualistic routine of flirtation, seduction, and adultery. The history of love has many an
enigma, but none more intriguing than this, that the very men and
women who spoke most nobly of subordinating their passions to
their reason were helplessly addicted to squandering their time and
money in amorous intrigues and ruining their health in excesses of
lechery.

The light of reason, in short, did not illuminate all of the human
soul; love in the Enlightenment was not as simple as it seemed. The
amiable, cynical view of sex and love may look charming when seen
from a great distance and sound delightful when set to Mozart's
music, but for those who lived with it, it must often have been
otherwise. Listen, for instance, to Madame d'Esparbès, speaking to
her distraught young lover, the Comte de Lauzun, who is in an
agony at learning that she has tired of their affair:

> Believe me, little cousin, being romantic does not succeed, but
> makes one ridiculous and nothing more. I have had a fancy for you,
> my child; it is not my fault that you have taken it to be a grand
> passion and convinced yourself that it would never end. It should
> matter little to you that this fancy has passed, and I have taken

another lover. You have many qualities to please women with; make use of them to do so; be convinced that the loss of one love can always be repaired by another, and that this is the means of being happy and agreeable.[1]

It is the pure authentic voice of enlightened love. The gracious, well-mannered words, though chilly, sound harmless; yet there is a tendency implicit in them which has not even a good name yet, but will gain one a century later from a practitioner of the ultimate development of this viewpoint, Marquis Donatien de Sade.

2

Gallantry and the "Aching Void"

G allantry had a long pedigree, particularly in France, but during the Age of Reason it underwent notable changes. From the time of Marguerite of Navarre on, it had meant Petrarchan affectations, allegedly painful emotions, intricate "services" and proofs of devotion, loquacious and didactic courting, and, perhaps at last, assignations and love-making. But the mysticism and affected emotionalism of all this was intolerable to the men of the Age of Reason. They still wanted to cluster about women who combined sex and intellect—but they sought a new kind of woman who could be detached and perfectly cool about love. Here is how one of the women they most admired wrote to her young lover, in about 1670, in terms perfectly expressing the new spirit:

Shall I tell you what makes love dangerous? It is the sublime idea we are apt to form of it. But to speak the exact truth, love, considered as a passion, is nothing but a blind instinct that one

[1] *Mémoires de M. le duc de Lauzun,* quoted in Edmond and Jules de Gon- court: *La Femme au Dix-Huitième Siècle,* p. 172.

must know how to appreciate properly—as an appetite which directs us toward one object rather than another without our being able to account for our taste. Considered as a relationship of friendship, when reason presides over it, it is no longer a passion, and indeed it is no longer even love.

That was Ninon de l'Enclos speaking—the greatest beauty, courtesan, and salonière of the latter half of the seventeenth century. In her home, men of intellect and breeding met regularly to exchange *pensées*, and to become her lover, if she beckoned. Ninon herself would placidly choose one of her admirers and inform him when he might begin to reign as her lover. His office would last a few weeks or months, and then he would be informed that the affair was over —but so charmingly and courteously that he remained a friend and a member of the salon. Ninon would then select the next favorite and notify him of his selection. None of her lovers was permitted to show signs of affection in public, either before being chosen or during the period of grace; each, however, was allowed to contribute to her upkeep.

Yet to none of them did this relationship seem like a form of prostitution. The distinguished men who were her friends were of the opinion that they had been in love with her and she with them; her lifelong friend, Saint-Evremond, congratulating her in her later years on a life well and richly lived, summarized the best side of gallantry in two sentences: "I consider you, in full life as you are, the happiest creature that ever was. You have been loved often enough to leave nothing untasted in pleasures, and wisely enough to avoid the disgusts of a languishing passion." Less than two centuries had passed since Castiglione wrote *The Courtier*, but it might as well have been twenty.

The most influential exemplar of rationalist gallantry was the young man who, at the very time of Ninon's zenith, took over the control of France and became its greatest king. He was, of course, Louis XIV, *le roi soleil*, the sun-king whose effulgence was so great that Father Hébert, a priest at Versailles who knew him intimately, wrote: "He is a very tall man, and very well proportioned; he is six feet tall as near as makes no matter," whereas in fact Louis, standing erect, was only five feet five. Father Hébert, however, and all of Europe, saw him with bedazzled and admiring eyes. In all things, Louis was the beau ideal of the aristocracy, and what he did in the matter of gallantry, each lesser man would try to do as best he could.

Louis had started out ungallantly by falling romantically in love, when still only a foolish lad of eighteen, with Marie Mancini, a niece of his prime minister, Mazarin. Like any country bumpkin, the boy-king thought that love was reason enough to marry her, but Mazarin and the Queen-Mother were horrified. They were fishing for larger game—the Infanta of Spain—and packed Marie off without further ado, lecturing the distraught Louis on his royal duty and the folly of romantic passion. Sullen and embittered, the young king married the Infanta and turned to gallantry.

Louis did not record his inner feelings, but one can judge much from the fact that thereafter he bedded impartially with chambermaids, peasant girls, and ladies of noble blood; it was only necessary that each make a suitable pretense of loving him, and he, being the greatest of gentlemen, did likewise. But if the pretense of love was important to Louis, equally important was the avoidance of all real feeling. He established a remarkable set of rules of etiquette at Versailles not only to enhance his stature, but to suppress all evidence of emotion in his court. Even to *tutoyer* (use the verb forms with "thou") in the King's presence was the height of bad manners. To stay away from court because of mourning was considered ill-bred or disrespectful, and to fail to conceal one's grief with gaiety and cheerfulness was highly improper. When a prominent court lady died suddenly, Madame de Maintenon described Louis's reaction to a friend: "The death of Madame d'Espinois," she wrote, "was a surprise and nothing more. The King rids himself of unhappy ideas as soon as possible."

Though he was the very embodiment of politeness and good breeding, Louis could treat his women with remarkable callousness. His homely Spanish wife genuinely loved him, but he required her to live on intimate terms with his mistresses and to keep a cheerful face about it. When he transferred his affections from Louise de la Vallière to Madame de Montespan and wished to conceal it from the world, he made La Vallière the confidante, and had her sit guard in the outside chamber while he sported in the bedroom with the new favorite. His *Mémoires* give little indication how he felt about either of them, but it contains advice to his son which is a good clue. "Our first thoughts," he wrote, "should always be toward the preservation of our glory and power. . . . A mistress is the most dangerous of favorites." He once told a group of his courtiers: "I command each of you that if you notice a woman, any woman in the world, gaining control over me, you will tell me at once. It will not take me twenty-four hours to rid myself of her."

Madame de Montespan, however, lasted for years, but in the end Louis tired of her tantrums, her jealousies, and her stormy scenes, and chose as his next mistress the lovely, dignified Madame de Scarron, whom he made Madame de Maintenon. She was three years older than he, calm, placid, and given to unremitting self-control; in three decades she never let him see the least boredom or annoyance on her face, but sought to please and cheer him. It little mattered that she was nearing middle age, and no longer a ravishing beauty. This liaison was the right one for him; when the Queen died in 1683, he even married Madame de Maintenon secretly, gave up outside gallant affairs, and became almost domestic. What was this woman like whom King Louis, still only forty-six, found so satisfactory—so much so that he quit all others for her, performed almost all his state business in her drawing room, and increasingly followed her sober and religious bent? She was handsome, charming, and polished; but a remarkably frank letter by the Abbé Gobelin, one of her spiritual advisors, yields this astonishing information: "She had a marked disgust for the state of marriage. . . . Despite the affection she bore for Louis XIV, she retained these revulsions; she submitted to the conjugal duties only with regret and . . . her spiritual director had to exhort her to conquer herself on these painful occasions." Aside from the act of physical union, how the King and Madame de Maintenon felt about each other is far from clear, for she carefully burned all letters addressed to herself, and left only her own, composed with great care and edited to a fare-thee-well. "I wish to remain an enigma to posterity," she once remarked, but not too enigmatically she retired from the King's side during his final illness and shut herself up at her girls' school at St. Cyr, apparently unconcerned and oblivious of his condition. This was the woman whom the handsomest and greatest king of Europe, after all his experience with gallantry, chose to marry when he was still in his prime, and whom he kept beside him for thirty-two years to give him what he evidently thought of as love.

Like Louis XIV, upper-class men and women of the late seventeenth and eighteenth centuries concealed their feelings by the aid of cold reason and carefully rehearsed manners; after a while, they almost forgot they had any feelings. Philibert, Count de Gramont, a gallant and extravagant playboy, came to England in 1662 after being exiled by King Louis. Gramont became quite friendly with two young aristocrats, Anthony and George Hamilton, and at the same time fell in love with their sister, Elizabeth, a court beauty who unfortunately had no great purse. The courtship progressed under the stimulus of her blond good looks and his smooth talk of marriage; finally it arrived at a critical, indeed irretrievable, stage. In December 1663, when Gramont was recalled by King Louis, and hurried off without her, the Hamilton brothers felt obliged to chase after him and only succeeded in overtaking him at Dover. With deep bows and ceremonious phrases, they assured him of their enduring respect and humble service, and inquired if perhaps he had not forgotten something. "Ah, true," said Gramont with admirable aplomb, undoubtedly taking a pinch of snuff, "I have forgotten to marry your sister."

Back they went together in the most amiable fashion possible, and seven months later Gramont became the father of a handsome legitimate son. Neither he nor the Hamilton brothers ever harbored any ill will about the incident, and, in fact, many years later Anthony Hamilton wrote a glowing eulogy entitled *The Memoirs of the Comte de Gramont*, retailing the Count's military and gallant adventures; with great good taste, however, Hamilton said nothing of the incident at Dover.

Gramont had been perfectly comfortable at Whitehall, for Charles II of England, having spent his years of exile at the French court, had brought its manners and morals back to England upon his restoration in 1660; there they were eagerly adopted as part of the reaction against the asceticism of the recent Puritan regime. He and his courtiers wore immense, curling, chest-length French periwigs, and when they bowed deeply, they tossed their curls back into place with a swooping movement known as "the French wallow." They spoke French fluently, danced gracefully, and observed a new and more formal etiquette, somewhat similar to that of Versailles. Yet at the very same time, being newly freed from Puritan regulation, they were wild and ruffianly to a previously unknown degree. The marks of a gentleman were arrogance, the bullying of lower-class people, and a reputation for drinking, wenching, and cheating at cards. Sir Charles Sedley, a typical Restoration rake, peeled off his clothes and, stark naked, harangued a crowd from the upper floor of a building in such obscene terms that they threw stones at the windows; the Earl of Oxford seduced an actress by rigging up a false marriage ceremony, and it took the King himself to fine him for it; and men of distinction like Sir John Coventry and John Dryden were beaten and wounded by hired thugs for having insulted or offended nobles too grand to demean themselves by fighting.

The several well-known vices, especially adultery, were practically a political necessity in the court of Charles II. The Puritans had opposed them all; debauchery, therefore, was the easiest proof of loyalty to the King. But social prestige was at stake, too; without adequate scandal and proof of sexual attractiveness, neither lord nor lady could reach the pinnacle of success. A nobleman named Henry Jermyn was the favored stallion of the 1662 season and Mrs. Theodosia Hyde, a court lady, was said by no less an authority on gallantry than the Count de Gramont to feel about him as follows:

> Mrs. Hyde had just married a man whom she loved. . . . However she was of the opinion that so long as she was not talked of on account of Jermyn, all her other advantages would avail nothing for her glory: it was therefore to receive this finishing stroke that she resolved to throw herself into his arms.

One must not gather from this that such couplings were accomplished quickly or crudely; with ladies of quality, the gentleman had to observe an elaborate ritual of courtship. Sir John Evelyn, himself something of a Puritan, described the process with evident distaste, but with reportorial care:

> You must often treat her at the play, the park, and the music; present her at the raffle; follow her to Tunbridge at the season of the drinking of waters, though you have no need of them yourself. You must improve all occasions of celebrating her shape, and how well the mode becomes her, though it be ne'er so fantastical and ridiculous; that she sings like an angel, dances like a goddess, and that you are charmed with her wit and beauty. . . . If the whole morning be spent between the glass and the comb, that your perruque fit well, and cravat strings be adjusted, as things of importance, with these and the like accomplishments, you'll emerge a consummate *beau*, or, in English, a coxcomb. . . . Thus you see, young sparks, how the style and method of woo-

ing is quite changed, as well as the language, since the days of our forefathers.[2]

Charles himself was the standard-bearer of English gallantry, as Louis XIV was of French gallantry. With his position and income as King, Charles could make a score to set other men's teeth on edge. He publicly acknowledged fourteen bastards, and history has the names of thirteen of his mistresses; there were many others whose names are lost. Being amiable and lazy, he generally chose his mistresses from among the females brought to him by his intimate advisors; but not being *too* lazy, he also indulged in a number of gutter escapades, including a famous visit to a brothel when his money was stolen and he very nearly got a beating for nonpayment before being recognized. The court rakes adored him for these follies, but the ordinary people of England were not so enchanted: the Duchess of Cleveland cost them £15,000 a year, the Duchess of Portsmouth £8,600, and Nell Gwyn, just as loving but made of common clay, £4,000. Nell was the most honest of them all, concerning royal love; she often called herself the King's whore, and once, being coolly treated by the Duchess of Cleveland, amiably clapped her on the shoulder and said: "I presume persons of one trade love not one another." Despite the handsome fees he paid, there is little evidence that Charles felt anything like tenderness or strong affection for any of them, and Bishop Gilbert Burnet, who knew the King well, said that despite his genial manner and outward bonhomie, Charles "did not think there was either sincerity or chastity in the world out of principle," and had a very ill opinion of mankind in general.

That same combination of elegance and animality, of stylized desire and cynical coldness, appears again and again in the annals of gallantry. A friend once chided the Count de Gramont, as follows: "Is it not a fact that as soon as a woman pleases you, your first care is to find out whether she has any other lover, and your second how to plague her; for the gaining of her affection is the last thing in your thoughts. You seldom engage in intrigues but to disturb the happiness of others; a mistress who has no lovers would have no charms for you." And a gentleman named Francis Osborn, advising his son against marrying a beautiful but poor woman, revealed the meaning love had for him in a crude anatomical witticism: "I have heard a well-built woman compared in her motion to

[2] Preface to *Mundus Muliebris* (a rhymed satire on women).

a ship under sail," he wrote, "yet I would advise no wise man to be her owner if her freight be nothing but what she carries between wind and water." But having delivered himself of twenty pages of sentiments comparable to this, Osborn added a postlude for any ladies who might have read the piece: his heart, he protested, "is no less ready to be your footstool in age than it was to be one of your triumphant chariots during youth." And that, in a word, is the spirit of gallantry.

Clearly, it was not just zestful, charming, and delightfully naughty. Even Madame de Maintenon once wrote to a young friend that her beauty, her pleasures, her royal favors and great years at court, had all left "an aching void." And for every Ninon de l'Enclos, whose life has busied generations of biographers, there were many women whose stories, being less agreeable and less titillating, have remained unknown except to scholars. One such was Mrs. Grace Worthley, a young beauty of good family who lost her husband in the Dutch War in 1665 and became the mistress of Henry Sidney, Earl of Romney. Sidney kept her in London where she was both comfort and ornament to him, until the passage of time and the advent of bigger game made her seem undesirable. Here are a few words from a letter she wrote to a cousin after she had been Sidney's mistress for nearly seventeen years and was in her fading forties:

> He treats me with a great deal of cruelty, which I think is very severe, first to have spent my precious youth as I have done, and now, for a reward of all my sufferings, to be abused and despised, and my son rejected as if he were none of his, and all this to please his great Mistress.[3]

About this time, Sidney cut her allowance nearly in half, had her forcibly turned away from his door by a constable, and tried to make her leave London so as to be out of his way. Finally she appealed to King Charles, who ordered Sidney to do his duty by his mistress. After Charles died, she was back in the same fix, and had to beg, threaten, and cajole Sidney year after year in this fashion:

> How happy should I now esteem myself if I could do or say something that would make you reassume your former good-nature! But do not misconstrue me, my Lord; I mean only that part of your good nature that would oblige you to do what is reasonable, and not to return to your embraces. . . . All that at present

[3] Probably the Countess of Sunderland, with whom Sidney was having an affair.

I desire your Lordship to do is let me have half a year's money next Monday. How poor and how ignoble a revenge is this of yours to me, a poor deluded woman. . . .[4]

And so it goes, year after year, until 1694. Then the letters ceased, though Sidney was still alive; one can only assume that Grace Worthley had quietly died, and so found the only lasting solution to the economic difficulties of gallantry.

3

A One-man Sample of Restoration Love

❀   ❀

❀

I f the early part of the Age of Reason was dominated by gallants and rakes, it also had its subdued Puritans, its stolid country gentry who were traditionally conservative in morals, and its men of decent and philosophic temperament such as exist in almost every age. Somewhere in the middle of all these types there was a median, an average kind of upper-class man; and by extraordinary good luck, during the first ten years of the Restoration, one of them wrote the world's most intimate, honest, and unbeautified diary. He was Samuel Pepys, fairly well born, fairly well-to-do (after a while), and both a fairly good husband and a fairly successful rake. Scattered throughout the six fat volumes of Pepys's coded memoirs is an unsparing portrait of one man's love life in Restoration England—an ill-blended amalgam of license and shame, exuberant sen-

---

[4] Both letters (and many more like them) were found in the Sidney correspondence, and printed in the introduction to Sidney's published letters, which appear under the title: *Diary of the Times of Charles the Second* (1843).

suality and feeble efforts at restraint, cheerful adultery and sincere marital affection.

Pepys came of minor gentry of Huntingdonshire and was reasonably well educated, but he lacked the arrogance and polished manner that only rank and wealth could give, and did not even learn to dance until he was twenty-eight. He even somewhat favored the Puritans for a while during the Civil War, but by 1660, when he was twenty-seven, he went along with the fleet that escorted Charles II from France back to England in glory. Through good connections, Pepys became Clerk of the Acts in the Navy and proved to be so devoted and accomplished an administrator that he eventually rose to the post of Secretary of the Admiralty. Though he was not very handsome (having a rather long bulbous nose and an over-heavy lower lip), and affected none of the extreme fopperies of the time (it took him days to muster up enough courage to wear his first ordinary periwig out on the street), he won the respect of his betters, mingled with them freely every day, and admired their looks, their habits, and their pleasures. As much as he could, he tried to act like one of them.

Before he began to model himself upon them, Pepys had done a very irrational and unaristocratic thing: he married for love. Having been enraptured by a fifteen-year-old French beauty, he wedded her without considering the fact that she had no property. For a while, he was mightily enamored of her; commenting years later on a new piece of music he had just heard, he wrote: "The wind-music . . . is so sweet that it ravished me, and indeed, in a word, did wrap up my soul so that it made me really sick, just as I have formerly been when in love with my wife." But he learned that, in the world of the wealthy and the rational, men and women asked other questions first and looked for love later. As a result, he so meddled in his younger brother's affairs, haggling and arguing for adequate dowry, that the latter died a bachelor. Samuel Pepys could even reflect, in one of his less charming moments, how ironic it was that "all my troubles should arise from my disorders in my family and the indiscretion of a wife that brings me nothing almost (besides a comely person) but trouble and discontent."

But she *was* pretty, and Pepys once remarked of himself in some astonishment: "A strange slavery that I stand in to beauty that I value nothing near to it." What he meant by this "slavery to beauty" was nothing metaphysical or pseudo-Platonic, but a simple, urgent response to almost any attractive female, from a court beauty to a streetwalker; he tried to make love to all of them, and often succeeded, being equally ready to use a bed in his own home, a carriage, or an unlit alleyway. Whether he caught hold of the maid while his wife was out shopping, or flirted with ladies at a court reception, he recorded everything unsparingly and without pretensions, and his utter candor has a charm about it, even in the tawdrier moments. In a public alehouse he had the bad taste to thoroughly paw Doll Lane, a trollop, yet the disapproving reader can only chuckle with him when Pepys ruefully comments: "She has a very white thigh and leg, but monstrous fat." The sight of a homely woman, whom he had been told was a great beauty, once put him in bad humor for a whole day; the sight of an attractive woman would make him gay, and if the occasion permitted, start him on an immediate flirtation. Even when the occasion was not appropriate, Pepys was often galvanized into action by the irresistible force of his slavery to beauty; on August 18, 1667, for instance, he went to St. Dunstan's Church,

> where I heard an able sermon of the minister of the place; and stood by a pretty, modest maid, whom I did labor to take by the hand and the body; but she would not, but got further and further from me; and at last I could perceive her to take pins out of her pocket to prick me if I should touch her again—which seeing I did forbear and was glad I did spy her design. And then I fell to to gaze upon another pretty maid in a pew close to me, and she on me; and I did go about to take her by the hand, which she suffered a little and then withdrew. So the sermon ended, and the church broke up, and my amours ended also.

No wonder it is easy to like him: he is always willing to laugh at himself.

Yet much about Pepys was far from being modeled along rakish lines. "God forgive me," he wrote one time after fondling a lady, "I had a mind to something more." He did not enjoy gambling; winning upset him almost as much as losing, and he prayed God not to tempt him. Though he loved the theater, he frequently swore never to go back when he had seen some particularly licentious comedy, but he always did return. He carried off his infidelities with suitable coolness, but once, when his wife sweetly and with deliberate malice asked him to read aloud a letter by Sir Philip Sidney that dealt with such matters, he was more troubled than he allowed her see: "My conscience told me it was most proper for me, and therefore was touched at it, but took no notice of it, but read it out most frankly, but it stuck in my stomach." His peccadilloes even bothered him privately, and although his diary was written in cipher, he fooled his conscience by turning some of the more lurid episodes into an idiotic jumble of schoolboy's foreign phrases, to wit: "Doll Lane, and con elle I went to the Bell Tavern, and ibi je did do what I would con elle as well as I could. She sedendo sobre thus far and making some little resistance. But all with much content and je tenai much pleasure com ista."

Like any bourgeois, Pepys was stodgily conservative about his wife's appearance in public; when she first donned a blond wig, he refused to let her wear it, and only with great reluctance did he let her begin to use black beauty-patches in the courtly fashion. Yet he was pleased when she showed up to advantage: "My wife, by my troth," he once wrote, "appeared I think as pretty as any of them; I never thought so much before." And also like a bourgeois, he took a great interest in household management, considering himself the immediate master of all affairs; the result was an interminable series of criticisms, scoldings, quarrels, and tears. He and his wife quarreled about many other things, too, and as often as he remembered, Pepys would act the real man of the seventeenth century, reducing her to abject submission merely by maintaining stony silence. Sometimes, however, he would call her names and swear at her, and occasionally might even frighten her into silence by making a fist at her ("She, poor wretch, was surprised with it and made me no answer all the way home.") Once in a while he went still further: "Find my wife in a dogged humor for my not dining at home, and I did give her a pull by the nose and some ill words." Yet there is also much in his diary that seems warm and affectionate:

> December 27th, 1663: . . . So home to dinner with my wife very pleasant, and pleased with one another's company, and in our general enjoyment one of another, better we think than most couples do. . . .
> February 25th, 1667: . . . Talking with pleasure with my poor wife, how she used to make coal fires, and wash my foul clothes with her own hand for me, poor wretch! in our little room at my Lord Sandwich's; for which I ought forever to love and admire her, and do.

Yet Pepys was too much a man of his time to take her problems seriously. Mrs. Pepys was childless and bored, and all Pepys could think of was that she lacked work to keep her busy. He made a few brief and ineffectual efforts to divert her with music, dancing, and geography, but once when she handed him a written statement about the boredom of her seclusion, he fell into a rage, tore it up, and for good measure tore up some of his old love letters to her. Towards the end of the diary (which Pepys abandoned, because of weakening eyesight, when he was thirty-six), there occurred a monumental struggle between husband and wife over the matter of Pepys's affair with Deb, his wife's personal maid. It went on and on for over a week, and culminated in a tear-streaked quarrel in the moonlit bedroom, lasting half the night. Deb was discharged, but Pepys hunted her out and indulged in more intimacies; his wife found out, and there ensued another terrible fight. And this time Mrs. Pepys won; Pepys signed an affidavit not to see or speak with Deb, and even declared, in the privacy of his diary, that he was

> most absolutely resolved, if ever I can master this bout, never to give her occasion while I live of more trouble of this or any other kind. . . . Did this night begin to pray to God upon my knees alone in my chamber, which God knows I cannot yet do heartily.

The London rake and moralistic Christian in one soul—a complicated combination, and sometimes an awkward one, but very likely the pattern of the typical upper-class male in the year 1668. If other men of that period appear in history to have been more urbane, cynical, and egocentric, it may be only that we have not had the chance to eavesdrop and hear them on their knees, wrestling with what they liked to call their "natural desires."

4

Love and Polish
in the Eighteenth Century

❀   ❀

❀

By the early part of the eighteenth century the Enlightenment had come of age. The educated and aristocratic classes had very generally subscribed to a new scientific and rational outlook on the world, replacing the mystical and intuitive ones of the past. The views of such men as Descartes, Galileo, and Newton about the physical world supplanted those of the Old Testament. A humane, amused, and tolerant view of man as a feeble but admirable animal took the place of sin-laden theologies which saw him as the guilty center of the universe. The ideal of human conduct was thought to be behavior in which cool, dispassionate reason guided every act, rather than emotion, revelation, or ancient custom.

On every side the rationalists found evidence of the logical and orderly nature of the physical world and of human character. The advances in astronomy, the growth of commerce, the emergence of stable monarchies, and the increase in material comforts all lent credence to the view that the universe was an excellent mechanism made by a Master Mechanic who wound it up, set it ticking in accordance with scientific and mathematical laws, and thereafter did not presume to interfere in its operation. Just as by detached reason He therefore was responsible for the conduct of both atom and star, so by reason ought man, His little likeness, govern himself and society—humanely, sensibly, and without prejudice.

The Enlightenment appealed to several groups in European society. Liberals and scientists rejoiced in it because of its rejection of ancient religious authority. The mercantilists found it good because it lent the sanction of philosophy to the present social order and justified the status quo. As Alexander Pope said, assuring everyone that the world was just as God meant it to be and needed no man-made improvements:

> And, spite of pride, in erring reason's spite,
> One truth is clear, Whatever is, is right.

But above all, the Enlightenment had the sympathy of the aristocracy, for it not only sounded their note of complacency, but expressed and justified their attitudes toward emotions, sex, and especially manners.

Never had there been such emphasis on manners, for an artificial code of formal behavior, applied consciously and deliberately, was the ideal technique for masking one's emotions and governing the irrational part of one's personality. Skill in the use of elegant courtesy, perfection in the maintaining of icy self-control, and the display of highly civilized politeness even in the tensest situations were the marks both of good breeding and of reason. Sometimes, to be sure, the overly civilized observance of politeness threatened to halt all normal human activities: the Duc de Coislin once saw a departing guest as far as his carriage, which was required; the guest, as also required, saw the Duc back to his own suite; but Coislin, the politest man of his time, then insisted with utmost assurances of his respect and devotion upon seeing his guest back to the carriage again, and the guest, seeing no other way to end the process, finally rushed out ahead of the Duc and managed to lock him in. Coislin, not to be outdone, leaped out the window and met him at the carriage. Having sprained his thumb in the leap, he then got it set by a surgeon, contested with the surgeon for the honor of opening the door for him, and sprained it again.

In England, manners continued to undergo refinements moderating the excesses and crudities of the Restoration period. Prior to 1703, at the fashionable resort of Bath, for instance, gentlemen wore their swords in public buildings, came to dances roaring drunk, talked vulgarly before ladies, and brawled and wenched without restraint. But by 1703 or 1705 Richard Nash ("Beau Nash") became the recognized Master of Ceremonies at Bath, and instituted new rules of deportment: gentlemen might not wear their swords, drunkenness was impermissible, and brawling, swearing, and undignified forms of flirtation were ruled out. Young dandies learned to bow and "make a leg" with all the Gallic grace in the world, offered each other snuff with matchless flourish, kissed each other on the cheek, and swore such pretty little oaths as "Why, blister me! Enfeeble me! Impair my vigor!" At other resorts, and in London, society rapidly changed in the same direction, and copied the manners of Bath and Paris.[5]

The emotional life of human beings almost disappeared behind the repressions of reason and the façade of stylized manners. Lord Chesterfield once cautioned his son never to say anything so crude to a bereaved friend as: "I am sorry for your loss," when good manners would call for: "I hope, Sir, you will do me the justice to be persuaded that I am not insensible of your unhappiness, that I take part in your distress, and shall ever be affected when you are so." Polished wit replaced overt anger: Richard Brinsley Sheridan, replying to an opponent in Parliament, said with flawless urbanity: "The Right Honorable gentleman is indebted to his memory for his jests, and his imagination for his facts," and when Chesterfield received the famous terrible letter of rebuke from Samuel Johnson, scorning his tardy patronage, he smilingly displayed it to friends and carefully pointed out in it certain excellent turns of phrase.

The customs of love likewise developed some bizarre aspects. A lady could receive visits from gentlemen while in bed or even in a covered bath; it was perfectly in order for a gallant to pretend to conceal tender feelings under such circumstances. Fond words and straightforward endearments were considered the *gaucheries* of inferior classes. In place of direct emotional expression, ladies learned from their French dancing-masters the code of the fan: it could be dropped, fluttered, closed with a clap, spread across a bosom, spread only partway across the bosom, or used as a weapon. Masks and masquerade balls were never more popular; anything was permissible if only emotion were concealed, and rules of etiquette observed. Casanova reported in his *Memoirs* that when he visited England, a strange lady once offered him a lift in her carriage, and though she refused to tell her name, allowed him to proceed from a squeeze of the hand to an inevitable conclusion before the ride was over; some time later, when he met her in someone's home and asked if she had

---

[5] The lower classes were meanwhile being improved by sterner methods. Dissenters (as Puritans were now called) and Anglicans joined hands in the formation of several Societies for the Reformation of Manners, one of which, between 1696 and 1730, brought about 99,380 prosecutions, almost all of lower-class people, for drunkenness, swearing, lewdness, and similar vices.

forgotten him, she frostily replied: "I remember you perfectly, but a frolic does not constitute an introduction."

The language used by eighteenth-century lovers is particularly intriguing. Words do not follow mere vagaries of fashion; the choice of language is governed by deep-seated forces of the human personality. It was not merely neo-classical style, but basic character structure, which made for the invariable use of such tepid abstractions as "witty nymph," "obliging modest fair," "endearing charms," "lively transports," and "pleasing flames"—expressions so conventional, polite, and formalized as to allow one to hint at emotion while nearly eliminating its power. Alexander Pope wrote some love letters to Lady Mary Wortley Montagu, and when she pretended he was merely being airily gallant, he protested in the rationalist equivalent of a throbbing confession:

> It would be the most vexatious of all tyranny if you should pretend to take for raillery what is the mere disguise of a discontented heart that is unwilling to make you as melancholy as itself; and for wit, what is really only the natural overflowing and warmth of the same heart as it is improved and awakened by an esteem for you.

Even in private amorous conversation, educated men and women used much the same sort of language and the same stilted, remote words and phrases. When young James Boswell was in London in 1762, he met and began visiting Mrs. Louisa Lewis, a pretty young actress, and hoped to have an affair with her. After some visits, he pleaded his passion and begged her to be "kind," a request she promised to think about. A week later he called on her to learn her answer, and since he copied down his own conversation as faithfully as he later did Samuel Johnson's, we have a chance to eavesdrop upon him and hear the very words an eighteenth-century gallant and a lady spoke, just as they spoke them, during that crucial scene. The dialogue went as follows:

> *Boswell:* The week is now elapsed, and I hope you will not be so cruel as to keep me in misery. (*He begins to take some liberties.*)
> *Mrs. Lewis:* Nay, Sir—now—but do consider—
> *Boswell:* Ah, Madam!
> *Mrs. Lewis:* Nay, but you are an encroaching creature! (*He deftly lifts up her petticoat.*) Good heaven, Sir!
> *Boswell:* Madam, I cannot help it. I adore you. Do you like me?
> *Mrs. Lewis (kissing him):* O Mr. Boswell!

> *Boswell (still struggling against her resistance):* But my dear Madam!
> Permit me, I beseech you.

At this juncture, Mrs. Lewis pointed out that her landlady might
come in at any moment, but she agreed to make Boswell "happy"
on Sunday at 3:00 p.m., when all would be safe; and this quaint
specimen of erotic semantics concludes thus:

> *Mrs. Lewis:* Whenever you cease to regard me, pray don't use me
> ill, nor treat me coldly. . . .
> *Boswell:* Pray, Madam, don't talk of such a thing. Indeed, we can-
> not answer for our affections. But you may depend on my behaving
> with civility and politeness.[6]

Boswell was duly made happy, but a week afterwards had a rather
different conversation with Mrs. Lewis equally remarkable for the
manners in which it clothes its subject matter:

> *Boswell:* Do you know that I have been very unhappy since I saw
> you?
> *Mrs. Lewis:* How so, Sir?
> *Boswell:* Why, I am afraid that you don't love me so well, nor have
> not such a regard for me, as I thought you had. . . . I have but too
> strong, too plain reason to doubt of your regard. I have for some
> days observed the symptoms of disease, but was unwilling to believe
> you so very ungenerous. But now, Madam, I am thoroughly con-
> vinced.
> *Mrs. Lewis:* Sir, you have terrified me. I protest I know nothing of
> the matter.

After some further talk, however, she admitted to having been infected three years earlier, but protested she had been entirely well
for the past fifteen months. She swore solemnly that she had been
ignorant of being still infected, and assured Boswell she was in
misery at losing his esteem and at being in jeopardy of getting a bad
reputation. Boswell rose to the occasion superbly.

> *Boswell:* I give you my word of honor that you shall not be discov-
> ered.
> *Mrs. Lewis:* Sir, this is being more generous than I could expect.
> *Boswell:* I hope, Madam, you will own that since I have been with
> you, I have always behaved like a man of honor.
> *Mrs. Lewis:* You have indeed, Sir.
> *Boswell (rising):* Madam, your most obedient servant.

Aside from such misadventures, the average rationalist, having
nothing but scorn for the glooms and fears of earlier forms of

---

[6] *Boswell's London Journal, 1762–1763,* pp. 115–16.

Christianity, no longer thought of woman as a painted evil and the gateway to hell; on the other hand, he disdained the mystical fantasies of Neoplatonism. But his view of woman, if realistic and sane, was far from including an acceptance of her as his equal, or as a whole human being. She was still, in the eyes of the upper-class male, an ornament and a toy, a legal incompetent, and a congenital nitwit; having no religious grounds for disliking woman, he justified her continued subservience in the Age of Reason by claiming she was inherently unreasonable.

"Your sex," wrote Jonathan Swift to that same young lady who was about to be married, "employs more thought, memory, and application to be fools than would serve to make them wise and useful. When I reflect on this I cannot conceive you to be human creatures, but a sort of species hardly a degree above a monkey." Even those amiable reporters of English life, Addison and Steele, repeatedly portrayed the frivolous, useless life of woman, ostensibly with the object of reforming it. Steele complained that the typical young girl was delivered straight from her nurse to the dancing-master and was "taught a fantastical gravity of behavior, and forced to a particular way of holding her head, heaving her breast, and moving with her whole body, and all this under pain of never having an husband, if she steps, looks, or moves awry." He was hardly exaggerating; a typical advertisement of a girls' boarding school in the time of Queen Anne listed the following as the subjects taught: "The needle, dancing, and the French tongue, a little music on the harpsichord, or spinet, to read, write, and cast accounts in a small way."

The best-mannered Englishman of the century provides us with an ideal example of how the rationalist gentleman regarded love and women. He was Philip Dormer Stanhope, fourth Earl of Chesterfield, whom we heard a few pages back enunciating a formula for condolences. Chesterfield, who lived from 1694 to 1773, was the very embodiment of the gentlemanly ideal. A distinguished diplomat and statesman, a man of letters, and a generous patron of writers (with the notable exception of Johnson), he valued, above all, good manners, a sense of taste, and the cultivation of personal polish. He once commented that the very essence of gentility lay in the easy and graceful use of the arms and hands. He never laughed aloud, deeming it uncouth to do more than smile. Even his enemy, Johnson, conceded that Chesterfield's manner was "exquisitely elegant," and most people, on meeting him, got the impression that he was distinguished in appearance; in actual fact, he was rather short, thickset, and had a broad, rough-featured face. He was, all in all, a triumph of art over matter.

Chesterfield disdained the simple lechery of the rake; any footman or porter, he felt, could do as much. Instead he practiced gallantry in the grand style, and in addition, during his time as ambassador to the Hague, he openly took a Frenchwoman, Mlle Elizabeth du Bouchet, as his mistress, and by her begot an illegitimate son, Philip Stanhope. At thirty-nine Chesterfield finally married, having been skillful enough to win the hand of Melusina von Schulemberg, an illegitimate daughter of the late George I, who was nearly forty and devoid of charm, but possessed a portion amounting to £50,000 plus an annual income of £3,000. The newly-weds lived separately in adjoining houses from the very first and Chesterfield celebrated his marriage by taking a great beauty, Lady Frances Shirley, as his new mistress. His wife seems not to have minded, since as might be expected of him, he treated her with perfect courtesy.

The private principles that guided his actions were all explained by Chesterfield in certain of the famous confidential letters he wrote to Philip Stanhope over a period of twenty years in an effort to make something of the boy, and which were published against his wishes. In one of them, written when his son was sixteen, Chesterfield confided to him the gentleman's real view of women:

> Women are only children of a larger growth; they have an entertaining tattle, and sometimes wit; but for solid, reasoning good sense, I never knew in my life one that had it. . . . A man of sense only trifles with them, plays with them, humors them, and flatters them, as he does with a sprightly, forward child; but he neither consults them about, nor trusts them with, serious matters, though he often makes them believe that he does both.

Nevertheless, he added, they have so great an influence on other men that they can make or break a man's reputation, and "it is therefore absolutely necessary to manage, please, and flatter them, and never to discover[7] the least marks of contempt, which is what they never forgive."

As his son grew older, Chesterfield began coaching him in the rudiments of gallantry. Women, he said, have only two passions—

[7] i.e., reveal or display.

vanity and love—and flattery is therefore the certain method of managing them. "He who flatters them most, pleases them best; and they are most in love with him who they think is most in love with them." He added a list of specific types of flattery, but despite his instructions, Chesterfield evidently felt that the boy was not making progress, and when young Stanhope was eighteen years old, Chesterfield began to urge him to attach himself to some older woman, long experienced in gallantry but now fading, who would be grateful for a young man's interest and would perfect his manners and gallant attentions. ("Nothing would do you more good than such a passion," he later added, making it sound almost medicinal.) But as the boy matured and failed to report any successful affairs of a high order, his father tried to guide his aim for him:

> I am assured that Madame de Blot, although she has no great regularity of features, is, notwithstanding, excessively pretty; and that, for all that, she has as yet been scrupulously constant to her husband, though she has now been married above a year. Surely she does not reflect that woman wants polishing. I would have you polish reciprocally.

Sensing that Philip lacked daring and confidence, his father assured him repeatedly that, given good manners, a man could seduce almost any woman with perfectly standard gallant techniques:

> Force, assiduities, attentions, tender looks, and passionate declarations on your side will produce some irresolute wishes at least, on hers; and when even the slightest wishes arise, the rest will surely follow. . . . If you are not listened to the first time, try a second, a third, and a fourth. If the place is not already taken, depend upon it, it may be conquered.

The end of the story is beautifully ironic. Despite the brilliance of the coaching he received, Philip remained only an affable sort of fellow, neither distinguished, gallant, nor especially graceful. He died in 1668 at the age of thirty-six, leaving his aging father to learn with dismay that he had for some time been secretly married to an unattractive woman of humble origin, with whom he had apparently been perfectly content and perhaps even happy.

5

The Trouble with Don Juan

❀   ❀

❀

In bewildering contrast to the philosophic talk of self-control and the discipline of politeness, there was another face to the eighteenth century—a face of barbarity, cynicism, and unpitying cruelty. In the early part of the century, the French government was still propelling its galleys by means of chained, whipped, human beings—not only criminals, deserters, and Turkish captives, but French Huguenots. The southern British colonies in America were building an economy based upon a system of slavery far more severe than that practiced by the imperial Romans. Throughout Europe, gambling was a general obsession, estates and fortunes being freely flung onto the gaming tables, and dueling was at a peak of popularity, gentlemen thinking it entirely proper and ethical to kill one another for trifling insults. Londoners of good breeding liked nothing better than going to Hockley-in-the-Hole to watch a cockfight or to see a bear or bull torn to bits by maddened dogs. Heavy drinking had never been so common; in London alone there were 17,000 gin shops at mid-century, and Hogarth's squalid scenes of mass alcoholism were not exaggerations. Men spoke about self-control through the use of reason, but the law specified 160 capital offenses in eighteenth-century England. Executions were held publicly, and nobles, merchants and riff-raff alike turned out in holiday mood to eat fruit and gingerbread, swill gin, and watch the lads swing.

Rationalist love, too, though often portrayed as lustily lecherous and amusingly naughty, had about it a distinct malevolence. In the seventeenth and eighteenth centuries, poets and dramatists in every major European country were inescapably attracted by the story of

Don Juan Tenorio, a semi-legendary libertine of fourteenth-century Seville whose adventures and philosophy they magnified and added to until his fictional figure loomed menacing and satanic, more real than reality. There had always been stories of seducers, but it took the Age of Reason to exalt the archetype, at once detesting and admiring him, fearing and emulating him. In their denial of medieval and Christian values, the descendants of the same aristocracy who had once idolized the mythical Tristan—adoring, courteous, true, and long-suffering—now idolized the mythical Don Juan —lustful, haughty, false, and sadistic. Like all myths, it was drawn larger than life, but there were men something like Don Juan in Europe, less vindictive and monomaniacal, but dedicated to the art of cold-blooded seduction; the Duc de Lauzun, the Duc de Richelieu, Bezenval, Sedley, and Bolingbroke are only a few examples of the type.

Edmond and Jules de Goncourt, who made a highly perceptive study of eighteenth-century woman from the perspective of the mid-nineteenth,[8] said that not only had love in the Age of Reason been reduced to mere sensuality, but that its strongest motive was a desire to seduce and desert, for malicious sport. "This warfare and this game of love," they wrote, "perhaps disclose the most profound characteristics of the century." The dedicated seducer concocted plans, feigned emotions, and played his part with the skill of an actor and the dedication of a soldier; but the crown of his victory was to do all this without the slightest emotional involvement, so that when the woman, conquered and submissive, begged at last: "At least, tell me that you love me!" he could affect a disdainful smile and refuse. This, according to the Goncourts, was the grand style of seduction—seducing by pure caprice, so as to abandon without compunction. No wonder the eighteenth century found so superlatively clever that maxim of La Rochefoucauld's: "If love is judged by most of its effects, it resembles hate more than friendship."

To some degree, the deep antagonisms between man and woman may have stemmed from the economics of aristocratic marriage, which built every union upon a foundation of financial bickering, bargaining, and mistrust. Eligible young men of good family openly hunted heiresses, offered themselves to the richest, and even advertised in the papers, naming the minimum amount required to make

[8] Edmond and Jules de Goncourt: *La Femme au dix-huitième siècle.*

a girl suitable. Squire Guise, a country gentleman in search of a wife, left this plain indication of the prevailing callousness:

> Being on the bench at quarter-session, a Justice of the Peace took me aside and asked me whether I would marry a woman worth twenty thousand pounds. This lady I had seen but never spoke to, and upon the whole readily accepted his offer.

Few offers were so speedily accepted, however; in the average courtship, representatives of both sides cold-bloodedly and doggedly haggled about every detail of jointure (the inheritance guaranteed to a widow from her husband's estate), portion (her dowry), pin money (her guaranteed personal allowance), and the inheritance by the grandchildren of money or land; love or mutual attraction of the prospective bride and groom was rarely an issue. Considering the possibilities for later dissatisfaction with one's bargain, it is little wonder that the system produced as much sexual antagonism as it did.

Not every society which based marriage on property-trading has produced Don Juanism. In the eighteenth century, however, the matter was aggravated by the idea that man should—and can—subdue and repress all his emotions, a notion Ortega y Gasset has called the greatest error of Western man from the Renaissance on. Only much later would man scientifically relearn what many men had always intuitively known: that the stifling of biologically inevitable emotions results in human sickness and in destructive conduct.

A common explanation of Don Juanism, derived from modern psychoanalytic practice, is that it arises from a deep-lying fear of impotence, which is in turn frequently traced to a heavily repressed mother-attachment. But this rationale, if meaningful for modern Don Juans, is much less so for those of the Age of Reason, particularly since the emotional ties between aristocratic parents of that period and their children were extremely thin. Indeed, the principal cause which underlay Don Juanism may have been the faulty family relationships of the aristocracy, who entrusted their children to servants and saw them for a few minutes of polite conversation each day, if that much. According to contemporary psychology, it is only when the parent-child relationship is intimate, warm, and generous that the child learns a pattern of love involving empathy, altruism, and kindness, and develops a conscience consonant with those traits. If, however, the parent-child relationship is cold, barren, and distant, the child will remain psychologically a self-centered, angry infant, his concept of love being that of a struggle to grasp, seize, and hurt the unloving beloved, and his conscience, stunted in its growth, will fail to inhibit him from taking revenge for his frustrations.[9] In such persons, love can mean at best a sensual delight with a modicum of friendliness; at worst, the sodomy, tortures, and obscene self-gratifications of the Marquis de Sade; and between these extremes, the half-genial, half-hostile lecheries of the actual Don Juans.

The best-known of the latter, and the only one who wrote out a complete record of his amorous experiences, was the Chevalier de Seingalt, better known as Giovanni Jacopo Casanova. Born in Venice in 1725, he was the son of an actor and actress of Spanish descent. Possibly the most important event of his life occurred when he was one year old; at that age, he was abandoned by his parents, who handed him over to be raised by a disinterested grandmother. His character early showed its bent: at fifteen he was expelled from the University of Padua for excessive gambling debts, and at sixteen from a Venetian seminary for immoral and scandalous conduct. The rest of his life was a series of variations on these themes.

Having a brilliant mind and a talent for impersonation, Casanova became not only a man of many talents, but a consummate adventurer who played perfectly the role of a gentleman of quality. He translated the *Iliad* into Italian rhyme, wrote two dozen books on mathematics, history, astronomy, philosophy, and belles-lettres, and conversed easily with men like Voltaire and d'Alembert. George III of England, Frederick the Great, Louis XV, and Catherine the Great were only a few of the monarchs who personally received him and welcomed him. He was variously secretary to an ambassador and a galley captain; director of state lotteries in Paris; diplomatic agent for Portugal; spy for the Venetian Inquisition; and above all, swindler and gambler. Time and again his adventures would follow the same inevitable pattern. Tall, sinewy, white of tooth, eloquent and elegant, he would arrive somewhere, make a dazzling social success, and win his way into an excellent position or post of confidence; after a while he would be found

[9] Several recent works deal with this phenomenon and offer abundant clinical and laboratory evidence; among them are psychoanalyst Abram Kardiner's *Sex and Morality*, anthropologist Ashley Montagu's *The Direction of Human Development*, and anthropologist Weston La Barre's *The Human Animal*.

out to be a rogue, or would get into some scrape; muffled and disguised, he would decamp and begin again elsewhere.

Three quarters of his *Memoirs*, however, are concerned with his love affairs, but like his business affairs these are marked throughout by rascality, showmanship, and a need—often forced by circumstances—for rapid movement and constant change. His first completed sexual experience consisted of coitus with two young sisters in one bed, all three of them enjoying the performance both as participant and spectator (Casanova was his own principal spectator then and ever after). He was always fond of this particular procedure, and in old age could reflect on it with benign wickedness:

> I achieved my best results, however, by attacking novices—whose moral principles and prejudices hindered the carrying-out of my intentions—in the company of another woman. I learned already in my early youth that young girls are difficult to seduce because they lack the courage, whereas in the company of a friend they easily surrender: the weakness of one excuses the fall of the other.

The fat volumes of his *Memoirs* are full of love affairs at this level. Casanova mentioned 116 mistresses by name and claimed that he had possessed hundreds of women. They ranged from noblewomen to chambermaids, and he made love to them standing, sitting, and lying down, in beds, alleys, on staircases, in coaches, and in boats. Typically, he would feel himself to be "passionately in love" a few moments after meeting a new woman; he would then launch himself upon any one of a hundred routines, using compliments, adoring words, gifts and money if necessary, stratagems of ambush if helpful or possible, and offers of marriage when all else failed. Finally he would bed the woman—and in the morning, or sometimes after a few days or weeks, he would be off on his way to the next one, for the prey, once taken, soon palled. It was the pursuit, the intrigue, the conquest that he found delightful, and a capitulation under duress was sometimes the sweetest of all. Casanova was once riding in a carriage with a pretty woman who had refused all his advances. Suddenly a severe thunderstorm broke over their heads; she clung to him in terror in the swaying coach, and then and there, wrote Casanova smugly, "my victory was most complete."

Some people find that the bulky *Memoirs* are a vast delicious meal, others that it rapidly produces surfeit and even nausea. The women in it form a surrealistic procession of lips, breasts, and thighs, but are scarcely individualized as human beings. Casanova himself must have felt ennui, for he required ever spicier dishes to stimulate him. "Madly in love" with a beautiful nun who had a semi-impotent lover, he put on one of his most prodigious displays of versatility and endurance after she told him the impotent man wished to watch through a peephole. He once met a young girl at the opera and was so smitten that he proposed marriage almost at once; before anything happened, he met her mother, who turned out to be an old mistress of his and who informed him that the girl was his own daughter. Only momentarily daunted, he hastened to bed with the mother, while the daughter shared their bed and watched them. Several years later he met the daughter again; this time she was married to an impotent marquis who wanted a child, and Casanova thereupon obligingly made love to his daughter three times and got her pregnant.[10]

In his forties he started collecting pornographic pictures, was "inflamed" by caressing a nine-year-old girl, and in the course of a swindle had sexual connection with a seventy-year-old marquise as part of an allegedly magical ritual. By the time he was forty-nine he had had at least eleven cases of venereal disease, and his powers had greatly waned or even vanished. In his aging years, when he was gouty, afflicted with prostatitis, and bored by his placid existence as librarian to Count Waldstein in Bohemia, he decided to live the good years all over again, and poured forth an unparalleled mass of recollections, without having changed his opinion or feeling about any of it. His final judgment of his entire life was contained in three words: "I regret nothing."

On a few rare occasions, however, Casanova seems to have felt a momentary awareness of the emotional impoverishment of his life, but the mood is fleeting. He wrote, for instance, how one night, in poor health and bad fortune, he stopped at an inn where thirteen years earlier he had been forced to part, with tears and suffering,

[10] The repetition of such themes as satisfying a woman whose lover or husband is impotent, making love to a woman while another watches, and indulging in the delights of incest has about it the suspicious sound of fantasy; one wonders if an aged man did not daydream about the acts he had never dared to do in actuality. European scholars, however, have verified a number of details in the *Memoirs*, identified some of the people involved, and found letters addressed to Casanova by a number of women. If some of his stories are fantasy, the larger number are evidently genuine.

from his young French mistress, Henriette, whom he loved with all the intensity of his Latin soul. Yet on this second visit to the inn he had completely forgotten the affair, the parting, and even the inn itself, until suddenly he saw on a window the prophetic words she had scratched there with a ring: "You will forget Henriette, too." Casanova's reflections at this point are immensely interesting:

> Overcome, I dropped into a chair. . . . Comparing the self I was now with the self I had been then, I had to recognize that I was less worthy to possess her. I still knew how to love, but I realized I had no longer the delicacy that I had had in those earlier days, nor the feelings which really justify the transports of the senses, nor the same tender ways . . . *but what frightened me was to have to acknowledge that I no longer possessed the same vigor.*

As much as anything else, this final comment is Casanova's own best evaluation of the meaning of love.

6

The Bourgeois Gentleman

❁   ❁

❁

The aristocratic and rationalist ideals penetrated eighteenth-century society deeply enough to make Casanova, a mere actor's son, into an excellent pseudo-aristocrat; even more remarkably, they infiltrated that stout bulwark of sentimentality, piety, and family life, the middle class, and produced in it a number of piebald specimens of mixed cultural values.

Intellectual salons, for example, had traditionally been held by ladies of noble rank or by the courtesans of noblemen, but in the latter half of the eighteenth century a number of salonières became prominent who were of neither category, and who even had certain distinctively bourgeois qualities. Madame Geoffrin, daughter of a dauphin's valet, was a virtuous, prim-looking woman who dressed simply, usually wore a modest lace cap on her head, and was thoroughly maternal in appearance; Madame d'Épinay, the wife of a tax collector, was not so virtuous nor so prim, yet she felt impelled to raise her child herself, a strikingly bourgeois action for a wealthy Parisienne of that time.

In England, a number of intellectual ladies known to history as the "Bluestockings" imitated the French salons beginning in 1750, and some of the most notable of them—Fanny Burney, Mrs. Hester Thrale, and Mrs. Hester Chapone, for instance—were serious intellectuals and perfectly moral wives of well-to-do middle-class citizens. They wore ordinary clothing to their meetings (hence the name "Bluestockings"), and ruled out cards, gambling, and other foolish pastimes. A tradition rooted in aristocratic flirtation had finally come fully around to the point where flirtation was no longer a part of it. Fittingly, the greatest luminary of their world was the ponderous pundit Dr. Samuel Johnson, a neoclassicist and rationalist, but a conservative, old-fashioned moralist all the same. Detester of "enthusiasm" and romanticism though he was, he summed up what was really a bourgeois reaction to the genteel ideal in his famous estimate of Lord Chesterfield's *Letters:* "They teach the morals of a whore, and the manners of a dancing master."

Voltaire, the friend of monarchs and chief prophet of the Enlightenment, was actually of sound bourgeois stock, his father having been a notary (a fact Voltaire preferred to say little about). All his life, this greatest propagandist of rationalism regarded passions as a prime source of human folly, and he once typically advised a wedding couple that the surest way to love forever was not to love each other too much. His well-known affair with the Marquise du Châtelet ("the divine Emilie") lasted sixteen years until her death and was carried on in the most enlightened fashion possible—with the tolerant consent of her husband, who for some years lived with them in a *ménage à trois*. Yet there was a distinctly bourgeois flavor about the way Voltaire and Emilie kept house together so long and so completely, and they were so thoroughly identified by the world as lovers that when they no longer made love and Emilie wished to break off so as to devote herself to a new affair, Voltaire would not let her for reasons of propriety. "He owed it to his public, he said, not to make a scandal which would cover him with ridicule and contempt," writes Nancy Mitford in her recent study, *Voltaire in Love*. "He thought it right to follow a straight line and to respect what he called, with his usual inaccuracy, a liaison of twenty years (really about fifteen)."

The prevailing ideas on love and women even had some influence in America, wherever the standard of living made it possible to emulate the British aristocracy. From New York to the South, the well-to-do gentry copied such English customs as fox-hunting, gaming, dances, and duels. Even in staid New England, an English traveler in 1740 remarked that aside from the theater and similar entertainments, the Boston gentry disported themselves in tempered emulation of the English:

> Both the ladies and the gentlemen dress and appear as gay in common as courtiers in England on a coronation day or birthday. And the ladies here visit, drink tea, and indulge in every little piece of gentility to the height of the mode, and neglect the affairs of the family with as good a grace as the finest ladies in London.

But that was only at the most elegant level of colonial society. More generally, the middle-class influence and the frontier philosophy caused great changes in the imported European ideas. Colonial libraries had a good sprinkling of rationalist writing on love and women, but typically the most popular books on these subjects were the conservative, moralistic ones, critical of the gallant life and full of sound, homemaking advice. Despite a considerable amount of intellectual scorn for romantic love, and the imitation and importation of English and French manners, marriage itself was generally praised in American books and magazines; even in the cities the frontier and pioneer feeling of a woman's immense usefulness and importance was still dominant.

One can see the hodge-podge of attitudes clearly in Benjamin Franklin. America's outstanding rationalist thinker came under the influence of the Enlightenment in his boyhood and adolescent years. Despite his New England background, he took a rationalist's guiltless view of sex, but had neither the money, skill, nor leisure for fancy gallantry; as a result, he took an obvious course, though he disapproved of it on purely practical grounds. "That hard-to-be-governed passion of youth," he later commented, "had hurried me frequently into intrigues with low women that fell in my way, which were attended with some expense and great inconvenience, besides a continued risk to my health by a distemper."

Too thrifty to waste his hard-earned money on a mistress, he turned his thoughts to marriage and approached it in the same cool, thoughtful spirit. Having started his own printing business in Philadelphia in 1728, he began to court a young lady with her parents' encouragement; after a suitable time, he candidly let them know "that I expected as much money with their daughter as would pay off my remaining debt on the printing-house, which I believe was not then above a hundred pounds." Bluffing, the parents said they did not have that much to give, and even denied Franklin the right to call on the girl. He rightly interpreted this as a ruse to get him to elope with the girl and forfeit all dowry, and was so annoyed by it that he would have nothing further to do with her even when the parents tried to draw him back.

He switched his interest instead to Deborah Read, a young woman he had courted years earlier. Unfortunately, in the meantime she had married a worthless fellow named Rogers who had deserted her and who was thought to have died. The situation was awkward: if Rogers had not died, another marriage would be bigamous, and if he had died, his wife's next husband might be liable for any debts he had left. The prudent Franklin therefore made only a common-law marriage with her, avoiding any ceremony or record. In his autobiography he summarized their relationship as follows:

> She proved a good and faithful helpmate, assisted me much by attending the shop, we throve together, and have ever mutually endeavored to make each other happy. . . . It was lucky for me that I had one as much disposed to industry and frugality as myself.

It was a workable, businesslike partnership, evidently devoid of inspiration or intensity. Deborah Franklin, though handsome, spirited, and devoted to Franklin's welfare, was not interested in his philosophic and scientific speculations, and was no intellectual company for him. He may have been fond of her, but was not strongly tied to her, for he spent what were the last ten years of her life in Europe without her.

From his middle years on, by which time he had become wealthy, famous, and sophisticated, Franklin adopted some of the airs of gallantry, but only at the verbal level. He corresponded warmly

with Catherine Ray for many years, but kept what he called "a
prudent but tender distance" between them. In London he acquired several young female admirers and treated them with affection and with gallant phrases, but his relationships with all of them
remained chaste. An old tradition holds that during his years in
France, he became a septuagenarian lecher; actually, he kissed the
ladies he met, allowed the audacious young Madame Brillon to sit
on his lap, and very pleasantly used to ask her for the ultimate favor
which she always very pleasantly refused. Far from being lecherous,
Franklin was merely being a good diplomat, and an amiable human
being. The rationalist gallant in him was evenly matched by the
New England Puritan.[11]

Franklin's writings on love, sex, and marriage, widely read and
quite influential in America, are a jumble of enlightened cynicism,
bourgeois earnestness, and vaguely Christian morality. The maxims in *Poor Richard's Almanack* range from "You cannot pluck roses
without fear of thorns, / Nor enjoy a fair wife without danger of
horns" to "A house without a woman and firelight is like a body
without soul or sprite." Franklin's typical attitude toward sex was
thoroughly rationalistic, yet not in the least licentious: "Rarely use
venery but for health or offspring," he wrote, "never to dullness,
weakness, or the injury of your own or another's peace or reputation." He was equally against marriage-by-infatuation and marriage purely for a good property settlement. The best-known of his
writings on love is the mildly scandalous *Letter to a Young Man on
the Choice of a Mistress*—a bit of Chesterfield in homespun—which
tells the young fellow to choose an older mistress because she will
be prudent, wise, infertile, and grateful. But it is really mostly
spoofing; first and last, Franklin urges the young man to get married instead, since marriage "is the most natural state of man, and
therefore the state in which you are most likely to find solid happiness."

So it went with the middle-class intellectuals: they borrowed
ideas and gestures from the Enlightenment and the aristocracy, but
lived for the most part very much like the bourgeoisie they really
were. In 1751, an impecunious young Englishman named Richard
Griffith, an amateur scribbler and rationalist, succeeded in seducing

[11] The case for the chastity of Franklin's
gallantries has been convincingly made by
Carl Van Doren, after a thorough sifting of
the evidence, in his *Benjamin Franklin*, pp.
234–42, 411–12, 653, and 639–41.

his philosophic friend, Miss Elizabeth Griffith (no relation), a young girl without dowry. Where Casanova conquered in a matter of days or even hours, the middle-class Griffith had required five years of talk, letters, pleas, schemes, and promises. As luck would have it, she became pregnant, appealed to him in anguish, and he did what the genuine libertine would never have done: he married her. They achieved a warmly sentimental marriage, and even built literary careers on their own sentimental love letters, which they shortly published. Nevertheless, when Griffith drew up a will in 1753, he still had some lingering pride in his by-gone dreams of libertinage and rationalism, for on the wrapper of the will he wrote:

> I was not over-reached into this match by art, nor hurried into it by passion, but from long experience of her sense and worth I reasoned myself into it. . . . I found I had so engaged her affections that no other man could make her happy, and so dallied with her character that only myself could repair it.[12]

It was the last defiant nose-thumbing of a wicked little boy, who has been trapped into becoming a respectable husband.

7

A Most Unlikely Love Story

And so we have before us a portrait of rationalist love drawn from life. Yet is there not something lacking? Some final stroke, some bit of shading, that will vitalize the expression and add the final illusion of reality? Perhaps we will find it in one more story of

[12] Quoted in J. M. S. Tompkins: *The Polite Marriage*, p. 1.

love—a brief one, a pathetic one, a wildly improbable one that could have happened only during the Enlightenment.

It begins in the fall of 1765, when, at the salon of the Marquise du Deffand in Paris, two human beings met who were the least likely of all protagonists of a love drama. The man was Horace Walpole, English gentleman: a fragile, refined bachelor of forty-eight, a Member of Parliament, a literary amateur, a devotee of refined manners, a collector of curiosa and relics of whom a friend once remarked that his house was a museum and himself the best-preserved mummy in it. His behavior was marked by extreme polish and artificiality; he would never even think of striding manfully into a roomful of people, but would enter in a fashionably delicate manner almost on tiptoe, his knees slightly bent, as if afraid of a wet floor. "Walking is not one of my excellences," Walpole himself confessed. "In my best days . . . I tripped like a peewit." Thin-lipped, high of forehead, and frail of build, he was plagued by gout and subject to fatigue; not surprisingly, he took great comfort in rationalist philosophy, and summed up his opinion of emotion in a famous sentence: "The world is a comedy to those who think, a tragedy to those who feel." Accordingly, he thought about everything, and found everything material for his wit, for despite his prissy and affected manner, with friends or fellow intellectuals he was a marvelous conversationalist (though some thought he prepared his remarks in advance), and one of the most prolific and entertaining letter-writers of all time. In a word, he was one end-product of the era—all manners, all intellect, all gentility, sterile, inbred, and on the way to extinction.

The woman of the story was the hostess herself, the famous salonière, Marie Anne de Vichy-Chamrond, Marquise du Deffand, whom Walpole was meeting for the first time—a birdlike wisp of a woman, seventy years old. No, it is no tasteless jest, no stupid error by the historian; these are indeed the two protagonists. When he first met her, she was already tiny and withered, her clear blue eyes totally blind these twenty-odd years, her chiseled profile still exquisite but her once-translucent skin now dry and pale, her frothy imperious wit surviving on a rich daily diet of intellectual conversation. In her youth she had married and shortly been separated from the Marquis du Deffand, but her beauty and extraordinary mind soon won her the honored position of mistress of the Duc d'Orléans, Regent of France; later she had long-term liaisons with a few other men of importance and high rank, was for some years the principal ornament and intellectual lady of the court of the Duchesse du Maine, and had for many years maintained one of the principal salons of the century at her quarters in Paris. Among her habitués were many leading aristocrats, intellectuals, and encyclopedists (Voltaire, Montesquieu, Madame de Staal-Delaunay and d'Alembert, for instance), and some of the major creative writers of the era. Still alive to every new idea, still restless, energetic, and endlessly eager to talk about everything, she reigned as queen in her salon, her barbed wit as keen as ever, her gestures as graceful and elegant as always even though her hands were now as frail as two dead leaves.

It was a day in October 1765, when Walpole first came to her salon to look and listen. He was mildly displeased to find such vivacity and such pleasure in cleverness on the part of so venerable a lady, and in a letter to his cousin, Henry Conway, he referred to her as "an old, blind debauchee of wit." Yet he was fascinated by the vitality and the charm of the spirit imprisoned in that faded body; he came again and again, and shortly was describing her to a friend as "the old, blind, charming Madame du Deffand." He talked to her for hours, visited her continually, and by late January wrote to his friend, Thomas Gray, that she

> . . . retains all her vivacity, wit, memory, judgment, passions, and agreeableness. She goes to operas, plays, suppers, and Versailles; gives suppers twice a week; has everything new read to her; makes new songs and epigrams, ay, admirably. . . . Her judgment on every subject is as just as possible; on every point of conduct as wrong as possible; for she is all love and hatred, passionate for her friends to enthusiasm, still anxious to be loved, I don't mean by lovers, and a vehement enemy, but openly.

For her part, Madame du Deffand found something rare, shy, and beautiful in the mind and soul of the crotchety, middle-aged bachelor; she responded to him with an outpouring of talk, effusions of flattery, and rapturous expressions of her feeling of *amitié* (friendship) for him that startled and frightened him. Yet it was Paris, and the salon habitués seemed to find nothing laughable or incongruous about the situation. Walpole was hypnotized into staying five months, and toward the end of that time he called on her daily, sat by her side during the salon gatherings, and in private even gingerly spoke of his own warm regard for her.

Then he had to go home, and the very touch of English soil produced a remarkable metamorphosis. Suddenly he was afraid of his involvement with her, shocked at his own actions, and genuinely alarmed lest English friends suppose he had been an old woman's lover and ridicule him for it. Meanwhile he was hotly pursued by letters in which she poured forth adulation, despair, and flattery in cascades of fluent rhetoric. What had seemed utterly charming in Paris seemed hideously inappropriate in England, and he wrote her, sternly scolding her for her indiscretions and romantic extravagances. She replied with warmth, but not the heat of anger: "Where, pray tell, did you get the idea that I am given to indiscretions and romantic transports? . . . I, the declared enemy of all that has the least resemblance to romance!" But two weeks later, completely forgetting this ringing declaration, she wrote in another vein, blurting out an incredible confession like an infatuated schoolgirl, even while pretending to find unobjectionable names and reasons for her feelings:

> I forget that I have lived; I am only thirteen. If you do not change and you come to find me again, my life will have been a happy one. You will wipe out all the past and I will date only from the moment when I met you. . . . Don't tell me that I have romance in my head —I am a million miles away from it, I detest it; everything which resembles love is odious to me, and I am almost glad to be old and hideous—not to mistake any profession of feeling for me, and happy to be blind, to be very sure that I am incapable of anything but the purest and most sacred friendship.

And only a few days after this palpitating message, she sent him one that was, in a way, still worse, since it plainly asked for pity and succor:

> All I can see is our separation, which it seems to me must be eternal. . . . I shall never see you again; it was not worth your coming here to revive me and help me, if it only meant making me die twice. You see how sad I am; it is really a kind of despair.

All of this produced in Walpole something akin to panic, and on May 20, 1766, he wrote her a shocking reply:

> On my return from Strawberry Hill[13] I find your letter, which gives me the utmost possible annoyance. Ought not your lamenta-

[13] Walpole's miniature mock-Gothic castle near Twickenham; he had just come back from there to his town lodgings when he wrote this letter.

tions ever cease, Madame? You make me repent my frankness.
. . . Really, if friendship is to have all the sorrows of love without its pleasures, I see no reason for trying it. . . . If you wish
our relation to continue, conduct it on a less tragic note.

So began what is surely the most incredible correspondence in
the annals of love—840 letters from her and nearly as many from
him over a fifteen-year period—filled with repeated outpourings,
confessions, quarrels, and apologies; on her part an endless stream
of emotional outbursts, on his a series of formal, cranky, and sometimes frozen replies ("*Je suis refroidi*," he actually wrote—"I am
refrozen"), unsuccessfully trying to make her hide or at least
moderate the intensity he found so upsetting and embarrassing.
(Walpole realized how these letters would sound to the world and
later asked for them back and burned them; only eighteen survive,
plus phrases or sentences from eighty-two others; Madame du Deffand's remain complete, not a word missing.)

To Walpole's most unconscionable attacks, Madame du Deffand
replied neither with icy scorn nor vitriolic rage, but a variety of
softer moods. Sometimes it was gentle sarcasm: "The English are
conceited and insolent. Declarations of friendship, of boredom, of
sadness . . . —they take all that for unrestrained passion." Sometimes it was with petulant tearfulness: "I think I have a friend, I
console myself by telling him my troubles, I take pleasure in
speaking to him of my friendship . . . and he is scandalized, ridicules me, and abuses me in every possible way!" Sometimes she
promised to reform: "You will find on your return (if you do return) that I am much improved. . . . I have a kind of fear and
respect for you that has very good effects." And sometimes she
resorted to exquisite flattery: "You make my setting far more
beautiful and happy than my noontime or my rising. I am only
frightened of not living long enough to see you again and tell you
all that I know not how to write you." And when, occasionally,
he would unbend a trifle, it would send her off into an ecstasy; once,
for instance, he wrote in a kindly vein to ask about her health and
got back this delirious burst of thankfulness:

Your insults, your roughness, even your cruelties, have never
blinded me to the goodness and the tenderness of your heart.
. . . Your letter has upset me so that I feel as if I were drunk.

If Walpole could not tame her, neither could he make himself
break it off. Indeed, he finally succumbed to the lure and visited her

for six weeks in 1767. In her own salon in Paris the transformation
in him again took place; once more he was the urbane charming
conversationalist, witty, gentle, and solicitous, offering his arm to
the frail little Marquise and acting as her prince consort. But when
he returned to England, he was *refroidi* again. It happened a third, a
fourth, and a fifth time, yet she never despaired or gave him up.
During his last visit to her, when she was seventy-nine, she could
still act like an impulsive girl: when he arrived, seasick, dirty, and in
need of a complete change, she rushed to his room at once, insisted
that her blindness made it permissible for her to stay, and chattered
gaily while he washed and dressed. They talked until 2:00 a.m.;
then she let him retire, but she was still full of things to say; when
he awoke in the morning, he found a long effusive letter awaiting
him which she had dictated while he was sleeping.

The entire affair was as baffling to her as it was to him; she
twisted her words and tortured her explanations, fearing always to
seem ridiculous. A letter she wrote about a year after they met is
typical of many others that indulged in the same confusions:

> It is a misfortune and a very great one, this friendship I have
> conceived for you. Ah! *mon Dieu*, how far it is from romance and
> how little you have known me to have suspected me of it! I love
> you only because of the esteem I have for you, and because I be-
> lieve I have found in you the qualities I vainly sought for fifty
> years in so many others.

But the letter is not unclear, after all. Whatever she may call it,
whatever she might deny it was, this was the one emotion Madame
du Deffand had never known in all her long, glamorous, gallant
life, and for which her unknowing heart had always been starved.
It was the bitterest of ironies that she was seventy when she first felt
it, and that Horace Walpole was the last man in Europe who could
return it. There may never have been a more hopeless love affair
in the world.

This, then, is the last stroke in the portrait; this is the final touch
that gives meaning. Love in the climate of rationalism could produce a frigid Madame de Maintenon, a rakehell Gramont, a cal-
culating Chesterfield, a libertine Casanova, and a sexless Walpole;
then, for good measure, it could give everything that was best
about the gallant life to a dazzling Madame du Deffand, only to let
her discover, hopelessly late, that all her life she had completely
lacked the thing she wanted most.

Chapter IX

THE ANGEL IN THE HOUSE

1 The Unmeaning of Romanticism

2 An Apostle of Romanticism
and His Gospel

3 The Practices of Romantic Love

4 Household Romanticism

5 Private Lives of Some Victorians

6 Emancipation and Confusion

7 Perfect Love and Some
of Its Imperfect Results

The Unmeaning of Romanticism

In his later years Lord Chesterfield, that paragon of good breeding and exponent of rational gallantry, grew deaf and lived in seclusion, largely out of touch with society. Perhaps it was just as well; before his death in 1773, the world of the absolute monarchs in which the Enlightenment had flourished was mortally ill. But even in advance of the wars and revolutions that destroyed it, the finely polished pattern of upper-class European life was being tarnished by influences a fastidious gentleman like Chesterfield could view only with revulsion. Factories were starting to befoul the good air, and businessmen with porky faces and soiled linen were growing wealthier than many an aristocrat. Some of these *nouveaux riches* tried to copy the ways of the upper class, but the more distressing spectacle was the upward infiltration of the tastes and customs of the lower and middle class. The Methodism of John Wesley—a reformer of morals who was so strict that he disapproved even of tea-drinking or lying abed of a morning—gained such ground in the latter half of the eighteenth century that the Established Church itself was following suit with a reforming movement known as Evangelicalism. The taste of chambermaids and merchants' daughters for the sentimental novels of Richardson and his imitators was spreading to people of the better sort. Throughout educated society, the urbane control of one's emotions was losing its popularity and being supplanted by a benighted, bourgeois attitude summed up in the word "sensibility"—a hyperemotional frame of mind, deeply affected by every event or thought. It became the style to exhibit languor, pallor, and a physical "decline" as proof of one's great sensitivity of soul, and some-

times an even more extreme result was attributed to it, as witness
this inscription on the Oxfordshire gravestone of a young lady:

> Her artless beauty, innocence of mind, and gentle manners
> once obtained her the love and esteem of all who knew her. But
> when nerves were too delicately spun to bear the rude shocks
> and jostlings which we all meet with in this transitory world, Na-
> ture gave way; she sank and died, a martyr to excessive sensibility.

Rationalist gentlemen like Chesterfield had wooed and philan-
dered with aplomb, considering love an excellent pastime, and they
had held a skilled style of seduction to be a necessary social grace.
Sensibility changed all that; men of the newer generation considered
love as a mighty force and a noble goal in life, but the higher they
prized it, the more they seemed to grow shy with women, inhibited, and fearful of rebuff. Men spoke of love in rhapsodic terms,
but shied away from sexuality; they began to prize not the dazzling
flirtatious woman, but the shy, virginal one, and themselves acted
just as shy, and nearly as virginal. In the very era when love poetry
again came into its own, a number of literary journeymen were re-
vising and purifying the love poetry of earlier eras; not only bawdy,
lusty, or passionate expressions were trimmed out, but even those
that might make the unwary reader think of sexual love, and, accordingly, one James Plumptre even emended Shakespeare's lyric
from "Under the greenwood tree/Who loves to lie with me," to
read "Under the greenwood tree/Who loves to work with me."

These were but a few of the signs of a major change in European
social ideals—a broad counter-trend to reason and neo-classicism
usually given the general title "romanticism." The label may itself
be the most confusing in the history of ideas, having been freely
pinned on unrelated areas of literature, politics, and psychology, on
events of brief duration and on movements lasting centuries, and
on such disparate phenomena as Rousseauism and horror novels,
free love and idealized chastity, Methodism and the Catholic revival,
and the French Revolution and the reaction that followed it. In
recent years, indeed, some scholars have at last thrown up their
hands in disgust and decided that the terms "romantic" and "romanticism" are an academic scandal and have become quite useless.

Fortunately for us, in the area of love these words are still meaningful and valuable. We have already seen romantic love in earlier
manifestations and observed its characteristics; in the late eighteenth
century it is this tradition that re-emerges from partial obscurity

and guides a larger fraction of society than ever before. And yet if it is still recognizable, it is not what it once was. The term "romantic love" refers really not to one thing, but to a loose aggregation of ideas and customs. As it passed down the centuries, some were continually sluffed off and others added; it is somewhat like the philosopher's much-darned socks, the fabric of which was eventually altogether changed, but which never lost their identity as a specific pair of socks.

One rarely thinks of the businessmen of the Industrial Revolution, for instance, as being the inheritors of a love tradition that was originated by the feudal knighthood, adapted to the needs of chivalry, and designed to provide extramarital adventures; and when one looks at the nineteenth-century family photograph of the round-bellied patriarch, stiff and unbending, surrounded by his well-scrubbed progeny and demure wife, it seems unlikely that he had been personally influenced by the eloquent preciosities of sixteenth-century Neoplatonism. Yet such was the case; the tradition of romantic love was clearly identifiable, but had become so modified that it suited the needs of a business-oriented society. To see how that society was able to blend feudal, Renaissance, and Puritan traditions, and why romantic patriarchalism seemed so important to it, we will concentrate our attention on an extreme and clear-cut example—Victorian love, or romantic love in nineteenth-century England, an archetypal pattern for much of Northern Europe and America.

If it may surprise one to find that the Victorians were the latter-day romantics, it may seem equally surprising that the romantics of Byron's own era were—with a few such notable exceptions as Byron himself—nearly as prissy and puritanical as the Victorians who would follow them. And though one usually thinks of the nineteenth century as being marked by high moral standards, a close-knit family life, and a tender, worshipful view of woman, it was also an age in which prostitution and deviation were endemic, the ancient structure of marriage was crumbling, and women themselves were making a determined revolt against their glorified status. Why all this was so we will understand better after doing our utmost to invade that sacrosanct shrine of shrines and mystery of mysteries, the Victorian bedroom.

2

An Apostle of Romanticism
and His Gospel

❈   ❈

❈

B ut the Victorian bedroom is neither easily seen into nor invaded; it was well shuttered and firmly locked. We need to
go back, and borrow both passkey and lamp from a pre-romantic
whose life illuminates nineteenth-century love although he died in
1778, whose ideas were immensely influential in conservative England though he had been a somewhat radical Genevan who lived
in France, and whose ideals were vastly admired although his personal life had been more or less shocking.

This was Jean-Jacques Rousseau, composer of operas and plays,
novelist, political theorist, educational reformer, and social philosopher. Every college student learns that he was one of the most
influential forces in fostering romanticism, political liberalism, and
sentimentality. Everyone knows of his nature worship, his concept
of the "natural man" spoiled and debauched by civilization, his pro-
republican theory of the "social contract," and his quarrels with the
rationalist *philosophes*. Generally by-passed in college, however,
are the unusually frank *Confessions* Rousseau wrote in later life,
recounting in detail not just his career, but his endless ailments, de-
pressions, and complaints of plots against him (David Hume described him unforgettably as a man not only naked in the world,
but without a skin), and in particular retailing his amorous history.
Extraordinarily, in the age when Don Juan was the fictional ideal,
Rousseau was pleased to recount about himself a series of sexual
and erotic tales involving incompetence, misadventure, and frustration. Sentimental tears, timidity, unsatisfied passion, and renun-

[300]

ciation seemed to him at once pathetic and noble; he wept for his shortcomings, and was thoroughly proud of them.

Rousseau was born in Geneva in 1712, the son of a watchmaker of French Protestant origin; his first piece of bad luck was the death of his mother nine days later. When he was a small boy, his father would sentimentally tell him about his dead mother's beauty, virtue, and goodness. "Jean-Jacques," he would say, "let us speak of your mother," and the small boy would knowingly reply: "Very well, father, then we are going to cry." Though Isaac Rousseau was fond of his son, he never let him forget that it was his birth that had killed his mother. "Ah, give her back to me!" he would cry out to Jean-Jacques, and the child would weep helplessly.

When the boy was ten, his father had to flee from Geneva. Jean-Jacques was farmed out in the succeeding years to an uncle and a tutor, and later apprenticed to an engraver. Some of his neurotic amorous proclivities began to appear quite early.[1] At the age of twelve, for instance, when he was boarding with a pastor named Lambercier, the pastor's sister threatened to whip him for misbehavior. He misbehaved anyhow, got whipped, and found to his astonishment that while it was painful, it was also peculiarly delicious. He loved her the more for the beating, and the very next time Mlle Lambercier beat him, she saw an evident symptom of his erotic feelings and thereafter refused to paddle him. It is tolerably obvious that this propensity stemmed from Isaac Rousseau's mishandling; the boy desperately sought to find a loving mother-substitute, yet expected punishment for having killed his real mother. For the rest of his life, Rousseau hungered for cruelty and beatings at the hands of women; fearing to ask for them outright, he transmuted his desire into an acceptable form by employing the older traditions of romantic love:

> To fall on my knees before a masterful mistress, to obey her commands, to have to beg for her forgiveness, have been to me the most delicate of pleasures. . . . This way of making love does not lead to rapid progress . . . [and] consequently I have possessed few women, but I have not failed to get a great deal of satisfaction in my own way, that is to say imaginatively. So it is that

[1] In some cases the dating of the episodes to follow does not coincide with that in the *Confessions*, but Rousseau's memory was inaccurate, and his paranoia far advanced, by the time he wrote it; scholars have managed, with considerable effort, to correct some of the discrepancies.

my sensibility, combined with my timidity and my romantic nature, have preserved the purity of my feelings and my morals, by the aid of those same tastes which might, with a little more boldness, have plunged me into the most brutal sensuality.

At sixteen, Rousseau ran away from the engraver, and a few miles from Geneva met a kindly curé who sent him to the home of a recent Catholic convert, the widow Louise Eleanore de Warens. Rousseau expected to find a pious, cranky old woman; instead, he came upon an angelic ash-blonde lady of about twenty-eight, whose sweet face and gentle manner captivated him instantly. For a while she housed and supported the short, nervous, black-eyed youth; then under her influence he went to Turin, studied Catholicism and became a convert, and after several years of vagabondage returned to her home at Annecy, the only place he felt happy and secure. Madame de Warens, whom he always called "Mamma," saw to it that her "Little One" got a decent education and a knowledge of music, and she secured him several government positions, each of which he muffed; but she always understood and forgave, and continued to take good care of him.

At twenty-one Rousseau, too shy to make advances to women, was still a virgin. At last the mother of one of his music students began to make some approaches toward him, and brought about one of the truly significant episodes of his life. Mamma, having learned of the impending situation, took him into the garden one beautiful day and told him, in the sweetest and kindest fashion possible, that promiscuity was dangerous; to save him from it, she proposed to grant him her own favors, but wanted him first to think it over for eight days. Rousseau could hardly answer her, so wild and vivid were his fancies. He had always considered Mamma extremely pretty, and the thought of the promised fulfilment threw him into a very fever of anticipation, but as the days passed he was all but sick with anxiety, fear, and even revulsion, a condition he found infinitely perplexing. "I loved her too much to desire her," he wrote half a life later, still perplexed. "That is the clearest idea I have on the subject."

The eighth day arrived; Rousseau went, all atremble, into her bedroom and learned his lesson. To appreciate the extraordinary emotions he felt, one has only to imagine the palpitating youth, in the moment of highest passion, murmuring "Mamma! Mamma!" His own comments on the episode are wonderfully revealing:

[I] found myself for the first time in the arms of a woman I adored. Was I happy? No; I tasted the pleasure, but I knew not what invincible sadness poisoned its charm. I felt as if I had committed incest and, two or three times, as I clasped her rapturously in my arms I wet her bosom with my tears. As for her, she was neither sad nor excited; she was tranquil and caressing. . . . She neither received sexual pleasure nor knew the remorse that follows.

It was the blueprint for romantic love—the burning but remorseful man, the frigid but charitable woman, the love-making compounded of yearning and tears, desire and guilt.

Tears and guilt notwithstanding, Rousseau remained Mamma's lover for some six or seven years, though one gathers that the actual sexual episodes were relatively infrequent and always colored by sinful overtones. Although Mamma remained perfectly kind and sweet despite Rousseau's instability and petulance, she finally took a better lover in 1738 or thereabouts, gently assuring Rousseau that she did not propose to deny him her favors and that he had only to share them with the new lover. Bursting into tears at her feet, he said that although he would always adore her, he would not so degrade her. "It is to our heart's union that I sacrifice my pleasures," he cried, but he chose this alternative so readily that perhaps it represented a relief; he stayed on in her house without discomfort another year before finally leaving to make his own way in the world.

In Paris, Rousseau began in his early thirties to achieve some success as an opera composer. Meanwhile, lacking the pleasures Mamma had provided, he took a fancy to Thérèse le Vasseur, a young, very shy, and simple girl who was a servant at the inn where he lived, and rather easily seduced her; what was more important, he found in her a companion who became attached to him by a doglike devotion. Telling her he would neither marry her (on some vague principle of rebellion against social custom) nor desert her, Rousseau began a permanent association with Thérèse, finally setting up housekeeping with her in a plain fourth-floor apartment and openly acknowledging her to his friends and the world.

What sort of woman was it that this greatest of the pre-romantics chose for his common-law wife? Neither a very pretty nor a charming one, and certainly not a clever one. Thérèse learned to write under Rousseau's prodding, but never to read properly; she never was able to tell time, count money, or name the months of

the year in proper order; and her malapropisms were so outrageous
that Rousseau compiled a little anthology of them for the amusement of one of his patrons. Five children were born of their union,
but since Rousseau felt that he could neither support them properly
nor write with children around the house, he turned all five over
to a foundling home. Although he and Thérèse wrangled somewhat in later years (particularly after Rousseau ceased being her
lover), he never left her; in fact, after twenty-five years of this
union, he married her in 1768, his middle-class origins and his boyhood Calvinism asserting themselves after all his years of intran-
sigence. As to what the relationship meant to him, he left this mys-
tifying summary:

> From the first moment I saw her until this day [circa 1770] I
> have never felt the least glimmering of love for her [and] no more
> desired to possess her than I had desired Madame de Warens. . . .
> The sensual needs I satisfied with her were for me purely sexual
> and had nothing to do with her as an individual. . . . Love did
> not enter into the feelings that attached me to the woman who has
> been dearest to me.

Famous at last as a writer and thinker, in his forties Rousseau
began to brood that he would die without ever having truly loved.
Day after day he would leave the country cottage in which they
were then living and go alone into the woods to spin daydreams of
love and tragedy; these he began to set down in the form of a
novel filled with painful and exquisite sentiments. In the middle of
this, a neighbor of his, Sophie, the Countess d'Houdetot, dropped
in at the cottage one day when her carriage got stuck in the mud
near by. She was an attractive vivacious woman of about twenty-
seven, with gentle features, a bubbling wit, and waving black hair
that she could let down to her knees. It was inevitable that Rousseau
should see in her the heroine of his novel, and in himself the hero;
moreover, since she had a lover named Saint-Lambert to whom
she was fervently devoted, and since Rousseau was suffering from
a chronic bladder ailment that made him all but impotent, his
chances of success in love were nil, and thus the entire situation was
perfectly suited to his inclinations. He fell in love with her wildly,
his emotion being so great as to produce trembling, palpitation, and
convulsive movements of the limbs; later he said that this was the
only real love of his life.

One perfect night, in the moonlit garden of her house, his tongue was fully unloosed and he poured forth with consummate eloquence all his emotions, weeping "intoxicating tears" at her knees, and making her weep likewise. But though she called him the most charming of lovers, she said she could not love two at one time and must remain faithful to Saint-Lambert. "I sighed and was silent," wrote Rousseau. "I kissed her. What a kiss! But that was all." And he supplied a rationalization which superbly covered the situation —an explanation that might have been written by Bernard de Ventadour, the Provençal troubadour who had sung the praises of pure ladies six centuries earlier:

> The light of every virtue adorned in my eyes the idol of my heart; to have soiled that divine image would have been to destroy it. . . . I told her a hundred times that, if it had been in my power to gratify myself, if she had put herself at my mercy of her own free will, except in a few short moments of madness I should have refused to purchase my own happiness at such a price. I loved her too well to wish to possess her.

This bizarre emotional life was in considerable part the product of neurosis, but Rousseau adapted it to a cherished ancient tradition, thereby idealizing and dignifying his disease. Moreover, it happened to reflect the growing sentiment and inclinations of his time, and his ideas therefore had immense success and influence among the liberals and intellectuals of late eighteenth-century Europe; so does fortune immortalize a man for his sickness in one age, and merely hospitalize him for it in another. Two works in particular carried Rousseau's ideas on love to the public. The first was *La Nouvelle Héloïse*, the novel he began before his unhappy love for Sophie, and completed after it, in 1761; the second was *Émile*, a novelized tract on education, published in 1762. The former told of the love of a man of low position and a girl of rank, her marriage (at her father's request) to a man of her own station, the sufferings of her lover, her purity as a wife and mother, and the partial easing of her lover's misery through the exercise of noble sentiments. *Émile* had little plot, but dealt with a young man's choice of an ideal wife and discussed the importance of domestic virtues and the proper upbringing of children.

Both novels, in short, put forth surprisingly conservative doctrines, considering Rousseau's cantankerous nature and untidy manner of life. Actually, all his thoughts about women and love were essentially old-fashioned and bourgeois, rather than radical and

avant-garde. Julie and Saint-Preux, for instance, the protagonists of
La Nouvelle Héloïse, were platonic lovers for a long while before
finally becoming physical lovers. Julie, after her marriage, became
an ideal wife and mother and was unswervingly faithful to her husband, even when Saint-Preux returned, his old love for her burning as brightly as ever. Much of Saint-Preux's sorrow at having lost
her stemmed from the fact that true love is unique, and not to be
found twice in life, each person having but one ideal soul mate.
This was a romantic concept of considerable age, and in Rousseau's
own time it already seemed hopelessly antiquated and barbaric to
rationalists; Dr. Johnson snorted that there were fifty thousand
women in the world a man might be as happy with as any one particular woman. *Émile* offered still more conservative doctrines. Its
major theses on woman are that her intellect is much inferior to
man's, and that she therefore requires a different kind of education;
that she should be weak and timid, and strive to make herself agreeable and obedient to her husband all the time; and that her proper
business in life consists of domestic affection, child-rearing, and the
cultivation of tender sentiments.

If there seems to be a striking inconsistency between his adoration of woman and his view of her as an acquiescent homebody, one
need not be surprised; in his private love life Rousseau had been
chronically inconsistent, and it had never bothered him. He wrote
ecstatically of the love he felt for Madame de Warens, but claimed
that the only true love he ever felt was for Sophie; he was sick for
Sophie's embraces, but believed that his love was too great to let
him possess her; he lived comfortably with a woman vastly inferior
to him, used her as concubine and housekeeper, and married her
only after marriage had lost its value for her; and having given
away his own children, he wrote sentimentally about home life and
child-rearing.

The truth was that Mamma, Thérèse, and Sophie represented
three aspects of woman that he strove to amalgamate; in his own
life he never succeeded, and even in fiction he scarcely managed it,
but he assured the world that it could and should be done. For well
over a century after the publication of his books, the middle class
and even some upper-class young men and women in Europe were
deeply under his influence; many of their problems in love and in
marriage were surely due to the fact that the amalgam was not much
easier for anyone else to make than for Jean-Jacques Rousseau.

3

The Practices of Romantic Love

❀   ❀

❀

Within a few years after Rousseau's death, many of the phenomena collectively called romanticism were flourishing
in Europe; in particular, the practices of romantic love which he
idealized were fast becoming the ruling fashion. Despite his ec-
centricities, he had not been speaking only for himself, but had
cogently expressed much of the domestic morality and sentimental
piety of the growing middle class. The sooty factory towns and
grubby counting-houses of the Industrial Revolution hardly look
like a fertile soil for the growth of that tender plant, romantic love.
In folklore and fiction, it is generally associated not with tradesmen, but with poets, musicians, rebels, and nonconformists; yet the
principal elements of romantic love had entered middle-class life by
the seventeenth century, and in that shelter survived the cold win-
ter of rationalism. When industrialization caused the middle class to
grow rapidly in size and power, its ideals of love and marriage began first to color and then to dominate Western thinking. Nonconformists like Rousseau were not really the typical romantics,
but only the extremists who put into words what the mercantile,
the professional, and the business people had long felt.

There were other reasons beside tradition for the sympathy the
middle class felt for the ideas Rousseau had espoused. His thoroughgoing individualism matched and expressed the general philosophy
of the bourgeoisie, especially that of Protestant England. Just as
laissez-faire economics and Puritan conscience were forms of individualism, so too was sensibility: it was individualism in the realm
of emotional life—a reliance on one's own inner feelings rather
than some external or rational standard. It is not so surprising after
all that the plant should have thrived in the soil of industrialism.

Rousseau's ideas, furthermore, appealed to the new middle class by their very earnestness and seriousness. His *Confessions*, though they tell of sexual transgressions, are soul-searching, serious, and almost entirely humorless. These were qualities the upward-striving middle class approved and prided itself on. Even before Rousseau's death, the *Sentimental Magazine* in England observed with approval that laughter and wit were going out of style, and by 1815 the *Edinburgh Review* was pleased to note that the change had gone still further:

> Our very advances in politeness have an undeniable tendency to repress all the extravagances of mirth or indulgence in humor . . . and to restore our original English taste for honest, manly good sense. . . . Artificial spirits and mere frivolous glitter, we believe, were never in so little request among us.

This latter-day Puritanism was not limited to the lower-class Methodists, but spread to the Church of England; it was an Evangelical reformer who persuaded George III in 1787 to close gaming houses, prosecute the drunk and the lewd, and suppress licentious publications. But no official edict was the cause of the closing of Ranelagh Gardens, one of London's famous pleasure parks, in 1803; it was, rather, the gradual conquest of England by a revived Puritanism that made Ranelagh's business wither away after sixty successful years.

Rousseau's paeans to the pure and the motherlike in woman also accentuated a growing middle-class emphasis on female delicacy and modesty. The earlier Puritans had called things by plain names, but the new Puritans and the Rousseauists became linguistic prudes. As early as the 1790's, no decent woman used good old expressions like "with child" or "brought to bed," but substituted "pregnant" and "accouchement," words which would spare tender sensibilities. By 1805 various expurgated classics were being put on the market, and the most famous of them appeared in 1818—Thomas Bowdler's *Family Shakespeare*, a version which excluded "whatever is unfit to be read by a gentleman in the presence of ladies." Although ladies' fashions continued to feature décolletage in upper-class circles, the romantic-bourgeois preference was for greater modesty; by 1798, in fact, a lady named Priscilla Wakefield, surveying the status of woman in a book, was all aflutter over the gross indelicacy of mortuary practice. "How shocking," she wrote, "is the idea of our persons being exposed, even after death, to the observation of a parcel of undertaker's men."

The typical romantic prided himself on the ability to fall tumultuously and passionately in love; at the same time, there runs throughout romanticism a persistent theme of sexual inhibition or limitation similar to Rousseau's, though seldom so severe. Goethe and Beethoven were both frequently very deeply in love, but succeeded in possessing few of the women they loved, and Keats, despite his sensuous poetry and his throbbing love letters, probably died a virgin. In 1798 it seemed perfectly reasonable to Reverend Thomas Malthus, fretting about the problem of overpopulation, to suggest that young people, though they fall in love, spend a number of years as abstinent lovers, marry late, and thus produce fewer children. Even to anti-Malthusians this seemed easy enough for women, for the emerging female ideal of the time was a sweet, tender, girl-mother (Madame de Warens again) in whom sexual desire seemed inappropriate, if not downright wicked. In a rape trial in 1804, Miss Rachael Lee, who had been abducted and ravished by two men, admitted that when resistance seemed pointless, she had flung away a magic charm supposed to preserve her chastity, and cried: "Now welcome, Pleasure!" In view of this shocking conduct, the judge dismissed the two alleged rapists forthwith, to loud huzzahs by the spectators.[2]

In place of sexuality, the romantics delighted in being demonstratively sentimental, melancholic, tempestuous, or tearful, according to the occasion. Tom Moore, the Irish poet, singing some pathetic ballads to an audience, so moved them that one by one they slipped off, reduced to helpless sobbing; Moore himself, equally moved by his own songs, at last bolted in a fit of tears. Brides were known to swoon at the altar, and ministers sometimes wept at the Table. Keats was moved by an urn and Shelley by the wind, but Coleridge was deeply stirred by a mere jackass and Wordsworth by things even more prosaic:

> *To every natural form, rock, fruit, or flower,*
> *Even the loose stones that cover the highway,*
> *I gave a moral life: I saw them feel,*
> *Or linked them to some feeling.*
>
> Prelude, III, 127–30

[2] M. J. Quinlan: *Victorian Prelude,* pp. 66–7, 154, 245–8; C. W. Cunnington: *Feminine Attitudes in the Nineteenth Century,* pp. 28–9.

When love was the cause, it produced cascades of rhetoric and frenzied actions. A young French medical student, distraught at not seeing the woman he loved for three weeks, wrote her as follows: "In the forest I shouted like a demon, rolled on the ground, crunched branches between my teeth. . . . In a rage I took my hand between my teeth and bit convulsively; blood spurted forth and I spat out at heaven a piece of living flesh. . . . I would have liked to spit out my heart at it."[3] It may be that emotional compensation is as simple as a law of physics: where the rationalists had repressed their emotions and acted out their sexuality, the romantics restrained their sexuality and poured forth their emotions.

One other compensatory device deserves mention—the development of the clinging-vine personality in women of the romantic period. Along with modesty, virtue, sweetness, and similar qualities, she was supposed to be weak, fearful, and anxious to lean on, and be dominated by, a strong kind man. Having no tradition of land inheritance, middle-class women had no marriage settlements and were wholly dependent on their husbands, any dowry being completely controlled by the husband, and divorce being all but impossible. Cleverness and education, never prized by the middle-class husband, went out of vogue, and "Bluestocking" became a term of reproach. Industrialism itself directly fostered the clinging-vine concept; the making of clothing, food, and medicine, and the teaching of children, were moving outside the home, depriving the middle-class wife of many of her functions, though leaving her cloistered—a situation paralleling that which we saw earlier with the women of Periclean Athens. An Edinburgh physician, Dr. John Gregory, advised his own daughters in 1774:

> The intention of your being taught needlework, knitting, and such like is not on account of the intrinsic value of all you can do with your hands, which is trifling, but . . . to enable you to fill up in a tolerably agreeable way some of the many solitary hours you must necessarily pass at home.

The reasonably well-off romantic did not need a woman-of-all-work as did his forefathers; he could therefore concentrate more on her value as a love ideal. Since, however, she was supposed to be uneducated, demure, frail, and modest, she was fading out as a person and becoming something of a wraith. The medieval troubadour

[3] G. M. Young: *Early Victorian Eng-*   *Romantisme et les moeurs*, p. 153.
land, Vol. II, p. 424; L. Maigron: *Le*

had met a similar situation by simply attributing the same divinity and perfection to any lady he loved. An analogous phenomenon took place in the romantie era: men sought an ideal woman rather than a real one, and pinned their ideal image on some girl of whom, because she had been so quiet and retiring, they knew very little.

William Hazlitt, the literary critic, is a case in point. In 1820, when he was forty-two and separated from his wife, he fell in love with his landlord's twenty-year-old daughter, a pretty, uncommunicative, uneducated girl. Each morning when she brought up his breakfast, Hazlitt would speak extravagantly and at length of his love for her, uttering innumerable statements like this: "Ah! enchanting little trembler! You are an angel, and I will spend my life, if you will let me, in paying you the homage that my heart feels towards you." He attributed to her every virtue, every beauty, every uplifting influence, and assured her that she could, if she would, remake his life for him. After each of his interminable speeches, the girl would reply in a monosyllable, or sometimes, extending herself, would make as long a statement as: "Indeed, you greatly overrate my power." Hazlitt supplied her with all the qualities he wanted her to have, and even was charmed by her lack of speech. "Her words are few and simple," he told a friend, "but you can have no idea of the exquisite, unstudied, irresistible graces with which she accompanies them, unless you can suppose a Greek statue to smile, move, and speak." His friends were not so ecstatic; Bryan Procter, a poet, met her through Hazlitt and saw her more plainly:

> Her face was round and small, and her eyes were motionless, glassy, and without any speculation (apparently) in them. Her movements in walking were very remarkable. . . . She went onwards in a sort of wavy, sinuous manner, like the movement of a snake. She was silent, or uttered monosyllables only, and was very demure.

Benjamin Haydon, another intimate of Hazlitt's, considered her nothing but a "lodging-house hussy" who would be the death of Hazlitt, and he wrote to a mutual friend: "He is really downright in love with an ideal perfection which has no existence but in his own head." [4]

[4] Hazlitt published the details of the affair anonymously under the title *Liber Amoris;* his statements quoted above appear on pp. 16 and 129; Procter's quote is from his *An Autobiographical Fragment,* pp. 181–2; Haydon's letter is quoted in P. P. Howe: *The Life of William Hazlitt,* p. 349.

For a year and a half Hazlitt loved her to distraction and believed her coolness to him was only the result of extreme maidenly modesty; he begged her to admit her feelings, but although she would sometimes sit on his lap and permit him a few chaste kisses, she would never admit anything and refused to promise to marry him. Nonetheless Hazlitt went to Scotland for half a year to obtain a divorce, but when he returned, he found her chillier and more uninterested in him than ever. He went berserk with rage and smashed things in his lodging-house room; then he went walking to calm down, saw her with another man, and discovered that she had had a lover all along. Suddenly she looked different to him; he saw her as a "lodging-house decoy" and a "callous jilt" who was small, indifferent-looking, and affected in manner. But disillusion did not mean the end of pain. For nearly two years he was despondent, disorganized, and almost unable to work properly. Mrs. Shelley, having run into him some time later, wrote to a friend: "I was never so shocked in my life; he has become so thin, his hair so scattered, his cheekbones projecting; but for his voice and smile I would not have known him." Hazlitt married a well-to-do widow shortly afterwards, but the marriage lasted only a short while; he lived the remaining five years without seeking or finding love again. Having judged so wrongly, he had had quite enough of it.[5]

As far as woman was concerned, her new role—that of the passive, quiescent, clinging vine—was a necessary adaptation to her changing problem of winning man. She was becoming less useful to him; it made sense, therefore, to attract him by flattering his ego through the claim of frailty and dependency. Hannah More, once a Bluestocking and a friend of Samuel Johnson, became later on a pious Evangelical and an exponent of the clinging-vine view. "To be unstable and capricious," she wrote to a friend in 1793, "I really think is but too characteristic of our sex; and there is no animal so

[5] The ability to imagine all the hoped-for perfections in a non-entity or someone relatively unknown was likewise the basis of the love-philosophy of Stendhal, who, incidentally, knew and admired Hazlitt. Stendhal called the process "crystallization"; just as a common twig (he said), if immersed for a time in salt water, becomes covered with glittering crystals, so does the ideal of a woman, residing in a man's mind, become the focus for a crystallizing of perfections and ideal attributes. Stendhal knew it to be a willful folly, but lived by it all the same. Being a Frenchman, he had more physical achievement in love than Hazlitt, but of the eleven women he adored in his life, the six with whom he had success all suffered from decrystallization after he won them; the perfect loves in his life were the ones who never yielded. See his *De l'amour*, pp. 6–7, 11, and 324*f*, and Howard Clewes: *Stendhal*, p. 32*f*.

much indebted to subordination for its good behavior as woman." Within a few years she was actively campaigning against all forms of female education that might give women interests outside the home. Even in America, where the frontier influence and the slower development of industrialization had retarded this view, the percentage of women who worked outside the home decreased markedly in the decades following the Revolution. In every country with a strong middle-class influence, men showed a new patriarchalism that went hand in hand with the feminine retreat. Napoleon stated flatly that "a husband ought to have an empire absolute over the actions of his wife," and saw to it that his Code embodied laws to that effect; Thomas Jefferson argued that the vote should never belong to women, since "the tender breasts of ladies were not formed for political convulsion"; and Keats, ecstatic about the new woman, burbled: "God! she is like a milk-white lamb that bleats/For man's protection."

The new-style patriarchs, unlike those of old, saw home life with their tender lambs as the be-all and end-all of existence. The footloose master, coming home when he wished and then only to attend to his own comforts, was an outmoded male ideal; the new one was that of a devoted stay-at-home husband. In 1829 William Cobbett, the newspaper publisher and parliamentary reformer, described the good marriage in terms that clearly anticipated, and even outdid, the much-touted "togetherness" of suburban home life in the late 1950's. In Cobbett's picture of nineteenth-century marriage (given in his book, *Advice to Young Men*), the wife stays at home to care for the house and tend the children; only the shameless woman trips around town paying idle visits and seeking diversion. The good wife's husband shares every available hour with her; he spends no time away from home except on business, always comes home punctually, plays with his children, helps his wife with the chores, and tells her of the affairs of his day. But there is no togetherness in the making of decisions; though the menu, furniture, and servants are her affair, he alone decides on their home location, their scale of living, their politics, the children's education, and other major questions. Still, his absorption in her and hers in him is complete and exclusive; Cobbett even disapproved of the custom of separating wives from their own husbands at dinner parties, and for that matter saw little point in dinner parties altogether or in entertaining in general. "What company," he asked, "can a young man and woman want more than their two selves, and their children, if they have any? If here be not company enough, it is but a sad affair."

It all begins to sound familiar. It is still romantic love, in a tradition eight centuries old—but newly domesticated, puritanized, and tailored to the measure of middle-class Anglo-Saxon culture; romantic love chastened, tamed, and grown cautious in its manners. In a word, it is nascent Victorianism.

4

Household Romanticism

❀   ❀

❀

The crown was set upon Victoria's head in 1837, but many of the attributes of Victorianism were already evident in England and elsewhere. In retrospect the nineteenth-century bourgeoisie look insufferably smug, complacent, and secure, but this is partly the effect of distance and nostalgia. The newly arrived middle class was, in fact, quite insecure in many ways. Its own industrialism was spawning a self-aware proletariat, and already agitators were loudly touting socialist ideas; farmers were counterattacking the growing power of the cities via uprisings and new political movements; and the rapid advance of the sciences was posing myriad questions that established religion could not answer. Most important of all, the free-for-all of economic liberalism was greatly accelerating that dissolution of ancient social ties, loyalties, and customs that had been going on ever since the Renaissance. "The Old has passed away," Carlyle wrote in 1831, "but, alas, the New appears not in its stead; the Time is still in pangs of travail with the New." And the travail only grew more intense. By the 1870's Matthew Arnold was lamenting the "break-up of traditional and conventional notions respecting our life, its conduct, and its sanctions, which is undeniably befalling our age." The era was far from being that fairyland of certainty and security we often imagine it to have been.[6]

The desire to find or achieve stability in a rapidly changing world led the Victorians to take many social actions of a constructive nature—political reforms, Sunday schools, hospitals, religious revivals, poor relief, and the like—but in private life it found its chief expression in the exaggerated worship of home life and in the domestication of romantic love. "This is the true nature of home," said John Ruskin, "—it is the place of Peace; the shelter, not only from all injury, but from all terror, doubt, and division." But home was more than shelter; in a commercial world where ancient loyalties and affections had dissolved, it was the only place where a man could prove to himself that he still possessed warm emotions and decent human feelings. As James Froude, a Victorian historian, wrote:

> When we come home, we lay aside our mask and drop our tools, and are no longer lawyers, sailors, soldiers, statesmen, clergymen, but only men. We fall again into our most human relations. . . . We cease the struggle in the race of the world, and give our hearts leave and leisure to love.

Anything threatening that shelter and refuge of warm emotion met violent hostility, be it talk of female suffrage, agitation for divorce reforms, free love experiments, or bloomers. And in May 1842, when the Commission on Child Labor prepared a report to Parliament on the terrible working conditions in the coal mines, Lord Londonderry was outraged because copies of the *Report*, containing what he called "disgusting pictorial woodcuts" of women and children hauling carts in the shafts, had reached the boudoirs of decent ladies and disturbed their domestic tranquility. It might also be added that Lord Londonderry himself owned a number of mines.

With the home being the only locus of emotional behavior and human kindness, woman's love was once again thought to be the source of ethical value. Typically, a popular manual for wives written by Mrs. Sara Ellis in 1843 stated that it was a wife's func-

[6] This is definitively documented by Walter Houghton in his recent study, *The Victorian Frame of Mind*. See especially chapters one, two, and three.

tion to "raise the tone" of her husband's mind and lead his thoughts
to dwell on a "higher state of existence" than his daily concerns.
Not for centuries had there been so general a belief that woman's
love uplifted and spiritualized man. Unlike the medieval troubadours and the Renaissance Neoplatonists, Victorian men thought
this improvement through love was exclusively a product of wedded domesticity, yet other than that their words sounded like
conscious echoes of the past. Robert Browning's plea to Elizabeth
Barrett—"Give me your counsel at all times, beloved: I am wholly
open to your desires, and teaching, and direction. Try what you
can make of me."—might almost have come straight from Andreas
Capellanus.

The same belief, in slightly different form, could even sometimes appear on the American frontier, where ordinarily one would
expect the valuation of woman to be more candidly procreative and
economic. In 1864 and 1866, for instance, Asa Mercer, a young college graduate who had moved out to the Oregon Territory, went
back East and arranged for the transport of several dozen unmarried females to the Puget Sound area, a project which later won
him election to the Oregon legislative assembly. His motives, however, had not been political, but thoroughly romantic: "I had been
taught to believe, and did believe," he later explained, "that practically all the goodness in the world came from the influence of
pure-minded women. At that time there was not a single woman
of marriageable age on Puget Sound . . . [and] the bachelor element was almost wholly beyond the reach of female influence
and its wholesome results."

The female, in such a view, had to be spotless and unimpeachable,
and every word or action that might conceivably have an immodest implication was therefore transmuted into a "respectable"
form. Even the word "pregnant" was now too blunt, and instead
ladies were said to be "in an interesting condition" or "visiting in
the country." Grown women would mincingly say of a newborn
baby that he "had been discovered under the gooseberry bush."
The anxieties of the ambitious middle class about its own social status and respectability led to the invention of numerous new taboos.
A gentleman could no longer offer a lady the leg of a chicken, but
only its breast—and he called even that the "bosom"; the books of
male and female authors were separately shelved in some Victorian
libraries; advertisements of ladies' underclothing always showed

them folded so one would be unaware of the crotch; and some women, when describing a pain to the doctor, would point out on a doll where the hurt was so as to be at one remove from making an indelicate gesture. The fictional Mrs. Grundy, a figure of satire in a play of 1798, had become the uncrowned ruler of English social mores half a century later, but Grundyism was by no means limited to England; there was a similar prudishness in France—a thing hard for the Anglo-Saxon to believe—and likewise in the United States. From the latter, in fact, comes the most delightful (though apocryphal) of all examples of prudery: according to Captain Frederick Marryat, a visiting Englishman, certain American ladies in an excess of modesty fitted up the legs of their pianos with crinoline pantalettes.

Ladies had been celebrated for purity before, but the extremes of the Victorian taboos were something new. So, too, was a notable new extension of modesty to bathroom functions, which had formerly been treated frankly; the result was that since modesty covered both excretion and sexuality, the two were more or less confused and identified with each other. Fear of nudity, of dirt, and of sexuality were all mingled in the minds of those who sought to be acceptable and respectable. They laid great stress on personal cleanliness, strenuously forced primitives and natives of tropical lands to put on English-style clothing, and generally felt that the sex act in marriage, though certainly not sinful, was an animal activity stemming from man's "lower nature," and was therefore "disgusting" or "indecent." A typical late Victorian, privately telling a doctor about his married sex life, candidly stated that he considered coitus with his wife a form of evacuation.

The emotional power behind prudery came from the romantic identification of the female with the pure mother ideal, and from the resulting inhibition of sexual desire. Conversely, the girl of the time, being a pure mother ideal, was forbidden to be sexually seductive in any way; she dared not even show any mild flirtatious interest in a man. "It is the privilege of the male, as superior and protector, to make a choice," the *Encyclopaedia Britannica* authoritatively stated in 1842. "The female preferred has no privilege but barely to consent or refuse." The young woman's permissible methods of attracting interest, or indicating her own interest, had shrunk almost to nothing. She might shriek delicately at the sight of a grasshopper, weep discreetly at a play or concert, or even, if the occasion merited it, faint (some manuals of deportment even taught the proper ways of fainting). But for the most part, her only way of showing any response to a young man's interested appraisal was, according to an etiquette book of the period, to summon up a "timid blush" or "the faintest of smiles lurking within the half-dropped eye."

Assuming that these feeble signals got across, and that the young man then obtained her father's permission to call on her, she might spend some time with him, talking, playing the piano, singing, or, on rare occasions, dancing—but always with a chaperone present; and even under these inhibiting conditions, his visits were limited in frequency, since they might otherwise produce "that undesirable familiarity which oftener lessens than increases esteem."

Somehow, despite these impediments, Victorian lovers eventually managed to convey to each other the knowledge that love existed in their hearts. The actual proposal might be made in writing to the father, but sometimes circumstances and a co-operative chaperone made a direct proposal possible. What such a proposal sounded like, or at least was supposed to sound like, may be judged from this sample declaration offered in an English manual of practical advice:

> If I can merit you by a love so chaste and illimitable as ever made the breast of man its tenement, you are mine already, my dear Miss Somersdown. . . . Heaven knows the purity of my intent and the affection which dictates it. . . . Your life of love with me shall be as near an approach to the utmost height of enjoyment as my pecuniary competence, my untiring zeal and infinite affection can make it. . . .[7]

What became of these purified and chaste sentiments on the bridal night and thereafter is not easy to discover; we are forced to imagine the quality of Victorian conjugal love on the basis of tangential hints. One woman, for example, who was married in the middle of the Victorian era and had borne several children, told Havelock Ellis when she was seventy that she had never seen a naked man in her life, and even those superlative lovers, the Brownings, are said never to have seen each other entirely nude. The typical attitude toward sensuous physical love can be inferred from the words of Tennyson's King Arthur (who hardly speaks in the

[7] *Courtship As It Is and As It Ought*   *History of Courting*, pp. 158-9.
To Be (1877), quoted in E. S. Turner:

tones of a fifth-century warrior): he knew of no greater power "to keep down the base in man" than "the maiden passion for a maid."

But if the base in man needed to be kept down by purifying love, woman supposedly had no such problem, for only prostitutes felt sexual desire or enjoyed sexual intercourse. This extraordinary idea was believed not only by poets, idealists, and prudes, but by a large number of physicians in various countries. Dr. William Acton, in a standard text on the reproductive system, said that the belief that woman had a sexual appetite was "a vile aspersion"; William Hammond, a surgeon-general of the United States, wrote that nine tenths of the time decent women felt not the slightest pleasure in intercourse; and at the University of Basel an eminent gynecologist named Fehling labeled sexual desire in young women "pathological." Even if a Victorian woman did feel those vile stirrings, she could only consider it shameful and degrading to yield to them; they were contrary to her nature. It was her business to lie still and be calm about the whole thing; in fact, in 1839 a highly successful English marriage manual written by a physician named Michael Ryan warned that female sterility was due, among other causes to "an excessive ardor of desire" or "passion strongly excited. . . . It is well known that complaisance, tranquility, silence, and secrecy are necessary for a prolific coition." [8]

From such scattered materials one can more or less visualize the Victorian act of love-making—hasty, ashamed, and uncommunicative, the husband "taking his pleasure" while the wife either was, or tried to seem, inert and passive. It is only natural that the Victorian bedroom was so heavily muffled, shrouded, and dark, for such surroundings must have somewhat reduced the embarrassment of performing so gross a function. This is not to say that Victorian marriages were loveless or unhappy, but that the quality of the love in them was partly, and in a special way, desexualized. The Victorians bred large families not because they were libidinous, but because of decreasing childhood mortality. Libido could not flourish where the woman's role was either that of a timid, virginal maiden or a sweet, pure mother, but never a sexual lover. Behind the sentiment that would later be expressed in the song, "I Want a Girl Just

[8] Acton, Hammond, and Fehling quoted in Havelock Ellis: *The Sexual Impulse in Women* (*Studies*, Vol. III), pp. 193–5; Michael Ryan: *The Philosophy of Marriage*, p. 260.

Like the Girl That Married Dear Old Dad," there operated both
an incest wish and an incest fear different in their trappings from
those which had affected the knight and the Renaissance courtier,
but comparable to them in power. Adolescent boys were endlessly
told to regard all women as mothers or sisters, more divine than
human; long engagements became ever more popular, possibly because a man who could worship a mother-sister divinity grew
shaky at the thought of copulating with her. In his mature years,
the Reverend Frederick Robertson recalled that, as a boy, when it
one day occurred to him that a pure young girl would someday
become his wife, he felt not rapture but pain at the thought of her
degradation.

But glorified and idealized as her role might seem, it was only a
new pretext for continued subjugation. And a new pretext was
needed. Formerly, one of the potent reasons for keeping woman
subordinate was that she had considerable productive importance
in the home. Industrialism robbed her of much of that, and to take
its place, there arose the fiction of female helplessness.[9] It was a
face-saving and ego-protecting device for woman; for man it was
the means by which he tried to make continued sense out of marriage in an era when its values were changing and its forms coming under attack.

Women carried out the scheme by making themselves literally
helpless through fashion. By the 1820's, Englishwomen had begun
to imprison themselves in laces, stays, and huge buckram-lined
sleeves. In the 1830's the English actress, Fanny Kemble, wrote
from Pennsylvania that American women too were lacing and pad-
ding themselves into virtual immobility. From the 1840's to the
1860's the crinoline and the huge skirt made nineteenth-century
woman not a two-legged human being but a seraphic image that
glided gingerly along to the sound of gentle rustling. So encum-
bered, she passed her time in the only pursuits convenient to this
condition. She gave the servants orders and instructed the children;
then she played the piano, read interminable novels, made anti-
macassars, painted on velvet, and shaped wax flowers. And then,
with time still heavy on her hands, she did things one finds hard to
believe: *Godey's Lady's Book and Magazine* for February 1864, for

[9] The loss of her productive importance was hardly true among the poor
or the frontier people in the United
States, but the helplessness of the female
was a social ideal, and even women of
the poorer or lower-middle classes
made a pretense of it whenever they
could.

instance, contains detailed instructions for making a netted ear-cover for a horse, decorated with eight charming tassels.

The role in which Victorian man had cast woman had its inevitable effect on man himself. Patriarchal he might be, stern to his children, frock-coated, mightily bewhiskered and not to be trifled with, but he played this part at the expense of his own sexual expressiveness and his own peace of mind. If he were a libidinous man, he was driven to resort secretly to brothels. If he were weakly sexed, the emphasis on the purity of woman might actually unman him. If he were an average man with an average drive, he might live his entire sexual life galled by the need for self-denial and self-restraint.

Doctors warned him against too early or too intense an enjoyment of his powers; intellectuals like Ruskin told him to conquer his lust through love; and even evolutionists found grounds to urge self-restraint, Tennyson telling him to

> *Arise and fly*
> *The reeling Faun, the sensual feast;*
> *Move upward, working out the beast,*
> *And let the ape and tiger die.*
> In Memoriam, cxviii

One of the wise men of the age—W. E. H. Lecky, the historian of moral development—said what must have been the regretful conclusion of many a thoughtful Victorian male:

> It must be owned that the progress of knowledge, which is usually extremely opposed to the ascetic theory of life, concurs with the theological view, in showing the natural force of this appetite to be far greater than the well-being of man requires.

5

Private Lives of Some Victorians

❁   ❁

❁

Despite all that we have seen, the private lives of the Victorians remain elusive and obscure, for we hardly ever learn how they actually behaved or felt behind closed doors. Novels of the period dealt with the love life of the Victorians, but only in a purified or sentimentalized fashion; biographies, on the other hand, either blandly pretended that there was no love life to record, or stated flatly that it was nobody's business. The novelist Anthony Trollope wrote an autobiography that filled two volumes, but on the subject of love he had only this to say: "If the rustle of a woman's petticoat has ever stirred my blood, of what matter is that to any reader?"

In the heat of emotion, the Victorians occasionally forgot to be so circumspect, and put their thoughts on paper, but almost invariably they or their families later expunged these revelations; only faint tantalizing traces remain, such as a note in Hallam Tennyson's biography of his father: "These extracts [on Tennyson's courtship] . . . are made from a series of letters from my father to my mother extending over three years. I have not felt able to include the many passages which would show the intensity of feeling expressed in these letters, but have burnt the correspondence according to my father's directions."

Yet in spite of the censor's fire, not all is hidden; there sometimes remain ashes or a scrap of bone from which one can sketchily recreate something. Hallam Tennyson does provide one or two clues by which we can estimate that "intensity of feeling" he speaks of. One evening in 1850, when Alfred Tennyson and his new bride were honeymooning in the Lake Country, Mrs. Tennyson went to bed early while the poet stayed up with two friends who had come to visit. The conversation came around to love, women, and Tennyson's bride in particular. The poet puffed his pipe thoughtfully, then slowly removed it and in his deep rich voice uttered a statement no bridegroom but an ultra-Victorian one could possibly have made: "I have known many women," quoth he, "who were excellent, one in one way, another in another way, but this woman is the noblest woman I have ever known."

Sometimes, too, the diligent scholar can, by heroic and patient reconstruction, recover evidence the Victorians thought they destroyed—only to be astonished at what they thought it necessary to conceal. Nathaniel Hawthorne wrote 164 letters to Sophia Peabody before and during their marriage; she preserved them for posterity, but spent a great deal of time carefully inking out a number of phrases and sentences, even making false blots above and below the line to mislead any prying scholar. Scholars pry all the same; a couple of decades ago several of them used a microscope, filtered light, and infinite patience, and after several years of recovering one character at a time, were able to read almost all of what gentle, maidenly, intellectual Sophia deleted.[10] And what was it like? Here is a typical deletion: "Shall there be no holy kisses in the sky? Shall I not still hold you in my arms, when we are angels together?" Why did she blot it? Apparently because she and Hawthorne were unmarried at a time when he indicated he had held her in his arms.

Later, but still before their marriage, he wrote to her from the Transcendentalists's co-operative at Brook Farm, saying: "There is a brook, so near the house that we shall be able to hear its ripple, in the summer evenings." This she allowed to stand, but canceled the rest of the sentence: "—and whenever we lie awake in the summer nights." She was equally cautious with letters written long after their marriage. "There is no thinking how much I love and desire thee," wrote Hawthorne while away on a trip; she struck out "and desire." There is perhaps only one truly surprising statement she canceled; as retrieved by the scholars, it shows Hawthorne writing from New York and saying, because he did not have the cash: "Thou shouldst not ask me to come to Boston for the purpose of sleeping a night in thy dearest arms." Sophia, of course, deleted the

[10] Randall Stewart: "Letters to Sophia," *Huntington Library Quarterly*, Aug. 1944.

words following "Boston" and purified herself, but the scholars with their microscope found her out; she was a woman, after all.

From such bits and scraps we gain an occasional flash of insight into Victorian love. One man, however, gives us much more than a flash: he not only experienced an ideal Victorian marriage, but made it his goal in life to write the definitive portrait of such a relationship. Coventry Patmore was his name; he is all but forgotten today although the Victorians liked his portrait of love and marriage well enough to buy a quarter of a million copies of it in his own lifetime.

Patmore, the son of a writer, was born in 1823 and early decided on a career in poetry. He took a position as an assistant librarian in the British Museum, and began diligently writing poetry in his spare time, but he had little success until after meeting and marrying Emily Andrews, for domestic love was to be his forte and his grand theme. Patmore, when he married her in 1847, was a tall, shy, somewhat stern young man of twenty-four with a sensuous mouth, powerful nose, long waving hair, and (when he thought about it) a Byronic expression. Emily was pretty, but her elongated face was always carefully composed into a grave, madonna-like expression, accentuated by hair which was parted in the middle and drawn down tightly on either side; Mrs. Carlyle, in some irritation, once grumbled that Emily Patmore tried to look like a medallion. Obviously they were typecast as the ideal Victorian couple.

Emily played to perfection the unassuming but omnipresent role of Victorian wife; when Patmore's friends—who included Tennyson, Ruskin, Carlyle, and Browning—came to call, she was always the hospitable charming housewife, listening appreciatively to male talk but unassumingly doing a bit of needlework the while. She herself had an urge to write, but appropriately produced only a book of child's verse, which she entitled *Nursery Rhymes by Mrs. Motherly*. She reared her own children with skill and care, lavished admiration upon her creative husband, accepted without complaint his varied moods of brusqueness, imperiousness, sensitivity, and dejection, and was his principal inspiration in life. It is therefore intriguing to see his personal estimate of her. In a private diary, he jotted down that she was unshakably mild, that she had a "milkmaid-like absence of pretensions" but a certain degree of "severity of feature," that her heart saw the right moral answer to every question, and that she could keep a house in a state of "gem-like neatness." His life with her, he wrote, was ideal and flawless; but with great honesty he confessed that it was easily forgettable, for after her death in 1862 he wrote himself the following note of reminder:

> Remember, above all, the 5,410 days she was my wife, and on each one of which, though nothing happened to be remembered, she did her duty to me, her children, her neighbors, and to God, with a lovely, unnoticeable evenness and completeness.[11]

This "unnoticeable evenness" was not the result of love alone, but of a complete and unquestioning acceptance on Emily's part of the role of the obedient woman; she once even wrote to Patmore in some amusement that a visitor, seeing "my appearance of instant submission to your slightest wish," had supposed it came from fear. It did not; Emily accepted his right to rule, and thus had no reason to fear him.

Early during this marriage, while recuperating from an illness, Patmore was struck by an idea he felt to be of major importance. In a state of great excitement, he told his friend and fellow poet Aubrey de Vere what he had suddenly realized—that poets through the ages, however much they had written of love, had overlooked or slighted the greatest theme of all—married love. He was dumbfounded to realize how universally they had failed to see this, and proposed to make good the lack himself; as he later put it:

> *The richest realm of all the earth*
> *Is counted still a heathen land:*
> *Lo, I, like Joshua, now go forth*
> *To give it into Israel's hand.*

The first product of this revelation was a long poem he wrote at blinding speed in a mere six weeks, and which was published as a separate book in 1854 entitled *The Betrothal*; it told of the conversations, moods, and ordinary incidents in the routine courting of a dean's daughter, first by one suitor and then by another. Two years later there appeared a second installment carrying the girl, Honoria, into marriage with her suitor, Felix; two more installments appeared in the next six years, painting in detail the unruffled tenor of marriage, the tragedy of her death, and the survival of love in the faithful husband. Patmore gave the over-all epic a brilliant title

[11] These private documents are quoted in Basil Champneys: *Memoirs and Correspondence of Coventry Patmore*, Vol. I, pp. 142–6.

—*The Angel in the House*—thus epitomizing in five words the
Victorian conception of woman and marriage. For the rest, the
monumental poem is anything but brilliant. Here and there occur
lyrics of reasonable merit, but for the most part Patmore had undertaken to celebrate in banal verse the minutiae of daily life, under
the impression that these were the essence of love. When the young
hero of the story writes to Honoria, for instance, his letter, suitably
rhymed, begins like this:

> *Dear Saint, I'm still at High-Hurst Park.*
> *The house is filled with folks of mark.*

Later one finds versified by the yard such material as a homely
wedding sermon, the honeymoon travel arrangements, and the
purchase of a pair of new shoes; lines such as these—

> *Our witnesses the cook and groom,*
> *We signed the lease for seven years more,*

—are all too frequent. Constructed of such realistic materials, the
sprawling work undertook to exemplify the familiar Victorian beliefs that love arises immediately when a man and maiden, pre-
destined for each other, finally meet; that love, whether successful
or not, "leaves the heart more generous, dignified and pure"; that
the supreme function of woman is to reign as the angel of the household, though despite her divinity she meekly and sweetly acquiesces
to her husband's wishes—and thus rules him by her very weakness;
and that conjugal sex relations are better than any others because
"life is sweetest when it's clean."

The *Angel in the House* became the most popular poem of the
era and a kind of national epithalamium. But after 1860 the Victorian frame of mind began to crack and disintegrate, and, before
he died, Patmore heard critics referring to him as a "laureate of the
tea-table" who wrote "humdrum stories," and even "goody-goody
dribble." The purely literary merit of his work to one side, though,
Patmore did succeed in portraying a typical Victorian marriage,
and although he denied that the Honoria of the poem was identical
with his own Emily, any comparison of the two makes it clear that
except for superficial characteristics they are the same and that
Patmore's own married life was the inspiration and source of material for the poem.

That being the case, the most interesting thing about Patmore is
the direction his life took after the completion of *The Angel in the*

House. It was finished in 1862, the same year Emily died; Patmore never again wrote in the same vein or style. Although he had portrayed Felix as being faithful to his love for his wife after her death, Patmore himself three years later, at the age of forty-two, married Marianne Byles, a forty-four-year-old spinster, serious, pious, and unbending, but wealthy enough to enable him to retire and give himself over to poetry. Although he rapidly managed to see in her all the same virtues he had seen in Emily, something in him was groping for a different solution to life; he became a Catholic like his wife, but simultaneously abandoned tea-table stories for poems dealing with the theme of sensual love versus spiritual love, and using irregular, free-moving verse forms. The result, published in 1877, was *The Unknown Eros,* a long work which came to Catholic conclusions only after extended passages of sensuous description. In his mid-fifties, this psalmist of placid marriage, this acolyte before the icon of the angelic wife, was consulting erotic reference books and producing lines such as these in which Psyche addresses her lover, Eros:

> *Kiss, tread me under foot, cherish or beat,*
> *Sheathe in my heart sharp pain up to the hilt,*
> *Invent what else were most perversely sweet;*
> *Nay, let the Fiend drag me through dens of guilt;*
> *Let Earth, Heav'n, Hell*
> *'Gainst my content combine;*
> *What could make nought the touch that made thee mine!*
> Bk. II, No. 12

Patmore's second wife died in 1880 after fifteen years of marriage; a year later, at fifty-eight, the tall, somber, greatly mustached poet fell in love and married once more. This time his wife was Harriet Robson, a woman a generation younger than he and a former schoolmate of one of his daughters. In this marriage, too, he seems to have been deeply affectionate and worshipful, but after some years he began to manifest a new and more significant symptom of unrest: without wishing to leave his wife, he conceived a grand passion for a married woman—Alice Meynell, the poet—and tried to win her. After all his thinking and pontificating about love, the seventy-year-old Patmore seemed to feel he had missed something all along. What he thought it was is not quite clear, but it must not have been pure Neoplatonic affection, for he made unsuccessful overtures to Mrs. Meynell and confessed to a friend that his feelings for her were "too much for the balance, peace, and purity of my religion." After she gently refused him, the aging Patmore, who should have been uplifted and enriched by his love (according to his own earlier doctrines), was instead desolate and wretched. Bundled in warm clothing on a sweltering July night, he complained to his son, Francis, that he was cold. His son said that that was impossible on so hot a night, but Patmore replied in the best romantic tradition: "Ah, it is a spiritual cold I feel." Love had been a pillar of fire, leading him a long way from *The Angel in the House*, but the Promised Land had never materialized. Now it was too late and he was lost, and would never know where he had been trying to go.

6

Emancipation and Confusion

"Chastity," said a wealthy English textile-manufacturer, "is sexual intercourse with affection." "I doubt not," wrote a French novelist, "that [marriage] will be abolished if the human race makes any progress towards justice and reason." "Yes, I am a free lover!" shouted an American lady lecturer to a heckler in the audience at Steinway Hall. "I have an inalienable, constitutional, and natural right to love whom I may, to love as long or as short a period as I can, to change that love every day if I please!"[12]

Paradox of paradoxes, only in the era of bourgeois dominion,

[12] The manufacturer, the novelist, and the lecturer were, respectively, Robert Owen, George Sand, and Victoria Claflin Woodhull.

when the wife was worshipped as the angel in the house, did free love become both a doctrine and an organized form of social protest. Nor was it a rare or isolated phenomenon, but part of a broad fight for greater rights for women and for emancipation from the purdah-like seclusion of the Victorian home. Throughout the century, an evergrowing army of people, including liberals, radicals, and some crackpots, fought for women's rights of one sort or another, and though most of the women of the period complaisantly accepted the role Victorian society assigned to them, many of them secretly hankered for some of the demanded freedoms and gladly accepted them when they were won. If helplessness was one female adaptation to a shrinking utility, militancy was the other alternative; woman could either barricade herself in the home with the myth of frailty, or struggle to get outside it and find some new definition of femininity.

Many a woman tried a little of each, but from the very first the aims of even the moderate feminists were confused and entangled with radical and seemingly dangerous notions. In 1792, Mary Wollstonecraft made the first comprehensive attack on bourgeois marriage and the subjugation of women in the form of a widely discussed book, *A Vindication of the Rights of Woman*. She was not against marriage as such, but against its existing inequities; she argued for increased social and economic rights and education so that in marriage women would be not submissive, pleasing housewives, but equals, capable of friendship with their husbands—a type of relationship she felt was surer and sounder than romantic adoration-and-domination of the female. These ideas might in themselves have seemed merely objectionable to the middle class, but coming from Mary Wollstonecraft they acquired the coloring of dangerous radicalism, for all the literate world knew that she had lived in Paris during the early years of the French Revolution, and been the unmarried wife of Gilbert Imlay, an American businessman, to whom she had borne a child. Seemingly pleased with this arrangement, she had even written the daring statement: "I am acquiring the matrimonial phraseology without having clogged my soul by promising obedience." Worse yet, she had thrown herself off a bridge in England when she learned that Imlay was unfaithful; still worse, after being saved by a boat and recovering, she next fell in love with the anarchist writer William Godwin. With him she again lived in unwedded bliss until Godwin, in an uncharacteristic fit of conformity, married her during her pregnancy.

From this point on, the woman's rights movement continued to incorporate radical elements. Shelley absorbed extremist political and social ideas from Godwin, wrote revolutionary pamphlets (some of which he sent to sea in bottles) and included in his *Queen Mab* a passionate defense of free love. Robert Owen, having practiced benevolent capitalism in his textile mill at New Lanark, became Utopian in his thinking and, beginning in 1825, poured most of his fortune into a short-lived social experiment at New Harmony, Indiana, where he tried to mingle communism, religious free thought, and egalitarian marriage. New Harmony failed, but from the 1820's to the 1840's there were, in the eastern United States, nine other Owenite and several dozen Fourierist communities, all of which mingled economic radicalism with experiments in modified love and marital relationships.

Although the woman's rights movement had been spawned by the industrial revolution, it was from the beginning allied with forces the bourgeois class could only fear and fight. The middle class had been all for increasing freedom while it had few rights of its own, but was ready to call a halt when the vote and the distribution of rights threatened to spread to the unpropertied class and to women. It was thus inevitable that these two dispossessed groups should either ally themselves, or seem allied in the minds of the rulers of society, who had all the proof they needed when Fourierists spoke of replacing marriage by some "new system of license" and Saint-Simonians justified the practice of "men and women giving themselves to several without ceasing to be united as a couple."[13]

The most alarming radicals, however, may have been those who offered their ideas in a mild, palatable form. Owen's son, Robert Dale Owen, leaving free love to one side, got himself married properly, but challenged the nineteenth-century marriage laws by making a written agreement with his wife and publishing it for all the world to see. In part, it read:

> New York, Tuesday, April 12, 1832
> This afternoon I enter into a matrimonial engagement with Mary Jane Robinson, a young person whose opinions on all important subjects, whose mode of thinking and feeling, coincide

---

[13] Later, the Marxists spoke of liberating both workers and women at the same time, but the tie-up of the two radicalisms was not their invention.

more intimately with my own than do those of any other individual with whom I am acquainted. . . . This ceremony involves not the necessity . . . of repeating forms which we deem offensive, insomuch as they outrage the principles of human liberty and equality. . . . Of the unjust rights which in virtue of this ceremony an iniquitous law tacitly gives me over the person and property of another, I can not legally, but I can morally divest myself.

Robert Dale Owen

Other parts of his statement repudiated a number of romantic concepts—the permanence of love, the clinging-vine nature of woman, and so on—but it was the challenge to man's rights over woman's own property and her body that was most fundamental and most dangerous. As late as the eighteenth century, women were actually not far advanced toward freedom from the female serfdom introduced a millennium and a half earlier by Teutonic tribesmen, compounded with Christianity, and later codified by feudalism. They still had few property rights or legal rights, no political rights, and very little status in intellectual, artistic, or business life. The Victorian male had no desire to change this situation, but only to intensify it. On economic grounds, too, he found it ideal; a subjugated wife, even if cranky, was simpler and cheaper to deal with than an equal at law who could decamp with her own property if displeased, or could sue for redress if mistreated.

Moreover, from the business viewpoint it made good sense: during much of the nineteenth century, subjugated womankind in English, French, and American industry were paid only one quarter to one half as much as male workers. It was only natural that any plea for female education or reform of marriage should seem to be linked with atheism, socialism, abolition, teetotaling, sexual immorality, and other despicable forces. But the counterattacks, even when couched in terms of ultra-romantic woman worship, began to sound ever more clearly like the slave-owner's paternalism; in fact, one of the typical condemnations of the woman's rights movement came from a Southerner, and was transparently analogous to the apology for slavery:

So long as she is nervous, fickle, capricious, delicate, diffident and dependent, man will worship and adore her. Her weakness is her strength, and her true art is to cultivate and improve that weakness. . . . In truth, a woman has but one right, and that is the right to protection. The right to protection involves the obligation to obey. . . . If she be obedient, she is in little danger of maltreatment: if she stands upon her rights, is coarse and masculine, man loathes and despises her, and ends by abusing her.[14]

Despite all resistance to it, the woman's rights movement inexorably gained ground all through the century; the very industrialization that had robbed woman of many of her essential functions left her time to yearn and fight for others. In 1833 Oberlin was the first man's college in the United States to admit women, and four years later Mount Holyoke, the first woman's college, was opened; in England the same process began in 1849 when Bedford College was established. In America the first Woman's Rights Convention met in Seneca Falls, New York, in 1848, and by the 1850's such respected intellectuals as the New England Transcendentalists were allying themselves to the movement; in England the Unitarians and other liberal elements were doing so likewise, and in 1869 John Stuart Mill's thoughtful work *The Subjection of Women* gave the stamp of absolute respectability to English feminism.

Meanwhile, women who had nothing to do with feminism and never dreamed of attending conventions or marching in protest parades were eagerly accepting by-products of the woman's rights movement. By the 1860's they began to discard their crinolines and gradually slimmed down their skirts until only the bustle was left. Once again they could and did begin to take exercise and play simple games of sport such as croquet and lawn tennis; and unchaperoned they could once again walk arm in arm with men, a thing impossible all during the crinoline period. A new "fast" girl, deplored by conservatives, appeared on the scene; she was flippant, gay, unsentimental, and even used such shocking words as "jolly."

All during the second half of the century, furthermore, a series of legal reforms were giving the lie to the myth of the angel's happiness in her house. In England, for instance, where divorce law had been so conservative and the procedure so expensive that only 184 divorces were granted between 1715 and 1852, a great divorce debate raged in mid-century and a new divorce law was enacted over violent opposition in 1857. It took the business of granting divorces out of the public hands of Parliament, gave it to a relatively private civil court, and eliminated the need for a preliminary ecclesiastical separation. The grounds remained few, but the right to obtain a divorce on those grounds was made unquestionable and the cost of doing so was greatly decreased. In the United States,

[14] George Fitzhugh: *Sociology for the South* (1854), pp. 213–20.

similarly, the general trend during the nineteenth century was to remove divorce suits from the legislatures, where it was awkward, expensive, and subject to political motivations, and put it in the hands of special courts; in addition, there was a general increase and broadening of the grounds for which it might be granted. Even in Catholic France, where divorce had been eliminated by the Napoleonic Code, it was restored in conservative form in 1884.

Victorian society furthermore found itself, willy-nilly, granting to woman economic privileges such as she had not had since the time of the Roman Empire. An act of 1857 granted a deserted wife the right to own any property she acquired after being deserted; prior to that, unthinkable as it may seem, a deserter could reappear and calmly seize whatever his wife had earned or been given in his absence. In 1870 and 1882 Parliament carried this further, granting all wives, deserted or not, ownership of whatever they earned after marriage or had owned before it; more than that, they won the right to make contracts, bring suit, and generally act as "persons" at law. In the United States, most jurisdictions had taken similar actions by 1900, and the same trend was visible in various European countries.

Even more valuable and influential were the rights, granted to woman by changing custom rather than by law, to support herself by her work without loss of self-respect or face, and to begin forcing her way not only into business but the various professions. Toward the end of the century one finds, for the first time, tracts and essays which argue that to remain single and to support one's self is better than to become the wife of a dissipated man. The right of lowly and of genteel women alike to work provided the means of escape from unhappy or loveless marriage, and the new divorce laws were used by ever-increasing numbers of women. In the United States, where the woman's rights movement was especially well advanced, the divorce rate showed an astonishing increase: between 1870 and 1905, while the population of the United States slightly more than doubled in size, the annual divorce total multiplied six-fold. The greatest rate of growth, almost predictably, was in the South, where the Civil War had broken up the feudal-romantic pattern of life and permitted the entry of industrialism with all its concomitant effects. Life with father, at the turn of the century, was not really life in a rigid patriarchy; by then, that was already only a nostalgic memory of earlier days.

In view of all these changes taking place at the very height of
Victorianism, the entire philosophy and practice of Victorian love
seem curiously unreal. Victorian love was at best a desperate rear-
guard defense against the inevitable changes made by industrial
civilization; it could be nothing more than a delaying action. Still,
why was woman not content with the romantic exaltation offered
her? Was it not enough to be honored, sung, and deified? Evidently
not, if such worship also meant her exclusion from all the other
areas of social and personal achievement. In the Victorian scheme,
woman was denied every form of status and achievement except
one, but in an industrial urban world that one was no longer as
meaningful as it once had been. She yearned, instead, for the achievements reserved for men, and her feminist spokeswomen argued that
she was the natural equal of man and deserved the same opportunities as he. But the very nature of this argument created in her
mind a confusion as to what part she could, or should, play in life;
the choice seemed to be between that of the unwed, childless, career
woman, and the subjugated, dependent, housewife-mother. If
there were some other answer, some other personality she could assume, Victorian women had no idea what it might be.

7

Perfect Love and
Some of Its Imperfect Results

❋   ❋

❋

Victorian love, wrote William H. Mallock, a late nineteenth-century novelist, was undoubtedly "far the highest" man had ever known; even Shakespeare, he said, had never been able to conceive of love in terms as sublime as those of Elizabeth Barrett Browning. His attitude was typical; most Victorians were convinced, by the analogies drawn from Darwinian evolution, that love had progressed undeviatingly upwards from a universal bestiality among primitives to the ultimate goal of sentimental monogamy.

In recent years the world has so lacked the seeming stability and optimism of the Victorian era that some people have become nostalgic and respectful of the Victorian world and its ways. Not long ago, for instance, the historian Esmé Wingfield-Stratford flatly stated (without offering statistics) that "the married lives of Victorians were, in an extraordinary number of instances, crowned with a happiness that no dreams of romance could have surpassed," and recent biographies have tended to make the Victorians seem genuinely estimable, well balanced, and content.

To some extent, it was true. Certainly a great majority of Victorians pledged their allegiance to a wholesome form of love directly concerned with the preservation of the family and the stability of society. But even in its heyday there were certain aspects of Victorian love which were neither "high," wholesome, nor indicative of contentment. The history of feminism, which we have just glanced at, is major evidence of the discontent and instability

inherent in Victorian love. Many other symptoms indicated that
not all was gold that glistened. In the second half of the century,
for instance, bourgeois morality was defiantly violated by an outburst of sensuality in literature—the "fleshly" and "erotic" poets
in England, Balzac and Zola in France, Whitman in America,
and many others. And there was more than mere sensuality:
often the writers displayed decadence and perversion, dwelling
on scenes of sadistic coition, gamy details of masochism, and
elaborate fantasies of the *femme fatale* or insatiable devouring
temptress; Swinburne, Gautier, Flaubert, and Wilde are only a
few of the cases in point.[15] And even where perversion was not
involved, the combination of love and death—typically, a product of unresolved incest-wishes, according to the late Dr. Ernest
Jones—was immensely popular, appearing on every level from
tear-jerking short stories in *Godey's Lady's Book* to the libretto
Wagner wrote for his own *Tristan und Isolde*.

Apart from legitimate literature, the great hunger for a fantasy
sex life that would make good the deficiencies of the real sex life of
the time manifested itself in a considerable increase in pornographic and indecent publications, prudish London being something of a European center for such materials. In America, meanwhile, when the conventional propriety was occasionally breached
by pornography in disguise, the reception was astonishing; Maria
Monk's *Awful Disclosures of the Hotel Dieu Nunnery of Montreal*, ostensibly an exposé, but actually a fraud designed for prurient
prudes, sold 300,000 copies, a remarkable record for the pre-Civil-
War period.

The symptoms were not only literary. During the century, there
was a notable increase in prostitution; estimates of the numbers of
prostitutes in mid-century London varied widely according to the
source (ranging from 7,000 to 80,000), but a few years later Taine,
an impartial Frenchman, claimed there were 50,000. His figure is
believable, for 42,000 illegitimate children were born in England in
1851, most of them to "fallen women." Even more noteworthy was
the existence, among the London brothels, of many which specialized in providing flagellation to a large clientele of men who, without it, were sexually inoperative; this taste was so character-

[15] This tendency was exhaustively illustrated and traced to its romantic origins by Mario Praz in *The Romantic*
Agony; see especially chapters four and
five.

istically Victorian as to receive the name, *le vice anglais*.[16] Against these ills bourgeois society struggled fitfully, seeking symptomatic relief, if not real cure, through police activities, the actions of antivice societies, purity crusades, and spasmodic efforts at the suppression of erotica. These countermoves, though most in evidence in countries with a Puritan tradition, appeared elsewhere too. As the historian G. M. Young has pointed out: "Much nonsense about 'the Victorians' is dissipated by the reflection that it was the French Government that prosecuted *Madame Bovary*"—and, he might have added, convicted Baudelaire for corrupting public morals with his sickly poems, *Les Fleurs du Mal.*

Beneath the placid exterior of bourgeois marriage, furthermore, there was much well-hidden misery. Toward the close of the era, Balzac, Breuer, Freud, and Havelock Ellis, among many others, collected evidence that wedding-night rape, vaginismus (painful vaginal spasm), frigidity, impotence, homosexuality, and other aberrations of sexual love were far more common than the official doctrine of nineteenth-century romantic love ever admitted. When even a leading American gynecologist said, before a convention of doctors in 1900: "I do not believe mutual pleasure in the sexual act has any particular bearing on the happiness of life," what could one expect of the average male? Doubtless not much, and it is therefore not surprising to find turn-of-the-century reports from different parts of northern Europe and America claiming incidences of female frigidity ranging from ten per cent to seventy-five per cent.[17]

We can actually see in clinical detail what one such woman's love life was like, thanks to the fact that by the end of the century the changing attitudes toward medical investigation had lifted some of the veils of secrecy, at least as far as concerned the recording of anonymous case reports. The case in point, reported by Havelock Ellis, is that of "Mrs. B.," an Englishwoman in her early thirties at the turn of the century, and characterized by Ellis as attractive, healthy, the mother of several children, and leading an active life. As a girl, she had been decently brought up; she was modest and thoroughly "pure," but fond of dancing and of male attention, and much given to romantic imaginings. Ignorant of sex until she fell

[16] Houghton: *Victorian Frame of Mind*, p. 366; G. M. Trevelyan: *English Social History*, pp. 490–1; Praz: *Romantic Agony*, pp. 421–3.

[17] Havelock Ellis: *Sex in Relation to Society* (*Studies*, Vol. VI), pp. 512, 525–7.

in love and became engaged, she feared to drive away her fiancé by excessive prudery and therefore let him fondle her breasts at length, but such was her state of inhibition that she desired neither this nor any other physical act except what she imagined lovemaking to consist of—lying in each other's arms all night and kissing. Reality came as a surprise, and her romantic lover assumed, in her eyes, a new look and personality:

> She was somewhat shocked and disgusted by the experience of the wedding night. It seemed to her that her husband approached her with the violence of an animal. . . . Coitus, though incomplete, took place some seven times on that first night. . . . For two months subsequently there was great pain during intercourse, although she suppressed the indications of this. . . . She has seldom obtained complete gratification. For a long time she disliked seeing or touching the penis, and the feel, and especially the smell, of the semen produced nausea and even vomiting. . . . Feelings of friendship for her husband have been [occasionally] potent in arousing the sexual emotions . . . [but] she has been for many months at a time without sexual intercourse. . . . She eventually discovered that her husband's abstinence from marital intercourse was due to infidelity. This led to a definite separation. She still occasionally experiences sexual desire . . . but she herself believes that her sexual life is at an end.[18]

So ended in failure the attempt by one couple, and, it would seem, a great many others, to make a reality out of the dream of Victorian love.

---

[18] Havelock Ellis: *Studies*, Vol. III, Appendix B, pp. 303–6.

Chapter X

THE AGE OF LOVE

All for Love, or the World Well Won

❀   ❀

❀

In the middle of the twentieth century, social critics seeking to identify the mood of their bewildering era pinned on it such labels as the Atomic Age, the Age of Conformity, and the Age of Anxiety. But another tag, suggested in the 1959 first edition of this book, was as relevant as any of those: the Age of Love. For at no time in history had so large a proportion of humanity rated love so highly, thought about it so much, or displayed such an insatiable appetite for word about it.

To be sure, in mid-century there were no Tristans, nor even any Jane Eyres, but only the likes of Stanley Kowalski and John's Other Wife; still, it seemed that never before had so many of the plays, novels, songs, and stories of an era centered about, or at least included, themes of love and sex. And this was true not only of fiction: the news media were crammed with reports of the romances, marriages, infidelities, and quarrels of the famous; in the love affairs of the celebrities, millions of the obscure lived out their own dreams. When Princess Margaret obeyed the call of duty in 1955 and gave up Group Captain Townsend, millions of people in the Western world were genuinely sad and sympathetic; when the Communist Czechoslovakian government, recognizing the supremacy of love in 1957, allowed its lady discus champion to marry an American hammerthrower, the citizens of Prague joyously turned the wedding day into a spontaneous citywide revel; and when in 1958 Crown Prince Akihito of Japan succeeded in breaking an ancient tradition to choose his fiancée on the basis of love, the youth of that nation all but rioted with enthusiasm, and the rest of the world was, if not exactly riotous, at least favorably impressed.[1]

The mid-century millions who were insatiably hungry for news and stories of love also tried diligently to make it an actual part of their own lives. As lovers, they were certainly not as graceful as the Renaissance courtiers, as lusty as the rationalists, or as sweetly eloquent as the Victorians; yet more than any of these, they considered love the *sine qua non* of the happy life. Americans, who made more of marrying for love than any other people, were also breaking up more of their marriages (close to 400,000 annually throughout the 1950's), but this signified not so much the failure of love as the determination of the disappointed not to live without it but to seek it in a second union. Large numbers of the world's people, while regarding American divorce with evident disapproval, seemed irresistibly drawn toward the same general conception of love and marriage. Communist East Germany, after a decade of attacking romantic love as "bourgeois trash," gave up the unequal struggle and urged its writers to produce love stories to meet the needs of its people; feminists throughout the Moslem world were throwing away the veil and warring against polygamy; and the love patterns of most Third World societies were beginning to disintegrate, to be replaced by Western models.

It is almost incredible that so many different peoples should have been attracted by a pattern of love that was essentially Western, strongly Anglo-Saxon, and relatively new on earth. In a manner scarcely found in earlier history, Western love in the mid-twentieth century was an effort to combine sexual gratification, affectionate and intimate companionship, and the procreative familial functions in a single relationship. Romantic attraction was considered the adequate, and indeed the only proper, basis for choosing one's marital partner; the sexual desires deliberately aroused in courtship were supposed to be held in check until after the wedding; the sexual drives of both partners were supposed to be completely and permanently satisfied within marriage even though there had been no testing period beforehand; and tenderness, mystery, arousal, and satisfaction were expected to survive in a milieu of household cares and childrearing problems, and the routines of 15,000 nights

[1] Some informed observers, however, thought that Akihito's action involved practical considerations: it might have been intended to persuade the world of Japan's new democracy, and to introduce new blood among the "six families."

together. All in all, according to anthropologists, it was one of the most difficult human relationships ever attempted; just as certainly, it was also one of the most appealing.

Much of the appeal was based on the aesthetic and morally elevated atmosphere of the ideal of modern love, yet with total inconsistency the very societies that were glorifying the synthesis of love and sex were at the same time commercializing and mechanizing sex. To judge by the content of the major news media, Western peoples were afflicted with endemic voyeurism and had an untiring morbid need to gaze at, and compare, the breast development of young actresses. The cigarette, clothing, and cosmetic industries continually intimated that their products would assure sexual conquest, the suggestion being frequently couched in terms referring to illicit seduction rather than marriage and companionship: typical perfume advertisements of the time said, "Not for the timid," "A whispered invitation for a man to be masterful," and "Depend on it—for anything!" In the name of science, sex was stripped of all emotional meaning and viewed as a purely mechanical activity; the tireless researcher Alfred Kinsey and his co-workers counted and tabulated millions of orgasms as if they were identical grains of wheat, assigning the same statistical value to one self-administered in the bathroom and to a one-minute backseat copulation as to the transcendent climax of a genuine love affair.

How is one to make sense of this inconsistent Age of Love? All over the world women wanted emancipation, thinking that among other benefits it would enable them to love and be loved in the modern way, yet over two thirds of America's supposedly emancipated women were staying home after they married, fearful that in shedding domesticity they might lose their femininity; at one college, female students uttered no mass cry of outrage when its president told them it was in their nature to be as satisfied by soufflés as by philosophy. The mid-century decades were an age in which not being married was taken as a sign of personal incompetence or even neurosis, yet during which millions of Americans chose to dissolve their marriages—some of them because (or so they swore in court) their mates played the television set too loudly, had noisy false teeth, or refused to let the cat share the nuptial bed.

It was an age in which the experts themselves were all at sixes and sevens about the whole subject of love. Some sociologists saw modern love in terms of greed, sensuality, and social ruin, while others saw it as the basis of egalitarian marriage and in tune with modern democracy; some anthropologists felt that lifelong fidelity was an unrealistic and unworkable concept, but any number of psychotherapists diagnosed infidelity as a symptom of neurosis and did their best to "cure" it.

Perhaps, however, these were not so much contradictory interpretations of the same phenomenon as compatible interpretations of different coexisting phenomena: men and women were so ambivalent about love and so much in the midst of transition from old orders to new ones that they picked and chose whatever patterns of behavior most nearly expressed their own wavering inclinations. In any case, it seems indisputable that they were even more perplexed about love than their ancestors had been at any time in the previous 2,500 years.

2

The First Sexual Revolution

❀   ❀

❀

Before looking more closely at behavior in the Age of Love, we need to go back briefly and remind ourselves of the process by which love broke away from the Victorian pattern. As we saw in the previous chapter, when the industrial middle class became socially dominant early in the nineteenth century, it established as the standard of European and American love a domesticated romanticism, prudish, patriarchal, and sentimental; but the same changes in the techniques of production and distribution that brought the businessman power over society also spawned a powerful feminist movement which successfully challenged his power over his wife and family.

Science, the humus of Victorianism, was also the seedbed of the revolution in love. For it was the new work in medicine, sociology, and anthropology that made sex once again a legitimate matter of study and caused sexual intercourse, so long viewed with shame and disgust, to be reconsidered as a necessary, health-giving, and even noble function. The revolution was anything but giddy and lighthearted about sex; its leaders were earnest, high-minded, and methodical, and in the process of liberating sexuality sometimes accomplished the almost impossible task of making pleasure seem a medical necessity.

It was, for instance, toward the end of combating emotional and mental disorders that, in the latter part of the nineteenth century, men like Krafft-Ebing, Forel, Weininger, and Havelock Ellis produced their studies of sexuality and sexual pathology. The same motive, rather than any bent towards licentious reveling, was responsible for the epochal discoveries of the Karl Marx of the sexual revolution, Sigmund Freud. Ironically, he originally had no intention of studying sexuality; he began his medical career as a neuro-pathologist, attempting to treat nervous disorders at first by electrotherapy (the administration of mild electric shock to parts of the body exhibiting symptoms), and later by hypnosis. In the late 1880's, working in collaboration with Dr. Joseph Breuer, also of Vienna, he found that a number of patients with severe nervous disorders were temporarily improved when they discharged their pent-up emotions under hypnosis. The matter might have rested there, with a modest improvement in symptomatic relief, but Freud was struck by the fact that the emotions vented during the hypnotic trance very often concerned sexual desires and fears that the patient, at all other times, was either unaware of or even vehemently denied having. From this early beginning, Freud was inevitably led along that road of investigation, discovery, and theoretical formulation which ended by his profoundly influencing Western conceptions of sex, love, morality, and human psychology. It was oddly paradoxical that this rather puritanical, romantic, and inhibited young man should become in the eyes of conservatives the licentious and prurient instrument of Satan; the apostle of the sexual revolution was himself chaste before his marriage, devotedly monogamous during it, and far from being a lustful satyr, was a man with a rather mild and prematurely terminated sex drive.[2]

Freud and Breuer published their findings in the book *Studies on Hysteria* in 1895, a date which in effect marks the discovery of the dynamic processes of the unconscious and the introduction of the concept into Western psychology. Not that Freud discovered the unconscious per se; philosophers and psychologists had speculated about it for two centuries. But by and large they thought of it as a mere repository of experiences and information waiting to be retrieved as needed; what Freud discovered was that the unconscious is a seething cauldron of fierce dynamic processes that profoundly affect conscious thought and behavior.

He soon found that if, without resorting to hypnosis, he encouraged patients to speak freely, abandoning all usual inner restraints on thoughts, they would produce a free-associative flow of talk that revealed far more of their problems and motivations than the material produced during a hypnotic trance. This was the origin of psychoanalysis; with this powerful tool for investigation and treatment, Freud made a number of discoveries in rapid succession and developed many of his principal theories. Although none of his findings led him to advocate or sanction anything like sexual libertarianism, they were thoroughly alarming to conservatives in the medical profession and elsewhere. People of many sorts felt that Freud's insistence on the paramount importance of the sex drive was vile and indecent, and were outraged by his claim that everyone's unconscious is a psychic closet stuffed with the skeletons of infantile, homosexual, incestuous, and perverse desires.

At first the medical profession tried to ignore Freud, but a decade after the book on hysteria appeared, when he was beginning to acquire a following and to receive international recognition, the opposition became overt. Particularly after the publication of his *Three Essays on the Theory of Sexuality* in 1905, Freud and his major ideas were for some years regularly denounced at medical meetings and in the press; various doctors castigated psychoanalysis as "mental masturbation," Freud himself as a "Viennese libertine," and his followers as candidates for lunatic asylums. All in vain; even before World War I, psychoanalytic theory was beginning to per-

[2] Such is the picture that emerges from the definitive biographies of Freud by Ernest Jones (1953–7), especially Vol. II, p. 386, and Peter Gay (1988), especially pp. 38 and 162–4.

vade psychiatry and psychology, and after the war it penetrated literature, philosophy, and the social sciences as well. It then was so thoroughly absorbed into popular thinking that psychoanalysts became familiar, friendly figures in television dramas, and perhaps more significantly, millions of parents read the ubiquitous baby book by Dr. Benjamin Spock and never winced at—or even noticed—the psychoanalytic concepts on almost every other page.

If Freud's ideas had arrived at the beginning of the nineteenth century, they might have had relatively little immediate effect; as it was, they came at a time of sexual redefinition and awakening attendant upon the successes of feminism. During the nineteenth century the feminists had slowly won a number of limited financial and social rights; now the long campaign was achieving certain of its major goals. Eleven of the western United States granted women the vote before World War I; Finland, Norway, and Denmark did so between 1906 and 1915; suffragettes marched down Fifth Avenue in 1912 and got the Bull Moose Party to endorse their cause, and Congress passed the Nineteenth Amendment in 1919, with ratification coming in 1920.

During this same period the more radical feminists were demanding and actually putting into practice some of the increased sexual freedoms which were only then becoming practicable. For with the breakdown of barriers to female employment, women could support themselves and remain free of the need to barter their love for lifelong maintenance. Olive Schreiner, the English feminist and writer, argued that only by total economic independence could sexual love be freed to become "the essentially Good and Beautiful of human existence." Ellen Key powerfully made the case for woman's right to maternity in or out of marriage. Putting these ideas into flamboyant practice, Isadora Duncan made herself the very symbol of flaming feminism: in America and Europe alike, she scandalized and fascinated the public by her rapt, interpretive dances performed only in a transparent veil, and by her well-advertised love affairs and her defiant unwed motherhood.

She was, to be sure, an extremist, but she exemplified a basic tenet of feminism—that sexual love should be an ecstatic experience for women. Indeed, Isadora was apt to ascribe cosmic importance to her own physical responses. When she was still a young virgin in Paris before the turn of the century, she introduced herself to Rodin one day, admired his work, and then privately danced for him at home in her diaphanous tunic. Not unreasonably, Rodin advanced upon her with glittering eye and bared tooth, whereupon she promptly took fright, threw on a dress, and sent him away thoroughly irritated. But for many years she reproached herself, feeling that she had cheated the entire world: "How often have I regretted this childish incomprehension," she wrote in *My Life*, "which lost me the divine chance of giving my virginity to the Great God Pan himself, to the mighty Rodin. Surely Art and all Life would have been richer thereby!" Belatedly she did her best by Art and Life with a series of other men, each love affair seeming to her like "the final resurrection" of her life, but each, by her own admission, ending badly. In her fading middle age, she married a young Bolshevik poet, Sergei Essenin, drank too much, quarreled bitterly, saw her popularity vanish, and was fortunate enough to die in an automobile accident in 1927 before things got worse.

Margaret Sanger, an American housewife and mother, was meanwhile waging a historic fight for woman's sexual freedom on a very different front—the control of pregnancy. As a visiting nurse, she had seen the squalid results of ungoverned fertility among the poor in the slums of New York City, and she felt that not only were health and happiness ruined by excessive childbearing, but that married love remained uncivilized and brutish as long as it could not be practiced without the fear of unwanted consequences. In France she collected birth-control information for a year; then in 1914, back in New York, she began publishing her data in a newspaper called *Woman Rebel*. It was sold mostly to labor and socialist groups, but her challenge was one all feminists could respond to: "A woman's body belongs to herself alone," she wrote, insisting that unless a woman had the absolute right "to dispose of herself, to withhold herself, to procreate or suppress the germ of life," all other feminist gains were empty.

Puritanical and Catholic elements alike were outraged. Sanger was arraigned for violating the Comstock Law, published a still more detailed pamphlet called *Family Limitation*, fled to England for a year, and then returned to stand trial. By that time feminists were solidly aligned with her, and the government, after delaying trial, dropped the case. In 1916 Sanger opened a birth-control clinic in Brooklyn, was arrested, and served a thirty-day sentence in the workhouse. But in 1918 the Court of Appeals put a new and more liberal interpretation on the dissemination of birth control information, and in 1923 she reopened the Birth Control Clinical Research Bureau; thereafter, clinics multiplied rapidly, despite continual opposition from the Catholic Church. By the late 1930's there were over three hundred of them in the United States, and a 1940 survey found that over nine tenths of upper-middle-class Protestant couples and nearly as many Catholic ones were making at least some efforts to regulate their own parenthood.[3]

Birth control, like divorce and feminism in general, was succeeding, in large part, because of a fundamental change in the nature of marriage and family life. The Industrial Revolution had been causing a gradual population shift from the country to the city, which became more rapid by the close of the century: in 1880 only twenty-eight per cent of Americans lived in cities, but by 1910 forty-six per cent did, and by the 1950's some two thirds lived either in cities or city-suburb complexes. The rural families of earlier centuries had raised much of their own food, built their own shelters, made their own clothes and medicines, and taught their own young; with the shift to the city, men began to work for wages, used the cash to purchase the goods and services they needed, and sent their children to public schools. Women were left with childbearing and housework but little other work that was irreplaceable or challenging. Men, if they chose, did not actually need women to survive in the city. As for children, they were no longer an economic asset with candle-making, cow-milking, and crop-harvesting value, but a costly luxury, valuable only for reasons of love and pride.[4] Margaret Sanger, after all, had been horrified by the problems not of fertile peasants but of fertile slum-dwellers. The Industrial Revolution had spawned the Victorian family in one century only to undo it in the next by giving the right to love priority over the act of begetting.

The inevitable result of separating lovemaking from procreation was to bring the traditional ideal of monogamous marriage under attack. The most frequent argument of the *avant-garde* was that, since love did not always last for life, the promise to love and be

[3] J. W. Riley and M. White: "The Use of Various Methods of Contraception," *Amer. Sociol. Rev.*, Vol. 5 (1940), pp. 890–903.

[4] Adam Smith reported in 1776 that an American child was worth £100 clear profit to his parents before he left home (in 1950's terms, at least $1,000 and possibly two to three times that much). For 1910 city-dwellers, in contrast, each child reared to maturity cost thousands of dollars, and by 1944 the per-child cost had risen to over $16,000 (see Metropolitan Life Insurance Company: *Statistical Bulletin*, January 1944, p. 100), and by the 1950's was nearing $25,000.

faithful for life was meaningless; it was the right of every human being to seek new love when the old one died. If children were involved, the marriage should continue, but with complete freedom by each partner to conduct outside love affairs. This general solution was proposed by a number of intellectuals, H. G. Wells, Bertrand Russell, and Havelock Ellis among them, who saw traditional restrictions on sexual freedom as an unreasonable, even outrageous, interference with human rights. Marriage, Ellis concluded, would conquer adultery in only one way—by absorbing and tolerating it. In the United States a somewhat different approach was taken by Judge Ben Lindsey in his widely publicized writings on marriage; he created a sensation in the mid-1920's when he suggested a form of legal but nonbinding union to be called "companionate marriage" and terminable at will by husband and wife, without going to court, as long as no children had been born. A more typically Jazz Age notion was put forth by Fannie Hurst, who advocated "visiting marriage," with separate households for husband and wife, and meetings by appointment—a proposal not likely to appeal to any but the well-to-do.

These and still other suggested modifications of marriage were widely discussed from the turn of the century on, but except for a handful of intelligentsia and radicals, not many tried to exercise their new sexual and romantic rights. Some of the most articulate advocates of emancipated marriage—Wells, Russell, D. H. Lawrence—themselves had rather untidy and painful personal lives; it often appeared that modernized marriage would satisfy one mate nicely, while making the other wretched.

The marriage of Havelock Ellis, that saintly, bearded scholar of sex, was a case in point; it seems more like one of the case histories of aberration in his own *Studies in the Psychology of Sex* than anything else. Ellis and the novelist Edith Lees fell in love and were married in 1891, but Ellis required her to agree in advance that they would always maintain separate homes, live by their own incomes, and retain complete personal freedom in outside relationships. Throughout their twenty-five years of married life, they generally spent half of each year together, the other half in separate lodgings. When the marriage was only a few years old, they ceased being physical lovers because of waning interest, according to Ellis's account in *My Life* (although there is some reason to suppose that Ellis himself may have been partially or largely impotent);

despite this, he wrote that their love for each other grew ever more intense and "passionate." In accordance with his modern ideas, Ellis told his wife in the friendliest possible fashion about his various love affairs, Platonic and otherwise, and in *My Life* he said again and again that Edith surmounted her initial jealousies and found security and genuine love in their marriage. Yet one has only to open this lengthy book at random to find Edith suffering, agonized, jealous, despondent, and always in the midst of some tear-streaked resolve never again to make a fuss; and always the trouble was Ellis's feelings for or relations with other women—never money, never politics, never religion, only love. As early as 1895 she was writing:

> *My poor boy*, my heart is aching and aching for you. . . . Oh! dear, oh, dear! *why* have you and I to keep making one another miserable, when no other person could ever be really as much to the other as you and I are?

In 1898, chin up (but quivering) she was sure things were going to be all right:

> I only have realized lately how much more I love you than I ever did, or you could not make me suffer so hideously. And though I may not yet comprehend you, you also don't quite see why I feel things; but all is sure to come right, for love carries folk through everything in the end.

So it went. Ellis seemed to feel constant improvement, enrichment, and spiritual exaltation in their love; the disinterested reader may see nothing but unvaried torment, and wonder why Edith continued to subject herself to it. Apparently she loved him far too much to break off with him, but despite her struggles to understand and accept his behavior, she could not help suffering for a reason the great scholar would not admit: namely, that love in the modern world is not painlessly divisible, that sex and affection, play and devotion, love affairs and marriage, cannot be easily or neatly maintained in separate compartments of the personality. When Margaret Sanger, during her flight from America, became Ellis's very dear friend, he wrote of her to Edith, whose reply said nothing of her own long years without his physical love and yet showed unmistakably the nature of her agony at not being her husband's choice:

> I have no heart or strength to write long letters. . . . It is not
> that you have ceased to care—it is—well, just what it is, and perhaps
> only a woman knows what that is. . . . That you cannot see it is
> the comedy—that I do is the bathos and the pathos in one. . . .
> God keep you and bless you in this new thing and may she make up
> for all our failures. Your comrade who loves you.

Not long after, she swallowed morphine unsuccessfully, then
jumped into a well and later out of a window, surviving both acts;
finally she died of a chill in 1916 and found the only state in which
she could cease to care.

There is, however, a postscript to the story, and an important
one. After his wife's death, Ellis took as his constant companion
and friend one Madame Françoise Cyon. His good friend, the poet
Hugh de Selincourt, living by Ellis's own recommendations, fell in
love with her and had an affair with her. Ellis, deeply hurt, broke
off with both of them. Mme Cyon, understandably dumbfounded,
eventually gave up de Selincourt and begged her way back into
Ellis's grace; even the poet, two years later, was readmitted to the
white-bearded Mosaic presence—but on the clear, if unuttered,
understanding that the emancipated theory of love be practiced
with someone other than the philosopher of love's consort.

While some of the sexual revolutionaries were philosophizing
about the improvement of love through adultery, many others
were fascinated by the purely mechanical aspects of the sex act; as a
corollary, they recognized the existence of female desire and, like
the suffragettes demanding the vote, loudly asserted woman's right
to orgasm. In 1918 Mrs. Marie Stopes, an Englishwoman who had
known the frustrations of an unconsummated marriage, published
her startling book *Married Love*, which had immense influence in
Europe and, later, in America. In terms that would have made any
Victorian lady faint away instantly, she ardently proclaimed that
the wife should be a full partner in sexual pleasure and should
obtain full gratification every time. It was doubtless a salutary reaction to what had long existed, but Mrs. Stopes, in her fascination
with the moment of climax, showed that odd tendency of the sexual revolutionaries to view the orgasm as a kind of excellent thing-
in-itself, detached from partner, meaning, and emotion. Often dis-
secting the act from its human context, she came up with many a
disembodied description of a woman's climax such as this: "The

critical pinnacle of the orgasm broke like the towering crest of a sun-sparkling wave."

In 1926 the Dutch physician Theodoor H. van de Velde issued his classic work *Ideal Marriage*, the philosophy of which was of the same type, placing on husbands a moral burden of no mean sort: "Every considerable erotic stimulation of their wives that does not terminate in orgasm, on the woman's part, represents an injury, and repeated injuries of this kind lead to permanent—or very obstinate—damage to both body and soul." That same year there appeared, in German, Wilhelm Reich's *Function of the Orgasm*, a work of maverick psychiatry whose author alleged that orgasm failure of either man or woman was the cause of major mental and physical diseases; later Reich even advocated masturbation as a way to combat cancer by promoting the flow of sexual energy. In the United States the psychiatrist Gilbert V. Hamilton made one of the first major statistical studies of married life and sexual conduct, paying particular attention to orgasm frequency in women; he reported that many women did not experience it regularly, and he claimed that this lack was a principal cause of weariness, ill health, adultery, and divorce. One might wonder how much of this was a sexual revolutionary's preconception, for he also admitted, with mild surprise, that the happily married women of his sample were only about seven per cent more orgasmic, on the average, than the unhappily married women.[5]

A similar attitude of detached biological concern was characteristic of the Lost Generation of the 1920's, who assumed the pose of hard-boiled pleasure-seekers. By their time, all circumstances conspired to support their stance: feminism had given a woman the right to put her foot on the rail, even in a prohibition speakeasy; World War I had created an atmosphere of cynicism combined with a desperate hunger to make up for wasted years; and the widespread dissolution of Victorian morality had left a vacuum unfilled by any new rules and standards. It was not only an American or Western phenomenon; in the Soviet Union, where nineteenth-century ideas had been even more abruptly repudiated, the state philosophically and legally encouraged sexual freedom, and made divorce and abortion no harder to get than a newspaper or a new

---

[5] The concentration upon orgasm as a separable entity was most remarkably exemplified in mid-century by the famous sexual studies by Dr. Alfred Kinsey, mentioned above, who, discarding all questions of love, counted all orgasms, in every conceivable context, as equal instances of "outlet" or relief from sexual tension.

hat. The reigning Communist attitude was that one should seek
sexual intercourse as one did a glass of water—to satisfy a physical
need—with no admixture of outmoded philosophy. Lenin was horrified by the "glass of water" theory and spoke out against it, but to
no avail.

In the United States, meanwhile, middle-aged people were likewise horrified by the young generation, who defiantly made bold of
their hip flasks and bootleg gin, wild rides and petting sessions,
loose talk and roadhouse parties. Even in the small towns of the
Midwest there was no escaping the sight of such goings-on, for the
movies and the radio had come into their own; no matter where
people lived, they were subjected to the impact of Clara Bow, the
"It" girl, and such edifying tunes as "Makin' Whoopee." Even the
aesthetic and intellectual *avant-garde* was committed to the tough,
cynical, and physical view of love; the new woman, being still in
part the same old woman, was therefore both witty and broken-
hearted, gay and pathetic. No one said it better than Edna St.
Vincent Millay:

> *I shall forget you presently, my dear,*
> *So make the most of this, your little day,*
> *Your little month, your little half a year,*
> *Ere I forget, or die, or move away,*
> *And we are done forever; by and by*
> *I shall forget you, as I said, but now,*
> *If you entreat me with your loveliest lie*
> *I will protest you with my favourite vow.*
> *I would indeed that love were longer-lived,*
> *And oaths were not so brittle as they are,*
> *But so it is, and nature has contrived*
> *To struggle on without a break thus far,—*
> *Whether or not we find what we are seeking*
> *Is idle, biologically speaking.*

3

*The New Romanticism:
Dashing and Sex*

❀   ❀

❀

The era of "It," however, was short-lived and superficial; its
bright, brassy, emancipated doctrines never really dominated
modern love except among the *avant-garde*, and then only briefly.
The bulk of Americans showed the influence of change in milder,
more bourgeois ways. In the middle of the 1920's, Robert and
Helen Lynd made their famous anthropological expedition into
darkest Indiana and studied the natives of Middletown (Muncie);
the natives, they found, had indeed lost their patriarchal and functional view of family life, but rather than replacing its moral code
with that of free love or emancipated marriage, they had switched
to what was becoming a typical American answer—divorce and
remarriage, or as it was sometimes referred to, progressive polygamy. Their attitude toward adultery was unchanged, but they were
getting six times as many divorces as they had in 1890. They had
genuinely accepted the modern conception of sexual enjoyment as
a human right, but basically they believed in romantic personal
love, not mere biology, and assigned it a major role in holding
society together.

In part, this represented simply the spreading out of middle-class
values to the whole society, for the great majority of Americans
were coming to think of themselves as "middle class," despite wide
variations in income, occupation, and habits; by the 1940's, studies
showed that seventy per cent of even the low-income groups
claimed to be of the middle class. But the importance ascribed to
love was more than a wide diffusion of middle-class tradition; the
isolation and anonymity of modern life made men and women

desperately long for firm ties, personal loyalties, and a sense of individual importance. Even D. H. Lawrence, that tormented exponent of sexual freedom, declared in the very last year of his life that it was not really sex that man needed. "It is a great blow to our self-esteem that we simply *need* another human being," he wrote in a magazine article. "I do not mean a mistress, the sexual relationship in the French sense. . . . It is in relationship to one another that [people] have their true individuality and their distinct being. . . . It is a living contact, give and take."

It was just such hunger for a larger definition of one's self, a reassurance of one's worth, that made romantic love more important than ever. The growing deluge of movies and of radio soap operas in the 1920's was characterized by themes of love, heartbreak, and eventual happiness, and however fictitious and trashy their portrait of life, the immense appetite for them indicated some considerable need on the part of the general population. The Depression only accentuated this trend, sweeping away the superficial follies and extremes of the previous decade, and making the comfort and reassurance of love more vital than ever; as in the latter part of the nineteenth century when Victorian certainties were disintegrating, there seemed only love to cling to, and Matthew Arnold's words, written in 1867, seemed to have a new relevance:

> *Ah, love, let us be true*
> *To one another! for the world, which seems*
> *To lie before us like a land of dreams,*
> *So various, so beautiful, so new,*
> *Hath really neither joy, nor love, nor light,*
> *Nor certitude, nor peace, nor help for pain. . . .*

The popular value placed on the emotional life was so high, in fact, that it became fashionable among social scientists to regard love as a kind of national disease. The anthropologist Ralph Linton's scathing appraisal of it in 1936 became something of a classic in the field:

> All societies recognize that there are occasional violent attachments between persons of opposite sex, but our present American culture is practically the only one which has attempted to capitalize on these and make them the basis for marriage. . . . Their rarity in most societies suggests that they are psychological abnormalities to which our own culture has attached an extraordinary value just as other cultures have attached extreme values to other abnormalities.

The hero of the modern American movie is always a romantic lover just as the hero of the old Arab epic is always an epileptic.

Many of the sociologists who were turning their attention to American love and marriage in the 1920's and 1930's used the term "romantic love" derisively or scoldingly to refer to the powerful, irrational emotions and expectations characteristic of the courtship period but not, presumably, of marriage. Whether or not this is a fair use, the term had clearly undergone important changes in meaning in half a century. In the twentieth-century version of romantic love, the whole concept of woman's part in courtship had changed radically; no longer was she the timid maiden, blushing and looking at the ground, hoping to be observed at church by some young man who would then ask her father if he might come calling. That marketing mechanism had worked adequately in stable small towns, but in the rapidly growing cities of the industrial era it left many a woman on the back shelf of spinsterhood, dependent on relatives or forced to seek the loveless compensation of feminism and factory work.

By the 1920's, however, when the ideal of shy, passive femininity had been largely discarded, a technical revolution in courtship became possible. It rested upon the spontaneous invention of dating —the most significant new mechanism of mate selection in many centuries. In place of the church meeting, the application to father, and chaperoned evenings in the family parlor, modern youth met at parties, made dates on the telephone, and went off alone in cars to spend their evenings at movies, juke joints, and on back roads. But the telephone and car, however essential to the new pattern, had not created it; they had been absorbed by it because they were so sorely needed. Society worked out the new procedure because it had to; young people urgently required a new way of developing themselves into marriageable persons through social experience, and a new broader exposure to possible mates in order to make the process of falling in love less risky.

The crucial part of dating, therefore, was its freedom from commitment in contrast to the Victorian entrapment known as "keeping company." Young people needed years in which to acquire their social skills and to experiment with relationships to the opposite sex; then they needed still more years in which to gingerly try out a series of tentative choices before settling upon one. The pattern that developed was strikingly different from the forms of sexual mingling and mate selection known elsewhere in the world. American children scarcely got beyond puberty when their mothers began to arrange a heterosexual social life for them via dancing classes and parties, but as soon as possible most of the control and initiation of the social life was handed over to the children themselves, who then made their own choices (subject to some parental pressures, of course), set up their own appointments, and sought to escape the parental eye as rapidly as possible. In backseats of cars, at senior proms, and in bull sessions, boys and girls tried to gather information about what it meant to be a male or a female. By their late teens, most of them had been through a "crush" or two, done a fair amount of necking, and in an increasingly large number of cases, some "heavy petting."

Eventually, these components would begin to coalesce into the more serious attachment known as "going steady"; at this point, finally, it became necessary to exhibit one's tentative choice to one's parents. The typical parental attitude towards a "steady" was one of wary, grudging acceptance—an understandable attitude, since parents had not selected the mate, yet could seldom exercise real veto power. But only a very small percentage of rebellious youths crossed religious, social, or color lines; for the most part, young people fell in love with other young people very much of their own background and position, and hence were rarely in serious conflict with their parents. In due course formal engagement followed, and then marriage, both of them involving the participation of the two families. Characteristically, however, this was only a superficial return to the bosom of the clan; the ideal was for the couple to rush off alone as soon as possible to experiment with their sexuality and their love unobserved, and to set up their own home, even if only in a drab single room, in order to have privacy. The freedom and isolation of the dating couple were, in other words, harmonious with the emerging image of married life, and it is not surprising that for several decades—roughly from just after World War I to and even beyond mid-century—the dating and mate-selection pattern was relatively stable.

Some social scientists sourly charged that dating was only simulated courtship behavior, its real purpose having little to do with love. The late Willard Waller coined the term "rating and dating complex" in 1937 and described it as a competitive game in which the primary goal was prestige and a high rating; boy and girl alike attained this by making a high score in getting dates with desirable people, and by sexual success—the latter, for the boy, consisting of obtaining thrills, but for the girl, of distributing as few of them as possible while remaining as enticing as she could. Critics of American love such as Margaret Mead and Geoffrey Gorer developed Waller's analysis still further. Dr. Mead said that dating was not courtship but a loveless contest designed to give the adolescent a feeling of success and popularity, neither of which could easily be acquired in our culture until later in life. She argued that the entire system worked to the distinct disadvantage of marriage; the young woman who had long practiced coyness and fended off approaches, for instance, was badly trained for the role of equal partner and joyously sexual wife.

Against Dr. Mead's view, some commentators pointed out that the Victorian premarital conditioning of the young woman had been a good deal worse. Moreover, although the theory of the rating and dating complex highlighted the tawdry aspects of dating, it ignored other more admirable ones; the competition, status-seeking, and personal gratification of the dating pattern did not rule out the existence of emotional attachments. The average mid-century American adult, thinking back to his or her own adolescence and youth, would recall most vividly and fondly the bitter-sweet memories of infatuation and not the score racked up, the long talk on a moonlight night or the walk hand-in-hand in the soft new snow rather than the backseat fumbling and the nervous efforts to advance the hand an inch or two.

A fair number of sociologists, therefore, disagreed with disapproving interpretations of the dating pattern and viewed it not only as a generally cheerful and happy activity of youth, but as an educational process that led gradually from playlike heterosexual behavior to companionship and love capable of initiating a marriage; so seen, it seemed an adaptation of older courting behavior to a new need. In 1951, Samuel Lowrie, a sociologist at Bowling Green State College, Ohio, asked 1,595 boys and girls in high schools and colleges why they dated. The anonymous (and so, probably, honest) responses indicated the young people's conscious reasons for dating. Only six per cent of the boys and one half of one per cent of the girls named necking. One out of four did, however, specify affection, a word which evidently had considerably more meaning and appeal to them. Very nearly as many others cited "to gain poise or ease," but only about half as many "to get to social affairs." All in all, Professor Lowrie concluded, reasons of the competitive-prestige type made up only about one quarter of all responses, while one third had to do with education and self-improvement, and well over a third with affection, courtship, and marriage.

One of the most valuable functions of dating was the chance it gave young people to learn something about each other's character, opinions, and plans for living—a need which had hardly existed in the stable small-town life of earlier centuries, when every young man was known, or known about, by nearly every young woman he was likely to court. In the early 1950's, a survey of typical college women in Ohio found that they had averaged four dates a week with their prospective fiancés in the period preceding engagement, but that their grandmothers had averaged only one a week. The granddaughters put their extra time to good use: fully half of them had discussed with their future husbands every one of the six major problem areas the survey asked about (money, children, where to live, religion, the wife's work, and the husband's occupation), but only 4.5 per cent of the grandmothers had done as well. One out of four grandmothers, in fact, had discussed none of the problem areas, while fewer than two per cent of the granddaughters were similarly reticent. Evidently, even if dating was competitive and status-seeking in its early, adolescent phases, it became increasingly task-oriented toward obtaining a good fit, and in its later phases even involved some relatively realistic testing of the conditions which might cause love to diminish or die in actual marriage. This, then, was the shape of the new romanticism: it was at once unromantic in the sense that it was practical, inquisitive, and cautious, and romantic in the sense that it sought a "right one" with whom love could be powerful, legitimate, and enduring.

The criticisms of dating may, though unfair, have carried much conviction with mature persons because of their fear that through dating the younger generation was becoming wild and sexually ungoverned. And the statistics collected by Kinsey and his co-workers did present parents with alarming evidence of change. To take a single example, of the females interviewed by Kinsey only fifteen per cent of those born before 1900 had ever petted to the point of climax by the time they were twenty-five, but of the women born in the first decade of the twentieth century, thirty per cent had done so, of those born in the second decade, thirty-four per cent had done so, and of those born between 1920 and 1929, forty-three per cent had done so. Only one in four of the women born before 1900 had had intercourse before marriage; half of those born after 1900 had. (The change was less marked for men, but most of the worry about Flaming Youth concerned women.)

The figures were impressive. Yet other data from the same study indicated that the change was not solely due, or even largely due, to wildness and thrill-seeking. Of the females who had had premarital coitus, nearly half had done so only with their fiancés, and another seven per cent with only one man; the overall amount of activity for women under twenty was on the order of once every five to ten weeks, hardly a riotous abandonment to sensuality. Similarly, several years before Kinsey's surveys the psychologist Lewis Terman reported, in a study of marital happiness, that fully two thirds of the women who were not virgins at marriage had had relations only with their fiancés. Given the prevailing American romantic expectations of marriage, this can be interpreted to mean that American women were coming to consider sexual expression legitimate where love existed (although, unlike their sisters in some European countries, they insisted that the love definitely be aimed at marriage).

Studies indicate, in fact, that young couples living in the milieu of mid-century American romanticism were not drawn to each other primarily by sexual attraction, nor was it chronologically the first source of attraction they felt. Ernest Burgess and Paul Wallin made a notable survey of a thousand engaged couples, all college students in the Chicago area, during the years 1937–39, and followed their subjects to and beyond marriage. The majority of all these people specifically replied, in answer to a question, that strong physical attraction had not been a conscious part of their initial interest in each other but that it had developed as time passed, and that in general it increased in intensity as the relationship itself became closer.[6] Over a third of the engaged couples had intercourse before marriage, and nine tenths of them considered that it strengthened their overall relationship. There was no evidence in either the Burgess-Wallin study or any of the Kinsey studies to show that premarital intercourse was hurtful to the ensu-

[6] Burgess and Wallin: *Courtship, Engagement, and Marriage,* pp. 117, 164.

ing marriage, and at least some evidence that it was correlated with good marital adjustment.

If dating had been geared primarily to thrills rather than to the romantic-marriage ideal, American youth would hardly have been strongly marriage-minded; what can be had for the price of a motel room need not be purchased at the cost of one's freedom. Yet in the very decades when family life was losing its personal survival value and Victorian morals were being discarded, young Americans were becoming ever more bent upon marriage and readier to undertake it in the expectation of rich emotional rewards. In 1890 only a little over half of all persons over fourteen years old were married; in 1950 roughly three quarters of males and two thirds of females over fourteen were. The median age at first marriage in 1890 was twenty-six for men and twenty-two for women; by the 1950's men were marrying at twenty-three and women at twenty.

To appreciate the extraordinary significance of these statistics, recall the conditions in the Roman Empire during the reign of Augustus Caesar. At that time, Roman women had won an economic and legal emancipation of sorts, the economic functions of home life had all but vanished for the well-to-do city dwellers, children had become a luxury rather than an asset, and sexual enjoyment was deemed a right and a natural privilege of every human being. All this seems generally comparable to the conditions of our own time; yet Augustus was grieved and concerned by the resulting preference of his Romans for bachelorhood, the infertility of marriage, the high divorce rate, and the deterioration of family life and morality in general; we recall his heroic efforts to enforce his Julian Laws and his tragic failure. In the mid-twentieth century there were no such laws, and none were needed; the same conditions had produced an almost opposite result.

Evidently, courtship in the new romanticism followed a complex prescription: one part youthful amusement, one part social striving, one part sexual attraction, one part infatuation and glamour, one part practical searching for a mate, and a number of parts of quasimystical expectation of love, joy, and personal fulfillment to come in marriage. How far the prescription was fillable, how far the great expectations in it were met in marriage and how far frustrated, were matters of endless debate among the experts, but not among Americans in general. When marriage failed, they precipitately drank of the magical elixir again, expecting that now it would work; and if their own marriages did not fail but only disappointed them, they smiled indulgently upon their romantic young as though, for them, the potion would surely prove effective.

4

The New Romanticism: Illusions and Realities

❊   ❊

❊

Van Nuys, Cal., Nov. 18—UNIVAC goofed 20 times as an electronic matchmaker but finally came up with a winner. Bob and Shirley Kardell are UNIVAC's lone success. The machine introduced them on the TV show "People are Funny," and declared them to be compatible marital partners. And so they were married.
                                                —*New York Post*, Nov. 18, 1958

However strong the faith of Americans in romantic love might have been in the Age of Love, it was far from pure and unalloyed. People were delighted to entrust to a machine, programmed with scientific marriage-prediction criteria, the task of selecting perfectly matched love candidates; yet they were still more delighted that ninety-five per cent of the time the machine failed to yield true love. For Americans were firmly of two minds about it all—simultaneously hardheaded and idealistic, uncouth and tender, libidinous and puritanical; they believed implicitly in every tenet of romantic love, yet well knew that things didn't really work that way.

Among the articles of faith in the American credo of romanticism, for instance, was what we might call the "one-person" theory, the romantic conviction that for each individual there is a "right one" waiting to be found (also thought of as "the only one in the world"). It was the task, and indeed the moral duty, of every unmarried person to wait or to search until that one was located. "Someday I'll find you" and "Somewhere in the world she is waiting for you" were two of a hundred familiar expressions of the belief. The romanticists of the late eighteenth century knew it as the doctrine of elective affinities, which, as we know, had its ultimate source in Plato. The one-person theory was combined, for mid-twentieth-century Americans, with the belief in free choice: it was up to man and woman alike to refuse all substitutes and to choose the right one on the basis of feeling "the real thing," unswayed by such ignoble considerations as geographical nearness, availability, or similarity of background.

Yet Americans, even young ones, were not utter fools and knew perfectly well that if a youth lived in Maine, the only one in the world for him did not live in Calcutta, and probably not even in California. Romanticism sometimes admitted this reality and waxed sentimental about the boy next door—a very reasonable love choice. Scientists proved the point: in a 1952 study of urban couples applying for marriage licenses, a sociologist found that more than half of the applicant pairs lived within sixteen blocks of each other at the time of their first date together. If somewhere in the world she was waiting for you, there was a fifty-fifty chance that you could walk that far in half an hour.

More important, scores of painstaking studies made in the era showed the importance of "homogamy" in mate selection: to an overwhelming extent Americans fell in love not with ideal persons freely found and freely chosen, but with persons narrowly limited to similar economic status, social class, religion, and educational level. The emotion might feel as strong, even under these circumstances, as if one had chosen from among all the world's people and as if the test of rightness overrode all practical determinants, but the realistic truth was that love was largely a matter of opportunity, similarity, and familiarity.

A second article of faith in the credo concerned the meaning of "falling in love"; generally people were supposed to be unsuspecting and unprepared for the attack, which occurred suddenly and powerfully either at first sight or soon afterwards, the victim being helpless in the grip of a superior force. Some enchanted evening one sees a stranger across a crowded room, and it happens, unmistakably and irresistibly. This belief was almost a required convention in popular fiction, television, and the movies; oddly enough a large number of the teachers in marriage and family courses in colleges seemed to believe it too, since they so consistently inveighed against it and warned their students against the pitfalls of rushing hastily into marriage because of violent romantic feelings. They pointed with alarm to news stories of lightning romances; the following one, for example, was cited in a sober 1950's sociological work from the *San Francisco Chronicle*:

> On Monday Cpl. Floyd H. Jackson, 23, and the then Mary Ella Skinner, 19, total strangers, boarded a train at San Francisco and sat down across the aisle from each other. Johnson didn't cross the aisle until Wednesday, but his bride said, "I'd already made up my mind to say yes if he asked me to marry him." "We did most of the talking with our eyes," Johnson explained. Thursday the couple got off the train in Omaha with plans to be married. Because they would need the consent of the bride's parents if they were married in Nebraska, they crossed the river to Council Bluffs, Iowa, where they were married Friday.

But most people, including the alarmists, were aware in some part of their minds that except in rare cases it really did not happen that way. Even the adolescent "crush" was not so precipitate or overpowering at its inception as it was said to be; the boy and girl did not so much fall in love as push themselves down a slide of love —after first looking the situation over. Realistically, most people knew what careful sociologists had reported: American boys and girls played cautiously at light love, or mock love, the boy "handing a line" and the girl playing whatever role best suited her (coquette, charmer, aloof one), until each was fairly sure the other was more or less equally interested and ready to fall. Then, and then only, did they wilfully submit to the inexorable force; then did they fall, but by design. Helpless passion, one-way love, and unrequited suffering belonged largely to fiction and to the medieval knight's long service of his lady. In the Age of Love, they existed chiefly in the form of the bobbysoxer's hopeless adoration of the remote idol, but among maturing young people they were more illusion than reality, believed in but not practiced.

As for the culmination of lightning romance in hasty weddings, that, too, was more myth than reality, according to the findings of various surveys of American marriage. It was a fact that at least two thirds of American husbands and wives had known each other two or more years before marrying; and it was also a fact that only one out of every six or seven love affairs became a marriage.[7] The myth that people fell in love and promptly rushed into marriage faded out of sight in the harsh glare of the data.

Supplementing these dry figures, sociologists of the time provided something new in the annals of love confessions—the clinical, undramatic, and artless interview, protected by anonymity and published not in the name of literature but that of scientific research. Here is what falling in love was like in the early 1950's, according to one college student whose story was selected by Burgess and Wallin as most nearly typical of the pattern they observed in their study of a thousand engaged couples:

> I had my first date with her about three months after we both started to work in the firm. One day we worked together on an assignment and we made a date for that Saturday night to go to a movie. At that time it was nothing but another date. I liked her general appearance and personality. . . . I would say that I was definitely interested our first night out. I know that on my first date I wanted more dates. . . . I would say that within the first two months we were going together I felt I was in love with her, and that I'd like to marry her. Our understanding was brought on very gradually, however. It was never actually stated, but I gave her my frat ring about nine months after we started dating and that was it. I don't know which of us fell in love first. I think it came on both of us in the same way. I think it just started out as plain dating, and gradually developed into love from there on.

Not exactly exciting, not very communicative, but it has the sound of truth and the feeling of authenticity.

Yet another article of the romantic credo held that love is blind, and that the lover neither observes his beloved's imperfections of character or beauty nor will admit them when they are pointed out. And certainly everyone knew that young adolescents often had mad crushes on inappropriate people, falling in love on the basis of wavy hair, a "heavy" look, a giddy manner, or a cream-colored convertible, rather than on the basis of more fundamental aspects

---

[7] The ratio of love affairs to marriages is from G. V. Hamilton: *A Research in Marriage*, Ch. 10. Later surveys yielded averages ranging from three to ten; a summary is in Robert R. Bell: *Marriage and Family Interaction* (1963 ed.), p. 122.

of the human being. But again, if we turn to the many mid-century field studies of dating and mate-selection rather than moralistic diatribes against romantic love, we find impressive evidence, heaped up in windrows of statistics and moraines of case histories, that during the years of dating and growing up most young Americans slowly discarded, or pushed into the background, their image of the ideal mate or dream mate. Often, to their own surprise, they found themselves falling in love with someone whose "type" they had never cared for but with whom they had found a workable degree of companionship and a comfortable sense of fitness, and with whom love derived from, rather than preceded, the recognition of these attributes.

Such maturing people described their emotions as "true" or "real" love rather than "puppy love" and "infatuation." Real love, though it might be myopic, was not blind, for among Burgess and Wallin's two thousand engaged people, two thirds of the men and three quarters of the women could name defects or things they wished were different in their partners. Some of the perceived defects concerned lofty matters such as too serious an attitude toward religion, too sharp a temper, or too great a tendency to stubbornness, but many were in the area of physical shortcomings which simply had to be accepted without hope of change, such as shortness, crooked teeth, and ears that stuck out a bit too much. Even nail-biting and dandruff were honestly named, and were evidently no impediments to love.

One other popular article of belief held that love conquers all. When Virgil long ago wrote *Omnia vincit Amor*, he was exercising poetic license, but Americans, intractably democratic and unreasonably optimistic, sincerely believed that the mighty force of love could overcome all obstacles, all reasoning, all ties that bind; love could easily best parents and professors, was superior to laws and in-laws, was greater than logic or logistics. The daughter of a coalminer who emigrated from Lithuania won a beauty contest and was seen and admired by Winthrop Rockefeller; what could be more inevitable than that they fall in love and marry? Americans were delighted; this was proof indeed that love surmounts all barriers and leaps easily across all chasms. But when Bobo and Winthrop separated a year later, Americans (having a remarkable ability to feel two ways about love) looked sourly wise and asked, what could one expect? And when five years later she got a divorce plus

$5,500,000, they snickered and avowed that all along they had known what she was up to.

The scientists of marriage were generally aligned with the public in this realistic (or cynical) side of their thinking. Sociologists computed to the last decimal point the effects of differences in cultural background, social class, personal tastes, and the like, finding them all hurtful to love; every difference increased the likelihood of unhappiness, maladjustment, and divorce. *Omnia vincit Amor* . . . but the truth was that everything conquered love. Marriage counselors, too, found that the unusual love choice—the person of another color, another country, another religion—was very often only a means of rebellion against one's parents. And at least some psychoanalysts regarded "being in love" as an obsessional state in which old forgotten angers, sadistic and masochistic tendencies, sibling rivalries, and the like all made the fond fool suppose himself in love when he was merely in the grip of his own unconscious motives.

In view of these several discrepancies between theory and actuality, a number of sociologists soundly belabored romantic love, and praised in unbounded terms its supposed opposite—conjugal or companionship love. They attributed to romantic love a number of follies, especially that of "idealization," the imagining or attribution of ideal beauty and ideal personality to some perfectly ordinary young man or woman. And indeed this is, historically, one of the classic characteristics of romantic love; we remember Ulrich von Lichtenstein's idiotic devotion to the cruel princess, Hazlitt's infatuation with the lodging-house serving-girl, and Stendhal's theory of "crystallization." To the sociologists, this was the core of romanticism and a distinctly malign and hurtful tendency.

"No marriage can be classified as wholly romantic or as based entirely on companionship," wrote Professor Burgess, ". . . [but] all our data bearing on the question point to the conclusion that, on the average, marriages resulting from comradely affection turn out happier than those chiefly inspired by romantic attitudes." "It is an ironic paradox," avowed Professor Ray Baber, "that this cult of romance, with its sincere desire to refine and beautify the marriage relationship, should do it more harm than good." Willard Waller (who took so dim a view of dating) even advocated a certain amount of quarreling in the early years of marriage in order to "liquidate the effects of the romantic complex" and thereby establish a firmer basis for the marriage.

But despite the collection of data to prove this thesis, the natural history of love does not justify any such sweeping attack on romantic love. To begin with, although it had changed its character considerably over a period of nine centuries, its earnest opponents were often still slaying medieval dragons. The uneasy and imperfect blend of illusion and reality, idealism and hardheadedness, which we have described under the name of "the new romanticism," was hardly identical in spirit with abject troubadour woman-worship, Rousseauistic idealization-plus-impotence, or Stendhalian crystallization.[8]

Some of the historical components of romantic love, notably the linking of love and death, and the impossibility of love's existing within marriage, had vanished altogether. Others, such as extreme idealization, remained in twentieth-century romantic love, but primarily in early puppy love and adolescent infatuation. The adolescent wanted to be in love and was surcharged with love before he had anyone in mind; it therefore took a mere face, of whose owner he knew nothing, to precipitate a very thunderstorm of adoration. Typically, as we have seen, during the process of dating and courtship some of these excesses disappeared and a degree of realistic testing and learning entered; nevertheless, the principal sources of attraction remained heavily romantic, including refined or beautified sexual desire, a sense of enrichment and fulfillment at feeling love and being loved, and a sense of completion at finding a soul mate.

In marriage, finally, the inhibition, mystery, and masking of defects typical of courtship came to an end. The sociologists who decried romantic love would have had us believe that this shedding of romanticization was a necessary loss, that true married love was based not on romantic love but comradeship, and that romantic love should be eliminated from the culture as much as possible; but in historical perspective it would seem that marriage did, in fact, incorporate certain other residual values of romantic love and that these were in large part responsible for its meaning and success.

[8] But many a mid-century family sociologist did so equate them; see, for instance, Winch's *The Modern Family*. He and others also cited the scholar Denis de Rougemont, who considered romantic passion and marriage irreconcilable, and traced the former back to the Albigensian heresy of the eleventh century, which linked love to a desire for sorrow and death. See above, pp. 148–9 and 170.

For one thing, before the advent of medieval courtly love the Catholic-Teutonic tradition made the husband godlike in his dominion over his wife. Courtly love reversed the roles and gave the woman sovereign, if make-believe, power over her suitor. The end result, after centuries, was to strike a rough balance, each partner in love trying to please and serve the other; and this, however rarely achieved, was considered the ideal of modern marriage.

For another, courtly love greatly refined sexual expression (often to the point of partial impotence), and linked it to devotion, deep feeling, gentleness, long service, and similar traits of behavior. This combination of characteristics originally existed only in illicit connections, but beginning in the Renaissance was gradually absorbed into Christian monogamy. The major absorption took place later, however, among the Protestant bourgeoisie, who badly needed romantic love as a cement for marriage to replace the sacramental bonds they had broken. The dominant love ideal of adolescents in the mid-twentieth century derived from this source, but so did that of adults. Everyone knew that adolescents were romantic, but even for the long-married couples—at least those with rewarding and successful marriages—love involved not only comradeship and mutual interests but tenderness, moments of intensity, waves of compassion, joyous sexual play, and occasional spells of candlelight and soft music. That many of the middle-aged did all this was the best-kept secret of the era; neither moviemakers, fiction writers, nor advertising men could bring themselves to admit that any but the young could feel and act so.

Yet another of the contributions of courtly love was its attribution of character improvement and ethical value to the experience of loving. The theme appears strongly in every incarnation of romantic love: the Neoplatonists made love the stairway to spiritual excellence, Puritans such as Milton considered wedded love the fulfillment of life, and the Victorians saw love as the redeeming experience that saved men from brutalization by business. Seen in this perspective, the ideal of marriage in the Age of Love was distinctly romantic, since it definitely allied love to ethical goals; men and women were overwhelmingly convinced that without married love, life was barren, selfish, ungenerous, and pointless. Even the critics of romantic love agreed on the ethical value of married love: psychiatrists viewed the ability to love givingly and generously as a sign of maturity, and anthropologists granted to love a life-preserving value (the scientist's equivalent of ethical good), since it met two creatures' emotional needs and in the process continued the species and the society. Some of the younger sociologists began to suspect that in large part modern companionship marriage—ostensibly opposed to romantic follies—owed its existence and continuation to the cohesive power of romantic love.[9]

The antithesis so often pictured in the sociological literature between romantic love and conjugal love thus appears to have been artificial, unhistoric, semantically unsound, and misleading. Romantic love in the Age of Love was evidently a continuing force in the life of men and women—an ever-changing but ever-present entity, altering slowly and smoothly from the wild, foolish, and self-centered love of young adolescents to the tempered, realistic, and mutual love of mature adults. Contradictory views of love co-existed in most people because it is the nature of the human being to be ambivalent about many things, and because even the most mature had not altogether conquered their juvenile desires; the foolish illusions they claimed to believe in were not a hurtful alien philosophy they could not live by but the unerased record of their youth and growth.

Romantic love might not be the ultimate or best way to choose a mate or build a marriage, but it was the only functioning one Americans of this era had. The subtle and fine adjustments required of a maturing marriage relationship could not be made without some stability, some force ensuring a continuation of the efforts, some motivation for doing so. But man and woman were no longer linked in marriage by patrimonies, indissoluble law, clanship ties, or social pressures; it was romantic love that first drew them into marriage, and then was the principal bond holding them together until they had forged other ties of habit, shared experiences, economic bonds, adaptation to each other's needs, and children.

Yet even after that, romance continued to give modern marriage its distinctive character, for despite the follies, disillusionments, infidelities, and divorces alleged to come from romantic love, without it men and women could not find in each other that unique,

[9] For typical mid-century sociological contributions recognizing the value of romantic love, see W. L. Kolb in *Social Forces*, May 1948; H. G. Beigel in *Amer. Sociol. Rev.*, June 1951; and J. F. Cuber in *Marriage and Family Living*, Vol. XI, p. 95.

difficult, and fragile blend of protector and protégé, child and parent, comforter and tempter, friend and lover, that had come to be implied in the word "husband" and the word "wife."

5

Love as Panacea

In other rationalistic and materialistic eras men and women treated love lightly and considered it nothing more than the agreeable sensations and sporting pleasure accompanying the effort to satisfy the sexual urge. In the Age of Love, despite the prevalent rationalism and materialism, they saw love not only as an elevating and noble human relationship but an essential one, since it alone satisfied a crucial human need that was no longer met by other human relationships as it had been in other times and places. That need was greatly exacerbated by the nature of twentieth-century society. Primitive human beings had lived in continual intimate contact with all the members of their village and been linked to scores of clan-relatives by a web of powerful loyalties and affections; marriage was only one of many supportive relationships, sex only the slaking of a hunger and, sometimes, an amusement. So, too, in the many forms Western societies took prior to modern times, men consorted with and were sustained chiefly by other men, women by other women; marriage was a practical convenience, love anything from a diversion to a source of inspiration, but neither marriage nor love, in any guise and separately or conjoined, was the primary emotional support of either sex.

But with the coming of industrialization and the growth of the modern city, traditional support networks disintegrated; the home and the family took their place, and accordingly in the Victorian period love—specifically, love in marriage—achieved an unprecedented significance. In the present century, as the development of modern society continued, love and marriage became even more important and more highly prized. The impersonality of industrial-urban society produced the central paradox of twentieth-century life that the sociologist David Riesman in 1950 aptly labeled "the lonely crowd." To the lonely, love seemed the cure for pain, the harbor for lost souls. No Greek youth pleasantly loitering all day with the ever-present gathering of men in the Athenian agora, no knight constantly surrounded by friends and retainers or lingering for years in the close-knit society of his liege-lord's castle, could have known anything like the feelings of the modern bachelor or career woman returning at evening to a rented room or tiny apartment, an anonymous cell in a vast prison where one could weep and be unheard, could die and remain undiscovered for days. No wonder the first sexual revolution, though it partly freed sex from guilt, did not free it from love and commitment.

The physical isolation and rootlessness of life in mid-century, however, was only one reason love assumed such great significance. Another was that society had come, as never before, to condition its members from earliest childhood to measure and evaluate themselves in terms of the amount of love they received. According to Freudian theory and the observations of child development researchers, the basic twentieth-century middle-class technique of rearing children was to give them love when they were good or did something well and to deny them love when they were bad or did something poorly. This, though it normally succeeded in socializing children, tended to make them chronically insecure about love and obsessed by the task of gaining and keeping it. Love had become the key to personal worth; the child interpreted every parental display of love as a reward for goodness, every withholding of it as punishment for badness.[10]

Children thus came early in life to identify success in general with personal worth, and to evaluate themselves according to their success in being liked and loved by others. In their teens, not yet

[10] Freud: *Group Psychology*, pp. 74–5; J. C. Flugel: *Man, Morals, and Society*, pp. 55–7; Talcott Parsons: *Essays in Sociological Theory*, p. 257; and many others.

having access to a career or to social prestige, they gauged their own merit by their popularity (a thin-spread form of love) or, as an alternative, by the intensity and overpowering quality of their youthful crushes. For to be in love even without being loved in return partly met the need, since it enabled one to fantasize winning the love of the wonderful loved one. Wonderful because the lover needed the beloved to be so. In psychological experiments, poor children, to whom coins were shown, later recalled them as being much larger than they really were (rich children did not make the same error); similarly, the teen-age boy, unsure of his merit and eventual status in our fluid society and needing love to provide a sense of worth, could see rare beauty and infinite charm in a giggling dumpling of a bobby-soxer, and the teen-age girl perceive manliness and sex appeal in a boisterous oafish youth. The dreaminess, new-minted optimism, and smug contentment of the adolescent in love meant that he or she had found two things to be of great value—the beloved, and the self.

The youth, however, when he started to earn a living or attained the social status of a college man with its attendant career expectations, began to achieve some small degree of success from those sources; his image of himself improved somewhat and the intensity of his need to bolster his ego through an idealized love object decreased accordingly. It was not only experience that, for him, introduced some realism into love during courtship but a diminished need to have love be a form of magic, solving his problems. Or rather, some of them, for at the very time he had his first successes, he also was apt to leave the parental home and to sense in full the isolation so typical of contemporary life.

Meanwhile, what of the young woman? After high school, whether she took a job or went to college her career expectations and thus her sources of self-esteem were nothing like the young man's. She was already aware that in all likelihood she would never have a career, make her mark, or seem important to any but a very few people; in consequence, love was even more important to teen-aged girls and young women than to teen-aged boys and young men, both at the dating and courtship level and after marriage. The young single female's addiction to romantic movies and the homemaker's to soap opera and romantic novels indicated that their need for love was greater than that of men. What Byron had written a century and a quarter earlier seemed truer than ever:

"Man's love is of man's life a thing apart, / 'Tis woman's whole existence."

Yet the difference in need between young men and young women was not all that great; it was these same young men, after all, who could not find bachelorhood a satisfying way of life and therefore married the young women. It was a time in which a variety of well-known social forces, plus the rapidity of social change itself, conspired to create psychological insecurity not only in adolescents but adults, male and female alike. Love came to have somewhat the character of a panacea, a medicine curative of anemia of the ego, loneliness, existential anxiety, and lack of purpose. And as these and other effects of industrialization and urbanization appeared in people in many areas of the world, love in the modern Western style became ever more appealing and widespread.

In America itself, the use of love as panacea reached new heights in mid-century. Parents thrust their children into dancing classes and parties even before puberty, and the young began to date at twelve and thirteen when masculinity and femininity were still only uncomfortable and unjustifiable poses. All too soon, they became obsessed with the importance of "going steady," and began doing so earlier and earlier, thereby reassuring themselves that they were worthwhile.

Having taken part in such activities from the age of twelve, they were ready earlier than formerly to marry and achieve still greater security. The decline in the age of first marriage which had begun at the turn of the century continued into its middle decades; between 1930 and 1950 the average age at first marriage dropped a year and a half for men and a year for women. *The Reader's Digest* of August 1957 expressed the popular view of this, seeing it through a roseate haze of optimism:

> The girl of 19 and the boy of 21 who walk down the aisle today, however, often are far different from the wild, eloping kids of a generation ago. Usually they have tested their affection and loyalty for each other during three or four years . . . [and] acquired an intimate knowledge and a deep tolerance of each other's habits, reactions and attitudes. Thus, marriage poses no overwhelming problems of adjustment.

But in truth the testing was superficial, since it took place only in the milieu of dating and since, moreover, adults so young hardly knew their own real needs and potential; to be valid, the testing would have had to be done in more realistic circumstances and at a more mature stage of development. Despite the optimism of the *Digest* and the wedding-loving American public, census data of the era showed that a young woman who married under twenty was three times as likely to be divorced as one who married between twenty-two and twenty-four; the data for men, though different, were comparable. The quest for love and the drive to marry may have been normal and healthful responses to emotional hunger but, like eating, could if overindulged result in pathology.

For the pressure to choose a mate and pair up early, despite limited knowledge of one's self and the other, increased the chance of falling in love on the basis of the unconscious meshing of dissimilar and opposite traits of personality, a source of attraction that, when exaggerated, often produced unwholesome marital relationships. Although sociological data showed that young men and women tended to fall in love with and marry those similar to themselves socially, intellectually, and in other ways that they were aware of, psychological studies showed that within these limits they were often unconsciously drawn to those whose emotional needs and characteristics complemented their own, bearing out to some degree the old adage that opposites attract. The achievement-oriented man or woman might choose a partner who was relatively quiescent and passive, the parentlike and caretaking person someone dependent and clinging, the steady and responsible person a flighty and impulsive mate, and so on. Most people thought they wanted someone just like themselves and chose a partner who was so in many external respects—but some of whose deep-seated personality traits dovetailed with, rather than matched, their own, and through whom they vicariously experienced characteristics they lacked. Cultural factors heightened the tendency; men and women, though they thought themselves modern and enlightened, were still powerfully influenced by ancient traditions of male and female personality differences and gender roles.[11]

Such complementarity of emotional needs was thought by many experts of the time to be a normal basis for love, yet all too often it resulted in what psychotherapists and marriage counselors called "neurotic marriage," productive of pain and symptom formation

[11] On "complementarity" theory, see Robert F. Winch: *Mate-Selection*, especially Ch. 6. A generation later, when the ancient social traditions were being dismantled, studies would find the theory of limited applicability, as we will see in the next chapter in the present book.

sufficient to ruin health and destroy careers. The people in such a marriage, though suffering, might be quite unable to do without each other or to cut themselves off from what they thought of as love. A typical case from the files of Family Service of Highland Park (Illinois) involved an exhausted, ailing man over whose face flickered a nervous desperate smile, and who told his story to the marriage counselor as follows:

> I had a premonition before I married Lucille that this is the way my marriage would turn out. I guess I was flattered that she chose me instead of some of the other guys. It was pretty tough competition. . . . I was just a nobody—and still am. In fact, if you listen to Lucille, I'm not only a nobody but a complete flop—as husband and as a man. . . . If I don't ask for a raise at work, she ridicules me. If I should happen to get a raise, she says it isn't enough and it proves I'm a sucker. . . . I've lost my last five jobs because she called me so often at work, talking endlessly and telling me off. She has thrown everything at me that she can lift. . . . We haven't lived as man and wife for twelve years.

His wife, a vigorous, voluble woman, frequently tearful but in blooming health, came in separately and told her side of it:

> Joe is a poor excuse of a man. He won't stand up to his boss and demand a raise. He won't argue with a clerk who overcharges him. . . . At times when I look at him, I get so mad I just can't control myself. Generally I just don't try. I just let him have it. . . . I wanted a strong, successful man I could lean on, depend on. What did I do instead? When I get after Joe, he gets a smile on his face that looks like the smile of Christ. . . . It's that damned smile that causes me just to throw whatever I can lay my hands on.

But when the counselor asked each one individually whether it might not be better to break up, their answers were remarkably similar. Joe, clearly horrified at the suggestion, replied with an air of explaining the obvious:

> Oh, I *couldn't* leave Lucille. I love her very much. I decided one night to leave and I did. But I couldn't sleep for thinking about her, wondering what she was doing and if she was all right. I was scared to come home because I knew she would be furious that I had left— and she was, but *I had to come home.*

Lucille, too, was aghast at the idea:

> What would I *do* if I left him? I would be absolutely *lost.* I have thought of it often enough, but when I try to imagine what it would

be like without him, I know I just couldn't go on without him. I would miss him, strange as it may seem. I just couldn't get along without him.[12]

In more eloquent terms the same pattern was brilliantly portrayed by Eugene O'Neill in *A Touch of the Poet*. The "poet" of the title is actually a low-born Irishman who had held a commission and fought under Wellington in the Napoleonic wars, but was cashiered for amatory indiscretion. He had moved to the United States, where he spent his years pretending to be an English gentleman. In the play, while he drinks, dresses like a lord, and rides a fine horse, his withered little wife runs the failing inn that is their sole support. She adores his swaggering gallantry, accepts his roaring abuse without a whimper, and ardently defends their ruinous relationship in several throbbing speeches to her daughter about the glory of love. The sad truth, known to playwright and marriage counselor alike (and nowadays labeled "codependence"), is that a human being may cherish a disease, cling to the source of his or her pain and self-destruction, and call the whole thing love; more than that, it may *feel* like love, and which of us can prove to him or her that it does not?

The panacea, in sum, often induced an addiction, with its attendant ills, that was no better than the ills it was supposed to cure. Infidelity is a case in point. We have seen that in many other times and places extramarital relationships were acceptable, normal, and even required; in the Age of Love, however, when fidelity was the professed ideal and the general practice, infidelity was often a symptom of some pressure or need over and above the normal.[13] This may be one reason Kinsey's data showed that men of the upper educational levels were apt to increase their extramarital activities in their late thirties. Many of them, at that age, were either reaching a career plateau or beginning to see that their potential success in life had fairly distinct boundaries, which is probably why roughly thirty per cent tried infidelity at that time as against only half that many in their early twenties. Like alcohol, it temporarily

---

[12] Case reported by Martha Winch, executive director, Family Service of Highland Park, in Winch, *Mate-Selection*, pp. 314–6.

[13] Fidelity was, indeed, the general practice in mid-century, though many have misread the Kinsey data to signify the contrary. Kinsey reported in 1949 and 1953 that half of all American husbands and a quarter of all American wives were unfaithful at some time or other during marriage, but his figures showed that many of these had had only one or a few scattered episodes of extramarital sex, a very different phenomenon from repeated, habitual, or practiced infidelity.

alleviated the sense of their limitations and induced an illusion of general well-being—at the cost, likewise, of multiple risks and aftereffects.

Most psychotherapists and marriage counselors considered the cause of both male and female infidelity to be neurotic needs. This view, based on the Freudian theory of the development of love from the selfish infantile level to the mature and giving level, was supported by statistical evidence: in one careful study of a sizable group of female psychiatric patients and a comparable group of normal women, six times as many of the patients as of the normal women had had extramarital affairs. To judge by contemporaneous case histories reported by marriage counselors, many of the men and women who believed they had found real love outside their marriages had chosen highly inappropriate persons with whom they were unlikely to be better off than with their marital partners. In the more successfully treated cases, therapy generally resulted in a revival of love and sexual enjoyment with the marriage partner, and a simultaneous fading of the glamour and intensity of the outside love affair.[14]

Thus once again, as so often in the past, love proved to be a thing of paradoxes. In a society that was not only mechanized and impersonal but in which religious and philosophic goals had lost much of their power, love met the emotional needs of the individual, gave a sense of security, and provided much of the impetus and inspiration to achievement. At the same time it had assumed in the eyes of many people the deceptive look of a cure-all. The immature, the discontented, the lonely, and the neurotic all dosed themselves with love; like most panaceas, it seemed for a while to lessen their ills but rarely cured them, and often, by the time its analgesic powers waned, it had allowed the ailments to progress beyond healing.

[14] For the psychoanalytic view of infidelity as due to neurosis or immaturity, see Abraham N. Franzblau: *The Road to Sexual Maturity*; for the study of normal women and psychiatric patients, Carney Landis *et al.*: *Sex in Development*, especially p. 97; and for case histories treated successfully, Emily Mudd *et al.*, eds.: *Marriage Counseling, A Casebook*, Ch. 6.

6

Who Is Woman? What Is She?

❀ ❀

❀

Most of the foregoing treats of the Age of Love in America as it equally affected men and women. Indeed, it was the intention of the feminists to make all of society's opportunities and benefits, love included, apply equally to both sexes; they expected that when they gained legal and educational equality, women would desire the same goals in life, work at the same jobs and careers, live and love as they saw fit, and marry and rear children without being relegated to the home and required to depend on men. They were sure that when that nirvana was reached, the abilities and personality of woman would be almost indistinguishable from those of man, and in the crop-haired, flat-chested Twenties even the differences in male and female appearance seemed to be diminishing.

But although the feminists had won some of their major goals, particularly the vote, by 1920, decades later modern woman was still by no means the equal of man. Quite apart from the fact that men stubbornly held on to their power and privileges in the worlds of work, academia, and politics, love itself was a major force hindering the achievement of equality; woman was afraid to be man's equal—afraid it would cost her the chance for love and leave her a juiceless old maid. Nor did she *have* to do the things he did, for in the name of love he would still pay her way and permit her to be dependent on him. And so she bought love at the price of remaining unequal, inferior, and discontented with her bargain all her life.

Her inequality was not, however, a matter of her legal status. After the many centuries of subjugation, she had become completely a person at law, with the same rights as the man to possess and control money, make contracts, use the courts, and vote for representatives. To be sure, a number of laws remained on the books which restricted her right to work, but they were minor and all ostensibly for her own good: in mid-century, seventeen states prohibited her from working in mines, eight would not let her mix or serve liquor in public bars, and almost all set limits on the number of hours she was allowed to work per day and per week. But the only important remaining legal inequity was in her favor, and more a matter of practice than actual legislation: in defiance of all the facts, it was still assumed by divorce courts throughout the land that, as soon as a woman married, she became permanently helpless and was entitled to lifelong support. And that was the core of woman's problem: she was painfully torn between the desire to use her hard-won rights and become as fully developed a being as man, and the desire to be man's temptress, darling, and dependent.

In the course of Western history, women had never been educated equally with men; in imperial Rome, at least among the upper class, she came the closest, but even then there was no genuine coeducation. In the twentieth century, however, girls went to the same public schools as boys and in fact by 1950 were averaging half a year more education than boys and in college earning over one third of all degrees. All this equipped them to want and to perform most of the kinds of work men do. And indeed, in the first six decades of the century the percentage of all women of working age who had full-time jobs more than doubled, reaching nearly forty per cent, while that of wives who worked had nearly quintupled, reaching thirty per cent. But what was far more remarkable was that decades after the major victories of feminism, seventy per cent of married women still did *not* work, nor did fully one quarter of all single women.

To a man, work meant not only money but what he *was*. Woman had won equal education and one third of all the jobs in this country, but work remained to her only something she did to earn money. The Department of Labor surveyed 9,000 working women in 1952 and found that only about three per cent worked because of job satisfaction; the rest did so purely for the money. The true career woman was in evidence in large Eastern cities and a few other places, and career women were always in the news, but they were still a rarity; in mid-century women made up only three per cent of America's dentists, six per cent of its doctors, and one per cent of its U.S. Senators, but sixty-nine per cent of its clerical workers. A generation earlier, female college students talked earnestly of becoming botanists, psychologists, or scholars; in the early 1950's, when more women went to college than ever, half had no intention of working after they married, another thirty per cent had vague hopes of combining marriage and motherhood with part-time work, and only twenty per cent were really bent on careers.[15] In the classroom the woman briefly flared up into a bright flame of talent, intellectual curiosity, and determination; then she graduated and fitfully subsided into an ember on someone's hearth.

Yet it was not easy for her to do so. Although there was no technique by which one could measure the total quantity of satisfaction or dissatisfaction in any society, the overwhelming consensus of such close observers as historians, psychiatrists, sociologists, and marriage counselors was that many American wives suffered from a chronic low-grade dissatisfaction with themselves and with life; they were bored, fearful of "going to seed," fatigued by their duties despite all the mechanization of housekeeping, and jealous of the lives their husbands led.

The central problem of mid-century woman, causing these dissatisfactions, was said by behavioral scientists to be "role conflict" or "role confusion." The modern woman did not really know what she wanted to be or should be; even if she knew, she also had reason for wanting to be, or thinking she ought to be, something very different. For she still lived in a man's society. Though no longer a thoroughgoing patriarchy, it was still a world in which men gave the family and its children their last name, ran most businesses and all governments, and were able to philander, gamble, or get drunk at the cost of being criticized but not ruined—none of which was true for women. It was a world in which nearly all prestige and importance accrued to men: of the people listed in *Who's Who*—the criterion of inclusion is that one be well known in some form of "useful and reputable achievement"—only six per cent were women. Even if this did not mean that homemaking was useless or disreputable, it unquestionably showed that it did not make one well known.

Some sociologists likened women to Jews, Negroes (as blacks were still called), and immigrants—persons caught between two

[15] The figures on college women were extracted by sociologist Mirra Komarovsky from a number of studies and surveys. See her *Women in the Modern World*, pp. 92–9.

worlds who live in the upper world but are not part of it, long to escape from their own group and are ashamed of their desire, yearn to enter the upper world but resent its members, and are both defensive and harshly critical of their own kind. Just as no one could lampoon a Jew like a Jewish comedian, so no one could paint the female character in as detestable colors as a caustic woman. And very much as Southern blacks used to grin, cackle, and shuffle in order to make the white man feel safe, young women, despite a century of feminist struggle and achievement, often adopted the role of the "sweet thing" and nitwit so as not to frighten men away. On two different campuses, roughly four out of every ten under-graduate women admitted to researchers that they "played dumb" with interesting men, deliberately misspelled words now and then, and on dates consciously adopted the "I-don't-care-anything-you-want-to-do" stance.

The potential male fear they were trying to allay was real enough. For men in America even more than in other Western countries, success, though broadly equated with love, was specifi-cally equated with masculinity. Many a male felt genuinely alarmed by a woman who could match wits with him, beat him in a debate, more quickly solve a problem in calculus, or write a better piece of advertising copy. He would snidely denigrate her to himself or other men as "cold" and "unfeminine," but at the unconscious level he felt a threat to his traditional male superiority and hence to his very potency. No wonder he shunned her; no wonder the ca-reer woman so often remained single.

But the noncareer woman was also caught between two worlds, and her jealousy of the male and suppressed desire to compete with him frequently reappeared after marriage in the form of attempts to dominate him by nagging, hostile criticism of his shortcomings and lack of success, and the like. The man often reacted as though it were literally his maleness which she criticized, which may well be why, according to the eminent psychiatrist Dr. Karl Menninger, for every woman who complained of her husband's excessive viril-ity, a dozen complained of their husband's sexual apathy or impo-tence.

If woman had believed wholeheartedly that her nature and char-acter were what men had long said they were, she might not have suffered from role confusions and conflicts. Suppose, for instance, she had agreed with all the things scornful and domineering men had said about her for 2,500 years. Suppose she believed herself to be less intelligent than he, weak, vain, and wanton, designed by God to live under man's dominion, and intended by nature to devote herself to making man happy. If she had thought all this, she could have tolerated her exclusion from the affairs of the world without burning resentment, could have accepted the nurturing and homemaking role as the best that fate had given her.

Her equal education, however, had not only made her want the rewards and privileges of the masculine world but shown her that she could do its worthwhile work as well as a man; moreover, the findings of psychologists had shown that her intelligence was the equal of his and that most of the differences between feminine and masculine abilities were socially dictated, acquired rather than innate. Sir Thomas More once found one of his daughters in tears over a difficult Latin text she was working on; gently he took it away from her and told her that such difficult mental effort was not for women. Three centuries later the Victorian poet Charles Kingsley wrote, "Be good, sweet maid, and let who can be clever." But to a century which had seen women like Marie Curie, Eleanor Roosevelt, Marianne Moore, Madame Pandit, Margaret Mead, and Suzanne Langer, Sir Thomas and Kingsley looked more like medieval gentlemen than a Renaissance one and a nineteenth-century one. It was not really her abilities twentieth-century woman was unsure of but her *nature*; even if she knew she had talents, she felt trapped in a recalcitrant body, a gentle prison in which it seemed abnormal, unnatural—and dangerous—to use those talents. The danger she most feared was that, if she did try to use them, she would become unlovable.

A bizarre resurgence of traditional ideas occurred in the wake of World War II, when men, returning to civilian life, wanted women to withdraw from their wartime gains in the world of work, and a chorus of voices was therefore raised assuring woman that to win love she had to accept the dictates of nature and content herself with being a fond, emotional, subservient homebody. It was particularly impressive when the voice was that of an extremely wealthy and successful career woman: Marlene Dietrich advised modern woman in the *Ladies' Home Journal* in 1954 to accept her husband's superiority without so much as the tiniest doubt, complaint, or wish of her own. "Love him," she urged, "unconditionally and with devotion. You chose him. He must be wonderful." In practical terms, Miss Dietrich explained, this meant adapting one's self completely to his needs and whims, worshipping him and treating him as the unquestioned lord and master of the house, pampering and comforting him, and devoting full time to making him happy without thought of one's self. Even Alfred Tennyson—even Tertullian —was not more patriarchal.

In the late 1940's and the 1950's there was a good deal of similar, if not so extreme, writing by social critics, educators, and others, but it was psychoanalysts who were the major intellectual power behind mid-century antifeminism. Oddly enough, Freud himself had been responsible; although he seemed an ally of the feminists two generations earlier, he had a thoroughly Victorian outlook on woman's proper role. In 1883, long before he had theoretical grounds for his beliefs, he wrote to his fiancée, Martha Bernays, as follows:

> It is really a stillborn thought to send women into the struggle for existence exactly as men. If, for instance I imagined my gentle sweet girl as a competitor it would only end in my telling her, as I did seventeen months ago, that I am fond of her and that I implore her to withdraw from the strife into the calm uncompetitive activity of my home. It is possible that changes in upbringing may suppress all a woman's tender attributes, needful of protection and yet so victorious. . . . Nature has determined woman's destiny through beauty, charm, and sweetness. . . .

This was run-of-the-mill nineteenth-century patriarchalism. But years later, when Freud was struggling to theorize about the character of woman, he decided that the determining factor in her psychological development was her realization that nature had failed to provide her with the admirable genitalia males possess. The result was, he reasoned, that she felt painfully inferior and by way of adjustment assumed a passive, submissive, and dependent role in life. The "normal" woman turned to dependency and domesticity; the woman who sought a career could only be suffering from neurosis or a "masculinity complex." Freud thus provided himself with a theoretical justification for those Victorian prejudices with which he was already equipped and took for natural laws the ephemeral opinions of his own time. Yet he seems to have sensed the weakness of his own rationalization, for years afterwards he said to a dear friend: "The great question that has never been answered and which I have not yet been able to answer, despite my thirty years of research into the feminine soul, is: *What does woman want?*"[16]

Many other psychoanalysts of the period accepted Freud's psychology of women but without experiencing his uncertainties. The noted Dr. Helene Deutsch, for one, in her two-volume *Psychology of Women*, presented a detailed portrait of the female personality that was based on the assumption that a "genital trauma" occurred when the girl realized her own shortage of external plumbing. The inclination of psychoanalysts of this persuasion was to urge women —as Freud did—to stay at home and *be women*. Perhaps the most popular contemporaneous exposition of this view was made in 1941 by the playwright and well-known analysand Moss Hart in the form of his entertaining but didactic show *Lady in the Dark*; the eponymous lady, a successful but unhappy editor, finds love and a sense of identity as a woman only when she cedes her top job to her male assistant, marries him, and presumably settles down in a healthful milieu of chintz, roast beef, diapers, and rosebushes.

An even more thoroughgoing advocate of traditionalism was the psychoanalyst Dr. Marynia Farnham, who labeled modern woman "the lost sex" and asserted that her neuroses and dissatisfactions were due solely to her failure in love—a failure stemming from her inability to be a real woman. The trouble, said Dr. Farnham and her collaborator Ferdinand Lundberg, was the lack of prestige accorded to real womanhood; they recommended that the federal government reestablish the dignity of womanhood by such means as giving honorary degrees and cash grants to good mothers, and by energetically advocating the doctrine that careers are "not generally desirable for women . . . [but are] the disordered fantasies of the masculine-complex woman." The individual woman, in their view, could find ample means of self-expression and achievement by returning to the handicraft stage of housekeeping, making her own bread, canning her own food, sewing her own curtains, and

[16] His theory of female personality is found in "Psychology of Women" in *New Introductory Lectures on Psycho-Analysis*. Throughout the era discussed in the present chapter, many psychoanalysts followed Freud in this view, but some, strongly dissenting, held that he mistook effect for cause and that penis envy was not so much an inevitable cause of woman's inferiority as one more proof that, in a man's world, she was socially disadvantaged and yearned to be a man, with all of man's privileges and advantages (including a penis). For a contemporaneous expression of this view, see Abram Kardiner: *Sex and Morality*, pp. 46–8. Other noted psychoanalysts sharply critical of Freud's psychology of women were Karen Horney and Clara Thompson; for a 1946 discussion of their views and similar ones, see Viola Klein: *The Feminine Character*, pp. 72–85.

the like. "Very possibly," wrote Dr. Farnham and Mr. Lundberg, "good food is no more susceptible of commercial exploitation than mother love. . . . The decline of woman's interest in food preparation parallels the decline in many of them of the capacity for affection."

But they might as well have used a broom to sweep back the incoming tide. Ruskin, Gandhi, and other reformers too had tried at various times to restore a lost morality by calling for a return to older ways; but when doing so meant giving up increased productivity and returning to a more difficult struggle for existence, people ignored the advice. Dr. Farnham and analysts with a like viewpoint might have convinced a few hundred patients to take their expensive advice, but the Industrial Revolution and its multifarious sequelae were not to be undone. Females of the poorer and even middle classes could not afford the luxury of playing frontierswomen; more than that, society itself could not survive the abandonment of the productive power that had helped fill the globe with people. In any case, it was far from certain that baking bread and canning peaches would produce true love; the twentieth-century man's motives in seeking a woman were not, as we have seen, those of a householder in search of a housekeeper but those of a person in need of emotional satisfaction and companionship.

And whatever the man wanted and needed, to the woman who for twelve years of school (and especially those who for four years in college) had been trained to be interested in the whole wide world, the routines of housework were suffocatingly dull and time-consuming. Even in the age of mechanization, a woman with three children and no servant had 28 beds to make per week, 170 pounds of food to prepare, and some 700 or more plates, glasses, and items of flatware to wash (which involved a lot of handling even with an automatic dishwasher). Next week it all started again. Important as her children and husband might be, the chores themselves took most of her time and energy; she might be pardoned for not finding in them an adequate meaning to life or definition of womanhood. The following letter from the twenty-five-year-old wife of a college instructor in a large city, offered by Professor Mirra Komarovsky as typical of many she received, exhibited nearly all the problems of modern woman in microcosm:

Believe me there is not enough stimulation in the incessant dishwashing, picking up, ironing, folding diapers, dressing and undressing the kids, making beds day in and day out. My social life with the other mothers on the park benches is depressing. I cannot get them away from the same old talk. . . .. My husband is very sympathetic and tries to help me on weekends, but he has his own work to do and must be allowed to do it if he is to advance in his job. I must confess I envy him. Here we were two college students, he a few years ahead, each interested in his own field. I majored in art and as you know even had some ambitions of my own. Now he still has a very interesting life. He meets in the course of the day some of the most interesting people in his field. Even his daily lunch at the Faculty Club is more exciting than anything that happens to me.

But the significant thing is that this young woman voluntarily accepted her self-denying role—mothers *could* work, if they really wanted to—in order to solve her role conflict dilemma, only to end up pitying herself and envying her husband. In such an atmosphere, love was lucky to thrive; lucky, even to survive.

For all the discomforts and frustrations of such a choice, in the post-war years and particularly in the smug, contented 1950's there was an unmistakable trend for women to accept their traditional place in the home, albeit without their ancient submissiveness. Not only did they marry younger but had children earlier and in larger numbers. The rise in fertility was by no means a phenomenon only of the upper-middle-class suburbs; in 1957 women of childbearing age throughout the nation had twenty-two per cent more children than only seven years earlier. The increase in the fertility of the youngest women was particularly striking: in 1957 those between twenty and twenty-four years old had thirty-two per cent more children than women of the same age range in 1950. The average family size, to be sure, increased only slightly, and there was no evidence of a movement toward the large old-fashioned family of early America. But childless or one-child families were becoming less frequent, while two-child and three-child families were increasing. As usual, the poor and the rich were having more children than the middle economic groups, but the national tendency was toward the three-child family.

The young American woman was thus muddling through her major dilemma by making several kinds of compromises, all only moderately satisfactory, and closing her eyes to another dilemma that lay ahead for her. By choosing early marriage and early motherhood, and abandoning any serious lifelong planning for career and work, she condemned herself in advance to nearly half a life of the so-called empty nest. Her three children would all be in school when she was in her early thirties, and the youngest would be a self-sufficient teen-ager when she was still under forty. At that juncture, with over thirty years of life ahead of her, at least twenty of which represented the very pinnacle of her powers as a personality, she would have nothing worthwhile to do—neither continued reproduction nor career—to give her a genuine purpose in life. Bored, useless, and disconnected, her emotional needs would almost certainly become greater than her familiar, preoccupied husband could meet. The Kinsey figures told the tale: the per cent of married women having extramarital relations was highest for women in their mid-thirties and early forties. The data did not reveal whether they found what they were seeking, but that they sought something more than mere "outlet" seems beyond reasonable doubt.

Some researchers of women's issues and moderate feminists suggested a rather more satisfactory compromise. Professor Komarovsky, Alva Myrdal, and others rejected the thesis that womanliness lies in homemaking and childbearing, but did agree that the well-being of society depends on adequate mothering of young children, and that the biology of woman predisposes her to find genuine fulfillment in childbearing and mothering; but these activities, they maintained, were not identical with housework, and chores were not a substitute for a purpose in life. They recommended that the young woman pursue a career or a job seriously until she felt certain she could resume it even after an extended furlough; then she could take leave to pursue her other role in life, working only part-time or not at all but making generous use of child-care facilities such as cooperative sitting pools, nurseries, and camps to gain leisure for herself so as to engage in stimulating activities. When her youngest child entered school, she could begin to reenter her working life part-time, and later full-time. If she devoted twenty-five years to it from the age of forty on, she would enjoy almost as long a career as men had a century earlier.

But all this was not yet actuality; it was only the recommendation and hope of some temperate feminists. Whether it would be the direction in which women's lives evolved no one could say with any certainty. In the 1950's, most American women were dealing with their role conflicts by accepting the conservative answer, with all its personal costs. In their uncertainty as to what they were or should be, they were making a definite choice with which, afterwards, many of them were far from happy. They had bargained away their other selves for love, and felt, too late, that they had paid too high a price for it.

7

Grand Design, with Flaws

For all the faults of the new romanticism, shortcomings of love as a cure-all, and discontents of women, in the 1950's it was possible to optimistically interpret the history of love as an erratic but purposeful progression upward. Despite reversals of direction during the Dark Ages and the Enlightenment, there had been a long-term movement towards the merging of romantic passion, sensuous enjoyment, friendship, and marriage. Seen in perspective, this evolution seemed so inevitable that the scholar Lionel Trilling spoke of "the dialectic of the history of love." Like the Victorians who smugly believed that their society was the highest form yet achieved by social evolution, many thoughtful observers in the middle years of the twentieth century considered their era's way of love close to being the ideal and ultimate at which history had been aiming all along.

Advertising art conveyed that Panglossian view by means of endless images of handsome young smiling Dad, pretty young smiling Mom, jolly freckled smiling children, in an environment of house, car, freezer, and perky smiling dog. Newspapers, television, and magazines reinforced the notion that the modern family was an amiable democratic team in which, from time to time, as one could infer from the misty mood of ads in which Dad was slipping a bracelet on Mom's wrist, romance existed and found its expression when the children were, at long last, asleep.

A quite different picture of mid-century marriage, however, was offered in the misogynistic polemics of the social critic Philip Wylie, the flood of alarming articles about divorce, and the acidulous portrayals by fiction writers of suburban boredom, demanding wives, harried and disenchanted husbands, and grubby experiments in adultery. All of these made it distressingly evident that, in the Age of Love, married love was something less than perfect. We have seen the positive values of marriage in this era; now we must note its conflicts and imperfections.

One, as we have just seen, was the dilemma of women, deeply rooted in the culture and to which there seemed to be no good answer but only, at best, a compromise. Equally basic was a conflict felt by man and woman alike, present in nearly every society but much exacerbated in mid-century America: the artificially created discontinuity, contradicting biology for society's sake, that required children to be thoroughly sexless during their formative years but abruptly become sexual as adults. The sexual impulses of children toward their parents were rigidly repressed at the same time that they were taught to love their parents and be affectionate toward them; therein lay the primary disconnection between love and sex, and the source of all those tangled, tortured arguments throughout the ages about the relationship between the two.

The Greeks had tried a solution-by-specialization, according to Demosthenes: their men had concubines, hetaerae, and wives for, respectively, sex, love, and housekeeping. But with the advent of ascetic Christianity, the primal disconnection became so severe that people supposed love and sex to be all but antithetical; even the amorous medieval knights had to keep love partly desexualized in order to be comfortable with it, and in the Victorian era, when love had been absorbed by marriage but wives were prized primarily as mothers, men had to repair to brothels in their lustier moods. In the twentieth century, our society still had an underlay of Christian condemnation of sex intermixed with and combatting the liberal and scientific attitudes engendered by the first sexual revolution. Each person's feelings were an unstable and inconsistent mixture of the two. In the first decade of life children learned that love was good and sex was bad; in the second decade that love was still better and that sex, though not bad, was a forbidden fruit; and in the third decade that love was better than ever and that sex was normal, healthful, and a major means of expressing one's higher sentiments in marriage.[17]

But after twenty-odd years of conditioning, the disconnections in their feelings were not easily repaired. The files of doctors and marriage counselors of the period were filled with case histories of young people who had entered marriage full of hope only to find that disgust, frigidity, impotence, vaginismus, and similar surprises blighted their love, and although the evidence indicated that these afflictions were less common than in Victorian times, they were still all too frequent. Even among supposedly normal people who had not been driven to seek professional help, studies found that by and large the sexual relationship was the slowest of the major areas of marital life to achieve satisfactory adjustment—this in a country that was fascinated by sex, highly valued sex appeal, and prided itself on its frankness and modernity in sex matters.

Contemporary marriage upheld the ideal of sexual equality between husband and wife, yet a contrary and conflicting value remained part of the pattern. Despite all the changes brought about by the sexual revolution, young women were still expected to be chary of their favors before marriage (while young men were expected to take all the sex they could get) and to be at once sexually attractive, yet reserved and inexperienced. Many a young woman, for all her freedoms, came to marriage astonishingly ignorant of the usual or average feelings of other women concerning sex; situations like the following—reported by a psychologist doing marriage counseling—were far more common than one would have supposed:

> *Mrs. N. (an attractive young woman from New England):* Do you think my husband is normal or is he oversexual? He wants it two or three times a week.

[17] The official position of the Catholic Church, that sexual love within marriage was justified solely as the means of reproduction, remained basically unchanged, but in 1958, the Archdiocese of New York, while reaffirming procreation as the God-designated purpose of marriage, added: "This does not deny secondary purposes for the exercise of the generative faculties of men, as the expression of love between husband and wife."

Counselor: Two or three times a week sounds very normal for a man his age. And I am sure that a great many wives would feel disappointed if their husbands didn't want it that frequently.

Mrs. N. (incredulous): You mean there are *women* who really want it that often?

Although physiological reasons for female frigidity were extremely rare, the extensive records of the Margaret Sanger Research Bureau and the findings of many researchers indicated that about one out of four women was sexually unresponsive, their feelings about the sex act ranging from indifference to intense disgust; among men, however, the proportion of total unresponsiveness was only about one per cent in youth, and did not match the female ratio until age seventy.

Not all the contradictions in marriage involved sex. One of the more serious was the disparity between the vastly increased importance of marriage and its greatly diminished structural strength. Gone were the bonds of law and religion that once made divorce all but impossible; gone from the family were its valuable food-raising, medicine-making, and other productive functions; gone, for the most part, were its responsibilities for education, defense, and security against age and disease. In place of all these functions, marriage now offered primarily sex, affection, and companionship; even the decision to have children was made largely on the basis of the pleasure they were expected to yield. Unlike food, marriage did not fill a vital need, and no one died for lack of it (although the married did live a bit longer than the single); it was a way to seek that highly valued but nonessential commodity, happiness. Having no vital functions that it alone could perform, a marriage stood or fell precisely according to whether it did or did not yield happiness —a fragile and slippery basis of existence. In past centuries an unhappy husband or wife sought ways to get along with minimum discomfort but did not live in constant fear of seeing his or her world shattered; in the Age of Love an unhappy husband or wife would lie rigidly awake in the night, turning over and over the sickening prospect of dissolving the partnership and beginning the long, dismal, uncertain process of building another one. In past centuries the functional family was a large, close association of loyal relatives who knew each other's troubles and were ready to help each other in any crisis, but the modern marriage of love required privacy and isolation, and when troubles or crises arose, husband and wife had to wrestle with them at home alone and assume the required look of good cheer as they stepped out the front door.

The weaknesses and hedonistic basis of modern marriage led to a number of gloomy predictions about it. In 1941, the sociologist Pitirim Sorokin offered this depressing forecast:

> Divorces and separations will increase until any profound difference between socially sanctioned marriages and illicit sex-relationship disappears. . . . The main sociocultural functions of the family will further decrease until the family becomes a mere incidental cohabitation of male and female, while the home will become a mere overnight parking place mainly for sex-relationship.

But at least during the next two decades his vision proved thoroughly wrong. Divorce rose sharply in 1946—a sweeping away of the incompatible marriages accumulated during the war—but during the 1950's the divorce rate held relatively steady at a level far below the 1946 peak; contrary to Sorokin's view, men and women continued to prize marriage as a source of love and emotional security. And in opposition to his prediction that marriage would become merely a convenient place for coitus, many mid-century experts held that the most distinctive characteristic of marriage in their era was the extent to which it created a merger or identification of the husband and wife with each other in nearly every aspect of their lives. They interacted so thoroughly in most of their roles and at most levels that their personalities seemed fused, each individual coming to have desires, think, and act in terms of the composite ego rather than of his or her own.

Yet though this was greatly prized in the Age of Love and made much of in the media under the label of "togetherness," it entailed a new and considerable cost. For where the merger became all but total over a period of years, so great a dependency was established that the illness of one spouse, or his or her absence on a trip, might produce in the other waves of irrational panic-like anxiety, while the death of one was an almost irreparable injury to the other. In primitive society or the societies of earlier centuries in Europe, the death of one's spouse was the loss of only a small fraction of one's self; now the fraction was a half and the bleeding remainder had all it could do to survive.

Apart from separation anxiety and death, the fusion of the selves over the years could also, ironically, produce a relationship in which there was no longer anything to give each other, no unexpected riches to offer, no private chambers of the mind from which to step forth refreshed and desirable into the partner's sight. Margaret Mead said that such husbands and wives had "become so much like a single person that, like most individuals in America, they feel the need of others to complete themselves, to reassure them that they are good, to rid them of the self-searching that comes from being left alone." The young lovers had been all in all to each other, utterly comforted in their isolation; the middle-aged couple might, in the same circumstances, feel desperately alone and in need of someone else to talk to, play cards with, just *be* with. Love was nourishing but could also be devouring; two could consume each other and have nothing left when hunger returned.

The integration of personalities, even when it avoided mutual consuming, created yet another conflict, this with what Dr. Kinsey repeatedly referred to as the "basic mammalian sexual pattern." By and large, faithful monogamy does not seem to be a natural pattern among human beings but a socially fabricated one, and even then rare to the point of seeming almost abnormal. Of one hundred and eighty-five societies analyzed in the Human Relations Area Files (a compilation formerly maintained at Yale University and later available at most major universities), only about five per cent were monogamies in which all outside sexual activity was disallowed or disapproved. Some behavioral scientists therefore viewed fidelity as difficult, unnatural, and greatly overpriced, and insistence on it as productive of hypocrisy, guilt, unhappiness, and broken marriage. These distressing results were particularly likely when marriage involved identification of the two selves, for infidelity is the sharing of a very intense experience with someone other than one's principal love partner and a breach of the merger. Even if the act remains wholly secret, it sets up in the unfaithful partner barriers and dark places into which the other cannot penetrate. Dr. Abraham Stone, a renowned sex expert and marital counselor in mid-century, reported that in nearly three decades of marriage counseling he had found infidelity almost never innocuous but practically always a source of guilt, withholding of the self, and impairment of personality interaction and total love.

The discontents and frustrated yearnings due to fidelity were thus part of the price paid for happiness and stability in marriage.

But the alternative had an even higher price. Men in the lower economic and educational groups were less apt to link sex to tender and affectionate relationships and, as Kinsey data showed, far more likely to indulge in extramarital coitus than men of higher education and economic status; this simplicity and freedom did not, however, make for stability or satisfaction in marriage as it had in some other societies and as Havelock Ellis and Bertrand Russell had hoped. For although the divorce rate was commonly thought to be highest among the neurotic, success-driven middle class, census data of the 1950's showed that in reality men earning less than $3,000 a year were two to four times as likely to be divorced as men earning over $4,000 a year.[18]

How are we to appraise the vitality and value of love in this era? Socially and biologically it was successful, for it was making marriage more popular than ever, yielding a more than adequate supply of children, and providing what seemed to be reasonable stability in family life, as judged by the fact that the divorce rate had leveled off. But in view of all its internal conflicts and tensions, was it successful in terms of its own major promise that it would bring happiness?

Many professional studies were conducted on this very point, but the results varied widely, with as few as forty-two per cent and as many as eighty-eight per cent of the husbands and wives in the different samples claiming to be happy in their marriages. These discrepancies had many causes, but the principal one was the inability of the researchers to make the word "happiness" precise or measure it in objective units. Despite this grave shortcoming, most of the results pointed in the same direction: a summary of them in 1955 suggested that about three quarters of the married people in the United States considered themselves happy in their marriages.[19] There is no way to prove that this figure exceeded the average happiness of Athenian men and women, medieval knights and ladies, or the good proper people of Victorian times, but the evidence we have seen should make us suspect, on a subjective basis, that it did.

Finally, that love in mid-century America, with all its inherent conflicts, was functional, immensely important, and generally re-

[18] William J. Goode: *After Divorce*, pp. 53–4.
[19] The summary was made by the sociologist Clifford Kirkpatrick; see *The Family as* *Process and Institution*, p. 448. The major surveys he summarized were those of Davis, Terman et al., Burgess and Cottrell, Lang, and Hamilton.

warding is evidenced by three data. The first: More than three quarters of all men and five sixths of all women married sooner or later, even though marriage was no longer an economic or practical necessity; it was, rather, necessary for emotional reasons. The second: With divorce generally easy to get and increasingly acceptable to society, three quarters of married Americans remained married until their union was ended by death; despite the costs and limitations of marriage, they preferred to accept what happiness it brought them than seek further for it. The third: Nearly all those who divorced when young, and a majority of those who divorced in middle age, married again; they had not been seeking to escape from marriage but only from loveless marriage.

Probably most of those who remained in a first marriage for a lifetime found it not a total realization of their daydreams but a realistic and acceptable substitute; so, too, with those who divorced and remarried, most of whom remained in their second marriages until death. Few of either group may have loved superbly, and few had really expected to, but many were moderately well pleased with the love they had. They were, after all, on Earth, not in Heaven.

Chapter XI
LOVE REMODELED

I

Love Becomes a Dirty Word

Love, as it had evolved by the 1950's, met the needs of modern men relatively well and of modern women middling well; though the Grand Design, as we called it in the previous chapter, was imperfect and sure to undergo alterations, it seemed likely to remain the blueprint for love in the industrial and post-industrial world.

But in the next two decades a number of unanticipated social upheavals caused love to be widely belittled, deprecated, and by some, deliberately avoided. A new wave of feminism, a renewal of the sexual revolution, a counterculture revolt against the Vietnam war and Establishment values, the civil rights movement, the trend toward wives' working outside the home, and a sharp upward turn in the divorce rate all led many men and women to see love as an obsolescent folkway, some psychologists and sociologists to label it an emotional disease, and radical feminists to condemn it as an insidious male technique for keeping women subjugated.

Denigration of love was, to be sure, nothing new. Lovers and poets had long railed at it in artful phrases: "a kind of warfare" (Ovid), "a flame to set the will on fire . . . a flame to cheat men into mire" (John Masefield), "the tyrant of the heart" (John Ford), "a madness most discreet, a choking gall" (Shakespeare), "the very god of evil" (Byron), and so on. But we need not take these ravings seriously; they were part of the traditional posture of the lover as one who is suffering—and loves it.

In the 1960's and 1970's, however, the disparagement of love was no lover's conceit, no fanciful plaint; love was disdained and assailed on realistic rather than poetic grounds. Only a few years after the love-obsessed 1950's, the devaluation of love—or at least of romantic love—was current among such diverse types as the intellectual *avant-garde* and teen-age dropouts, family sociologists and sexual swingers, research psychologists and radical feminists, Maoist terrorists and idealistic commune-dwellers.

The sexual libertarians and leftist radicals held that love was the ruling elite's way of channeling sexual desire into marriage; they called love "bourgeois crap" and "Victorian bullshit." The motto of Vietnam era peaceniks, "Make love, not war," was an exhortation to copulation, not romance, as the alternative to conflict. Epitomizing the new view of sex and love, one teen-aged girl said to her father, after he had lectured her about the importance of love as a prerequisite to sex, "I don't want to hear about any of that love stuff. It's garbage, just plain garbage. If a guy wants to make it with a girl, he'll say anything."[1]

A different but equally negative view was voiced by many family sociologists and psychologists, who saw love as a symptom of inadequacy or neurosis. They said things like, "Love is the fear of losing an important source of need gratification," "Persons who marry demonstrate greater feelings of ego deficiency than do persons who remain single," and "Considering personality inadequacy to be one of the origins of love can scarcely be questioned." Others, though recognizing that love could be a healthy form of behavior, said that its more intense forms—passionate or desperate love of the kind idealized in drama, poetry, and fiction—were the result of personality defects, affective disorders, or addiction. Among the many pejoratives they applied to such relationships were "perverted love," destructive passion," "morbid dependency," "deficiency love," "inferior love," "masquerade of love," "puppy love," "soul sickness," and "pseudo-love."[2]

But it was radical feminists who made the most scathing attacks. Germaine Greer charged that "men have reduced heterosexual contact to sado-masochistic patterns by exploiting love and fantasies of romance." Kate Millett asserted that romantic love supposedly elevates the status of women but is in reality a stratagem by which men conceal and justify women's traditional subordination

---

[1] Quoted in Lillian Rubin: *Erotic Wars*, p. 75. Dr. Rubin heard the story in the 1980's but it typifies how many teen-agers felt from the late 1960's on.

[2] The negative views of psychologists and sociologists are quoted in Murstein: "A Tax-onomy of Love" (unpublished paper), and in Stanton Peele: "Fools for Love," in Sternberg and Barnes: *The Psychology of Love;* the compilation of pejoratives is from Dorothy Tennov: *Love and Limerence*, p. 117.

and economic dependence on them. Ti Grace Atkinson was the most savage: "The psychopathological condition of love is a euphoric state of fantasy in which the victim transforms her oppressor into her redeemer. 'Love' is the natural response of the woman to the rapist. . . . Marriage means rape and lifelong slavery. Love has to be destroyed."[3]

Despite these criticisms and vilifications, love did not disappear during the 1960's and 1970's; nearly all single young men and women, and most of the not-so-young and middle-aged who had been divorced, continued to hunt assiduously for the right someone and, often, to find him or her. The marriage rate actually rose during the 1960's and remained high during the 1970's; so did the remarriage rate of the divorced; trashy romantic novels were sold by the millions and love in any number of variations remained a major topic of films, plays, novels, and advertisements; and in a nationwide Roper survey of 1966 three quarters of married couples named love as the major reason for marrying and ranked it far above sex or children.

But the idealism of the Age of Love had gone somewhat rancid. Many single men and women now were embarrassed to use the word "love"; they would say that they were "seeing someone," "involved," or "in a relationship," but not that they were "in love." One of the most popular rock songs of the 1960's was the lighthearted and cynical "Why Do Fools Fall in Love?" Sentimental love stories remained a staple of Hollywood but the best-known portrait of married love in the 1960's was that of the superficially fond but deeply hostile and mutually destructive couple of Edward Albee's drama and film *Who's Afraid of Virginia Woolf?*

Many men and women preferred relationships that were amiable rather than loving. *Open Marriage* (1972) by Nena and George O'Neill, widely taken to recommend limited extramarital relationships, sold nearly four million copies.[4] Group marriage, a dilution

[3] Germaine Greer: *The Female Eunuch;* Kate Millett: *Sexual Politics;* Ti Grace Atkinson: "The Institution of Sexual Intercourse" and "The Oppressed Majority Demands Its Rights."

[4] The public interpretation of the book as recommending extramarital sex was in error, according to Nena O'Neill. In the 1984 edition, she said—George O'Neill had died a few years earlier—"We suggested that fidelity could be seen in the light of the larger loyalty the partners had to each other and to their mutual growth, rather than as ownership of the mate or exclusivity. We suggested that some couples, who had developed the necessary trust, open communication, and feeling of primariness in their marriage, *might*, as individuals, have a supplementary relationship with another person that did include sex" (p. 227).

of emotional relationships as well as a source of sexual variety, was a favorite topic in women's magazines and on talk shows. In many of the hundreds of communes that sprang up in remote areas, the sharing of partners, often by scheduled rotation, distributed feelings thinly. Extramarital relationships were endlessly discussed in all the media, and affairs that did not involve deep feelings and supposedly would not disrupt marriage were recommended by some experts in human relations as valuable enrichment of life. Thousands of people experimented with mate-swapping, group-sex parties, and sex clubs, all these being ways to engage in sex without running any risk of falling in love. One man confided to a friend, after his first experience of a group-sex party, that what most astonished him was not the sight of well-bred middle-class men and women stripping and coupling while others watched but the response of a woman to whom, overcome by a rush of tenderness after an intense coition, he had said, "I love you!"—whereupon she gently pressed a finger to his lips and said, "Ssh! You mustn't say that here."

2

The Second Sexual Revolution

❀   ❀

❀

It was not only mate-swappers and group-sex libertines who felt nothing but lust or, at most, a kind of friendliness toward those they lay with. The new sexual revolution that swept the nation in the 1960's had as its goals not only freedom to have sex with more than one partner and to indulge in variant kinds of erotic activity, but also freedom from the traditional requirement to love one's sexual partner or partners.

Although the first sexual revolution had sought to rid sexual pleasure of guilt and even to make intercourse outside of marriage acceptable, nearly all the early sexual revolutionaries took it for granted that love was an essential part of the sex act. By the 1920's they had achieved many of their aims and the revolution died down; as the Kinsey Reports of 1949 and 1953 and later sex surveys by others showed, there was relatively little change in American sexual attitudes and behavior from the 1920's through the 1950's.

But then the sexual revolution flared up again, and so fiercely that it has generally been termed "the" sexual revolution, as if no other had preceded it. The new sexual revolution was due to a confluence of causes—the several social developments and upheavals already named—that generated disenchantment with and disrespect for traditional bourgeois and puritanical values and customs. Among the more conspicuous forms this took were "dropping out," living on the street and in crash pads, addiction to marijuana, LSD, and other psychedelic drugs, and street-corner begging; searching for ultimate answers in primitive utopian communities, mystical cults, and EST and other outlandish pseudotherapies; participating in antiwar demonstrations and massive rock concerts; taking part in underground terrorist attacks on war-related research centers and corporate headquarters; and of course, violating society's sexual standards and flouting its traditions of romantic love and marriage.

The new sexual revolution was not, however, limited to the alienated and those in revolt. Many who were active in or sympathetic to the civil rights movement also joined or aided efforts to repeal laws that criminalized adultery, and oral and anal sex even between consenting spouses, and to expand the rights of adults to read, write, and publish materials that were overtly erotic or pornographic. Quite a few affluent and upwardly mobile people, and others who only dreamed of being so, saw the sexual revolution as part and parcel of the good life. *Playboy*, founded by Hugh Hefner in 1953 and hugely successful by the 1960's, appealed to young and middle-aged men for whom work and success were the means to the pleasurable life and its rewards: good clothes, sleek cars, gourmet food, and liberated sex. Hefner himself wrote a seemingly endless series of articles in the magazine expounding the "Playboy

Philosophy," a hedonistic and unfettered view of sex and other pleasures; he paid lip service to affection and love, but the sexual freedom he espoused, unlike the "free love" of the first sexual revolution, did not require love as a prerequisite or envision it as an inevitable outcome of sex. (Hefner lived by his own guidelines for over three decades, experiencing, he estimated, about a thousand sex partners before finally marrying one of them several years ago and adopting a more conventional lifestyle.)

The new sexual revolution swiftly brought about far greater changes than the first one. Sex research, formerly beyond the pale, suddenly became respectable; staid foundations and the government funded surveys and studies of premarital and extramarital sexual behavior, prostitution, and homosexuality. Some of the research made history by using methods that would formerly have landed its practitioners in jail: to study human sexuality, Dr. William Masters and Mrs. Virginia Johnson watched couples having coitus in the laboratory through one-way mirrors and, at various stages of the process, entered the chamber to inspect, measure, and record the condition of their organs. The naked female breast, formerly portrayed only in arty or pornographic magazines, became a commonplace in popular ones. By the early 1970's *Playboy*, in a historic breakthrough, displayed the female pubis; other magazines soon followed suit and a few even moved on to male frontal nudity. Respectable authors, among them Philip Roth and John Updike, included in their novels explicit scenes of masturbation, coitus, fellatio, and cunnilingus, and shortly many writers were giving specific details of the odors, colors, and textures of the parts involved in these acts such as had previously been found only in locked-away works of pornography. On stage and in films simulations of sexual acts grew ever more daring, and X-rated films including actual sex acts became widely available in larger cities and through the mail. What used to be called "marriage manuals" were now sex manuals addressed not only to the married but all who wanted to maximize sexual pleasure; many of these guides, openly sold in bookstores and achieving bestseller status, recommended such erstwhile unmentionable practices as simultaneous oral sex, anal penetration by finger or penis, anilingus, bondage and discipline, and group sex. Dr. Alex Comfort, in his 1972 bestseller, *The Joy of Sex*, dutifully mentioned that great sex is "sex with love," but having given it that nod, wrote as though sexual pleasure is an excellent thing regardless of who one's partner is.

These public changes were matched in private by comparable changes in the attitudes and behavior of most of the young and single, many of the middle-aged and married, and even a few of the elderly of either status. In a Roper poll of 1959, more than half of a national sample had said that premarital intercourse was not all right either for men or women. By 1972, in contrast, a major national sex survey funded by the Playboy Foundation found that 84 per cent of men felt that premarital sex was all right for men and 81 per cent for women if there was strong affection between partners; even lacking strong affection, 60 per cent said it was all right for men and 44 per cent for women. Although women were more conservative, anywhere from 37 to 73 per cent felt that premarital intercourse was all right for men and 20 to 68 per cent for women, depending on the degree of emotional closeness.[5]

Actual behavior was changing as much as attitudes. Kinsey, interviewing volunteers in the 1940's, found that about a quarter of unmarried males had not yet had intercourse by age twenty-five; in 1972 this was true only of 3 per cent. Kinsey reported that one third of unmarried females had had premarital intercourse by age twenty-five; two decades later, over two thirds had. The repertoire of sexual variations used by both the unmarried and the married had also greatly widened, particularly among younger persons: positions such as woman-above or rear-entry, formerly considered either exotic or perverse, were in wide use, fellatio was routine, and although in the 1940's only a minority of men had ever mouthed a woman's genitals, in 1972 nearly two thirds (four fifths among young college-educated men) had done so. Anal intercourse was so rare in Kinsey's time that he could offer no data on it; by 1972, anywhere from a sizable minority to a majority of younger Americans, and a small minority of older ones, had tried it and some did it more or less regularly.

Some sex researchers saw these changes as a shift from "person-centered" sex to "body-centered" sex. Not that sex had been wholly sundered from love; the 1972 survey showed that for most

[5] Although the Playboy Foundation funded the survey, it exercised no influence over its content or conclusions. The survey was conducted by a national marketing organization and its findings reported by the author of this book; see Morton Hunt: *Sexual Behavior in the 1970s*. Several smaller surveys by social scientists in the 1960's and the 1970's yielded similar data on many issues.

people sex was most acceptable when affection existed between the partners. Yet every study of sexual behavior and love made in the 1960's and 1970's found that increasing percentages of Americans condoned sex by unmarried people who felt for each other only mild affection or none. As was to be expected, it was the young who most strongly endorsed this view; in the 1972 survey, 71 per cent of men aged eighteen to twenty-four said that sex was all right for men and 56 per cent for women despite the absence of strong affection; among women in the same age group, 47 per cent sanctioned sex for men without strong affection, 29 per cent for women.

Casual or "recreational" sex, as it was called—anything from regular encounters with a partner one liked to one-night stands with strangers—became common, even if not the predominant mode, among young singles and the separated and divorced. To be sure, many women and some men felt "empty," let down, or ashamed after a sexual episode with a partner with whom they had no emotional connection, but it took only a modicum of friendliness to make them feel all right. A typical statement by one young woman: "What's bad is when you do it and afterward you want him to go away as soon as possible because you and he have nothing to say to each other. But when it's someone you know, a fellow who's a friend, and you still like each other afterward, it's fine."

Others, however, suffered no post-coital sadness after sex with a partner for whom they had no feeling, and some actually preferred their sex totally unemotional. As a twenty-seven-year-old salesman interviewed for the 1972 survey said, "What matters to me most is balling absolutely wildly with somebody new—real knockout stuff, really breaking through and getting to her, and getting the maximum possible turn-on for myself. The only thing I won't try is getting involved emotionally, because that would limit me." A twenty-two-year-old secretary said, "I haven't had all that many men, but I just love sex. I used to have a man friend who would meet me for lunch and a quickie, and that was practically the wildest of all, because it was like anything goes; it wasn't love, it was just passion." Reminiscing not long ago about love in the 1970's, Bruce Weber, an editor of the *New York Times Magazine*, wrote:

We were a lusty, if callow, bunch, not least because we thought we could afford to be. Encouraged by the expansive social mores spawned by the sexual revolution, fortified by the advent of a widespread availability of birth control, and fundamentally unaware of germs, we interpreted sex, for our convenience, as pure pleasure shared by "consenting parties." If it feels good, do it. Remember that?

Unlike the young and single, many married and older people were alarmed by the new sexual freedom. Conservatives and religious fundamentalists, of course, were scandalized and outraged by it, but many relatively liberal parents of the young and some social scientists feared that the new sexual freedom would prevent the unmarried from developing serious relationships and marrying. If Freud was right that love is "aim-inhibited sexuality"—that sexual desire dammed up by custom is transformed into love—the abandonment of sexually inhibiting rules might do away with love. And if love fell victim, would not marriage too? And if marriage, would not the family—and therefore society? But this was all speculation; there was no scientific evidence on the matter. Some social scientists argued that sex early in a relationship tended to short-circuit intimacy and interfere with the development of closeness and commitment; others, equally knowledgeable, held that premarital intercourse was an effective means of building emotional intimacy.

Making the future of love still more uncertain was the fact that another great social upheaval seemed almost sure to severely prune back love or even rip it up, root and all, and cast it on the compost heap of history. Or else, perhaps, reshape it and give it new vitality.

3

What Does Woman Want—Now?

❀   ❀

❀

That other upheaval was, of course, the second wave of feminism—a movement so powerful and dramatic that, like "the" sexual revolution, it is generally called "the" women's movement, as if there had been no other.

In mid-century, as we have seen, women's lives were plagued by role conflicts and painful compromises. Partly liberated from their ancient subordination and tasting equality with men in some areas of life, they found it exasperating to have to play the passive role in courtship and dating, and much worse, particularly for those who had been to college, give up their ambitions and larger interests and to become submissive housewives and mothers. In the classroom they had been the peers of men, and at work, they were part of the larger world (though rarely allowed to climb the ladder of success), but married and with children they watched their husbands go off into that world every morning and then spent the day with running noses and dirty diapers, laundry, unmade beds, shopping, cleaning, and late in the afternoon, preparations for dinner and the welcoming home of the family provider and hero.

During the conservative pro-domestic 1950's, existing feminist organizations were relatively inactive and women's discontents remained largely bottled up. But a tremor hinting at the repressed energy was felt in 1961 when *Sex and the Single Girl*, by Helen Gurley Brown, was published. A flippant, saucy little work, it told young working women that their lives need not be limited to domesticity, that they need not be dependent on men, and that they should make the most of the "bachelor girl's" opportunities for flirtation, romance, and sex. The book rapidly became a bestseller and was much talked about; though not a call to social action, its success indicated that many young women were eager to hear of alternatives to domesticity.

Meanwhile, industriously making notes in a scholars' room at the New York Public Library was an unlikely revolutionary, a discontented housewife, mother, and magazine writer named Betty Friedan. The fruit of her labors, *The Feminine Mystique*, published in 1963, was an all-out assault on the injustices of women's lives and on the myths of femininity and masculinity that served to keep women in their place. The book, sober, well researched, and seething with anger, became not only a bestseller but a manifesto, a call to arms. Friedan's battle cry: "We can no longer ignore that voice within women that says, 'I want something more than my husband and my children and my house.'" Love and its sequelae—marriage, children, and household—were not enough; the something more was career, equal opportunity, and all the rewards they could yield.

The message galvanized discontented and frustrated women throughout the nation. They began voicing their discontent in the media and at home, and joined consciousness-raising and other feminist groups, especially the newest, angriest, and most active of them, the National Organization for Women (NOW), founded by Friedan in 1966. By the end of the 1960's the women's movement, with Friedan as its leading spokesperson, was in full swing, fighting in legislative halls, the courts, and the media for a long list of goals, particularly equal pay, equal access to graduate and professional schools, and equal job opportunities. More broadly, the movement attacked all those traditional customs and attitudes by which men maintained their power, superiority, and privilege: treating women as physically frail, emotional, timid creatures who had to be cherished and protected; had limited mental abilities and were incompetent at managing money and rewiring lamps, and were suited by nature to be men's dependents, assistants, and servants. The women's movement, says the sociologist Lillian Rubin in *Erotic Wars*, was a "gender revolution"—an uprising aimed at redefining the roles and meaning of womanhood—and manhood. Our concern being the history of love, we will pass by the complex story of the movement's struggles, factional battles, achievements, and failures, and look at the ways in which women active in the movement and those sympathetic to it sought to alter their sexual and emotional behavior towards men and that of men towards them.

Some men sympathized with the demands of activists in the movement for equal rights and for the elimination of men's customary sexual innuendoes and condescension towards women. Many others, however, threatened by the feminists' goals, found women who were assertive or refused to play the old prescribed parts "unfeminine," and were disgusted and infuriated by some of the ways in which feminists dramatized their views. One way was "bra burning"—a public event, common in the early years of the movement, in which feminists set fire to their brassieres to show that they liked their breasts as they were and not, as men preferred, hiked up and made firm and pointy. Other women cut off their long hair and stopped shaving their legs to symbolize their feminist consciousness and contempt for traditional seductive wiles; in the magazine *Everywoman,* one strong-minded feminist asserted woman's "right to be plain" and to abandon the "pretty" ideal. At parades and demonstrations, feminists burned pornographic magazines and books that, in their opinion, degraded women and incited men to sadistic sex acts. Some women met in small groups to combat their shame about their own sexual parts; using hand mirrors, they looked at and strove to admire their labia, vaginas, and cervixes. Others met in groups to practice reaching orgasm by means of masturbation; many felt that gratifying themselves was safer and more certain than seeking gratification from men. A cadre of daring activists threw bricks through porn-shop windows, set off a stinkbomb in the auditorium where the Miss America pageant was to take place, and squeezed Crazy Glue into the locks of the main doors of the Stock Exchange at 4 A.M. Some feminists founded cults of goddess worship, arguing that human beings had worshipped goddesses until male priests and leaders of society substituted gods; others called themselves "witches" and formed covens for the practice of exotic forms of worship.

Relatively few men knew women who took part in these cutting-edge activities, but many saw numerous disturbing changes in the behavior of the women in their lives. Millions of women who belonged to no feminist organization considered themselves feminists and recognized for the first time in their lives their resentment of many male attitudes and behaviors, and made their views known to the men around them. Many a man was disconcerted and angered when, holding a door open for a woman or helping her to a chair at a table, he was rewarded by a scowl or snappish remark for a gesture she saw as meant to symbolize his strength and her weakness. Many a man who prided himself on being courteous to women was annoyed to find that his good manners were viewed with disdain and dislike. The single man used to invite the single woman out, take her to the restaurant of his choice, and pay the bill; now he might be informed in one way or another that only an insensitive macho clod would decide where to go and assume he should pay (and expect some reward). A man used to think it was flattering of him to make suggestive remarks to a woman co-worker or one he was dating, or to pat her behind, or, under the table, ease his hand onto her thigh; now, for his pains, instead of a giggle or a gentle push he got a furious look and caustic words.[6]

And so, along with the movement's substantive victories—scores of women's rights bills were enacted in the 1970's—it was altering many elements of the daily behavior of males in search of sex and love. Dating in the 1950's mode had become outmoded, at least among college students, and since they now lived in adjacent or shared dormitories or apartments, been replaced by continuing and casual contacts. (For lack of a good new term, however, "dating" continued to be used for the new kind of informal meeting and going out together.) The former emphasis on dating as a popularity contest gave way to a new concept of dating as partly recreation and partly testing and preparation for marriage. Formerly, decisions about where to go, what to do, and when to try to initiate sexual activity were made largely by the man, even as they would later be in marriage; now he was likely to find his companion insisting on sharing the decision making, and getting chilly if he resisted. Both sexes used to think it appropriate for the man to see how far he could get sexually and for the woman to yield as little as possible; now it wasn't clear what he was supposed to do or when. If he tried too soon, he might be harshly rejected and called a "male chauvinist pig"; if he didn't try, he might be thought cold, timid, or homosexual. Nor was it clear how to behave if what he felt was infatuation or love. The strong silent man of tradition, the

---

[6] Not that women's new attitude eliminated such male behavior: sexual harassment has remained a common problem in the workplace and in universities to this day, as evidenced in the 1991 hearing concerning Clarence Thomas's nomination to the Supreme Court and in the 1992 charges by a number of women employees of Senator Bob Packwood that he had tried to force himself upon them.

"aw shucks, ma'am" hero, was becoming an absurdity, a relic; the new ideal man touted by women's liberationists was androgynous —less manly, more womanly, though just how to be so was nowhere spelled out. Confusingly, too, in bed he was not to "take his pleasure" as his forefathers had done—yet neither was he to pridefully exercise his skills to "give pleasure," as earlier feminists had said he was obliged to do, but now saw as one more form of male control and expression of male superiority.

If all this bewildered many men, it also bewildered many women. They were particularly unsure what their attitudes should be toward the new sexual freedoms. The sexual revolution was bringing them a fairer share of sexual rewards: they were more easily aroused by erotic movies or books, more responsive to and pleased by erotic caresses, more often and regularly orgasmic, freer to enjoy acts that formerly had filled them with fear or disgust. Some feminists rejoiced in their new freedom, engaged in sex promiscuously, took part in orgies, and defended pornography for its "turn-on" value. But a number of the most militant feminists (among whom were a number of surfacing lesbians) saw heterosexual intercourse as the very symbol and essence of male oppression of the female. Buoyed by Masters and Johnson's claim that the clitoral orgasm was as powerful and satisfying as the vaginal, they assailed the male preference for penis-in-vagina sex as essentially political:

> Before Masters and Johnson, men defined feminine sexuality in a way as favorable to themselves as possible. If woman's pleasure was obtained through the vagina, then she was totally dependent on the man's erect penis to achieve orgasm. . . . The definition of feminine sexuality as normally vaginal, in other words, was a part of keeping women down, of making them sexually as well as economically, socially, and politically subservient.[7]

Others, exulting in their newly prestigious clitoral orgasmic capacity, now regarded as gross the biologically normal effort of the male to insert himself and hammer away until release. This attitude was voiced by lesbian radical feminists but also by some heterosexual feminists—Shere Hite, for one, in her bestselling *Hite Report on Male Sexuality* (1981)—who characterized the male coital movements as distasteful and aggressive "thrusting."

This was only part of a more serious flaw the hard-line feminists

[7] Susan Lydon: "Understanding Orgasm," *Ramparts*, December 14–28, 1968.

found in men, namely, their inability to express love or, in fact, to love at all, a doctrine promulgated in the 1970's by some radical feminists (Shulamith Firestone flatly asserted, "Men can't love") and by a number of feminist social scientists. Some said men's incapacity was due to the way they were socialized, others that it was biologically based; in either case, most men were said to lack tenderness, nurturance, emotional attachment, passion, romance, expressiveness, and caring—all traits characteristic of female love. A feminist who loved a man, says Robin Morgan in *The Anatomy of Freedom*, even if he was trying to become androgynous, might be looked on with contempt by other women and be ashamed of her choice of lover.

To the extremists, the implication of their belief that love was a mechanism for maintaining the oppression of women was plain: Kate Millett said that the radical feminist "will reject love, firmly but regretfully, occasionally raucously." Those feminists who nevertheless sought it sometimes publicly confessed that the experience had been wretchedly disappointing: the feminist psychologist Phyllis Chesler, in her searing portrait of male psychology, *About Men*, includes brief sketches of ten of her love affairs with men, all of which ended in their betraying, abusing, abandoning, or boring her. Among her comments on men's love:

> Most men experience any and all expressions of female emotion as overly intense and threatening, as a form of attack, as an attempt at female control. . . . It is *because* men believe that women, creatures-without-a-penis, are not human beings—that women are devils or angels, goddesses or whores—that many men *do* have a genuine urge to "protect" women. They "protect" women, that is, from the consequences of being treated as extra- or superterrestrial beings. They "protect" women into corners where the harm they may do men is at least limited, minor, or limited to minors.

Despite such assessments of the male animal, most liberated women continued looking for and falling in love, but they and the men in their lives experienced numerous difficulties, some small and some large, in working out the new egalitarian love relationship. Who phones whom? Should he pick her up and later take her home when they go out, or should they meet where they're going? Who should give the signs—and what signs?—of emotional and sexual arousal? What words, sounds, and requests may he—and may she—make during intercourse, and what ones would the other

find unappealing or disgusting? Who does what in marriage? Will
he still be the primary provider? If not, and if she is a careerist, will
she resign her job if his career calls for relocation—or he if hers
does? How will they divide the homemaking chores—and more
difficult, the childrearing chores? Who, for instance, will stay
home and be a nurse when a child is running a fever? Despite a
flood of articles, lectures, and debates about the evolution of marriage, role-sharing, and even househusbanding, the old patterns
were deeply ingrained in people's thinking, corporate policies, and
male and female expectations; minor changes were achieved but at
inordinate cost in tension and conflict.

The young liberated woman who wanted to pursue a career,
preserve her independence, and avoid the trap of domesticity, had
a new attitude toward love—not the radical feminists' hostility to it
but a revaluation of love and home life: they were no longer the
center of her existence but only an important part of it. She was,
accordingly, readier than her predecessors to break away from a
disappointing marriage rather than cling to it as if it were a life
preserver without which she would drown. She would *not* drown
but swim on her own—and look for another love; the divorce rate
rose throughout the 1960's and 1970's but nearly all of the divorced hunted for new partners and over four fifths eventually
remarried.

Even some leaders of the women's movement—but not the radical feminists—felt that love, for all its new perplexities, remained a
vital part of their expanded way of life. Robin Morgan, poet, author, and contributing editor to *Ms.* magazine, devoted a sizable
chunk of her book *The Anatomy of Freedom* (1982) to her twenty-
year-old marriage to a bisexual poet, telling of shared pleasures and
shared worries, passionate moments and humdrum days, their support of each other in times of trouble, their periods of shouting and
weeping and raging at each other, and their idiosyncratic intimacies: she says (referring to the two of them in the third person),
"Some of their best conversations take place when one of them is
sitting on the toilet. This is one example of where love has it all
over romance."

Not that Morgan belittled romance; she said that although she
had been called a man-hater, she was in fact "a hopeless, un-
salvageable, politically incorrect romantic." Many of the details of
her marriage bear that out, as does her account of a brief affair she

had with an attractive artist while away from home at an art colony one summer. She had trusted the "sexual vibrations," yielded to impulse and curiosity, and managed "at considerable cost, to break through into a new kind of sexual empowerment, sexual energy, sexual intelligence." She felt and looked radiant, but couldn't leave well enough alone:

> I was also a romantic . . . so it was not enough: the purely aesthetic, the sexual joy, release, abandon, and plain *fun*. No, I had to invite "love" in (not just amicable affection, mind you, but passion) —although the thought of any permanent relationship with this person did give me indigestion. I had to write poems about it. I had to, immediately on my return home after a month, Tell All to my husband—a freethinking man of intellectual and sexual courage as well as curiosity, a man deeply committed to antisexist politics, who might have taken the news calmly (even supportively?), had I not implied a compare-and-contrast analysis.

Her husband became "melodramatically unhinged," told their friends about it, and had a retaliatory affair with another woman; for a year there was much screaming, sobbing, door-slamming, and reconciling, followed by more screaming, sobbing, and door-slamming. But finally the crisis was over and they were together again. Morgan characterizes their marriage afterward: "Mellowness . . . the blessedness of the daily, the treasuring of the common, the ordinary, the forgettable. Mellowness."

Some, perhaps most, feminist activists valued realistic love but decried romance. That, at any rate, came to be the view of Gloria Steinem, who started out in the women's movement thirty years ago by getting a job as a Playboy Bunny in order to write a magazine exposé, later co-founded *Ms.* magazine, and ever since has been a major spokesperson of the women's movement. When she was young, says Steinem in *Revolution from Within* (1992), she kept falling in love with rather decent men with whom she "remained friends even after the intensity of romance was gone." (Why all the affairs waned and ended she doesn't say.) In her college years and for some time afterward, it seemed to her that each man she was interested in might be the man she would marry because, as she then thought, "I would *have* to marry eventually if I was to be a whole person." There was, however, a great stumbling block:

> Since we really believed then that a husband would decide the rest of our lives, marriage became a decision almost impossible to

make. If it closed off all other decisions, then it was like a little death. *I'll definitely get married,* I kept on thinking, *but not right now. There's this one thing I want to do first.* . . . Fortunately, feminism came along to help me and millions of others try to become ourselves, with or without marriage; to understand, in the brilliant phrase of some anonymous feminist, that we could "become the men we wanted to marry."

From then on, she was on a nonstop treadmill of traveling, organizing, fund-raising, working on *Ms.*, and having love affairs with men who were her friends beforehand and remained so afterward. At last, in her late forties, wearied by the life she was leading, she met and fell in love with a dynamic, wealthy, powerful, and wholly self-sufficient man unlike anyone she had been involved with. Strangely, she found herself willingly regressing to an old, long-discarded pattern: she let him make all the decisions, listened to his talk, laughed at his jokes, went to events with him at his wish looking appropriately glamorous, and in general, played an old-fashioned role. "The only problem," she says, "was that, having got this man to fall in love with an inauthentic me, I had to *keep on* not being myself." But that proved frustrating and debilitating; after two years, realizing that she had deceived him by deceiving herself into believing that that kind of romantic affair could make her feel complete, she ended the relationship.

These days, Steinem is firmly antiromantic:

> Clearly, romance can arrive with all its obsession whenever we're feeling incomplete. . . . I think the truth is that finding ourselves brings more excitement and well-being than anything romance has to offer. . . . The internal wholeness that allows one to love both one's self and another, freely and joyously, is hard to find anywhere. On the other hand, the personal wreckage caused by romantic obsession is a feature of our everyday landscape.

But she does not minimize the value and rewards of love, at least the kind she seeks, and recounts with pride and pleasure a later affair she had with a black Southern physician who was as good a listener to her as she to him, was as comfortable with her female experiences as she with his male ones, and shared her tastes in books, music, foods, political values, and lovemaking: "It felt as if we had always known each other, yet also as if we were just exploring and exploding into a new part of ourselves." Then, like her other loves, the relationship faded into a post-affair friendship.

Steinem's explanation: she traveled too much, he had too little respite from work; he fell seriously ill for a while, triggering off in her old anxieties that originated with her mother's long illness; they worried too much about the same kinds of things and needed others with different perspective. After a year or so of painful times, they became "part of each other's chosen family" but no longer lovers. Ever since, they have both had other partners—an area of their lives they do not discuss with each other—but have remained close, in touch, sharing each other's lives and experiences.

Though Steinem has never married or had children, she believes that today's women and men have a better chance of succeeding at love than their forebears. For love now has wider possibilities than formerly: women need no longer limit themselves to a man who can support them and is older, taller, earns more, and weighs more; women and men can open themselves to loving not only each other but people of their own sex; they are freer than formerly to explore sexuality and sensuality as part of the pleasurable language of love; and above all, they can move from love to love throughout the changing stages of their lives:

> It's possible to raise children with a loved partner and then move on amicably to a new stage of life, to love someone and yet live apart, to forge new relationships at every phase of life, even at the very end—in short, to enjoy many different kinds of love, in a way that doesn't hurt but only enriches.

Our long trek through the history of love entitles us to differ with Steinem's evaluation of romantic love; what she is criticizing is not romantic love per se but the unreal and magical aspect of it known as infatuation, an early and temporary stage in the course of a love affair. Some of the more important and enduring elements of romantic love, however, especially the high worth ascribed to the beloved and the sense of merger of the two selves, have been absorbed into marriage and cohabitation. As for Steinem's evaluation of what real love is or can be today, we may question whether it meets the needs and emotional capabilities of most contemporary women and men or only of those whose personal attributes and opportunities enable them to do without marriage and to engage in love affairs, one after another, throughout life.

But enough of such speculations; let us turn back to actual history and see what has become of love three decades after the onset of the second sexual revolution and the second women's movement. And an odd and paradoxical story it is: these and other social changes first eroded and partly dismantled love, only to modify and repair it later so that it meets the needs of most contemporary men and women.

4

Love Moribund

Although the sexual revolution and the women's movement downgraded love in some ways during the 1960's and 1970's, there was reason to think that they would improve it in others. If men and women were freed from sexual inhibitions and guilt, their lovemaking should become more intense and joyous; if they became more nearly equals, they should be capable of greater sharing, empathy, and intimacy. And in fact there is evidence that such changes were taking place.

Sexual surveys, as already noted, showed that women were becoming increasingly arousable and orgasmic, and that marital sex was becoming more varied, frequent, and satisfying. Other studies found that men, after many centuries of preferring women who seemed less intelligent than themselves, were developing more egalitarian tastes: three small surveys of college men in the late 1960's and early 1970's found that most of them were attracted to women who were intelligent and competent. An ambitious study, begun in 1972, of steadily dating couples from four Boston-area colleges measured their sex-role traditionalism by means of a series of statements to which they were asked to respond on a six-point scale ranging from strong agreement to strong disagreement. Here are three of the statements:

> When a couple is going somewhere by car, it's better for the man to do most of the driving.

> If both husband and wife work full-time, her career should be just as important as his in determining where the family lives.

> It's reasonable that the wife should have major responsibility for the care of the children.

Overall, the women disagreed moderately and the men mildly with traditional attitudes; five sixths of the women and more than half the men were egalitarians or moderates.[8]

Other researchers, observing actual behavior in real-life circumstances, reported that even so traditionally masculine a form of behavior as the pickup was showing signs of egalitarianism. Researchers Timothy Perper and Susan Fox doggedly spent 300 hours in singles bars unobtrusively watching single men and women pair up; as always, they saw, the man was usually the first to speak—but rarely did so unless the woman had made the first move by glancing at him once or twice or standing near him. As one woman told Perper, "At some point the man should get the hint and take it from there."

Some studies made at about the same time found that it was still men who asked women out on a first date and paid the way but that thereafter women sometimes took the initiative and even insisted on splitting the bill, behavior that would have been unthinkable in their mothers' time. Even more surprising was the implication of a 1967 study by the sociologist William Kephart that either men were becoming more idealistic, or women less so, about love: he asked a sample of college men and women if they would marry someone who had all the traits they wanted in a mate but whom they did not love; two thirds of the men, but only one quarter of the women, said they would not.

Yet despite such findings, other evidence suggested that love was

[8] Charles T. Hill, Zick Rubin, et al.: "The Volunteer Couple: Sex Differences, Commitment and Participation in Research on Interpersonal Relationships," *Social Psychology Quarterly*, Vol. 42 (1979); Letitia Anne Peplau, Charles T. Hill, and Zick Rubin: "Sex-Role Attitudes in Dating and Marriage: A 15-Year Follow-Up of the Boston Couples Study," *Journal of Social Issues*, in press.

losing its former urgency and power. In 1945 there had been 12.2
marriages per 1,000 population but from that postwar peak the rate
had drifted steadily downward to 10.6 in 1970 and 10 in 1976.[9]
The marriage rate drops off in hard times, but the long-term decline from 1945 to the late 1970's bears no relation to recessions.
Not only were more people choosing never to marry but those
who did marry were doing so later—in the mid-1950's the median
age of women at first marriage was 20.1 but by 1980 22, while that
of men went from 22.5 to 24.7—an indication that the need for
marriage was less compelling than formerly.

To some extent, the decline was offset by the growing acceptance
of cohabitation (living together unwed)—in 1960 considered daring or even somewhat scandalous, in 1980 widely accepted and
thought nothing of except in conservative circles. In 1960, according to the U.S. Bureau of the Census, there were only 439,000
such couples, in 1970 there were 523,000, but during the next ten
years the figure trebled, reaching 1,589,000 in 1980. Some people
with liberal views on love and marriage said that cohabiting lovers
were husbands and wives in all but a legal sense, but the data
indicate that many of the relationships were either frail or flawed:
those who eventually married—sixty per cent of such couples—
were more prone to divorce than married couples who had not
lived together, and the rest, who did not marry, broke up after an
average of only eighteen months together.

Even more noteworthy as an indication of the waning importance of love was the increase in the proportion of men and women
of the most marriageable ages who neither married nor lived with a
partner. (It also indicated the growing acceptability of living alone.)
In 1960, 698,000 males aged fifteen to forty-four lived alone; in
1970, 1,207,000; and in 1980, 3,849,000, a more than fivefold increase in a mere twenty years. The increase was nearly as great
among women: from 636,000 in 1960, to 953,000 in 1970, and
2,588,000 in 1980.

A possible interpretation of the marriage, cohabitation, and living alone data might go as follows: The innumerable little changes
in courting behavior, the growth of self-esteem in women, the

---

[9] The total number of marriages rose by
thirty-four per cent over this period because
of the increase in the total population, but
what indicates the popularity of marriage is
the rate per thousand adults, especially in
the most marriageable age range. Data are
from the National Center for Health Statistics, *Vital Statistics of the United States*, various issues.

abandonment of feminine self-deprecation and feminine wiles, and the new willingness of unmarried women to have intercourse with men they merely liked or found appealing were dismantling the cultural construct called love. Many men were finding sex so easily available that they no longer had to persuade themselves they loved a woman when they desired her. Many women were finding that occasionally socializing and sleeping with men was less taxing and more satisfactory than living with them. The acceptability of co-habitation, combining satisfactions with relative freedom to escape, was dulling the desire to love deeply and the development of com-mitment. Love, so long a mysterious and magical attraction be-tween very different kinds of human beings, was becoming akin to a friendly, collegial, buddy relationship—agreeable and rewarding but no longer all-important.

Very likely; but there was also a more practical reason why love was losing some of its power to bind men and women. Though women were still being paid less than men for equal work and given little chance at the better jobs, they were increasingly choos-ing to work not only while single but when married; before World War II only a fifth of the female population had been in the labor force, but by 1980 over half were, and for younger women the percentages were far higher. What has this to do with love? Much: A woman who is wholly dependent on a man can easily persuade herself that despite his faults and her discontents she does love him; a woman who knows she can support herself is more likely to face the facts and to recognize her true feelings.

And to act upon them. As more and more women entered the labor force, the divorce rate, which had settled back from its 1945 peak of 3.5 per 1,000 population to 2.2 in 1960, began climbing again, reaching 3.5 by 1970 and 5.2 in 1980; at that level, about half of all first marriages were ending in divorce. It is also true that men, few of whom any longer depended on their wives to help bring in the crops and make their clothing, were increasingly ready to abandon unsatisfying marriages. Divorce analysts can name a large number of causes of marital breakup, ranging from incompat-ibility to infidelity, but demographers regard women's employment as the major factor in the rising divorce rate. As women became increasingly able to survive on their own, they were increasingly ready to leave marriages in which, for whatever reason, love had withered or turned sour; men, too, felt less compunction about leaving a loveless marriage if they knew their wives would be able to get along without them.

But the divorced were people who had been motivated by love to marry, and after a period of recovery nearly all of them began acting much like young singles, searching, flirting, dating, offering artful presentations of themselves, experimenting sexually, and succumbing to waves of infatuation and hope. Yet having known the emotional suffering, the legal wrangles, and the social embarrassment frequent in divorce, they were often terrified of love when they seemed to find it. A woman might be excited about a man after a few evenings together and then, suddenly feeling as if she was about to be trapped, make excuses the next several times he called or behave in ways that chilled his interest in her. A man might be entranced by a new woman until, all at once, he experienced overwhelming panic and fled, as in this paradigmatic case (the speaker is a thirty-eight-year-old woman, the time 1966):

> A couple of years ago I made a blind date with a lawyer from out of town. He walked in, we took one look at each other, and the sparks flew. There was something we both felt that was like nothing I had known in two years as a divorcee. We went to dinner but never noticed the food. We couldn't talk enough, we got misty-eyed again and again, and choked up. We went to his hotel room and talked and necked almost all night. I don't go to bed with anyone all that fast, but I would have gone with him without any hesitation if he'd asked me. He told me that we would be married, and I wasn't even surprised—it was just that natural and inevitable. He took me home at five a.m. and said he'd phone at nine, when my kids had left for school. I was exhausted, but I couldn't sleep a wink. It had really happened to me at last, and all I could do was paint scenes of the future. I got up with the kids at seven-thirty, and watched the clock —it never ran so slow. At eight-thirty I was excited. At ten of nine I was as fidgety as could be. Nine o'clock, and I was perspiring. Five after. Ten after. My heart was palpitating and I was feeling funny in the stomach. Well, I waited by that phone all morning and all afternoon, and it never rang. Not that night, either. Not ever. I never heard from him. I was shattered. It took months before I got over it, and I still feel a little sick telling about it even now.[10]

Although such experiences were common—though few as extreme—the divorced, as their numbers grew, were increasingly likely to pair up and remarry; by the 1970's, five out of six divorced

[10] From Morton Hunt: *The World of the Formerly Married*, pp. 175–6.

men and three out of four divorced women were remarrying.[11] But for them married love was even more vulnerable than for people marrying for the first time; they were more likely, though not by a large margin, to divorce again than those in first marriages.

The declining marriage rate, rising divorce rate, and the difficulty of working out egalitarian husband-and-wife roles made many thoughtful people begin to think that marriage could not survive unless it underwent a metamorphosis, though there was no agreement as to what its new form would have to be. Under modern conditions, what arrangements could induce men and women to want or need to marry and make their marriages endure? In most other times and places, they married for practical and social reasons; although they sometimes loved each other, love was neither essential to, nor the binding force of, marriage. In America, however, by the 1950's love had become the primary reason for marrying—but by the 1960's and 1970's, with sex so available and cohabitation increasingly acceptable, marriage was becoming unnecessary; creature comfort and companionship were ever easier to come by without risking deep feelings and commitment.

By that time a number of sociologists, psychologists, feminists, and others were saying that marriage was obsolescent and soon would be extinct. Others said it would soon give way to common-law unions or to five-year renewable contract marriages. Still others said it could survive only in radically redesigned form—sexually open marriage, group marriage, or two-couple mergers of sexual, emotional, and economic resources; or with totally egalitarian sharing of roles, each partner doing as much housekeeping and child-care as the other; or even in role-reversed form, the man being a househusband and the woman the wage earner. Still others said that no one form would prevail but that love and marriage would undergo mutation into a variety of forms: in *The Future of Marriage* (1972), Jessie Bernard, a feminist sociologist, said that since nothing in human nature favors one kind of marriage over another, love and marriage would probably survive in the form of an array of options—childless liaisons for the young, "temporarily permanent" marriages for the more mature during childrearing years, traditionally monogamous marriages for some, sexually freer

[11] Young divorced women's chances of remarrying were roughly the same as those of young divorced men, but with increasing age their chances grew increasingly smaller than those of men, chiefly because men's shorter life expectancy causes an ever-larger surplus of women in each older cohort.

and even polygamous marriages for others, marriages with separate households, weekend marriages, and so on.

As Pope asked, "Who shall decide, when doctors disagree?"

5

Love Surviving

H istory shall decide.

The predictions of the imminent demise of love and marriage have not come true, but neither have the predictions that they could survive only by assuming radically new forms. Love, after being castigated for two decades as obsolete myth, neurotic symptom, and male scheme for subjugating women, endures; although Ovid, Eleanor of Aquitaine, and D. H. Lawrence might be puzzled by some of its modern characteristics, they would recognize it. Marriage remains the major choice among alternative lifestyles; although our grandparents would be startled by some of its present-day aspects, they would know what it is.

What accounts for the survival of love and marriage in modified but not transfigured form? A century from now, historians may see the answer in perspective; from today's too-close foothold, it appears to be the result of a number of disparate causes.

One, many people think, is that the fear of sexually transmitted diseases, especially AIDS, has counteracted the sexual revolution and restored the power and appeal of monogamous love. This hypothesis is only weakly supported by the available data. Sexually transmitted diseases spread widely throughout the nonmonogamous population during the free-wheeling 1960's and 1970's without checking casual sex. Nor did AIDS when it appeared in 1981 and was first thought to be a disease of homosexuals. The latter, however, did react to some degree: within a few years, as scores of thousands of them sickened and died, there was much talk in gay circles about giving up cruising and trying to form close monogamous attachments; like Saint Paul telling the Corinthians that it is better to marry than to burn, they told themselves that it would be better to love than to die of AIDS. But how many gays ever formed love relationships out of the fear of AIDS is unknown.[12]

By the latter 1980's, AIDS was spreading among heterosexuals and clearly was eventually going to be as common among them as among gays. That grim news does not seem to have changed the behavior of teen-agers. Currently, nearly half of them—girls as well as boys—now have intercourse by or before sixteen, two thirds by nineteen, and with more than one partner (the Alan Guttmacher Institute says that thirty per cent of today's teen-aged women have had four or more partners); furthermore, four out of ten times teen-aged boys do not use condoms. People in their twenties or thirties, however, are better informed and more in control; according to various observers, they are now afraid of casual sex and have it less often. Most sex clubs closed in the late 1980s; lately, the business has been reviving, but only a minority of clubs are frequented by heterosexuals and all urge or even require their customers to practice safe sex.[13] A noteworthy new folkway: Many

[12] Even before the advent of AIDS, a major study of homosexuals reported that most of them wanted a steady relationship but for a variety of psychological and social reasons few ever managed to have one; see Alan P. Bell and Martin S. Weinberg: *Homosexualities*. It appears, however, that in recent years more gays have been living together as couples, though whether this is the result of fear of AIDS or of greater openness about homosexuality is not clear; see Steven Seidman: *Romantic Longings;* Marshall Kirk and Hunter Madsen: *After the Ball;* and David P. McWhirter and Andrew M. Mattison: *The Male Couple*.

[13] See Bruce Weber: "Alone Together: The Unromantic Generation," *New York Times Magazine*, April 5, 1987; Lillian Rubin: *Erotic Wars;* Steven Seidman: *Roman-*tic *Longings;* and Simon Sebag Montefiore: "Love, Lies, and Fear in the Plague Years," *Psychology Today*, September/October 1992. The March/April 1993 issue of the Alan Guttmacher Institute's journal, *Family Planning Perspectives*, published the results of a new national survey of men in their twenties and thirties by a research team at the Battelle Human Affairs Research Centers: the researchers found that the men's median frequency of intercourse was only once a week and median number of sexual partners since beginning sexual activity only 7.3—hardly a year's or even a month's worth for the driven swingers of the 1960's. On sex clubs, see Mireya Navarro: "In the Age of AIDS, Sex Clubs Proliferate Again," *New York Times*, March 5, 1993, sec. B, pp. 1, 5.

single women now buy and carry condoms to present to a partner at the appropriate moment. This is no trivial innovation in the history of love. The former pursuer is now checked by the formerly pursued, who, even if as eager as he, asks, "Have you got something . . ." If he hasn't, she digs into her purse and hands him one, and he girds himself and continues, no longer masterful raptor but tractable partner.

More important, because of the fear of disease, many who used to prefer only casual relationships now halfheartedly think they'd be better off with a close and exclusive one. "Maybe there's a silver lining in all this," one twenty-five-year-old man said to Bruce Weber, "maybe AIDS will bring back romance." A fatuous remark: it may be true that if people delay having sex until they get to know each other somewhat, real feelings will have time to develop, but it is unrealistic to think that chronically promiscuous people can be remade into loving ones by fear, and thus far there is no hard evidence of it.

In all probability, the survival of love and marriage is due not to the fear of AIDS but to a broad movement of public opinion and behavior toward centrist positions on social issues. To spell out the causes of that shift is beyond the purview of this book; we may note, however, that it is part of the natural course of reformist and liberationist movements to slow down after a while, and even to regress somewhat. The civil rights movement, the counterculture movement, the sexual revolution, and the women's movement all did so by the 1980's, partly because they had achieved many of their goals and partly because by then conservative and rightist forces were mounting increasingly powerful counterrevolutionary attacks on all of them.

As part of the moderation within the women's movement, a number of those who had been in the forefront of it in the 1960's, although still working for an expansion of women's rights, softened their views of men, love, and marriage. In her book *The Second Stage* (1981), the founder herself, Betty Friedan, attacked the more radical feminists who had taken over NOW after she left its presidency in 1970; among their errors, she said, was a failure to recognize the importance of the family, which she urged women to rediscover "as the base of their identity and human control." In *Sex and Destiny* (1984), the former firebrand Germaine Greer advocated premarital chastity and birth control by means of abstinence, and pictured the old-fashioned peasant wife as a role model. Even the tough-minded feminist Robin Morgan said in *Anatomy of Freedom* (1982), "We questioned the institution of marriage in the 1960's and early 1970's . . . [but] now, in the 1980's, we are witnessing a curve back toward marriage—or at least toward committed relationships."

She might have added "and toward older ideas of feminine appeal." The unisex costume formerly favored by liberated women—shapeless bluejeans, denim shirts, work boots—was losing popularity, and sexier styles, including uncomfortably high heels, plunging necklines, impractically short skirts, beads and fringes, and elaborate makeup, were becoming fashionable again. There were many such indications that love, in modified forms, was regaining popularity and prestige; among others were the importance newly ascribed to love in studies and surveys, and its omnipresence and centrality in fiction, film, and television dramas. Significantly, too, attacks on romantic love as the product of neurosis or inadequacy gave way to a flood of self-help books telling readers how to recognize and escape from neurotic or faulty love and find the real thing. Examples include *If This Is Love, Why Do I Feel So Insecure?* by Carl G. Hindy et al.; *Smart Women, Foolish Choices,* by Connell Cowan and Melvin Kinder; and *False Love, and Other Romantic Illusions,* by Stan J. Katz and Aimee Liu.

The revaluation of love did not, however, result in a return to the previous generation's concept of male and female roles. The changes that had come about in dating, for instance, embodied the contemporary view of women's abilities and rights, and have remained in place. Women take for granted today what were daring advances of the 1970's: they have no hesitation about telling a date what they'd like to do; few feel any need to act coy or kittenish or to act cutely bewildered by political, scientific, or economic issues; they feel free to phone a man they have dated, invite him out, and insist on splitting the costs of an evening. When it comes to sex, however, most men and women still expect the man to make the first moves; men, when asked by researchers, are likely to say that women are entitled to as much sexual freedom as they themselves but will admit that they dislike women who "come on too strong sexually." Generally it is not until a man has dated a woman several times or become her lover that he is not threatened by her indicating that she's in the mood for sex, and it is only within marriage, according to a 1988 study by Elaine Hatfield and associates, that most men would like the woman to initiate sex more often, act wilder, and talk dirty.

There has, however, been a significant return toward the former ideal of the union of sex and love, and for reasons other than fear of AIDS. In fact, the shift began, at least among relatively well-educated people, before heterosexuals had reason to be afraid of AIDS. In 1969 only 14 per cent of the men and 29 per cent of the women in a *Psychology Today* reader survey had said that sex without love had no appeal for them; in 1983, when the magazine did another such survey, more than twice as many men (29 per cent) and half again as many women (44 per cent), and a clear majority of those under twenty-two, said so. One-night stands and fleeting encounters still exist, but, says Lillian Rubin, "The dominant ethos, and the values men and women now give voice to, call for sex between two people who have some kind of emotional connection, even if it's a relatively transient one." A night with a stranger is infra dig, with a friend is all right, and with a person one loves is excellent.

Teen-agers, in particular, once again justify sex by means of love —but now without pretending or supposing that it means commitment and eventual marriage. Rubin cites, as typical, a sixteen-year-old girl who told her, "We love each other, so there's no reason why we shouldn't be making love." Did that mean, Rubin asked her, that she and the boy had made a long-term commitment to each other? The girl hesitated, looked doubtful, and finally said, "Do you mean are we going to get married? The answer is no. Or will we be together next year? I don't know about that; that's a long time from now. Most kids don't stay together such a long time. . . . Just because we don't expect to get married doesn't mean we're not in love, does it?"

Often, indeed, if one teen-age lover talks of commitment or marriage, the other may cool off and break away. As one youth told a researcher, "I said I wasn't able to give her the time and the part of myself that she wanted—she was reaching out for me, and I ran away from it. I'm 19, and I felt I needed to experience more things." Some find the satisfactions possible in present-day dating relationships all they need or think they will ever need; a young woman whose affair had withered away told the researcher:

We had been seeing each other every weekend, and calling each other every day. However, around January, he began doing things with his friends more on the weekends. I knew something was wrong—Bob wasn't as open. I didn't say anything for several months about it, but eventually I asked Bob if it was another person —he said, "No, but let's talk." I found out that back in January he'd been talking with a friend who said "I think Sue needs to get married." Bob had decided that we needed to deal with that—he told me that he never wanted to marry (but if he had ever wanted to marry, it would have been me). At this time I told him that I could live with that, that I was willing to continue the relationship without that kind of commitment, and when I began to feel uncomfortable with that, I'd let him know.

In May, we had a disagreement—he thought I'd been sending him mixed messages—stating I didn't need a commitment but continuing on with the relationship just like before. We ended the relationship at this point.[14]

Even though young people in such relationships do not say that they mean to marry, they expect their parents to understand that, since they're in love, they're sleeping together. When one of them is an overnight guest in the other's family home, they assume they will share a room with the parent's knowledge and unspoken approval or at least consent. In most parts of the country, unmarried couples, when traveling, feel no embarrassment about rooming together; at motels and resorts they no longer bother with fake rings or sign in as "Mr. and Mrs."; what was *avant-garde* thirty years ago in Hollywood and Manhattan is now acceptable in Podunk. And if there are years of college ahead or careers that take priority, loving and sleeping together is enough for the young people; they don't find it necessary to think of themselves as future husband and wife.

Another notable development is the further growth of cohabitation. The number of unmarried couples living together has more than doubled since 1980, reaching 3,039,000 in 1991—almost six per cent as many as existing marriages. Living together is a kind of halfway house to married love. Romance and passion thrive on deprivation, and when lovers meet only from time to time, they do so with urgent need, seize each other, feast on each other, cannot hear enough of or tell enough to each other. But those who live together, eat together, spend all or most of their leisure time to-

[14] Both cases are from an unpublished doctoral dissertation by Sally A. Lloyd quoted in Rodney M. Cate and Sally A. Lloyd: *Courtship* (Newbury Park: Sage Publications, 1992).

gether, and sleep together every night interact less intensely and on a wide range of mundane issues: the shortage of clean sheets, the overflowing garbage pail, a minor urethral disorder or temporary bout of diarrhea, how much one of them owes the other for food or rent, who will do which errands tomorrow, who has to work late and wants the other to make dinner.

For some, careers outrank love. Bruce Weber, after interviewing sixty-odd young people several years ago about love and marriage, summed them up as the "unromantic generation"—career-minded, practical and materialistic, and putting success ahead of love and marriage. He chose, as his lead specimen, a Dallas live-together couple in their mid-twenties: Clark Wolfsberger, a marketing and management junior executive, and Kim Wright, who worked in an advertising agency. They told Weber they were in love—but, Clark Wolfsberger added, "We don't need much time together to confirm our relationship." Both said they intended to be married by thirty—but possibly not to each other: "Kim's a great girl," said Wolfsberger, "I love her. But she's very career-oriented. I am, too, and with our schedules the way they are, we haven't put any restrictions on each other. I think that's healthy."

"He might want to go back to St. Louis," Kim Wright said. "I want to go back to Chicago. If it works out, great. If not, that's fine, too. I can handle it either way."

Weber felt that such low-intensity, uncommitted love is typical of modern young lovers. But his sample was small and gathered by methods that did not assure representativeness; while his couples did illustrate one facet of modern love, there is reason to think that most young couples are more intimately and strongly bound. One piece of evidence already noted: Six tenths of cohabiting couples do eventually marry. More evidence: in a mid-1980's survey, over 80 per cent of a sample of college men and women said they would not marry a person they were not in love with (in 1967, you will recall, two thirds of the men and only a quarter of the women said so). A recent study asked college men and women who were not married or engaged to name the person with whom they had the closest relationship; more than half specified neither a parent, sibling, nor best friend but a romantic partner. Finally, researchers and family counselors hear much the same range of experiences and problems from unwed couples as they do from the married—a whole panoply of petty discontents and disagreements, but also the centrality of the emotional relationship, their deep need of each other, their sharing of hopes, fears, and goals, and their view of each other as the most important person in their life.

The love of most unwed couples is thus deeper, more committed, and more a joining of purposes than the romantic love of the dating couple; moreover, it is permeated by all the ordinary irritants of everyday life, a rigorous test of its soundness. The unmarried couples who live together are practicing a form of quasimarriage, terminable without court action if it fails but convertible to more committed and legal form if it succeeds. Such trial marriage was advocated by the visionary Judge Ben Lindsey in 1927 and by anthropologist Margaret Mead in 1966; though never enacted into law by any legislature, it meets the needs of modern lovers and has become a reality.

Most of the men and women in such relationships are part of the Census category "never-married" (the others live either with family or friends, or alone, or in institutions). The never-married are one of the fastest growing segments of the population: in 1970, 16 per cent of adults 18 and over had never married, but by 1991 the figure was up to 23 per cent, half again as large. This may look like evidence that marriage is on the way out, but the Census term ought to be "not-yet-married"; men and women are delaying marriage (in 1991 median age at first marriage had risen to 26.3 for men, 24.1 for women), but eventually over 90 per cent do marry. Although the marriage rate has declined in recent years and at 9.4 per 1,000 population in 1991 was lower than at any time since 1966, it was still higher than in the years 1955 to 1966—or than at the turn of the century. Indeed, if cohabitation is considered a form of trial marriage, one might argue that the marriage rate is stabilizing.

Unlike earlier eras, in which there was a dominant pattern of marriage, today there are a number of patterns: the classic marriage of two young people setting out to make a home for themselves and have a family; the marriage of young divorced or widowed people in which one moves into the other's home, and the children of one partner (or sometimes both) are present, complicating—and often damaging—the love relationship; the marriage of middle-aged divorced or widowed people whose children are grown and gone, and who are somewhat like young cohabiting couples in their freedom and privacy; and many others. But within all these types a major determinant of the nature and quality of the love relationship is the degree to which the gender roles of husbands and wives are traditional or nontraditional.

A substantial minority of American marriages are still more or less traditional, the husband being the breadwinner and wielding considerable power over family decisions, the wife being the housekeeper and mother, and interacting much as husbands and wives did half a century or more ago. This kind of marriage predominates among conservative segments of the population and late middle-aged or elderly people. Since we have seen such marriages earlier, one detail, like a match struck in a dark room, will serve to remind us of their size and shape: In many such a marriage the wife receives a weekly allowance from her husband and has no access to, and little if any knowledge of, his income or investments; she may even know almost nothing about what he does for a living, as is the case with the wives of stock manipulators, CIA operatives, and Mafiosi, among others.

The majority of marriages, however, are nontraditional to some degree. Two decades ago, much of the talk about the need for new forms of marriage was concerned with loosening the bonds of monogamy; the popular term for the new forms, mentioned above, was open marriage or, more accurately, sexually open marriage. Some experts and many commentators predicted that this adaptation would be common by now, but none of the variations of sexually open marriage suggested or tried out in the go-go years proved workable for more than a few couples. Although extramarital sex is even more common now than in 1972, virtually all of it is kept secret from the spouse.[15] Most attempts at sexually open marriage, in which each partner freely tolerates the other's outside liaisons, have run aground on the rocks of jealousy, hurt feelings, fear of loss, and emotional insecurity. Nena O'Neill, coauthor of *Open Marriage* (1972), herself says that today sexually open marriage is the lifestyle of very few.

The marital lifestyle of many, however, is nontraditional in that both partners have careers, and consequently, the balance of power, decision making, and marital roles are much modified. If a wife works solely to boost family income and has no career inter-

[15] In the 1972 survey, about a quarter of all wives and half of all husbands had had at least one extramarital experience; several informal recent surveys indicate that today that is true of about half of all wives and three quarters of all husbands. See Helen Fisher: *Anatomy of Love*, pp. 85–6.

est, the marriage may still be traditional in many ways, but if she is at all career-oriented, the marriage is almost sure to be fairly non-traditional. Some partners preserve so much independence—separate bank accounts, different last names, separate work and sleep schedules—that they are much like unwed couples. Others seek to be conjoined and close, but their closeness is limited by their ambitions and the requirements of their careers. If they are high achievers in demanding, fast-moving fields such as advertising, corporate law, or politics, they must patch their life together with the help of a cleaning person, a nanny or baby-sitter, frozen foods, and frequent dining out. Several years ago writer Dinah Prince sketched a number of such marriages in *New York* magazine. Here are two of them:

> In a Brooklyn brownstone, corporate lawyer Chuck Richard is greeted by his wife, Cynthia Larson, on their phone machine. "I am not going to be home. Go ahead and eat," says Cynthia, a photographer. As the couple try to coordinate two unpredictable work schedules, they live on take-out food in an apartment where three laundry bags fill up before a wash. With the recent birth of their first child, they face the task of integrating a third erratic schedule into their lives. . . .
>
> On the phone in their midtown Manhattan offices, lawyers Wendy and David Hashmall regularly plan for a romantic Thursday evening out. First they arrange for a baby-sitter to take over from the nanny who cares daily for their three-year-old daughter. Then they choose a movie they both want to see. They almost always conclude by standing each other up.
>
> "We say, 'Let's use the time to work, and I'll meet you at home at ten and we'll order in,'" Wendy says.

Extreme cases, admittedly. But even in less-stressed contemporary marriages there is often a divergence of interests and a barrage of outside demands that give the couple little time together and sometimes wholly preempt it, supposedly only for the day but in fact day after day and week after week.

Equally hard on love is the inequitable division of labor carried over by habit and inertia from traditional marriage. If husband and wife both work but cannot afford ample paid help, it is the wife who still bears the major burden of homemaking and child care. Most men "help out," but by and large when they come home they read the paper, play with the children, or watch TV; when women come home, they do the laundry, bathe the children or help them with their homework, straighten up the house, and make dinner. A recent study found that wives employed outside the home spend twenty-six hours a week on housework, their husbands thirty-six minutes. The inequity in the costs and benefits of marriage makes many a wife resentful and angry, plus guilty at being angry; the mixture of feelings can be toxic to love.

The answer being worked out by an increasing number of couples is to share the chores of marriage, though not necessarily identically; the man may do the heavier tasks—vacuuming the house, lugging groceries, mowing the lawn—and leave lighter ones to his wife. Some couples do try to share all chores equally, but it is hard to cast off habits and attitudes rooted in traditions many centuries old. As Elaine Hatfield and Richard L. Rapson say in *Love, Sex, and Intimacy:*

> Both men and women may find themselves demanding a transformation and then, perversely, sabotaging real change when it occurs. Husbands may "forget" to wash the pans; the ants notice their lapse. Women often get so irritated at—"Where does this go? And this?" "Sure I'll bring in the groceries. Just give me five minutes. . . . Whoops. I forgot. Did the ice-cream melt? Sorry"—that they give up. "Get out of my kitchen! I'd rather do it myself!" they scream. Women, on the other hand, are equally good at sabotaging change. Some delight in taking the moral high ground. They complain that he does not help. But when he tries, nothing is ever good enough. She insists he do it *her* way ("How can you put the forks tine-down in the washer? Don't you know they have to be tine-up?" "Everyone knows cups have to be hung on little hooks.") She gloats at his every failure. Not surprisingly, the men refuse to help. Change is always difficult.

If task sharing, with all its exasperations, were the chief goal of modern marriage, the marriage rate would surely be sinking fast, the divorce rate rising; neither is the case (the marriage rate is sinking slowly, the divorce rate is rising slowly). But task sharing is the format, not the goal; every recent survey has shown that what people seek in marriage is emotional security, a confidante, a sex partner, creature comforts, family life, and above all, love. In our unsentimental and hard-boiled age, few married people speak freely, or at all, about the love they and their spouse feel for each other; they seem, in fact, not to be keenly aware of it unless they lose it through divorce or death. But some fortunate husbands and wives are sharply conscious of it during the overnight absence of the partner on a business trip, or even during the working day; these are the people who feel a surge of gladness when they see each other at the end of the afternoon and feel whole again, like Plato's mythical halves of the original human being come together.

The love of such husbands and wives (and of most unmarried cohabiting couples) is not what they felt when they first fell in love. Everyone has always known this, though few have said it as succinctly as La Rochefoucauld: "There are good marriages but no delicious ones." But the love in today's good marriages is a kind of love that was rare, if it ever existed, in earlier eras; marriage researchers call it "companionate love." Although it embodies the values of romantic love, it is quite different from romantic love of the agonized, impassioned, yearning kind. A number of research studies have shown that the romantic and passionate phase of love lasts up to three years, slowly metamorphosing into a calmer and cooler, but closer and deeper form.[16] The closeness and the overall level of marital happiness diminish during the childrearing years, particularly when children are in their teens, but after they are gone, companionate love regains its intimacy, marital happiness increases, and some couples even feel a return of occasional romantic feelings. At least, so it is with couples who, today, are middle-aged. One can only hope that the love of today's young couples will replicate that developmental history.

Companionate love reaches its peak today in those marriages in which people merge their bank accounts and investments,[17] divide the tasks equitably, carefully save time to talk, fight, play, and make love, yet find ample room in their careers, friendships, and outside interests to feel unconfined by marriage and to have experiences to bring home and share with each other. Today's companionate husbands and wives, when asked to define their relationship, often use such words as "partners," "buddies," and "really good friends,"

[16] Walster and Walster: *A New Look at Love*, chs. 6 and 7; Hatfield and Rapson: *Love, Sex, and Intimacy*, chs. 2 and 4. Why romantic-passionate love does not last has been much debated; sameness of the sexual diet and daily encounters with commonplace problems are often said to be antipathetic to romance, but Ellen Berscheid, a long-time researcher of love, suggests that the state of being romantically "in love" is intense and stressful, and like other alarm or emergency reactions, cannot be sustained for long without risk of physical harm or death ("Some Comments on Love's Anatomy," in Sternberg and Barnes: *The Psychology of Love*, pp. 370–1).

[17] Many marriage counselors view the merger of financial assets as a sign of genuine commitment. But where there are children by a previous marriage, or where state divorce law would require a division of property that would wreck one partner's going business, a prenuptial agreement erecting financial barriers may be valuable.

but the terms fall far short of reality; the emotional and sexual content of marriage makes their love far more pervasive, important, and self-defining than even the closest friendship. A clumsy term comes a bit closer: "we-ness."

Despite the evidence that love has come back into style and is again a prime desideratum for the majority, it is not for a minority. In 1990, ten per cent of all men and seven per cent of all women of prime marriage age (twenty-five to forty-four)—substantially more than ten years earlier—were living alone. The increase has been greater among women than among men—not surprisingly, since studies show that the more they earn, the less they want to marry. As Jane Gross of the *New York Times* recently reported, "[the] experts say that increasingly it is women who now look skeptically at marriage, often viewing it as a bad bargain if they have gained financial and sexual independence." Barbara Foley Wilson, a demographer at the National Center for Health Statistics, told Gross that "women are learning to be self-sufficient and they are choosing singleness rather than losing their independence"; Frances Goldscheider, a sociologist and editor of *Demography* magazine, said that women's growing lack of interest in marriage is "the real revolution" of the last twenty years. One successful woman executive epitomized the matter by saying that, after being divorced, "I could do anything I wanted for the first time in my life."

There are no research studies on the part love plays in the lives of the men and women who prefer to live alone. Impressionistic reports indicate that a number of them have love relationships that they keep walled off from the rest of their lives and limited to occasional nights or weekends, plus many phone conversations. Others go for long periods without a lover, though they may have one-night stands or get-togethers with a friendly sex partner. One may wonder whether some or many of the women and men who prefer this lifestyle are emotionally stunted, but there are no data on the matter; it is evident, however, that love of the kind that exists in marriage or cohabitation is not their preference, or at least ranks low among their goals.

The growth in the proportion of adults living alone, never married, or divorced, and the decline in that of the married—sixty-one per cent in 1991, down from seventy-two per cent in 1970—might seem to indicate that love, at least of the committed sort, is on the way to becoming a historical curiosity. But the figures are misleading since so many of the never-married and divorced will eventually marry. Marriage used to be a state in which one spent his or her adult life; today in America it is a state very many pass into and out of for parts of their adult life. The sociologist William J. Goode persuasively argues in his important new study, *World Changes in Divorce Patterns*, that family life centered about marriage has lost much of its former value to the individual. One's best interests used to lie in being loyal to the family, the main source of power and economic goods, but today those benefits are to be found elsewhere; accordingly, the present trends are toward avoiding long-term investments in the family: "It has simply become too fragile to assure payoffs that are eventually adequate or satisfactory . . . People have moved somewhat toward the belief that investments in oneself are more likely to be profitable over the long haul." But if the practical value of family life has diminished, its emotional value has not: Men and women still want to live together in love, and for the great majority of them that still means as married partners. Marriage is no longer, as it once was, the only desirable way of adult life, but for most people it remains the most desirable. Moreover, any sampling of present-day American media products—films, TV sitcoms and dramas, novels, clothing ads in magazines and newspapers, magazine feature articles, personal ads, and news stories about Hollywood celebrities, candidates for elective office, and the British royal family—reveals what is almost an obsession with the subject.

Love has proven too delectable, rewarding, and sustaining to most women and men to be discarded; in various remodeled forms, it has regained much of its old status. Much changed and greatly diversified but still bearing key elements of its ancestry, love is alive and well—and for a large majority of people, still the most important and most mysterious aspect of the human condition.

6

"I Don't Want the Answer"

❋　　❋

❋

The mystery of it should have long ago aroused the curiosity of psychologists and engaged them in research, but for many years they studiously ignored love as a research topic. Harry Harlow, in his 1958 presidential address to the American Psychological Association, chided his colleagues: "So far as love or affection is concerned, psychologists have failed in their mission. The little we know about love does not transcend simple observation, and the little we write about it has been written better by poets and novelists."

At that time, most psychologists regarded the study of love as frivolous in comparison to research on such topics as perception, memory, and problem solving, and the few who did take up Harlow's challenge were looked at with scorn by most of their colleagues. And by one powerful image-maker. Senator William Proxmire, who periodically sought publicity by ridiculing what he considered government-funded boondoggles, chose in 1975 to savage the work of Elaine Hatfield (then Elaine Walster) and Ellen Berscheid, who had a modest grant of $84,000 from the National Science Foundation to investigate passionate and companionate love. In a press release that the media gleefully made much of, Proxmire said:

> I object to this not only because no one—not even the National Science Foundation—can argue that falling in love is a science; not only because I'm sure that even if they spend $84 million or $84 billion they wouldn't get an answer that anyone would believe. I'm also against it because I don't want the answer.
> I believe that 200 million other Americans want to leave some

[440]

things in life a mystery, and right at the top of things we don't want
to know is why a man falls in love with a woman and vice versa.

But although Proxmire's paean to ignorance reaped a harvest of
publicity, research on love continued and grew in volume. After
World War II, many psychologists had been obsessively concerned
with the study of hatred and violence, but in the 1960's and 1970's
they began turning their attention to "prosocial" behavior—cooperation, sharing, friendship, helping, altruism, and love. To understand the nature and roots of love seemed to a growing number of
them to be of great intellectual interest; moreover, such understanding, they felt, would surely help people improve both the
quality and the durability of their intimate relationships. Research
on love grew slowly during the 1970's, explosively in the 1980's,
and today is a "hot topic" in psychology. In this short time scores
of major studies and many hundreds of lesser ones have yielded a
mass of insights, many of which have been mentioned, about particular aspects of love, such as what attracts people to other people,
what kinds of people are most powerfully affected by romantic
feelings, how men's love differs from women's love, and hundreds
of others.

People who took Senator Proxmire seriously probably felt, as he
did, that science cannot measure and analyze something as impalpable and poetic as love, but in fact there are a number of tried-
and-true techniques for doing so. One is the use of case histories:
researchers interview volunteers and try to spot events or influences in their histories that are plausible causes of their adult love
behavior. Of course, such cause-and-effect connections are only
conjectural; proving them requires a cumbersome amassing of
cases and correlation of data. For instance, if a number of women
who love much older men had fathers who abandoned the family
when they were little, and if no women who love older men had
fathers who remained at home, there would be a credible case for
cause and effect. But such findings are expensive and time-consuming to come by; furthermore, a multitude of influences are at work
simultaneously in every person's life, and only complex statistical
analysis can show which one or combination is the most likely—
but never the certain—cause of a given result.

A related but less chancy method is the use of case histories of
patients in psychotherapy. This is somewhat akin to an experiment;

if the therapist's methods, suggestions, and interpretations improve the patient's love relationship, the therapist's assumptions concerning it would appear to be confirmed. For example, virtually all researchers of contemporary love maintain that intimate and self-revealing communication is one of its essential characteristics—modern love has little in common with that of Dante, who never spoke a word to his Beatrice—and if a therapist trains a couple to talk to each other more revealingly and their relationship improves, it is reasonable to feel that the hypothesis has been validated.

Much scientific study of love employs even more controlled and rigorous research methods. One genre gathers evidence by means of personality tests and other paper-and-pencil measures, and looks for statistically significant relationships among the data. In the 1950's, for instance, as we heard earlier, the sociologist Robert Winch gave dating couples personality tests, statistically analyzed their answers, and concluded that people tend to fall in love with others whose traits supply what is lacking in themselves (the passive person chooses an active one, the introvert an extrovert, and so on). But later studies by others, using similar methods, found little support for the theory and even some evidence for the opposite theory, that people fall in love with persons like themselves in personality. Eventually, a fine-grained statistical analysis by Robert Sternberg and Susan Grajek of Yale University yielded a satisfying resolution: both theories are right—couples are similar in certain respects, complementary in others. Though hardly earth-shaking, the finding explains why there can be two such well-accepted but opposite folk observations as that like seeks like, and opposites attract.

Much of this kind of research relies on the scores of "love scales"—paper-and-pencil tests measuring certain components of love. One scale that has been widely used was devised in 1970 by Zick Rubin, then at Harvard, who also developed a "liking scale"; by means of the two, he could measure and discriminate between the feelings of a volunteer toward various people in his or her life. To create the scales, Rubin asked a number of undergraduates which of a long series of statements would pertain to a boyfriend or girlfriend, and which to a platonic friend of the opposite sex. Through factor analysis—a statistical sorting technique—he extracted thirteen items for a love scale and thirteen for a liking scale. The love scale contains such statements as:

I would do almost anything for ———.

If I could never be with ———, I would feel miserable.

One of my primary concerns is ———'s well-being.

The liking scale contains such statements as:

In my opinion, ——— is an exceptionally mature person.

I think that ——— is one of those people who quickly wins respect.

——— is one of the most likable people I know.

Such scales are often used in conjunction with interviews; the aim is to locate formative events in the subjects' lives that tie in with how they score on the scales. A recent notable example is a study by the psychologists Philip Shaver and Cindy Hazan, who, combining the data of personality tests and love scales with what they learned in the interviews, found that the way people feel and behave in love is related to how they interacted with their mothers when they were infants. Previously, child psychologists had demonstrated three kinds of infant-mother attachment by having a mother leave her toddler alone in a strange room for a few minutes and then return: If she was usually warm and reassuring, the infant would be glad to see her return and go to her to be held; if she was usually emotionally inexpressive, the infant would ignore her and turn away; if she was inconsistent in her behavior, the infant would be angry and, if she tried to hug him or her, would hit or kick her. The first is a "secure" attachment, the second an "anxious-avoidant" attachment, the third an "anxious-resistant" attachment. Shaver and Hazan hypothesized that there were comparable kinds of adult love, and devised the following scale to measure it in their volunteers:

Which of the following best describes your feelings?

I find it relatively easy to get close to others and am comfortable depending on them and having them depend on me. I don't often worry about being abandoned or about someone getting too close to me.

I am somewhat uncomfortable being close to others; I find it difficult to trust them completely, difficult to allow myself to depend on them. I am nervous when anyone gets too close, and often, love partners want me to be more intimate than I feel comfortable being.

I find that others are reluctant to get as close as I would like. I often worry that my partner doesn't really love me or won't want to stay with me. I want to merge completely with another person, and this desire sometimes scares people away.

The result: As Shaver and Hazan had predicted, these three prototypes of adult attachment—secure, avoidant, and anxious/ambivalent—were directly related to the type of infant-mother attachment each person had experienced. While all romantic love experiences have certain elements in common, they said, in their sample about a quarter of the adults had a fear of intimacy; about a fifth were insecure, fearful of possible loss, and jealous; and somewhat more than half were secure and at ease in love relationships. (Despite the traditional differences in how men and women love, they found no differences in the numbers of men and women who fit into each category.)

In contrast to the use of tests and interviews, many researchers conduct experiments of various kinds by means of which they can observe actual behavior, although for ethical reasons they attempt neither to induce nor to disrupt major love relationships. An example: Zick Rubin asked couples to fill out his love scale and later to come to his laboratory for an experiment; while they were waiting for it to begin, Rubin covertly observed and recorded the amount of time the couple made eye contact with each other. The experiment they were supposedly going to take part in never took place; the real experiment was the one in which they were the unwitting subjects whose behavior was being observed. Partners who had scored high on Rubin's love scale—that is, agreed strongly with most of the statements—made much more eye contact than those who had scored low; high scorers were also more likely to look into each other's eyes simultaneously, low scorers to look when the other was looking elsewhere.

In a 1965 experiment Elaine Hatfield tested the hypothesis that low self-esteem makes one particularly receptive and responsive to affection. She had a number of college women take three personality tests and then gave them bogus feedback: in private conferences, she told some that they had weak personalities, were basically immature, and felt inadequate, and told others very positive things about themselves. In each case, having given the volunteer these supposed findings, she left the room on an errand, and a handsome male graduate student—an accomplice—entered, ostensibly to wait for her. He chatted with the female subject, became friendly and interested in her, and invited her to dinner and a movie the next weekend. Later, each woman was asked for her impressions of the graduate student: those whose self-esteem had been injured by the false test reports were distinctly more attracted to him than those whose self-esteem had been boosted. (As is customary, the deceived students were then told the truth about the experiment and the reasons why the deception and misinformation had been necessary.)

In another experiment, Hatfield and several assistants undertook to find out what traits initially attract young men and women to each other. They invited nearly 800 first-year college men and women at the University of Minnesota to a dance, telling them that a computer would match them with a date who was just right for them. They asked the students what they looked for or were drawn to in a partner; without exception the students named intelligence, personality, and social skills. Before the dance, the researchers collected data on these traits in each student, but actually assigned partners randomly. At the dance, the assigned partners met, talked, danced, and got to know one another, and during intermission were asked in confidence what they thought of their dates and whether they would want to see them again. When the answers were analyzed, it turned out that the sole trait determining how well the students liked their dates and how eager they were to see them again was looks; intelligence, personality, and social skills made no difference.

The researchers Donald Dutton and Arthur Aron had an attractive female assistant approach men students as they were crossing either a swaying suspension bridge over a deep canyon or a solid cement bridge. The assistant asked each man to complete a questionnaire and write a brief story, supposedly for a research project on conservation, and gave him her name and phone number in case he wanted to know more about it. The men she talked to on the swaying suspension bridge were more likely to call her and ask for a date, and to write stories with sexual imagery, than the men on the low firm bridge. The researchers interpreted this to mean that men on the alarming bridge had felt anxiety and mistaken it for the first stage of sexual attraction. Other experiments have shown, similarly, that anxiety, fear, embarrassment, jealousy, loneliness, and even grief can arouse or enhance feelings of attraction or love.

By the painstaking review of existing information on 166 primitive and developed cultures, the anthropologists William Jankowiak and Edward Fischer recently concluded that romantic love is not, as widely believed, a phenomenon found only in Western civilization. They found evidence of it, either in descriptions of behavior or in the form of folk tales and legends, in nine tenths of the cultures they reviewed. In most, however, it had nothing to do with marriage, although lately there is a tendency in some of the cultures for romantic love to lead to marriage—an idea that older people find either ridiculous or shocking.[18]

The analysis of blood and urine samples has produced some interesting information about the biological underpinnings of love. Michael Liebowitz, a psychiatrist at the New York Psychiatric Institute, has found that "love junkies"—people addicted to wild and inappropriate romantic passions—have an abnormal craving for a high produced by phenylethylamine (PEA), an amphetamine neurotransmitter produced by the brain, and that when this craving is controlled by drugs, the addiction wanes. Normally, the PEA high is too stressful to be sustained continuously without damage, and in healthy people, therefore, infatuation is of limited duration; long-lasting attachment love, on the other hand, is associated with the production of endorphins (morphine-like neurotransmitters), which yield a calmer, steadier, good feeling. Still, while particular neurotransmitters may provide the motive power for different kinds of love, they do not determine specific ways of feelings and behaving; we learn from the society around us and our own experiences to love in any one of a number of different styles.

The goal of some researchers has therefore been to identify those styles and develop a taxonomy of love. Like early naturalists, some have simply looked at a host of specimens—in literature, biography, and psychotherapy case histories, among other sources —and grouped them according to apparent similarities; then, administering love scales and personality tests to groups of volun-

---

[18] Jankowiak and Fischer's paper, read at an anthropological meeting is reported in Daniel Goleman: "After Kinship and Marriage, Anthropology Discovers Love," *New York Times*, Nov. 24, 1992, p. C1.

teers, they have sought to validate their grouping. John Alan Lee of the University of Toronto identified six basic styles of love in literary and other sources, and also in a sizable sample of volunteers: infatuated, affectionate, playful, manic, practical, and selfless. Robert Sternberg of Yale University went at the matter differently: he began with a theory that love has three components—intimacy, passion, and commitment—which, in various combinations, should yield eight kinds of love; he then tested a number of volunteers and found what he expected. The eight kinds, which bear little relation to Lee's six, are: nonlove (none of the components), liking (intimacy only), infatuated love (passion only), empty love (commitment only), romantic love (intimacy and passion), companionate love (intimacy and commitment), fatuous love (passion and commitment), and consummate love (all three).

This sampling of recent love research may leave many readers ambivalent—intrigued by the specific findings but frustrated that they yield no grand and overarching theory that makes sense of the multifarious phenomena of love as Newton's laws and, later, Einstein's did of the many phenomena of physics. But it is hardly to be expected that there would be a theory of love of such clarity and scope so soon. Men and women have been puzzling about love for 2,500 years that we know of and possibly ever since the development of the modern brain 40,000 years ago, but research on love began only three decades ago and has been in full force little more than a dozen years. In time, researchers and theorists will see farther and more clearly; in time there may be a Newton or Einstein of love who will make it all plain to us. Until then, we may grudgingly agree with Sir John Suckling:

> But love is such a mystery
> I cannot find it out:
> For when I think I'm best resolved,
> I then am most in doubt.

7

Conclusion

❀   ❀

❀

In our lengthy meander through the history of Western love, we have seen how love became deeper and more important as primitive clans grew into city-states and then into nations, agricultural and feudal societies turned into industrial ones, and theocracy yielded slowly to democracy. We have noted the shaping of love by family structure and woman's position, the molding of love by philosophy and the growth of leisure, the flourishing and proliferation of love by urban loneliness and insecurity. But all these factors only modify love and determine the limits of its significance; none is the prime mover that sets it in motion and furnishes its momentum. Though they have directed, deflected, or enlarged affectional needs in a variety of ways, we may still wonder why there are such needs at all and from what source they draw their strength.

Many answers have been suggested in modern times. We saw that Freud believed the origin of love and source of its power to be biological: the imperious sex drive, socially constrained, is transmuted into the acceptable form of love. This view is still held by some researchers of the subject: Ellen Berscheid recently commented that she does not know what romantic love is but "if forced against a brick wall to face a firing squad who would shoot if not given the correct answer, I would whisper 'It's about 90 per cent sexual desire as yet not sated.' "

A quite different biological theory was recently offered by Helen Fisher, an anthropologist at the American Museum of Natural History: As the human brain became ever larger, she says, babies had to be born earlier, before the head got too large for the birth canal; since newborns were therefore helpless and in need of care for several years, only men who, by innate inclination, bonded to their mates and stayed with them for some years to protect and feed them were likely to have progeny that survived. Evolution eliminated the hit-and-run lover and selected the faithful and protective one.

Most psychologists would demur on the grounds that specific behavior patterns, such as pair-bonding to a mate, are not coded in our genes; nearly all innate aspects of human nature are only propensities that must be developed by experience. Most theorists of love have therefore been concerned with the psychology of love rather than its neurological or biochemical substrate. Some have accounted for love in terms of realistic but unflattering motives: A few decades ago the psychoanalyst Edmund Bergler offered the sourly cynical theory that all love originates in self-love and is a reflecting back from someone else of one's own self-worship—a kind of emotional moonlight mistaken for the light of the sun. More recent but equally unflattering is the "equity theory" or "social exchange theory" of love propounded by Elaine Hatfield and others: We love when the benefits of the relationship outweigh its costs; only in unhealthy or neurotic love do we spend more than we get.

Some theorists have taken quite the opposite view. The psychoanalyst Erich Fromm held that the power of mature love comes from its allowing one to become parentlike (or godlike) and giving without thought of return, and Abraham Maslow, a noted humanistic psychologist, distinguished between "deficiency love" (an effort to remedy one's shortcomings through loving and being loved by another person) and "being love" (achieving maximum personal development through loving another and helping that person develop).

Many social scientists account for love in terms of learning theory: they see it as a behavior pattern acquired from one's family and society. Some sociologists have said that love is in large part "cultural expectation"; biological needs may provide the drive but in no way determine the outcome. Similarly, some psychologists argue that, although the body responds to outside influences with various kinds of arousal, the feelings of arousal are nonspecific until we learn to attribute certain of them to another person and call them love; as La Rochefoucauld acerbically said, "There are people who would never have loved if they had never heard love talked about." So, too, Shaver and Hazan, Shaver, arguing that the three basic styles of loving are related to the three kinds of infant-mother attachment, are explaining love as learned behavior.

How are we to choose among these many theories? All have merit, but they differ widely and often are mutually contradictory. But perhaps several or most are true, since love is not one thing but many: an emotion but also a social bond, an individual behavior pattern but also a cultural construct, sometimes a wild hunger but sometimes tenderness and understanding, in some cases a symptom of disease but more often the outcome of health and maturity. For all our new knowledge, a comment made more than a century ago by Sir Henry Finck, a Victorian behavioral scientist, remains true: "Love is such a tissue of paradoxes, and exists in such a variety of forms and shades, that you may say almost anything about it that you please, and it is likely to be correct."[19]

Having seen all that you have seen, you can decide for yourself, if you like, which of the foregoing theories of love comes closest to the truth. But you need not; we set out together to collect and describe specimens, not to derive a theory or prove a philosophy, and have limited ourselves, except in part of this final chapter, to observing how love is manifested rather than seeking its quintessence. We have seen that love sometimes harms and sometimes benefits men and women, that it can be only a game but again almost a religion, that at times it is a cruel sport and at other times a partial remedy for life's ills. We have watched it passing down the centuries and found modern love to be a composite of much that has gone before, a mélange of ancient and modern, mystical and rational, sacred and profane. Not in the sense of having attained any ultimate insight, but in the sense of having *seen* love in all these embodiments, we can say, like Virgil's shepherd in his moment of illumination: *Nunc scio quid sit Amor*—Now do I know what love is.

---

[19] Henry Finck: *Romantic Love and Personal Beauty* (London: Macmillan, 1891), p. 224, quoted in Berscheid, q.v.

Notes on Sources

✿ ✿

✿

"A man will turn over half a library to make one book," said Dr. Johnson. Even if this is a trifle exaggerated, space does not permit me to give a complete bibliography of the sources consulted, much less of those I might have looked at but decided to pass by. But for the benefit of any who may wish to extend their reading on the subject of this book, I have listed here chapter by chapter almost every source mentioned in the text or footnotes, giving bibliographical information for those not easy to find, and for modern works; in addition I have included the other principal sources I drew on, even when not specifically named or alluded to in the text or footnotes.

CHAPTER I: *Introduction*

FOR GENERAL DISCUSSIONS of the nature of love from several very dissimilar contemporary points of view, see the works listed below by Huxley, Ortega y Gasset, and Fromm, and the little anthology by Montagu, *The Meaning of Love*. Montagu's *The Direction of Human Development* and La Barre's *The Human Animal* are both excellent interdisciplinary studies of human nature and culture, and both discuss love from the biological, sociological, and psychological viewpoints. Of the general histories of love, the one by Lewinsohn (published too late to be cited or used in this book) is excellent, though its emphasis is more on sexual mores than the emotional meaning of love itself. Taylor sketches sexual history in the West in psychoanalytic and sociological terms, and much sexual and marital history is scattered throughout the old but indispensable work of Ellis. The monumental work by Westermarck, and the briefer one by Müller-Lyer are dated, but give a still-useful panorama of marital patterns among primitives and civilized peoples. Love among the primitives, as reported by more modern anthropologists, can be found in the works by Danielsson, Firth, Kaberry, Mead, Richards, and Schapera; the somewhat older books by Briffault and Malinowski take opposite points of view and are both still useful, and the still older one by Sumner continues to be an indispensable mine of data. The questions of the relation between fiction and reality, and the unreliability of fiction as primary evidence of human behavior, are discussed by Jones, Lesser, and Lucas.

Bölsche, Wilhelm: *Love-Life in Nature*. London: Jonathan Cape; 1931. First published in German in 1900.

Briffault, Robert: *The Mothers*. New York: The Macmillan Company; 1927. A massive three-volume anthropological study of sex and love.

—— and Bronislaw Malinowski: *Marriage: Past and Present*. Boston: Porter Edward Sargent; 1956. A reprint of a series of radio debates in 1930 on primitive love.

Danielsson, Bengt: *Love in the South Seas*. New York: Reynal & Co.; 1956.

Descartes, René: "The Passions of the Soul," in *Selections*, edited by R. M. Eaton. New York: Charles Scribner's Sons; 1927.

Ellis, Havelock: *Studies in the Psychology of Sex*. Philadelphia: F. A. Davis; 1901–28. Of the seven volumes, Vols. I, III, IV, and VI are particularly useful for the historian of love.

Firth, Raymond: *We, the Tikopia*. London: George Allen & Unwin; 1936.

Freud, Sigmund: *Civilization and Its Discontents*. London: The Hogarth Press and The Institute of Psycho-Analysis; 1939.

Fromm, Erich: *The Art of Loving*. New York: Harper & Bros.; 1956.

Huxley, Julian: *New Bottles for New Wine*. New York: Harper & Bros.; 1957. Has an excellent chapter on love.

Jones, Ernest: *Essays in Applied Psycho-Analysis*. London: The International Psycho-Analytical Press; 1923.

Kaberry, Phyllis M.: *Aboriginal Woman, Sacred and Profane*. London: George Routledge & Sons; 1939.

La Barre, Weston: *The Human Animal*. Chicago: University of Chicago Press; 1954.

Ladies Dictionary, The (anon.). London: J. Dunton; 1694.

Lesser, Simon O.: *Fiction and the Unconscious*. Boston: Beacon Press; 1957.

Lewinsohn, Richard: *A History of Sexual Customs*. New York: Harper & Bros.; 1959.

Lodge, Henry Cabot: *Studies in History*. Boston: Houghton Mifflin Co.; 1884.

Lucas, F. L.: *Literature and Psychiatry*. Ann Arbor: University of Michigan Press; 1957.

Malinowski, Bronislaw: *The Sexual Life of Savages in North-Western Melanesia*. New York: Halcyon House; 1929.

Mantegazza, Paolo: *The Physiology of Love*. New York: Cleveland Publishing Co.; 1894.

Mead, Margaret: *Coming of Age in Samoa*. New York: New American Library; 1949.

Montagu, M. F. Ashley: *The Direction of Human Development*. New York: Harper & Bros.; 1955.

——, ed.: *The Meaning of Love*. New York: The Julian Press; 1953.

Müller-Lyer, F. C.: *The Evolution of Modern Marriage.* London: Allen & Unwin; 1930. First published in 1913.

Ortega y Gasset, José: *On Love.* New York: Greenwich Editions; 1957.

Plato: *Symposium.*

Plutarch: *Conjugal Precepts.*

Putnam, Emily: *The Lady.* New York: Sturgis & Walton; 1910.

Richards, Audrey J.: *Bemba Marriage and Present Economic Conditions.* Livingstone, Northern Rhodesia: The Rhodes-Livingstone Institute; 1940.

Schapera, I.: *Married Life in an African Tribe.* London: Faber & Faber; 1940.

Sewall, Samuel: *Diary of Samuel Sewall: Collections of the Massasetts Historical Society,* 5th series, Vols. V–VII (1878–82).

Sumner, William Graham, and A. G. Keller: *The Science of Society.* New Haven: Yale University Press; 1927. Written, in large part, prior to 1906.

Taylor, G. Rattray: *Sex in History.* New York: Vanguard Press; 1954.

Westermarck, Edward: *The History of Human Marriage.* New York: The Allerton Book Co.; 1922. First published in 1889.

CHAPTER II: *Dilemma in Greece*

AMONG THE GENERAL SECONDARY SOURCES which include useful introductions to Greek love are the books listed here by Durant, Robinson, and Wright; the older works by Blümner, Gulick, Mahaffy, and Tucker sometimes sound a trifle Victorian, but are still excellent standard references. The primary sources have already received special singling out in the text. On the subject of Greek character structure and the distinctions between shame cultures and guilt cultures, see the works by Benedict, Dodds, and Piers.

Aristotle: *De Generationa Animalium,* II, i, iii. *Ethica Nichomachea,* VII, iv, and VIII, iii. *Politica,* II, iv.

Athenaeus: *The Deipnosophists,* Book XIII.

Benedict, Ruth: *The Chrysanthemum and the Sword.* Boston: Houghton Mifflin Company; 1946.

Benson, E. F.: *The Life of Alcibiades.* London: Ernèst Benn; 1928.

Blümner, H.: *The Home Life of the Ancient Greeks.* New York: Cassell & Co.; 1893.

Butler, Samuel: *The Authoress of the Odyssey.* London: Longmans & Co.; 1897.

Demosthenes: "Against Neaera," and "Erotic Oration."

Diogenes Laertius: "Socrates," in his *Lives.*

Dodds, E. R.: *The Greeks and the Irrational.* Berkeley: University of California Press; 1951.

Döllinger, J. J. I.: *The Gentile and the Jew in the Courts of the Temple of Christ.* London: Gibbings & Co.; 1906. Originally published in 1857.

Durant, Will: *The Life of Greece.* New York: Simon and Schuster; 1939.

Finley, Moses I.: *The World of Odysseus.* New York: Viking Press; 1954.

Greek Anthology (Anthologia Graeca). With a translation by W. R. Paton. New York: G. P. Putnam's Sons; 1916–18.

Gulick, C. B.: *The Life of the Ancient Greeks.* New York: D. Appleton & Co.; 1902.

Herodotus: *Historiae*, III, 118 (on Intaphernes).

Homer: *Iliad. Odyssey.*

Jones, W. H. S.: *Greek Morality.* London: Blackie & Sons; 1906.

Keller, A. G.: *Homeric Society.* New York: Longmans, Green & Co.; 1902.

La Barre, Weston: *The Human Animal.* Chicago: University of Chicago Press; 1954.

LaCroix, Paul: *History of Prostitution.* Chicago: P. Covici; 1926.

Lyra Graeca, edited and translated by J. M. Edmonds. New York: G. P. Putnam's Sons; 1928. Contains all of extant Sapphic fragments, and all the classical biographical evidence about her.

Machon. Quoted extensively in Athenaeus, q.v.

Mahaffy, J. P.: *Social Life in Greece.* London: Macmillan & Co.; 1925. First published in 1874.

Piers, Gerhart, and M. B. Singer: *Shame and Guilt.* Springfield, Ill.:

C. C. Thomas; 1953.

Plato: *Charmides. Laws. Lysis. Menexenus. Phaedrus. Republic. Symposium.*

Plutarch: "Alcibiades," "Demetrius," and "Pericles," in *Lives. Conjugal Precepts. Of Love.*

Robinson, C. E.: *Everyday Life in Ancient Greece.* Oxford: Oxford University Press; 1933.

Sappho. See *Lyra Graeca*, Vol. I, for biography and extant poems.

Theocritus: *Idylls.*

Tucker, T. G.: *Life in Ancient Athens.* Chautauqua: Chautauqua Press; 1917.

Weigall, Arthur: *Sappho of Lesbos.* New York: F. A. Stokes Co.; 1932.

Westermarck, Edward: *The Origin and Development of the Moral Ideas.* London: Macmillan & Co.; 1917.

Wright, F. A.: *Greek Social Life.* London: J. M. Dent; 1925.

Xenophon: *Oeconomicus. Memorabilia. Symposium.*

CHAPTER III: *Bread and Circuses, Love and Games*

A GOOD MODERN SURVEY of Roman sexual customs and love can be found in the book by Carcopino; the old work by Friedländer is still marvelous and gives some special attention to sex and love. For biography, topical studies, and general background, the standard sources include Pauly, Daremberg, and the *Cambridge Ancient History.* Lecky's history of morals is Victorian in tone, but remarkable for scholarship. Goodsell's history, covering much of the same ground, is briefer and modern in tone.

Boak, E. R.: *Manpower Shortage and the Fall of the Roman Empire in the West.* Ann Arbor: University of Michigan Press; 1955.

Buchan, John: *Augustus.* Boston: Houghton Mifflin Company; 1937.

Cambridge Ancient History, Vol. X (especially for Antony and Cleopatra).

Carcopino, Jerome: *Daily Life in Ancient Rome.* New Haven: Yale University Press; 1940.

Catullus: *The Poems of Catullus*, edited and with comments by William A. Aiken, in translations by various hands. New York: E. P. Dutton & Co.; 1950.

Cicero: "Philippics" and "Pro Caelio" in *Orations. De Legibus*, iii. *Letters to Quintus* in *Letters to Friends.*

Daremberg, C. V., and E. Saglio, eds.: *Dictionnaire des Antiquités*

Grecques et Romaines. Paris: Hachette; 1877–1919.

Dio Cassius: *Dio's Roman History* (Loeb Classical Library), lv (on Julia).

Durant, Will: *Caesar and Christ.* New York: Simon and Schuster; 1944.

Ferrero, G.: *The Greatness and Decline of Rome.* New York: G. P. Putnam's Sons; 1907.

Fowler, W. W.: *Social Life of Rome in the Age of Cicero.* New York: The Macmillan Company; 1909.

Frank, Tenney: *Aspects of Social Behavior in Ancient Rome.* Cambridge: Harvard University Press; 1932.

Friedländer, Ludwig: *Roman Life and Manners Under the Early Empire.* Seventh edition. New York: E. P. Dutton & Co.; n.d.

Goodsell, Willystine: *A History of the Family as a Social and Educational Institution.* Revised edition. New York: The Macmillan Company; 1934.

Haywood, Richard: *The Myth of Rome's Fall.* New York: The Thomas Y. Crowell Company; 1958.

Highet, Gilbert: *Poets in a Landscape.* New York: Alfred A. Knopf; 1957.

Horace: *Epodes. Satires.*

Juvenal: *Satires,* esp. No. 6.

"Laudatio Turiae": in M. Durry: *Laudatio Turiae: Éloge Funèbre d'Une Matrone Romaine.* Paris: Belles Lettres; 1950.

Lecky, W. E. H.: *History of European Morals.* New York: D. Appleton & Co.; 1869.

Livy: *Roman History,* Bk. XXXIV.

Lucretius: *De Rerum Natura,* Bk. IV.

Macrobius: *Saturnalia,* Bk. II (on Julia).

Ovid: *Amores. Ars Amatoria. Tristia* (contains letters written from exile).

Pauly, A. F. von, and G. Wissowa: *Real-Encyclopädie der Classischen Altertumswissenschaft.* Stuttgart: J. B. Metzler; 1894–1919.

Pliny the Younger: *Letters.*

Plutarch: "Antony," "Cato the Younger," "Caesar," and "Cicero," in *Lives.*

Polybius: *Histories,* XXXIV, ii–iii.

Putnam, Emily: *The Lady.* New York: Sturgis & Walton; 1910.

Sellar, W. Y.: *Roman Poets of the Republic.* London: Oxford University Press; 1905.

Seneca: *De Beneficiis,* iii. *De Clementia,* i. *Ad Helviam,* x.

Seneca the Elder (L. Marcus Seneca): *Controversiae,* iii.

Suetonius: *Augustus* and *Julius Caesar* in *Lives of the Caesars.*

Tacitus: *Annals,* iii, 24–5. *Dialogue Concerning Oratory.*

Tucker, T. G.: *Life in the Roman World of Nero and St. Paul.* New York: The Macmillan Company; 1910.

Wright, F. A.: *Catullus; the Complete Poems.* London: George Routledge & Sons; 1926.

CHAPTER IV: *It Is Better to Marry Than to Burn*

AMONG VARIOUS GENERAL HISTORIES which give some attention to the Christian influence on love, the *Cambridge Medieval History* and Bury are worth looking at, though neither is recent; Lecky and Westermarck are indispensable classics. Lot and Boak pay special attention to the declining Roman society and the mood it engendered. The two *Dictionaries* are very generally useful for topics and biographies, as is also the *Encyclopaedia of Religion and Ethics.* Baring-Gould offers a massive compilation of saints' lives, referring back to original sources, but is frequently inaccurate and unscholarly. Westermarck and Cadoux both survey Hebrew and early Christian attitudes toward sex, woman, and love, and the details of clerical unchastity and papal corruption are exhaustively documented by such varied sources as the *Cambridge Medieval History*, Lea, Lecky, McCabe, Milman, and Westermarck.

Ammianus Marcellinus: *Ammianus Marcellinus*, translated by John C. Rolfe. Cambridge: Harvard University Press; 1937. Vol. II, Book XXII, discusses Emperor Julian (the Apostate).

The Ante-Nicene Fathers, edited by A. Roberts and J. Donaldson. New York: Charles Scribner's Sons; 1899–1900.

The Apostolical Constitutions: in *Ante-Nicene Fathers*, Vol. VII.

Athanasius: *Stories of the Holy Fathers . . . Compiled by Athanasius, Archbishop of Alexandria, Palladius*, etc., translated by E. A. W. Budge. Oxford: Oxford University Press; 1934.

Augustine: *Confessions. City of God. Treatises on Marriage.* (In *Fathers of the Church* series.) New York: Fathers of the Church; 1947.

Baring-Gould, Rev. S.: *The Lives of the Saints.* London: John C. Nimmo; 1897.

Battenhouse, R. W., ed.: *A Companion to the Study of St. Augustine.* New York: Oxford University Press; 1955.

The Bible.

Boak, A. E. R.: *Manpower Shortage and the Fall of the Roman Empire in the West.* Ann Arbor: University of Michigan Press; 1955.

Brittain, Rev. Alfred, and Mitchell Carroll: *Women of Early Christianity.* Philadelphia: Rittenhouse Press; 1907.

Bury, J. B.: *History of the Later Roman Empire.* London: Macmillan & Co.; 1923.

Cadoux, Cecil J.: *The Early Church and the World.* Edinburgh: T. & T. Clark; 1925.

Cambridge Medieval History, Vol. III.

Chrysostom, St. John: "Letters to Theodore," in *Nicene Fathers*, Vol. IX.

Clement of Alexandria: *Stromata*, in *Ante-Nicene Fathers*, Vol. II. Includes his discussion of heretics. *Paedagogus*, in *Fathers of the Church* series: New York: Fathers of the Church; 1947.

Cyprian: *Epistle* lxi in *Ante-Nicene Fathers*, Vol. VIII.

Dictionary of Christian Antiquities, edited by W. Smith and S. Cheetham. "Agapeti," "Betrothal," etc. Boston: Little, Brown & Co.; 1875.

Dictionary of Christian Biography, edited by H. Wall and W. C. Piercy. Boston: Little, Brown & Co.; 1911.

Eginhard (also known as Einhard): *Life of Charlemagne.* New York: American Book Co.; n.d. (but copyright 1880 by Harper & Bros.).

Ellis, Havelock: *Sex in Relation to Society*, Vol. VI of *Studies in the Psychology of Sex.* Philadelphia: F. A. Davis; 1901–28.

Encyclopaedia of Religion and Ethics, edited by J. Hastings. "Agapetae," "Chastity," "Marriage," etc. New York: Charles Scribner's Sons; 1908–26.

Ephraem, St.: "Life of Saint Mary the Harlot," in *Vitae Patrum*, q.v.

Gregory (the Great), Pope: *Epistles*, in *Nicene Fathers*, Vol. XIII.

The Dialogues of St. Gregory. London: Philip Lee Warner; 1911.

Gregory of Nyssa: "De hominis opificio," in *Nicene Fathers,* Vol. V.

Gregory of Tours: *History of the Franks.* Oxford: Clarendon Press; 1927.

Jerome, St.: *Against Jovinianus; Epistles* xxii, xxxviii, xlviii, cvii, cxxii; Preface to *Ezekiel,* all in *Nicene Fathers,* Second Series, Vol. VI.

Julian (the Apostate): *The Works of Emperor Julian* (see especially *Misopogon*). New York: The Macmillan Company; 1913.

Kligerman, Charles: "A psychoanalytic study of the *Confessions* of St. Augustine," *Jour. Amer. Psychoanal. Assn.,* Vol. III, July 1957.

Lea, H. C.: *Historical Sketch of Sacerdotal Celibacy.* Boston: Houghton Mifflin Company, 1884.

Lecky, W. E. H.: *History of European Morals.* New York: D. Appleton & Co.; 1869.

Lot, Ferdinand: *The End of the Ancient World.* New York: Alfred A. Knopf; 1931.

McCabe, J.: *Crises in the History of the Papacy.* New York: G. P. Putnam's Sons; 1916.

Menninger, Karl: *Man Against Himself.* New York: Harcourt, Brace, & Co.; 1938. Includes a psychoanalytic discussion of martyrs and ascetics.

Milman, H. H.: *History of Latin Christianity.* London: John Murray; 1872.

Nicene Fathers. A Select Library of the Nicene and Post-Nicene Fathers edited by P. Schaff. New York: Christian Literature Co.; 1887–1900.

Palladius: *Historia Lausiaca,* in *Vitae Patrum,* q.v.

Russell, C. E.: *Charlemagne, First of the Moderns.* Boston: Houghton Mifflin Company; 1930.

Socrates ("Socrates Scholasticus"): *Ecclesiastical History,* in *Nicene Fathers,* Second Series, Vol. II.

Tacitus: *Germania,* 18.

Tertullian: "On the apparel of women" ("De Cultu Faeminarum") and "To his wife" ("Ad Uxorem"), both in *Ante-Nicene Fathers,* Vol. IV.

Theodore of Canterbury: *Penitential,* in A. W. Hadden and Wm. Stubbs: *Councils and Ecclesiastical Documents,* Vol. III. Oxford: The Clarendon Press; 1871.

Todd, James H.: *St. Patrick, Apostle of Ireland.* Dublin: Hodges, Smith & Co.; 1864. Contains the story on Scuthin and Brendan.

Verba Seniorum (by various compilers), in *Vitae Patrum.*

Vitae Patrum, edited by J. P. Migne. Paris, 1849–50. (Appears as Vols. LXXIII–LXXIV of Migne's *Patrologiae Cursus Completus,* Ser. Lat.). An excellent and easily located English translation of selections from the *Vitae Patrum* is by Helen Waddell, and entitled *The Desert Fathers.* Ann Arbor Books: University of Michigan Press; 1957.

Westermarck, Edward: *Christianity and Morals.* London: Paul, Trench, Trubner & Co.; 1939.

——: *The Origin and Development of the Moral Ideas.* London: Macon; 1917.

CHAPTER V: *The Creation of the Romantic Ideal*

AMONG THE MANY SOCIAL HISTORIES portraying the general background against which courtly love appeared, Painter is one of the best and most recent, and the works by Coulton, Durant, May, and Vossler are all stuffed with helpful details. Of books paying special attention to troubadours and courtly love (either in a chapter or throughout), those by Kelly, Lewis, De Rougemont, Schultz, and Taylor are especially noteworthy, and display a variety of viewpoints. Andreas and Chrétien provide the two best medieval discussions of the subject; many others, in Provençal, are included in Raynouard, and Smythe gives a sampling of troubadour verses translated into modern English.

Andreas (Andreas Capellanus, or Andrew the Chaplain): *The Art of Courtly Love*, translated by John J. Parry (from *Tractatus Amoris et de Amoris Remedio*). New York: Columbia University Press; 1941. Parry's introduction is excellent.

Aquinas, St. Thomas: *Summa Theologica*, Supplement of: LXXXI, 3. *Summa Theologica*, II, ii, Quaest. CLIV, Art. 4.

Bernard, St.: Sermon XI, in *Life and Works*, translated by S. J. Eales. London: John Hodges; 1896.

Briffault, Robert: *The Mothers*. New York: The Macmillan Company; 1927.

Butler, P.: *Women of Mediaeval France*. Vol. V of *Woman, in All Ages and in All Countries* (by various authors). Philadelphia: The Rittenhouse Press; 1907–8.

Cambridge Medieval History, Vol. III.

Chaytor, H. J., Rev.: *The Troubadours*. Cambridge: The University Press; 1912.

Chrétien de Troyes: *Le Chevalier de la Charrette*, in English as *Lancelot* in *Arthurian Romances*, translated by W. W. Comfort. London: J. M. Dent & Sons; 1913.

Coulton, G. G.: *Life in the Middle Ages*. Cambridge: The University Press; 1930.

——: *Medieval Panorama*. New York: Meridian Books; 1955.

Dante: *La Vita Nuova. La Divina Commedia*.

De la Tour Landry: see Landry.

Denomy, Father Alexander J.: "Fin' Amors: The Pure Love of the Troubadours," *Mediaeval Studies*, Vol. VII (1945), p. 139f.

——: *The Heresy of Courtly Love*. New York: The Declan X. McMullen Company; 1947.

Durant, Will: *The Age of Faith*. New York: Simon and Schuster; 1950.

Gesta Karoli Magni ad Carcassonam et Narbonam, edited by F. E. Schneegans. Halle: Max Niemeyer; 1898.

Huizinga, J.: *The Waning of the Middle Ages*. New York: Doubleday Anchor Books; 1956.

John of Salisbury: *The Statesman's Book (Polycraticus)*, translated by John Dickenson. New York: Alfred A. Knopf; 1927.

Kelly, Amy: *Eleanor of Aquitaine and The Four Kings*. Cambridge: Harvard University Press; 1950.

Kroeger, A. E.: *The Minnesinger of Germany*. New York: Hurd & Houghton; 1873.

Landry: *Le Livre du Chevalier de La Tour Landry*, edited by A. de Montaiglon. Paris: Bibliothèque Elzévirienne; 1854.

Lee, Vernon (pseud. of Violet Paget): *Euphorion*. Boston: Roberts; 1884.

Lewis, C. S.: *The Allegory of Love*. Oxford: The Clarendon Press; 1936.

Lucka, Emil: *Eros; the Development of the Sex Relation through the Ages*. New York: G. P. Putnam's Sons; 1915.

May, Geoffrey J.: *Social Control of*

Sex Expression. London: George Allen & Unwin; 1930.

Neumann, Freidrich: "Ulrich von Lichtenstein's Frauendienst," in *Zeitschrift für Deutschkunde*, 1926, p. 373f.

Owst, Gerald R.: *Literature and Pulpit in Medieval England*. Cambridge: The University Press; 1933.

Paget, Violet: see Lee, Vernon.

Painter, Sidney: *French Chivalry*. Baltimore: Johns Hopkins Press; 1940.

Raynouard, F. J. M.: *Choix des Poésies Originales des Troubadours*. Paris: F. Didot; 1816–21.

De Rougemont, Denis: *Love in the Western World*. New York: Pantheon Books; 1956.

Schultz, Alwin: *Das Höfische Leben zur Zeit der Minnesinger*. Leipzig: S. Hirzel; 1889.

Smythe, Barbara, translator: *Trobador Poets*. New York: Duffield; 1911.

Taylor, G. Rattray: *Sex in History*. New York: Vanguard Press; 1954.

La Tour Landry: see Landry.

Ulrich von Lichtenstein: *Ulrich's von Liechtenstein Frauendienst*, edited by R. Bechstein. Leipzig: F. A. Brockhaus; 1888. For a modern German translation, see *Der Frauendienst des Minnesängers Ulrich von Liechtenstein*, translated by Michelangelo Baron Bois. Stuttgart: Robert Lutz; n.d.

Vossler, K.: *Mediaeval Culture*. New York: Harcourt, Brace & Co.; 1929.

CHAPTER VI: *The Lady and the Witch*

IN THE RENAISSANCE (and thereafter) the available materials are so plentiful that it is not possible to list more than a fraction of the sources used. In particular, biographies are so numerous that I will limit myself, for the most part, to naming only works containing accounts of several lives in one volume, since individual biographies are easy enough to find.

A general introduction to the social history of the period can be found in Durant, Einstein, and the *Cambridge Modern History*, among many others. More specifically, Maulde's old work and Kelso's two recent ones give much space to Platonic love in theory and practice, while the theory and practice of the inquisitors concerning women is given in detail with rich documentation from the original sources by Jones, Lea, and Zilboorg. Castiglione and Sprenger, both readily available in English, are the two most valuable Renaissance documents giving the opposing points of view, and a vast number of lesser works dealing with the many questions of woman, sex, love, and married life are cited and quoted in Camden, Powell, and Stenton.

Aubrey, John: *Brief Lives*, edited by A. Powell. London: The Cresset Press; 1949.

Bligh, E. W.: *Sir Kenelm Digby and His Venetia*. London: Sampson Low, Marston & Co.; 1932.

Boulting, William: *Woman in Italy*. New York: Brentano's; 1910.

Bromberg, Walter, M.D.: *The Mind of Man*. New York: Harper & Bros.; 1937.

Burckhardt, Jacob: *The Civilization*

of the Renaissance in Italy. New York: Harper & Bros.; 1929. Reprint of a classic, still valuable.

Cambridge Modern History, Vol. I (1957 edition).

Camden, Carroll: *The Elizabethan Woman*. New York: Elsevier Press; 1952.

Castiglione, Count Baldesar: *The Book of the Courtier*, translated by L. E. Opdycke. New York: Charles Scribner's Sons; 1903.

Chambers, E. K.: *The Mediaeval Stage*. Oxford: Oxford University Press; 1903.

Cupid's School: Wherein Young Men and Maids May Learn Divers Sorts of New, Witty, and Amorous Compliments. By W. S. London: 1632.

Digby, Sir Kenelm: *Private Memoirs of Sir Kenelm Digby*, edited by Sir Nicholas Nicolar. London: Saunders and Otley; 1827.

Durant, Will: *The Renaissance*. New York: Simon and Schuster; 1953. Deals with Italy only.

——: *The Reformation*. New York: Simon and Schuster; 1957.

Einstein, Lewis: *The Italian Renaissance in England*. New York: Columbia University Press; 1902.

——: *Tudor Ideals*. New York: Harcourt, Brace & Co.; 1921.

Garcon, Maurice, and Jean Vinchon: *The Devil*. London: Victor Gollancz; 1929.

Hansen, Joseph: *Zauberwahn, Inquisition und Hexenprozess im Mittelalter*. München: Oldenbourg; 1900.

Henry VIII: *The Love-Letters of Henry VIII*, edited by Henry Savage. London: Allan Wingate; 1949.

Historia Regis Henrici Septimi, edited by James Gairdner (Great Britain Public Record Office: *Chronicles and Memorials of Great Britain and Ireland during the Middle Ages*). London: Longman, Brown, Green, Longmans and Roberts; 1858.

Innocent VIII, Pope: Papal Bull, *Summis Desiderantes Affectibus*, available in English in the Introduction to Sprenger, q.v.

Jones, Ernest, M.D.: *On the Nightmare: The International Psycho-Analytical Library, No. 20*. London: Hogarth Press; 1949.

Kelso, Ruth: *The Doctrine of the English Gentleman in the Sixteenth Century*. Urbana: University of Illinois Press; 1929.

——: *Doctrine for the Lady of the Renaissance*. Urbana: University of Illinois Press; 1956.

Lea, H. C.: *History of the Inquisition of the Middle Ages*. New York: S. A. Russell; 1956. Reprint of a classic.

Marguerite, Queen of Navarre: *The Heptameron*. New York: Alfred A. Knopf; 1924.

De Maulde la Clavière, R.: *The Women of the Renaissance*. New York: G. P. Putnam's Sons; 1900.

Paston Letters, The, edited by James Gairdner. Westminster: A. Constable & Co.; 1895.

Pastor, Ludwig: *The History of the Popes*. London: Kegan Paul, Trench, Trubner and Co.; 1910.

Pollard, A. F.: *Henry VIII*. London: Longmans, Green & Co.; 1951.

Powell, Chilton L.: *English Domestic Relations, 1487–1653*. New York: Columbia University Press; 1917.

Raleigh, Sir Walter: "Instructions to His Son," in *Remains of Sir Walter Raleigh*. London: 1675.

Saltini, G. E.: *Tragedie Medice e Domestiche (1557–87), Narrate sui Documenti*. Firenze: Barbera; 1898.

Sprenger, Jacob, and Henry Kramer: *Malleus Maleficarum*, translated by Rev. Montague Summers. [London]: John Rodker; 1928.

Stenton, Doris Mary: *The English*

Woman in History. London: Allen & Unwin; 1957.

Taylor, G. Rattray: *Sex in History*. New York: Vanguard Press; 1954.

Thorndike, Lynn: *History of Magic and Experimental Science*. New York: The Macmillan Company; 1923–41.

Zilboorg, Gregory, M.D.: *The Medical Man and the Witch During the Renaissance*. Baltimore: Johns Hopkins Press; 1935.

CHAPTER VII: *The Impuritans*

FOR A GENERAL INTRODUCTION to the Reformation, both Durant and Smith are readable and thorough; more specifically the social history of Puritanism in New England is covered in Wish. The over-all modifying and reshaping influence of the Reformation upon the laws and customs of marriage, divorce, fornication, and adultery is sketched rapidly by Goodsell, and in minute detail by Howard. Harkness gives much special detail on the experiment in Geneva. The surprising liveliness of Puritans in New England is dealt with by Lawrence, Morgan, and Oberholzer, through the convincing method of liberal citation and extracting of court cases, private correspondence, diaries, and the like.

Bainton, Roland: *Here I Stand*. (On Luther.) New York: Abingdon-Cokesbury Press; 1950.

Bradford, Governor William: *Of Plymouth Plantation*, edited by Samuel Eliot Morison. New York: Alfred A. Knopf; 1952.

Calvin, John: *Institutes of the Christian Religion*, translated by H. Beveridge. Edinburgh: T. & T. Clark; 1869.

Durant, Will: *The Reformation*. New York: Simon and Schuster; 1957.

Essex County Archives: *Salem Witchcraft, 1692*.

Funck-Brentano, Frantz: *Luther*. London: Jonathan Cape; 1936.

Gataker, Thomas: *A Good Wife God's Gift—A Marriage Sermon*. London: 1620.

Goodsell, Willystine: *A History of the Family as a Social and Educational Institution*. New York: The Macmillan Company; 1934.

Haller, William: "Hail Wedded Love," ELH (English Literary History), Vol. XIII, June 1946.
—— and Malleville Haller: "The Puritan Art of Love," *The Huntington Library Quarterly*, Vol. V, Jan. 1942.

Hanford, J. H.: *John Milton, Englishman*. New York: Crown Publishers; 1949.

Harkness, Georgia: *John Calvin*. New York: Henry Holt; 1931.

Howard, G. E.: *A History of Matrimonial Institutions*. Chicago: University of Chicago Press; 1904.

Hutchinson, Lucy: *Memoirs of the Life of Colonel Hutchinson*. London: J. M. Dent; n.d. This Everyman edition includes Mrs. Hutchinson's *Life of Mrs. Lucy Hutchinson*, which, though only a fragment, is useful.

Lawrence, Henry W.: *The Not-Quite Puritans*. Boston: Little, Brown & Co.; 1928.

Luther, Martin: *Tischreden*. Weimar: Hermann Böhlaus Nachfolger; 1912–21. (These six volumes are part of *Dr. Martin Luthers Werke: Kritische Gesamtausgabe*, same publisher.) See esp. *Tischreden* Nos. 3, 49, 55, 975, 1161, 1472, 1563, 1965, 2047, 2733a, 3523,

6567, 6925 and 6928. Also, the essay on married life in Weimar *Werke*, X–2, 276.

——: *Dr. Martin Luther's Sämmtliche Werke*, edited by G. Plochman and J. Irmischer. Frankfurt and Erlangen: C. Heyder, und Hender & Zimmer; 1826–57. Especially Vol. LX, 110 (*Tischreden* No. 1588).

——: *The Table-Talk of Martin Luther*, translated by Wm. Hazlitt. London: G. Bell & Sons; 1902. See Nos. 737, 752.

Masson, David: *The Life of John Milton*. New York: Peter Smith; 1946. Reprint of a classic.

Mather, Cotton: *Diary of Cotton Mather (1681–1708)*: *Mass. Historical Soc. Collections*, 7th Series, Vols. VII–VIII. Boston: Published by the Society; 1911.

May, Geoffrey J.: *Social Control of Sex Expression*. London: Allen & Unwin; 1930.

Miller, Perry: *The New England Mind*. New York: The Macmillan Company; 1939.

Milton, John: *The Doctrine and Discipline of Divorce*, and *Tetrachordon*, both in *The Works of John Milton*, Vol. III. New York: Columbia University Press; 1931.

——*Apology*, in *Complete Prose Works of John Milton*, Vol. I. New Haven: Yale University Press; 1953.

Morgan, Edmund S.: *The Puritan Family*. Boston: The Public Library; 1944.

——: "The Puritans and Sex," in *The New England Quarterly*, Vol. XV, Dec. 1942.

Muir, Edwin: *John Knox*. New York: The Viking Press; 1929.

Oberholzer, Emil: *Delinquent Saints*. New York: Columbia University Press; 1956.

Powell, Chilton L.: *English Domestic Relations, 1487–1653*. New York: Columbia University Press; 1917.

Rogers, Daniel: *Matrimonial Honor*. London: 1642.

Schaff, Philip: *The Swiss Reformation*. New York: Charles Scribner's Sons; 1892.

Sewall, Samuel: *Diary of Samuel Sewall: Collections of the Massachusetts Historical Society*, 5th Series, Vols. V–VII. Boston: Published by the Society; 1878–82.

Smith, Preserved: *The Age of the Reformation*. New York: Henry Holt & Company; 1923 and 1936.

Whately, William: *The Bride-Bush*. London: 1617.

Winthrop, Governor John: *The History of New England from 1630 to 1649*. Boston; Little, Brown & Co.; 1853.

Wish, Harvey: *Society and Thought in Early America*. New York: Longmans, Green & Co.; 1950.

CHAPTER VIII: *The Contact of Two Epidermises*

Smith and the *Cambridge Modern History* are two of the many general works on the era here portrayed. For greater detail on French social history, see the works by Lewis and Russell, and on English social history see Ashton, Traill and Mann, and Trevelyan; all these books quote copiously from original sources. On the subject of rationalist love in particular, the pre-Freudian work by the Goncourts remains wonderfully perceptive. As indicated in the chapter itself, my own interpretation draws upon modern

ideas of the psychodynamics of family life and personality growth
as found in Kardiner, La Barre, Montagu, and elsewhere.

Ashton, John: *Social Life in the Reign of Queen Anne.* London: Chatto & Windus; 1925.

Bertrand, Louis: *Louis XIV.* New York: Longmans, Green & Co.; 1928.

Boswell, James: *Boswell's London Journal, 1762–1763.* New York: McGraw-Hill Book Co.; 1950.

Cambridge Modern History, Vol. V.

Casanova, Jacques (or Giacomo, or Giovanni Jacopo): *The Memoirs of Jacques Casanova de Seingalt,* translated by Arthur Machen. New York: A. & C. Boni; 1932.

Chesterfield, Philip Dormer Stanhope, Earl of: *Letters to His Son,* edited by O. H. Leigh. New York: Tudor Publishing Co.; n.d.

Dobson, Austin: *Horace Walpole.* London: Oxford University Press; 1927.

Du Deffand, Madame: see Walpole.

Earle, Alice Morse: *Colonial Dames and Goodwives.* Boston: Houghton Mifflin Company; 1895.

Evelyn, John: *Mundus Muliebris,* in *Miscellaneous Writings of John Evelyn.* London: Henry Colburn; 1825.

Franklin, Benjamin: *Autobiography of Benjamin Franklin,* a restoration of a fair copy by Max Farrand. Berkeley and Los Angeles: University of California (in cooperation with the Huntington Library); 1949.

——: *Poor Richards Almanack,* published as "The Sayings of Poor Richard," edited by P. L. Ford. New York: G. P. Putnam's Sons; 1890.

Goncourt, Edmond et Jules de: *La Femme au Dix-Huitième Siècle.* Paris: G. Charpentier; 1882.

Gramont: see Hamilton.

Halsband, Robert: *The Life of Lady Mary Wortley Montagu.* Oxford: The Clarendon Press; 1956.

Hamilton, Count Anthony: *Memoirs of Count Grammont* [sic]. Edinburgh: John Grant; 1908.

Kardiner, Abram: *Sex and Morality.* New York: The Bobbs-Merrill Company; 1954.

Kesten, Hermann: *Casanova.* New York: Harper & Bros.; 1955.

La Barre, Weston: *The Human Animal.* Chicago: University of Chicago Press; 1954.

De Lenclos, Ninon: *Lettres de Ninon de Lenclos.* Paris: Librairie Garnier Frères; n.d.

Lewis, W. H.: *The Splendid Century.* New York: William Sloane Associates; 1954.

Magne, Emile: *Ninon de Lanclos.* London: S. W. Arrowsmith; 1926.

Maintenon, Madame de: *Correspondence Générale de Mme. de Maintenon,* edited by T. Lavallée. Paris; 1865–6.

Mitford, Nancy: *Voltaire in Love.* New York: Harper & Bros.; 1957.

Montagu, M. F. Ashley: *The Direction of Human Development.* New York: Harper & Bros.; 1955.

Osborn, Francis: "Advice to a Son," in *The Works of Francis Osborn.* Ninth edition. London: 1689.

Pepys, Samuel: *The Diary of Samuel Pepys,* edited from Mynors Bright with an introduction by J. Warrington. London: J. M. Dent; 1953.

Russell, Phillips: *The Glittering Century.* New York: Charles Scribner's Sons; 1936.

Shellabarger, Samuel: *Lord Chesterfield and His World.* Boston: Little, Brown & Company; 1951. First published in England in 1935.

Sidney, Henry (Earl of Romney): *Diary of the Times of Charles the Second,* edited by R. W. Blencoe. London: Henry Colburn; 1843.

Smith, Preserved: *A History of Modern Culture,* Vol. II. New

York: Henry Holt & Company; 1934.

Spectator, The: Nos. 2, 66, and 154; and The Tatler, No. 40.

Swift, Jonathan: "A Letter to a Young Lady, on Her Marriage," in Vol. IX of Prose Works of Jonathan Swift, edited by Herbert Davis. Oxford: Basil Blackwell; 1948.

Tompkins, J. M. S.: The Polite Marriage. Cambridge: The University Press; 1938.

Traill, H. D., and J. S. Mann, eds.: Social England, Vols. IV and V. New York: G. P. Putnam's Sons; 1909.

Trevelyan, G. M.: English Social History. New York: Longmans, Green & Co.; 1942.

Van Doren, Carl: Benjamin Franklin. New York: Viking Press; 1945.

Walpole, Horace: The Yale Edition of Horace Walpole's Correspondence; edited by W. S. Lewis. New Haven: Yale University Press; 1937–55. Includes Mme du Deffand's letters to Walpole.

Wilson, John H.: Nell Gwyn: Royal Mistress. New York: Pellegrini and Cudahy; 1952.

CHAPTER IX: *The Angel in the House*

OF THE VERY MANY HISTORIES of England in the Romantic and Victorian periods, the relevant sections of Wingfield-Stratford's *The History of British Civilization* are perhaps the most readable; many others, easily available, are more scholarly in format, but need not be listed here. On the characteristics of pre-Victorian society, Quinlan is a good recent study, rich in detail. On Victorian society itself, Wingfield-Stratford's *Those Earnest Victorians* and the book by Young are both useful, but Houghton is far and away the most thorough, detailed, and richly documented study available and includes the best modern discussion of Victorian love. (The best nineteenth-century discussions of it are by Ruskin and, of course, Patmore.) The woman's rights movement is treated in Calhoun (old, but indispensable), Ditzion (literary more than historical), Goodsell, and Stenton. Ellis frequently deals with the sexual and emotional ailments of the era, and Pearl lovingly gathers up all the evidences of its vices (and somewhat exaggerates them for effect).

Bagley, C. B.: "The Mercer Immigration," Quarterly of the Oregon Hist. Soc., Vol. V (1904).

Benson, Mary S.: Women in Eighteenth-Century America. New York: Columbia University Press; 1935.

Calhoun, Arthur W.: A Social History of the American Family. Cleveland: Arthur H. Clark Co.; 1918.

Champneys, Basil: Memoirs and Correspondence of Coventry Patmore. London: George Bell & Sons; 1900.

Clewes, Howard: Stendhal. London: Arthur Barker; 1950.

Cobbett, William: Advice to Young Men. London: 1829.

Cunnington, C. W.: Feminine Attitudes in the Nineteenth Century. London: Wm. Heinemann; 1935.

Dexter, Elisabeth A.: *Career Women of America, 1776–1840.* Francestown, N.H.: Marshall Jones Co.; 1950.

Ditzion, Sidney: *Marriage, Morals, and Sex in America.* New York: Bookman Associates; 1953.

Ellis, Havelock: *The Evolution of Modesty; The Sexual Impulse in Women;* and *Sex in Relation to Society,* in Vols. I, III, and VI of *Studies in the Psychology of Sex.* Philadelphia: F. A. Davis; 1901–28.

Encyclopaedia Britannica, 1842 edition: "Love."

Fitzhugh, George: *Sociology for the South.* Richmond: Morris; 1854.

Froude, J. A.: *The Nemesis of Faith.* London: J. Chapman; 1849.

Goodsell, Willystine: *A History of the Family as a Social and Educational Institution.* New York: The Macmillan Company; 1934.

Green, F. C.: *Jean-Jacques Rousseau.* Cambridge: The University Press; 1955.

Gregory, John, Dr.: *A Father's Legacy to His Daughters.* London: A. Millar; 1788. First published in 1774.

Hazlitt, William: *Liber Amoris, or The New Pygmalion.* London: Mathews & Lane; 1893. First published in 1823.

Houghton, Walter E.: *The Victorian Frame of Mind, 1830–1870.* New Haven: Yale University Press; 1957.

Howe, P. P.: *The Life of William Hazlitt.* London: Martin Secker; 1922.

Klein, Viola: *The Feminine Character.* London: Kegan Paul, Trench, Trubner & Co.; 1946.

Maclean, C. M.: *Born Under Saturn.* (Biog. of Wm. Hazlitt.) London: Collins; 1943.

Maigron, Louis: *Le Romantisme et les Moeurs.* Paris: H. Champion; 1910.

Malthus, Thomas: *An Essay on the Principle of Population.* London: Reeves & Turner; 1872. First published in 1798.

Owen, Robert Dale: Marriage letter printed in Calhoun, q.v.

Patmore, Coventry: *Angel in the House* and *The Unknown Eros,* both in *Poems,* edited by F. Page. London: Oxford University Press; 1949.

Pearl, Cyril: *The Girl with the Swansdown Seat.* New York: New American Library; 1958.

Praz, Mario: *The Romantic Agony.* New York: Meridian Books; 1956.

Procter, Bryan W. ("Barry Cornwall"): *An Autobiographical Fragment.* Boston: Roberts Brothers; 1877.

Quinlan, M. J.: *Victorian Prelude.* New York: Columbia University Press; 1941.

Reid, J. C.: *The Mind and Art of Coventry Patmore.* London: Routledge & Kegan Paul; 1957.

Rousseau, Jean-Jacques: *The Confessions of Jean-Jacques Rousseau.* London: Penguin Books; 1953.

Ruskin, John: "Of Queens' Gardens," in *Sesame and Lilies.* London: Cassell & Co.; 1907.

Ryan, Michael, M.D.: *The Philosophy of Marriage.* Philadelphia: Lindsay & Blakiston; 1867. First published in 1839.

Stendhal: *On Love.* Garden City, N.Y.: Doubleday Anchor Books; 1957.

Stenton, Doris Mary: *The English Woman in History.* London: Allen & Unwin; 1957.

Stewart, Randall: "Letters to Sophia," in *Huntington Library Quarterly,* Vol. VII (Aug. 1944). Nathaniel Hawthorne's censored letters.

Tennyson, Hallam: *Alfred Lord Tennyson.* London: Macmillan & Co.; 1897.

Trevelyan, G. M.: *English Social*

History. New York: Longmans, Green & Co.; 1942.

Turner, E. S.: *A History of Courting*. New York: E. P. Dutton & Co.; 1955.

Wingfield-Stratford, Esmé: *The History of British Civilization*. Lon-

don: George Routledge & Sons; 1928.

————: *Those Earnest Victorians*. New York: Wm. Morrow & Co.; 1930.

Young, G. M., ed.: *Early Victorian England, 1830–1865*. London: Oxford University Press; 1934.

CHAPTER X: *The Age of Love*

This chapter, revised for the present edition, continues to draw largely on material available during the era, although some recent sources of data and biography have been added. The surveys and studies to which the chapter refers or on which it draws are so numerous that, with a few exceptions, I list only secondary sociological and psychological textbooks in which the bulk of the primary sources are cited. Among works of this type are those by Baber, Burgess and Locke, Folsom, Kirkpatrick, Nimkoff, and Winch's *The Modern Family*. Winch's *Mate-Selection* contains a summary of studies of homogamy and heterogamy in the pairing of lovers, as of 1958; for later data on the matter, see Hatfield and Rapson. Statistics on marriage, divorce, fertility, and women workers come from the U.S. Census Bureau and the U.S. Department of Labor Women's Bureau.

Baber, Ray E.: *Marriage and the Family*. New York: McGraw-Hill Book Co.; 1953.

Beigel, Hugo G.: "Romantic Love," in *Am. Sociol. Rev.* Vol. XVI (1951).

Bell, Robert R.: *Marriage and Family Interaction*. Homewood, Ill.: Dorsey Press; 1963, 1975.

Burgess, Ernest W., and Leonard S. Cottrell: *Predicting Success or Failure in Marriage*. New York: Prentice-Hall; 1939.

———— and Harvey J. Locke: *The Family*. New York: American Book Co.; 1953.

———— and Paul Wallin: *Engagement and Marriage*. Philadelphia: J. B. Lippincott Company; 1953.

Calverton, V. F., and S. D. Schmalhausen, eds.: *Sex in Civilization*. New York: The Macaulay Co.; 1929.

Cuber, J. F.: "Can We Evaluate Marriage Education?" in *Marriage and Family Living*, Vol. XI (1949).

Cyon, Françoise: see Delisle.

Davis, K. B.: *Factors in the Sex Life of*

Twenty-Two Hundred Women. New York: Harper & Bros.; 1929.

Delisle, Françoise: *Friendship's Odyssey*. London: Wm. Heinemann; 1946.

Deutsch, Helene: *The Psychology of Women*. New York: Grune & Stratton; 1945.

Dietrich, Marlene: "How to Be Loved," *Ladies' Home Journal*, Jan. 1954.

Duncan, Isadora: *My Life*. New York: Liveright Publishing Corporation; 1933.

Ellis, Havelock: *The History of Marriage*, in *Studies in the Psychology of Sex*, Vol. VII. Philadelphia: F. A. Davis; 1928.

————: *My Life*. Boston: Houghton Mifflin Company 1939.

Farnham, Marynia: see Lundberg.

Flugel, J. C.: *Man, Morals, and Society*. New York: International Universities Press; 1945.

Folsom, J. K.: *The Family and Democratic Society*. New York: John Wiley & Sons; 1943.

Franzblau, Abraham N.: *The Road to Sexual Maturity*. New York: Simon and Schuster; 1954.

Freud, Sigmund: *Group Psychology and the Analysis of the Ego*. London: The Hogarth Press; 1922.

———: "Psychology of Women," in *New Introductory Lectures on Psycho-Analysis*. London: The Hogarth Press; 1933.

———: Letter to Martha Bernays, in Jones, q.v.

Gay, Peter: *Freud: A Life for Our Time*. New York: W. W. Norton & Co.; 1988.

Goode, William: *After Divorce*. Glencoe, Ill.: The Free Press; 1956.

Hamilton, G. V.: *A Research in Marriage*. New York: A. & C. Boni; 1929.

Hatfield, Elaine, and Richard L. Rapson: *Love, Sex, and Intimacy: Their Psychology, Biology, and History*. New York: HarperCollins Pubs.; 1993.

Jones, Ernest, M.D.: *The Life and Work of Sigmund Freud*. New York: Basic Books; 1953–7.

Kardiner, Abram: *Sex and Morality*. New York: Bobbs-Merrill Co.; 1954.

Kinsey, Alfred C., et al.: *Sexual Behavior in the Human Male*. Philadelphia: W. B. Saunders Co.; 1948.

——— et al.: *Sexual Behavior in the Human Female*. Philadelphia: W. B. Saunders Co.; 1953.

Kirkpatrick, Clifford: *The Family as Process and Institution*. New York: The Ronald Press; 1955.

Klein, Viola: *The Feminine Character*. London: Kegan Paul, Trench, Trubner & Co.; 1946.

Kolb, William L.: "Sociologically Established Family Norms and Democratic Values," in *Social Forces*, Vol. XXVI (1948).

Komarovsky, Mirra: *Women in the Modern World*. Boston: Little, Brown & Co.; 1953.

Lader, Lawrence: *The Margaret Sanger Story*. Garden City, N.Y.: Doubleday & Co.; 1955.

Landis, Carney: *Sex in Development*. New York: Paul B. Hoeber; 1940.

Landis, Judson T.: "Length of Time Required to Achieve Adjustment in Marriage," *Am. Sociol. Rev.*, Vol. XI (1946).

Lang, R. O.: Unpublished study on happiness in marriage, quoted in Burgess and Cottrell.

Lawrence, D. H.: *We Need One Another*. New York: Equinox; 1933. A reprinting of two magazine articles.

Linton, Ralph: *The Study of Man*. New York: Appleton-Century; 1936.

Lowrie, S. H.: "Dating Theories and Student Responses," *Am. Sociol. Rev.*, Vol. XVI (1951).

Lundberg, Ferdinand, and Marynia F. Farnham, M.D.: *Modern Woman: The Lost Sex*. New York: Harper & Bros.; 1947.

Lynd, Robert S. and Helen M.: *Middletown*. New York: Harcourt, Brace & Co.; 1929.

Mead, Margaret: *Male and Female*. New York: New American Library; 1955.

Mudd, Emily, et al.: *Marriage Counseling: A Casebook*. New York: Association Press; 1958.

Myrdal, Alva, and Viola Klein: *Women's Two Roles: Home and Work*. London: Routledge & Kegan Paul; 1956.

Nimkoff, Meyer F.: *Marriage and the Family*. New York: Houghton Mifflin Company; 1947.

Parsons, Talcott: *Essays in Sociological Theory, Pure and Applied*. Glencoe, Ill.: The Free Press; 1949.

Reich, Wilhelm: *The Function of the Orgasm*. Vol. I of *The Discovery of the Orgone*. New York: Orgone Institute Press; 1942–8.

Riley, J. W., and M. White: "The Use of Various Methods of Contraception," *Am. Sociol. Rev.*, Vol. V (1940).

Sorokin, Pitirim: *Social and Cultural Dynamics*. New York: American Book Co.; 1941.

Stopes, Marie: *Married Love*. London: A. C. Fifield; 1918.

Sullivan, Mark; *Our Times*. New York: Charles Scribner's Sons; 1926–35.

Terman, Lewis M., et al.: *Psychological Factors in Marital Happiness*. New York: McGraw-Hill Book Co.; 1938.

U.S. Bureau of the Census: *Characteristics of the Population*, in *Census of 1890, 1940, 1950*.

———: Current Population Reports, Population Characteristics Series (Series P-20, Nos. 450 and 461), *Marital Status and Living Arrangements, March 1990* and *March 1991*.

———: Labor Force Series, 1951–8.

U.S. Department of Labor: Woman's Bureau *Bulletins*, Nos. 157, 209, 239.

Van de Velde, Theodoor: *Ideal Marriage: Its Physiology and Technique*. New York: Covici Friede; 1930.

Waller, Willard: "The Rating and Dating Complex," *Am. Sociol. Rev.*, Vol. II (1937).

———: *The Family: A Dynamic Interpretation*. New York: The Cordon Co.; 1938.

Whelpton, P. K., and C. V. Kiser: *Social and Psychological Factors Affecting Fertility*. New York: Milbank Memorial Fund; 1950. Includes data given in a series of articles by same authors in various issues of *Milbank Memorial Fund Quarterly*, 1943–9.

Winch, Robert F.: *Mate-Selection*. New York: Harper & Bros.; 1958.

———: *The Modern Family*. New York: Henry Holt & Company; 1952.

CHAPTER XI: *Love Remodeled*

THE CHANGES IN MALE-FEMALE RELATIONSHIPS since 1960, and hence in love, have been so extensive and complex that only the principal sources used are listed here. Details of the sexual revolution are drawn largely from Crosby's *Reply to Myth*, Hunt's *Sexual Behavior in the 1970s*, and Hatfield and Rapson's *Love, Sex, and Intimacy*. The discussion of the women's movement leans chiefly on the books by Susan Faludi, Robin Morgan, Lillian Rubin, and Gloria Steinem, plus other works listed here or cited in the footnotes. Most of the many studies and experiments mentioned in sections 3 through 6 will be found here under the principal researcher's name; others are cited in the works by Fisher, Hatfield and Rapson, and Sternberg and Barnes, in which they can be located via the indexes.

Atkinson, Ti Grace: "The Institution of Sexual Intercourse," *Notes from the Second Year: Women's Liberation*. New York: Radical Feminism; 1970.

———: "The Oppressed Majority Demands Its Rights," *Life*, December 12, 1969.

Bell, Alan P., and Martin S. Weinberg: *Homosexualities: A Study of Diversity Among Men and Women*. New York: Simon & Schuster; 1978.

Bernard, Jessie: *The Future of Marriage*. New York: World Publishing; 1972.

Berscheid, Ellen: "Some Comments on Love's Anatomy," in Sternberg and Barnes, *The Psychology of Love*, q.v.

Chesler, Phyllis: *About Men*. New York: Simon & Schuster; 1978.

Crosby, John F., ed.: *Reply to Myth: Perspectives on Intimacy*. New York: John Wiley & Sons; 1985.

Dutton, Donald, and Arthur Aron: "Some Evidence for Heightened Sexual Attraction Under Conditions of High Anxiety," *Journal of Personality and Social Psychology*, Vol. 30 (1974).

Faludi, Susan: *Backlash: The Undeclared War Against American Women*. New York: Crown Publishers; 1991.

Fisher, Helen E.: *Anatomy of Love: The Natural History of Monogamy, Adultery, and Divorce*. New York: W. W. Norton & Co.; 1992.

Freeman, Jo, ed.: *Women: A Feminist Perspective*. 3d ed. Mountain View,

Calif.: Mayfield Publishing Co.; 1984.

Friedan, Betty: *The Feminine Mystique.* New York: W. W. Norton & Co.; 1963.

Goode, William J.: *World Changes in Divorce Patterns.* New Haven: Yale University Press; 1993.

Greenblat, Cathy Stein, and Larry C. Baron: "Male-Female Differences in Romantic Love." Unpublished paper, n.d. [ca. 1980].

Greer, Germaine: *The Female Eunuch.* New York: McGraw-Hill Book Co.; 1971.

Gross, Jane: "Divorced, Middle-Aged and Happy: Women, Especially, Adjust to the 90's," *New York Times*, December 7, 1992.

Hatfield, Elaine: "The Effect of Self-esteem on Romantic Liking," *Journal of Experimental Social Psychology*, Vol. 1 (1965).

———, E. Aronson, et al.: "The Importance of Physical Attractiveness in Dating Behavior," *Journal of Personality and Social Psychology*, Vol. 4 (1966).

———, and Richard L. Rapson: *Love, Sex, and Intimacy: Their Psychology, Biology, and History.* New York: HarperCollins Pubs.; 1993.

———; S. Sprecher; et al.: "Gender Differences in What Is Desired in the Sexual Relationship," *Journal of Psychology and Human Sexuality*, Vol. 1 (1988).

Hazan, Cindy, and Philip Shaver: "Romantic Love Conceptualized as an Attachment Process," *Journal of Personality and Social Psychology*, Vol. 52 (1987).

Hite, Shere: *The Hite Report on Male Sexuality.* New York: Alfred A. Knopf; 1981.

———: *Women and Love: A Cultural Revolution in Progress.* New York: Alfred A. Knopf; 1987.

Hunt, Morton: *The World of the Formerly Married.* New York: McGraw-Hill Book Co.; 1966.

———: *Sexual Behavior in the 1970s.* Chicago: Playboy Press; 1974.

———, and Bernice Hunt: *The Divorce Experience.* New York: McGraw-Hill Book Co.; 1977.

Huston, Ted L., ed.: *Foundations of Interpersonal Attraction.* New York: Academic Press; 1974.

Jay, Karla, and Allen Young: *The Gay Report.* New York: Summit Books; 1979.

Kephart, William M.: "Some Correlates of Romantic Love," *Journal of Marriage and the Family*, Vol. 29 (1967).

Kirk, Marshall, and Hunter Madsen: *After the Ball: How America Will Conquer Its Fear and Hatred of Gays in the '90's.* New York: Doubleday; 1989.

Lee, John Alan: "A Typology of Styles of Loving," *Personality and Social Psychology Bulletin*, Vol. 3 (1977).

———: "Love-Styles," in Sternberg and Barnes, *The Psychology of Love*, q.v.

Liebowitz, Michael R.: *The Chemistry of Love.* Boston: Little, Brown & Co.; 1983.

McWhirter, David P., and Andrew M. Mattison: *The Male Couple: How Relationships Develop.* Englewood Cliffs, N.J.: Prentice-Hall; 1984.

Millett, Kate: *Sexual Politics.* New York: Doubleday & Co.; 1970.

Morgan, Robin: *The Anatomy of Freedom: Feminism, Physics, and Global Politics.* Garden City, N.Y.: Anchor/Doubleday; 1982.

Murstein, Bernard I.: "A Taxonomy of Love." Paper presented at 1977 conference of the National Council on Family Relations.

O'Neill, Nena, and George O'Neill: *Open Marriage: A New Life Style for Couples.* New York: M. Evans & Co.; 1972, 1984.

Otto, Herbert A., ed.: *Love Today: A New Exploration.* New York: Association Press; 1972.

Peele, Stanton: "Fools for Love," in Sternberg and Barnes, *The Psychology of Love*, q.v.

————, and Archie Brodsky: *Love and Addiction.* New York: New American Library; 1977.

Perper, Timothy, and Susan V. Fox: "Flirtation and Pickup Patterns in Bars" (1980), cited in Hatfield and Rapson, *Love, Sex, and Intimacy,* q.v.

Pope, Kenneth S., and Associates: *On Love and Loving.* San Francisco: Jossey-Bass Pubs.; 1980.

Prince, Dinah: "Marriage in the '80's," *New York,* June 1, 1987.

Reiss, Ira: "Explanations of Premarital Sexual Permissiveness," in Crosby, *Reply to Myth,* q.v.

Rubin, Lillian B.: *Erotic Wars: What Happened to the Sexual Revolution?* New York: Farrar, Straus & Giroux; 1990.

Rubin, Zick: "Measurement of Romantic Love," *Journal of Personality and Social Psychology,* Vol. 16 (1970).

————: "From Liking to Loving: Patterns of Attraction in Dating Relationships," in Huston, Ted L., ed., *Foundations of Interpersonal Attraction.* New York: Academic Press; 1974.

Seidman, Steven: *Romantic Longings: Love in America, 1830–1980.* New York and London: Routledge; 1991.

Shaver, Philip, and Cindy Hazan: "Adult Romantic Attachment: Theory and Evidence," in D. Perlman and W. Jones, eds., *Advances in Personal Relationships,* Vol. 4 (1992). See also Hazan and Shaver, supra.

Steinem, Gloria: *Revolution from Within: A Book of Self-esteem.* Boston: Little, Brown & Co.; 1992.

Sternberg, Robert J.: "A Triangular Theory of Love," *Psychological Review,* Vol. 93, No. 2 (1986).

————, and Michael L. Barnes, eds.: *The Psychology of Love.* New Haven: Yale University Press; 1988.

————, and Susan Grajek: "The Nature of Love," *Journal of Personality and Social Psychology,* Vol. 47, No. 2 (1984).

Tennov, Dorothy: *Love and Limerence.* Briarcliff Manor, N.Y.: Stein & Day Pubs.; 1979.

U.S. Bureau of the Census: Current Population Reports, Population Characteristics Series (Series P-20, Nos. 450 and 461), *Marital Status and Living Arrangements, March 1990* and *Marital Status and Living Arrangements, March 1991.*

————: Current Population Reports, Special Studies (Series P-23, Nos. 162, 163), *Studies in Marriage and the Family,* 1989, and *Changes in American Family Life,* 1989.

Walster, Elaine, and G. William Walster: *A New Look at Love.* Reading, Mass.: Addison-Wesley Pub. Co.; 1978.

Weber, Bruce: "Alone Together: The Unromantic Generation," *New York Times Magazine,* April 5, 1987.

Index

ABOUT THE AUTHOR

MORTON HUNT, who specializes in psychology, is the award-winning author of eighteen books, including The Universe Within, The Compassionate Beast *(Anchor Books), and most recently,* The Story of Psychology *(Anchor Books), as well as hundreds of articles. He lives in East Hampton, New York.*